"Growing up is a hard process, and it is especially daunting with the growing challenges that emerging adults face in all sectors of their lives. Varda Konstam has written a poignant book on the romantic lives of emerging adults, charting their often circuitous journeys from tentative forays in dating to the development of caring and nurturing partnerships. This very well-written book comes alive with vivid case examples and with the richness of current psychological research. This is a must read!"

—David Blustein, Professor of Counseling Psychology,
Lynch School of Education, Boston College

"Defying researchers' tendency to promote simplistic, headline-grabbing perspectives of emerging adults, Varda Konstam provides a nuanced and contemporary view on the process of becoming an adult. Konstam actively embraces the complexity and contradiction that is the hallmark of this developmental period, as young people begin to define themselves more squarely in relation to those around them. There remains much to know about the nature and significance of relationships—both successful and unsuccessful—but this book represents an important step forward."

—Moin Syed, Associate Professor of Psychology,
University of Minnesota

"A timely text on emerging adult romantic relationships and experiences. Readers will particularly enjoy the excellent synthesis of the developmental literature with novel and critical qualitative data. Professor Konstam does an excellent job highlighting the complex and dynamic nature of emerging adult romantic lives, while ensuring a high level of readability. A must read for anyone intrigued by emerging adult romantic relationships and experiences."

—Manfred H.M. van Dulmen, Associate Dean and Professor of
Psychological Sciences, Kent State University

D1450652

EMERGING ADULTHOOD SERIES

Series Editor

Larry J. Nelson

Advisory Board

Elisabetta Crocetti
Shagufa Kapadia
Koen Luyckx
Laura Padilla-Walker
Jennifer L. Tanner

Books in the Series

Forthcoming Books in the Series

The Romantic Lives of Emerging Adults

Getting From *I* to *We*

Varda Konstam Ph.D
Professor Emerita
Department of Counseling and School
Psychology
University of Massachusetts Boston

OXFORD
UNIVERSITY PRESS

OXFORD
UNIVERSITY PRESS

Oxford University Press is a department of the University of Oxford. It furthers
the University's objective of excellence in research, scholarship, and education
by publishing worldwide. Oxford is a registered trade mark of Oxford University
Press in the UK and certain other countries.

Published in the United States of America by Oxford University Press
198 Madison Avenue, New York, NY 10016, United States of America.

Library of Congress Cataloging-in-Publication Data
Names: Konstam, Varda, author.
Title: The romantic lives of emerging adults : getting from I to we / Varda Konstam.
Description: New York : Oxford University Press, [2019] |
Includes bibliographical references and index.
Identifiers: LCCN 2018015686 | ISBN 9780190639778 (pbk. : alk. paper)
Subjects: LCSH: Young adults—United States. | Sexual minorities—United States. |
Interpersonal relations. | Friendship. | Love.
Classification: LCC HQ799.7.K66 2018 | DDC 305.242—dc23
LC record available at https://lccn.loc.gov/2018015686

9 8 7 6 5 4 3 2 1

Printed by Webcom, Inc., Canada

This book is dedicated to all of my inspirational students.

CONTENTS ▲

SERIES FOREWORD ◢

The *Emerging Adulthood Series* examines the period of life starting at age 18 and continuing into and through the third decade of life, now commonly referred to as emerging adulthood. The specific focus of the series is on flourishing (i.e., factors that lead to positive, adaptive development during emerging adulthood and the successful transition into adult roles) and floundering (i.e., factors that lead to maladaptive behaviors and negative development during emerging adulthood as well as delay and difficulty in transitioning into adult roles) in the diverse paths young people take into and through the third decade of life.

There is a need to examine the successes and struggles in a variety of domains experienced by young people as they take complex and multiple paths in leaving adolescence and moving into and through their twenties. Too often the diversity of individual experiences is forgotten in our academic attempts to categorize a time period. For example, in proposing his theory of Emerging Adulthood, Arnett (2000, 2004) identified features of the development of young people including *feeling in-between* (emerging adults do not see themselves as either adolescents or adults), *identity exploration* (especially in the areas of work, love, and world views), *focus on the self* (not self-centered, but simply lacking obligations to others), *instability* (evidenced by changes of direction in residential status, relationships, work, and education), and *possibilities* (optimism in the potential to steer their lives in any number of desired directions). Although this is a nice summary of characteristics of the time period, the scholarly examination of emerging adulthood has not always attempted to capture and explain the within-group variation that exists among emerging adults, often making the broad generalization that they are a relatively homogenous group. For example, emerging adults have been categorically referred to as "narcissistic," "refusing to grow up," and "failed adults." While there certainly are emerging adults who fit the profile of selfish, struggling, and directionless, there are others who are using this period of time for good. Indeed, there is great diversity of individual experiences in emerging adulthood. Hence, there is a need to better examine various beliefs/ attitudes, attributes, behaviors, and relationships during this period of time that appear to reflect positive adjustment, or a sense of flourishing, or conversely those that lead to floundering.

For example, recent research (Nelson & Padilla-Walker, 2013) shows that young people who appear to be successfully navigating emerging adulthood tend to engage in identity exploration, develop internalization of positive values, participate in positive media use, engage in pro-social behaviors, report healthy relationships with parents, and engage in romantic relationships that are characterized by higher levels of companionship, worth, affection, and emotional support. For others who appear to be floundering, emerging adulthood appears to include anxiety and depression, poor self-perceptions, greater participation in risk behaviors, and poorer relationship quality with parents, best friends, and romantic partners. Thus, while various profiles of flourishing and floundering are starting to be identified, the current work in the field has simply provided cursory overviews of findings. This series provides a platform for an in-depth, comprehensive examination into some of these key factors that seem to be influencing, positively or negatively, young people as they enter into and progress through the third decade of life and the multiple ways in which they may flourish or flounder. Furthermore, the series attempts to examine how these factors may function differently within various populations (i.e., cultures and religious and ethnic sub-cultures, students vs. non-students, men vs. women, etc.). Finally, the series provides for a multi-disciplinary (e.g., fields ranging from developmental psychology, neurobiology, education, sociology, criminology) and multi-method (i.e., information garnered from both quantitative and qualitative methodologies) examination of issues related to flourishing and floundering in emerging adulthood.

It is important to make one final note about this series. In choosing to employ the term "emerging adulthood," it is not meant to imply that the series will include books that are limited in their scope to viewing the third decade of life only through the lens of emerging adulthood theory (Arnett, 2000). Indeed, the notion of "emerging adulthood" as a universal developmental period has been met with controversy and skepticism because of the complex and numerous paths young people take out of adolescence and into adulthood. It is that exact diversity in the experiences of young people in a variety of contexts and circumstances (e.g., cultural, financial, familial) that calls for a book series such as this one. It is unfortunate that disagreement about emerging adulthood theory has led to a fragmentation of scholars and scholarship devoted to better understanding the third decade of life. Hence, although the term "emerging adulthood" is employed for parsimony and for its growing familiarity as a term for the age period, this series is devoted to examining broadly the complexity of pathways into and through the third decade of life from a variety of perspectives and disciplines. In doing so, it is my hope that the series will help scholars, practitioners, students, and others better understand, and thereby potentially foster, flourishing and floundering in the lives of young people in the various paths they may take to adulthood.

▲ The Romantic Lives of Emerging Adults: Getting From *I* to *We*

With the average age of marriage being higher than it has ever been before, the prevailing notion is that the twenties are all about the individual rather than relationships. Such a simplistic notion fails to capture the role of romantic relationships in the lives of young people during the third decade of life. Without a doubt, a central quest of emerging adulthood is for young people to form their identity as an individual. However, the process of identity development does not occur in an individual bubble disconnected from the social world of relationships. Throughout the twenties, romantic relationships play a significant role in the lives of individuals including the longing that many have to be in one (i.e., a romantic relationship), the perplexity that many have to get out of one, the consternation felt by many of how to balance one with the pursuit of education and careers, the emotional pain for many at the termination of one, and, for many, making decisions today in preparation for one in the future. In each of these scenarios, whether "in" or "out" of a relationship, the day-to-day lives and overall well-being of many may very well be tied directly to the role that romantic relations play in their lives (i.e., longing for, happy in, balancing of, wanting out of, preparing for, hurting from the termination of, etc.). When viewed in this way, it becomes clear that examining the romantic lives of young people is essential in our pursuit to understand factors that lead to flourishing and floundering during the third decade of life.

This is exactly the reason why *"The Romantic Lives of Emerging Adults: Getting from I to We"* by Dr. Varda Konstam makes such a significant contribution to this book series with her in-depth look into multiple aspects of the romantic lives of emerging adults. Again, the notion of identity development is typically seen as an individualistic process whereby a person seeks answers to the question "Who am I" as an individual. Dr. Konstam, however, paints a much more complex picture of identity development as she examines how young people protect and develop the *I* identity (the identity as an individual) while also working towards and building an identity of *We* with another person. These simultaneous processes of development occur while young people engage in a variety of relationships that vary in levels of commitment (i.e., ranging from casual sexual relationships to marriage) throughout the third decade of life. Indeed, a strength of the book is the way in which it illuminates how the "experimental experiences with premarital commitment" (i.e., multiple forms of romantic relationships) build the bridge between the development of the *I* orientation to a *We* orientation. For example, the book highlights the concept of sacrifice which is seldom examined in the discussion of emerging adults' romantic relationships (as opposed to marriage). The ability to sacrifice in a relationship does not automatically happen when one marries so when does a readiness and ability to sacrifice occur and what role does experience in romantic relationships in emerging adulthood play in this process? These are the type of novel questions she addresses as she sheds important light (via both quantitative data and the "voices" of young people) on the complex role that romantic relationships have in the lives of young people as they build their *I* identity and their *We* identity. She likewise examines the important role of media in emerging adults' romance, the challenges of balancing romance in the pursuit of a career, and the challenges and potential for either growth or stagnation brought about by break-ups of romantic relationships. Finally, and notably, is a chapter that examines the romantic lives of emerging adults who identify as

LGBTQ (lesbian, gay, bisexual, transgender, queer). Taken together, this book provides a comprehensive look into some of the most important and interesting aspects of the romantic lives of emerging adults. In doing so, Dr. Konstam not only reviews existing literature but moves our understanding of this important area forward by presenting new data and, finally, brings it all to life with the voices of young people who lend their lived experience in romantic relationships to the book. In a series that is devoted to examining flourishing and floundering in the diverse paths young people take into and through the third decade of life this book lends novel insight into the role that romance plays in explaining and understanding those paths.

Larry J. Nelson
Series Editor

ACKNOWLEDGMENTS ▲

Depicting the romantic lives of emerging adults has been an ambitious and demanding project. Feeling in between, during a developmental period of self-focus, instability and uncertainty, emerging adults are faced with the daunting task of working toward the consolidation of a romantic identity. Understanding that the choices they make have significant implications for their overall well-being, emerging adults forge forward in a cyber-dominated romantic arena seemingly offering unlimited access, freedom, and opportunity to explore and grow emotionally, yet often causing them to feel insignificant and disposable. In an interconnected, yet unstable and fluid world, emerging adults frequently perceive romantic exploration as treacherous.

In writing a book devoted to the romantic lives of emerging adults, I have encountered many individuals whose contributions merit acknowledgment. Their diverse perspectives and insights have led me to a more textured and nuanced understanding of the field.

In 2013, I assembled a team to tackle a project on the impact of divorce; over the prior 3 years we transitioned to focus on romance. Throughout the 5 years we have worked together, two members of the research team, Teyana Curran and Samantha Karwin, emerging adults themselves, have been steadfast in their commitment to this work. Our weekly lively and passionate discussions sustained us through periods of bewilderment and confusion, alternating with periods of clarity and breakthroughs. Teyana and Samantha each brought a unique, complementary set of skills, perspectives, and experiences which enhanced our efforts. I am eternally grateful to have had the privilege of working with them. The fruits of our combined labor are reflected throughout this book.

The contributions of Selda Celen-Demiritas, an emerging adult from Turkey and a third member of the group, have likewise been instrumental. In the coming years, I look forward to watching Selda grow into a highly productive independent investigator and clinician.

I would also like to acknowledge the contributions of two additional team members, Bonnie Andrews and Kimberly Bryant. Each provided a unique perspective and skill set and I have appreciated their insights and contributions to the project.

The unwavering support of Larry Nelson, the editor of this series, has been instrumental to the completion of *The Romantic Lives of Emerging Adults: Getting From* I *to* We. I have learned to rely on his mastery of the field, sound academic judgment, and sophisticated understanding and commitment to all facets of the publication process. A consummate professional, his encouragement and contagious enthusiasm for academic discourse cannot be overstated. I am also grateful to Andrea Zekus and Courtney McCarroll at Oxford University Press for their support and encouragement.

My colleagues in the field have also provided me with insight and inspiration. A special thank you goes to Drs. Paul Amato, Ofra Mayseless, Elizabeth Morgan, Mike Pratt, Moin Syed, Shmuel Shulman, and Amber Vennum.

Finally, I want to thank my family—my husband Marv and our two children, Amanda and Jeremy Konstam, for their insights and generous support. It is not coincidental that I began my journey into this broad field when our children were emerging adults, themselves. Baffled by the choices they were making, I was forced to rethink and recalibrate many assumptions about this developmental period. They were spark plugs for my continuing professional and emotional growth, and for that I am eternally grateful. I feel deeply fortunate to have them in my life.

THE ROMANTIC LIVES OF EMERGING ADULTS ▲

1 ▲

The Romantic Lives of Emerging Adults
Getting From I *to* We

▲ Introduction

> *Perhaps in the absence of sheer necessity, direction*
> *is hard to find. Or perhaps . . . [emerging adults] feel*
> *the need to extend the chaos and take longer than*
> *one would expect of them to grow up, sensing that*
> *the future is indeed quite unpredictable, recognizing*
> *the dramatic acceleration of events that has occurred,*
> *and following the dictates of nature that suggested*
> *that the young, unformed, pliable creature has a*
> *better chance of evolutionary survival than the*
> *one that matures too quickly and becomes frozen,*
> *unable to adapt to a drastically alien environmental*
> *condition, the . . . twenty-first century.*
> —Flach, 1988, pp.70–71

Contradictions abound when trying to characterize today's generation of emerging adults. They have been depicted in both the academic literature and popular culture in divergent ways. Emerging adults seem at once to be more fearless and yet more anxiety-ridden than generations past; more practical and yet more irresponsible; more globally aware and yet more isolated (Konstam, 2015). While popular "wisdom" suggests that they are narcissistic, entitled, easily distracted, self-absorbed, and impatient—traits that certainly do not position them to be "successful" romantic partners—they are also depicted as seeking authentic and growth-oriented romantic relationships that are based on trust and mutual respect. More than previous generations, these emerging adults seem to be trying to achieve purpose, meaning, and balance in their work and romantic lives (Mayseless & Keren, 2014; Willoughby & James, 2017). When they marry, they want to marry for love. But at their current stage of development, entangled as they are in the metamorphosis from adolescence to adulthood, their romantic lives are fraught with complexity and ambiguity.

Computer-mediated communication (CMC) is both an aid and a hindrance to emerging adults. They are relying on technology to an unprecedented extent to help manage their social and romantic lives. On the one hand, smartphones and social media create enormous romantic conveniences; on the other, these CMC tools are allowing relationships to become more superficial, disposable, and confusing.

Challenged by a harsh, unstable, and global economic environment that is in transition, emerging adults, ages 18 to 29, sense the uncertainty around them. The rules that previously enabled them to function and thrive in familiar environments, such as school and family, no longer apply. They are experiencing a "serious disjuncture" between the demands of adolescence and the developmental tasks associated with emerging adulthood (Cote, 2000, p. 29).

That pressure is taking its toll. Many emerging adults are ridden with anxiety about the future (Arnett, 2014). College counseling centers throughout the country are deluged with students in need of psychological services (Center for Collegiate Mental Health, 2015). A 2012 survey conducted by the American Psychological Association (APA) found that 19% of emerging and young adults ages 18–33 reported having been diagnosed with a depressive disorder (Jayson, 2013). In a study conducted by Arnett and Schwab (2013), it was found that more than 56% of emerging adults, 18–29 years of age, reported that they "often feel anxious." The anxiety was attributed in large part to career instability (Arnett, 2014). However, it must be pointed out that nearly half of emerging adults are not experiencing anxiety and that, over time, most emerging adults find their way and flourish (Padilla-Walker & Nelson, 2017).

As the United States is struggling to find meaning in a vision that unites us as citizens, emerging adults are also struggling to find purpose, meaning, and goals, both collectively and individually. They are taking a longer time to construct an identity that includes commitment to both career and partner, and they are doing so in the context of an unpredictable shifting global economy with a paucity of guidelines to inform their choices (Shulman & Connolly, 2013; Konstam, 2015).

In terms of our understanding of the romantic lives of emerging adults, there is a void regarding what happens between the end of adolescence and the emergence of adulthood (Shulman & Connolly, 2013). First, in order to gain a solid footing, we must understand emerging adulthood itself and the meanings emerging adults attach to this period of development.

Arnett (2000, 2006) observed that emerging adults are in a highly unstable stage of life. They are experimenting with choices and working toward identity formation and consolidation in multiple important domains. He identifies five developmental markers of individuals negotiating this transitional period, which typically includes individuals 18 to 29 of age:

1. It is the age of *identity explorations*, of trying out various possibilities, especially in love and work.
2. It is the age of *instability*.
3. It is the most *self-focused* age of life.
4. It is the age of *feeling in-between*, in transition, neither adolescent nor adult.
5. It is the age of *possibilities*, when hopes flourish, when young people have an unparalleled opportunity to transform their lives. (Arnett, 2004, p. 8)

Arnett (2004) does point out, however, that an emerging adulthood characterized by exploration and experimentation is the specific terrain of individuals from middle- and upper-class backgrounds who are pursuing either a college degree or a career that *requires* a college degree. Individual and sociocultural factors intersect and shape the transition to adulthood (Hendry & Kloep, 2010); these factors can either encourage or impede individuals from using this period to explore and experiment. For those emerging adults with fewer economic options and less social capital to explore multiple educational, vocational, and romantic paths, this period of experimentation can become truncated. Such emerging adults are likely to assume adult roles during this life stage (e.g., through having to take a "permanent" job or through parenthood), roles that are likely to prevent them from further exploration. Delaying adult roles may not be a "luxury" they can afford.

How do contemporary emerging adults define adulthood and what criteria do they use in determining whether a member of their peer group is an adult? Today's emerging adults are endorsing individualistic and adaptive psychological criteria (Arnett, 2000; Nelson & Luster, 2016). They do not believe that being married and having children are necessary criteria for adulthood. However, being accountable, self-supporting, and responsible for one's actions *are* considered key markers of adulthood (Nelson, Padilla-Walker, Carroll, & Madsen,

2007; Nelson & Luster, 2016). Interestingly, over time, many emerging adults incorporate more traditional markers into their own definition of adulthood, such as marriage and children (Lowe, Dillon Rhodes, & Zwieback, 2013, as cited in Sharon, 2016). This sometimes-bewildering fusion of the old and traditional with the new is one of the most distinguishing characteristics of emerging adulthood.

▲ Why This Book

How can we best understand today's emerging adults and the meanings they assign to their romantic experiences and expectations? How do they think about themselves, their casual relationships, their more enduring romantic relationships, and marriage? During this transitional period of their lives, emerging adults face more developmental tasks than they do at any other stage of life (Caspi, 2002). They are feeling the pressure to solidify the sense of *I*, and they know their future may depend on how they respond to this pressure (Gala & Kapadia, 2013). Thus, many of them are postponing the structuring of careers, relationships, and other life domains—a seemingly natural response to the complex, unpredictable environment they find themselves encountering.

As if forming a viable *I* were not challenging enough amidst today's unguided range of options, many emerging adults are also learning to form a *we* identity as part of a romantic couple. Emerging adults follow a variety of pathways toward sustained romantic commitment. They may enter and leave a series of short-term romantic relationships, some stable, some unstable (Shulman, Seiffge-Krenke, Scharf, Boiangiu, & Tregubenko, 2016). They may elect to pursue steady long-term relationship(s) (Rauer, Pettit, Lansford, Bates, & Dodge, 2013) or experiment with casual sexual encounters and relationships (Claxton & van Dulmen, 2016). They may opt out of committed relationships entirely or pursue some combination of these choices. There is no one path toward a *we* identity, should that be a goal. And for many emerging adults in the United States, working toward resolving a career or educational identity may preclude or prolong exploration of a *we* identity.

What are emerging adults looking for in their romantic relationships? What are their values and beliefs about romantic commitment and how do they enact these perspectives in terms of their romantic lives?

Emerging adults are not a monolithic group and the paths taken toward adulthood are diverse and fluid, not unlike the external exigencies they are navigating. Long-term commitments such as marriage, for some, seem to be in conflict with the constant refining and redefining of the self that emerging adults feel called upon to negotiate. And yet most still desire long-term committed relationships. They are likely to view their single status as a preparatory stage, and when (and if) they find the "right" partner, their expressed preference shifts accordingly. However, they also value the process of developing an autonomous identity. They recognize that the *I* identity must be protected and developed even as a couple is becoming a more solidified *we*.

Emerging adults make a wide variety of missteps and miscues on the way to satisfying romantic relationships, but many, if not most, of these "errors" can lead to positive outcomes in the long run. Over time, most emerging adults do gain clarity around their romantic lives, though a minority continue to be mired in confusion and uncertainty through the third decade. How do emerging adults navigate this tumultuous decade? How do they transition from an *I* orientation to a *we* orientation and what choices do they make along the way to help them get there? These are examples of the questions this book will attempt to answer, or at the very least further illuminate.

In trying to understand emerging adults, the contradictions abound. For example, while a majority of emerging adults in the United States declare that they are committed to traditional notions of romantic commitment, their behaviors often seem to belie their stated values and goals—for example, in their practice of casual sex and their delay in entering long-term committed relationships. We will attempt to deconstruct their sometimes perplexing behaviors and provide multiple lenses to help us understand these apparent contradictions. Throughout this text, we will examine the key issues that inform emerging adults' choices and dilemmas (e.g., commitment, sacrifice, CMC). We will attempt to disentangle facts from unhelpful myths that have been associated with this generation of emerging adults. We will be mindful of the complexity of their romantic lives, the seemingly boundless choices before them, and the lack of structure and protocol that exists to inform their choices. We will come to better understand why some emerging adults are linear and direct in their approach, others more experimental and meandering, and still others seem lost without a throughput that informs their behaviors and choices.

The Romantic Lives of Emerging Adults: Getting from I to We will present original research data in addition to examining the existing literature. The content represents an attempt to cover the major areas of research, expand upon the existing literature, and generate new contributions in areas that have received inadequate attention and/or remain elusive. The voices of 29 emerging adults, interviewed extensively by the author and a team of graduate students, will be heard throughout this text in the hopes of adding depth and clarity to the issues discussed, lending support and dimension to existing theory, and suggesting new areas of study and inquiry. (Details of the methodology and sampling of this study and analysis of data can been found in the appendices.)

▲ Structure and Content

Structurally, each chapter begins with an introduction of the topic related to the romantic lives of emerging adults and examines some of the most relevant theory and literature in that area. Original data about the topic is presented based on extensive interviews with the 29 participants including categorizing, analyzing and summarizing the data. Following that section is an attempt to digest the original research and frame it in the context of existing theory and literature. In most chapters, a special topic of interest is then presented, a topic that typically is not adequately represented in the literature. Finally, with the exception of Chapter 5, a "close-up look" at one or more participants whose experiences are particularly relevant to that chapter's topic is presented and discussed. The hope is that by presenting these in-depth, chapter-closing "case studies" the chapter topics will be brought to life more vividly.

We will begin our journey in Chapter 2 with a foundational topic: identity formation in emerging adulthood. How does one form both an individual and a "couple" identity in a world where there is such great flux, uncertainty, and ambiguity of rules and guidelines, and at a time in life when many developmental tasks are clamoring for attention? Much of the work of individual identity formation ideally takes place before one is ready to adopt a relationship identity. This transition from *I* to *we* is, in fact, one of the key defining aspects of emerging adulthood (hence, the subtitle of this book).

The ability to make a romantic commitment, the subject of Chapter 3, is a crucial prerequisite for forging a strong couple identity. Most emerging adults, despite the way they have been characterized as noncommittal, are looking, ultimately, for commitment in romance. Through their "experimental" experiences with premarital commitment, they have opportunities to learn many of the relational skills they can use to build long-term committed relationships, including marriage.

Closely related to commitment is the concept of sacrifice, which is the topic of Chapter 4—a topic not well represented in the existing literature. In order to be ready to make a meaningful romantic commitment, one must be fully cognizant of what one is ready and willing to give up—for example, spending time with single friends and having casual sexual encounters. Today's emerging adults, as reflected by our research group, are highly sensitized to the notion of sacrifice. In fact, their grasp of the magnitude of sacrifice seems to be a main reason that many emerging adults are delaying serious romantic commitment until they feel authentically ready. Hence, the purpose of this chapter will be to explore how sacrifice is viewed and lived among emerging adults who are living in an age of possibilities, when so many options are seemingly open to them.

No discussion of romance among today's emerging adults can take place without including the topic of CMC, the focus of Chapter 5. For emerging adults engaging in romance, CMC is not a fringe consideration, but a central one; hence this topic is accorded a full chapter. Never before have technological tools—texting (and sexting), social media, Skype, dating apps—played such an integral role in how romance is sought and managed on a day-to-day basis. Without understanding the way emerging adults integrate CMC with romance, it would not be possible to fully comprehend the meanings they assign to their romantic experiences and expectations.

It is CMC that largely empowers today's emerging adults to enjoy unprecedented freedom around casual sex, the focus of Chapter 6. Presently, a host of casual romantic options such as friends-with-benefits and hookups have become acceptable, including some (such as booty calls) that rely on the immediacy of today's communication technology. The relationship of casual sex to attachment style is examined here, as is the potential effect of casual sex on one's long-term relationships and individual psychology.

Breaking up is another aspect of the romantic lives of emerging adults that is frequently mediated by CMC. In Chapter 7, we will examine not only *how* emerging adults break up—including the role social media plays—but *why*, and what the future consequences of breakups may be. Partly due to social media, the dissolution of relationships is marked by a great deal more ambiguity for today's emerging adults than for generations past. The type of narrative one adopts about a breakup can inform and determine whether a breakup will represent growth or stagnation.

One of the reasons emerging adults are taking longer to commit to marriage than past generations is the new set of realities they face in the workplace. Chapter 8 is devoted to work and romance and their coordination. We will examine the challenges emerging adults face in forming identities in both the work and the romance domain, at a time when they are still struggling to complete the task of cementing individual adulthood. Because of the uncertainty and difficulty today's emerging adults face in finding dependable, well-paying careers, many of them are electing to focus on career first and relationships later. Hence, the purpose of this chapter will be to understand how the dynamics of work and romantic love interact for today's emerging adults and how today's vocational challenges are affecting the way emerging adults view and approach long-term romantic commitment.

Chapter 9 addresses the romantic challenges and experiences of individuals who identify as LGBTQ (lesbian, gay, bisexual, transgender, queer). In a society that is still heteronormative, there is a lack of general understanding about the romantic lives of emerging adults who identify as LGBTQ and about what some of the basic terms (e.g., transgender, transsexual, transvestite, and "trans") mean. Stigma—overt, covert, and internalized—continues to be a major issue for LGBTQ identified emerging adults, and one that affects both their romantic relationships and their identity development. However, they are inclined to harbor the same basic romantic goals as other emerging adults—that is, to find a partner and establish a trusting, growth-oriented, long-term relationship—but they often face more obstacles and complexity on the way to their goals. In this chapter we will explore both the commonalities and the differences LGBTQ emerging adults experience in romance as compared to mainstream heterosexuals, with an eye toward improving our overall understanding.

Most emerging adults, however, do foresee a day when they will be ready to make a long-term commitment to a partner, for many specifically in the form of marriage. Despite the fact that emerging adults are delaying marriage and/or choosing other relationship options such as singlehood and cohabitation, 80% still see marriage in their futures and are optimistic about it. Chapter 10 explores the beliefs that emerging adults hold about marriage—*getting* married and *being* married. Marital horizon theory and marital paradigm theory ground the discussion.

Understanding the meanings emerging adults attach to marriage helps us to understand their romantic behaviors and attitudes in the years *leading up* to marriage. Despite the fact that most emerging adults do not marry during this period of development, there are some who do, and many of these marriages do not succeed. In Chapter 11, which focuses on divorce, we will examine some of the reasons marriages fail for emerging adults.

In keeping with the book's planned structure, we will end the present chapter with the first of these close-up encounters. Here, we will focus on Sandra. In many ways, she is romantically representative of the emerging adult population. She has had some bad experiences in romance, but is using those experiences to help her refine what she ultimately wants in a long-term relationship. In this way, we can see that, even *problems* in romantic relationships can lead to positive outcomes. Sandra uses CMC to aid in her love life, but, like many emerging adults, is somewhat ambivalent about its benefits versus drawbacks. Though she wants to meet a man who will treat her better than past partners have, she has not yet developed the capacity to fully identify the behaviors and attitudes of her own that may be getting in the way of realizing her romantic goals.

▲ Sandra: Wary (and Weary) but Hopeful

Sandra self-identifies as a heterosexual Black Hispanic female, 26 years of age. She is currently enrolled in a master's program in computer science, holds a full-time job in the field, and seems well on her way toward achieving her professional goals. Romantically, Sandra has experienced a series of frustrating and unsatisfying relationships. From her perspective, the men with whom she has been involved have been "selfish," "noncommunicative," and "unwilling to express their feelings" (including their feelings about her, even during intimate sexual encounters). She longs for a partner who makes her feel "important" and "cared about" and who is motivated to "please" her. And she is optimistic that CMC will help her find him.

Currently she describes herself as being in a self-protective mode: just lately, she has taken some time off from "dating." She ended her most recent relationship because she felt she needed to protect herself and her "heart." Sandra has been able to set limits on past romantic relationships; however, there remains a simmering anger toward the men she has dated. She attributes her past relationship failures to "bad luck" and does not appear to link the failures to her own behaviors, the behaviors of her previous partners, and/or any patterns that may have emerged in her cumulative dating experiences. Sandra asserts that "being in a relationship" is "better" than "feeling alone and lonely"— a stance that might be viewed as a formula for making hasty and ill-advised partnering choices.

Sandra's ideas about an ideal partner have shifted over time:

> In the past, I expected my boyfriends to do things for me, take me out to nice places, have a nice car, be well known/important, 'that guy'. . . Now my expectations are the complete opposite and more realistic. . . . I want someone who has a career and is not financially dependent on me or their mother, someone who is hardworking, spontaneous, and adventurous. A partner I can talk to, who is more of a friend than a lover, because sleeping with someone is easy, but being a friend takes effort. I need to feel secure and [know] that my partner has my best interests at heart and is not just trying to get what they want. [I would like to meet] someone who is genuine, respectful, and loyal.

It seems that Sandra *has* developed some insight into the type of man with whom she is more likely to be happy; this is forward progress for Sandra. She has learned about compromise, too. Compromise is at the heart of a relationship, according to Sandra. "Without compromising," she says, "there is no foundation, there's nothing being built on." Sandra has a vision regarding the relationship she is hoping for:

> I want it to be genuine and they're just listening to me and I'm listening to them because I really do care. . . . I picture a romantic relationship being a very thoughtful and considerate and caring and very, like, sensitive towards anything I say. It's not just like, "Oh, whatever" [when] you're having a bad day; it's . . . "Oh my gosh, I'm sorry, is there anything I can do to make you feel better?" That's where the answer is. You know?

Currently, Sandra's future plans do not include being married or having children. She states that it is much easier to leave and enter relationships without children—seemingly reflecting an assumption that future relationships, like her past ones, will be impermanent.

Sandra, like many of her peers, has used CMC to aid in her search for more satisfying romantic choices. Being a minority Black Hispanic woman, CMC empowers her to "communicate" with a greater pool of potential partners. With respect to dating apps, she assesses that they have had both positive and negative effects on her romantic life:

> I think that technology has been good. It's the good and the bad that come out of it. . . . It is good because you're able to communicate more with people from everywhere that you could not communicate with before, [whereas in the days before dating apps], you would have to go out to meet someone. And then if you do go out, in this city, you meet up with the same people all over again because . . . they keep going to the same places. And that's kind of like not really meeting anyone.
>
> If [you're] reaching out to someone across the world, or someone that's, like, on the other side of the state, or the other side of town from you . . . technology has been . . . really good in helping people in relationships [find] that person.

As for social media, Sandra speaks about her past enthusiasm for "letting the world know that she is in relationship and that it is going well." However, she is now wary of having her relationship open to the world, only to be dissected on social media when it "goes bad." She feels that the relationship becomes even more vulnerable when everyone offers their opinions:

> It's good but at the same time when things go bad and things get aired out, that's when things get ugly on social media. So it's good in ways and it's bad, but it depends on what you use it for.
>
> [It] could also, like, screw you over because . . . everyone seems to, like, just value everyone's opinion. And it's like living your relationship through social media. It's never going to work because everyone's going to have an opinion regardless if it's good [or if] it's bad. They're going to always find fault . . . [with] something. And if you keep living that way . . . living your relationship through social media, then it's . . . never gonna be able to bloom, to blossom.

Sandra states that at critical junctures, when conflict is at play within a couple, it is particularly important to hunker down, rely on one's interpersonal resources, and work things through so that the relationship is able to "bloom" and "blossom."

Although Sandra expresses disappointment in her previous romantic relationships, she is guardedly hopeful about the future. Despite her negative experiences with the men she has been in relationship with, she maintains an optimistic stance and believes that relationships can grow. She clearly prefers to be in relationship than to be alone. However, Sandra appears to have a blind spot about how she comes to select partners, typically ending up with men who are unable to give her what she says she is seeking: respect and care. Sandra has shifted her perspective in terms of what she is looking for in a potential partner. However, she does not seem to be in touch with her anger when she speaks about past romances, an anger that is likely to tinge the quality of her future relationships. Perhaps, over time, she will gain insights about herself in relationship and, with or without the help of CMC, develop the ability to find the type of man she would like to be with. Although Sandra has not met anyone that she admits to seriously liking, she remains optimistic that love will "blossom."

One of the reasons for introducing Sandra in this introductory chapter is that her story touches on many of the issues we will be exploring throughout the book—marriage, CMC, compromise, the interplay of career and romance, and the desire among emerging adults for long-term commitment. Sandra does not "speak for her generation," however, and that is why she is just one of the many voices we will hear from in this book. There is not one version of emerging adulthood but many overlapping variations (Arnett, 2010; Larson, Wilson, & Rickman, 2009; Shweder, 1998). In fact, as we will observe through the reviewed literature, the original research, and the case studies, diversity seems to be *more* pronounced during this transitional, experimental, and exploratory period than in any other stage of life. However, there are also common themes that emerge; common attitudes, values, and experiences that emerging adults share. Both the commonality and the individuality of the emerging adults you will meet in this book will contribute to a richer understanding of emerging adults and how they live and love.

▲ References

Arnett, J. (2000). Emerging adulthood. A theory of development from the late teens through the twenties. *American Psychologist, 55,* 469–480. doi:10.1037/0003-066X.55.5.469

Arnett, J. (2004). *Emerging adulthood: The winding road from the late teens through the twenties.* New York, NY: Oxford University Press.

Arnett, J. (2006). Emerging adulthood: Understanding the new way of coming of age. In J. Arnett & J. Tanner (Eds.), *Emerging adults in America: Coming of age in the 21st century* (pp. 1–3). Washington, DC: American Psychological Association.

Arnett, J. (2010). The cultural psychology of a new life stage. In L. J. Arnett (Ed.), *Bridging cultural and developmental approaches to psychology: New syntheses in theory, research, and policy* (pp. 255–275). New York, NY: Oxford University Press.

Arnett, J. J. (2014). *Emerging adulthood: The winding road from the late teens through the twenties* (2nd ed.). New York, NY: Oxford University Press.

Arnett, J. J., & Schwab, J. (2013). *The Clark University poll of emerging adults, 2012: Thriving, struggling, and hopeful.* Worcester, MA: Clark University.

Caspi A. (2002). Social selection, social causation, and developmental pathways: Empirical strategies for better understanding how individuals and environments are linked across the life-course. In L. Pulkkinen & A. Caspi (Eds.), *Paths to successful development: Personality in the life course* (pp. 281–301). New York, NY: Cambridge University Press. doi:10.1017/CBO9780511489761.012

Center for Collegiate Mental Health. (2015). *2015 Annual Report.* Penn State University. University Park, PA. Retrieved from http://ccmh.psu.edu/wp-content/uploads/sites/3058/2016/01/2015_CCMH_Report_1-18-2015.pdf

Claxton, S. E., & van Dulmen, M. H. M. (2016). Casual sexual relationships and experiences in emerging adulthood. In J. J. Arnett (Ed.), *The Oxford handbook of emerging adulthood* (pp. 245–261). New York, NY: Oxford University Press.

Cote, J. (2000). *Arrested Adulthood: The changing nature of maturity and identity.* New York, NY: New York University Press.

Flach, F. (1998). *Resilience: How to bounce back when the going gets tough!* Long Island City, NY: Hatherleigh Press.

Gala, J., & Kapadia, S. (2013). Romantic relationships in emerging adulthood: A developmental perspective. *Psychological Studies, 58*(4), 406–418. doi:10.1007/s12646-013-0219-5

Hendry, L. B., & Kloep, M. (2010). How universal is emerging adulthood? An empirical example. *Journal of Youth Studies, 13*(2), 169–179. doi:10.1080/13676260903295067

Jayson, S. (2013, February 7). Who's feeling stressed? Young adults, new survey shows. *USA Today.* Retrieved from http://www.usatoday.com/story/news/nation/2013/02/06/stress-psychology-millennials-depression/1878295

Konstam, V. (2015). *Emerging and young adulthood: Multiple perspectives, diverse narratives* (2nd ed.). Cham, Switzerland: Springer International.

Larson, R. W., Wilson, S., & Rickman, A. (2009). Globalization, societal change, and adolescence across the world. In R. M. Lerner & L. Steinberg (Eds.), *Handbook of adolescent psychology: Contextual influences on adolescent development* (3rd ed., Vol. 2, pp. 590–622). Hoboken, NJ: Wiley.

Mayseless, O., & Keren, E. (2014). Finding a meaningful life as a developmental task in emerging adulthood: The domains of love and work across cultures. *Emerging Adulthood, 2*(1), 63–73. doi:10.1177/2167696813515446

Nelson, L. J., & Luster, S. S. (2016). "Adulthood" by whose definition? The complexity of emerging adults' conceptions of adulthood. In L. J. Arnett (Ed.), *The Oxford handbook of emerging adulthood* (pp. 421–437). New York, NY: Oxford University Press.

Nelson, L. J., Padilla-Walker, L., Carroll, J. S., Madsen, S. J., Barry, M. C., & Badger, S. (2007). "If you want me to treat you like an adult, start acting like one!" Comparing the criteria that emerging adults and their parents have for adulthood. *Journal of Family Psychology, 21*(4), 670–674.

Padilla-Walker, L. M., & Nelson, L. J. (2017). Flourishing in emerging adulthood: An understudies approach to the third decade of life. In L. M. Padilla-Walker & L. J. Nelson (Eds). *Flourishing in emerging adulthood: Positive development during the third decade of life* (pp. 3–13). New York, NY: Oxford University Press.

Rauer, A. J., Pettit, G. S., Lansford, J. E., Bates, J. E., & Kodge, K. A. (2013). Romantic relationship patterns in young adulthood and their developmental antecedents. *Developmental Psychology, 49*(11), pp. 2159–2171. doi:10.1037/a0031845

Sharon, T. (2016). Constructing adulthood: Markers of adulthood and well-being among emerging adults. *Emerging Adulthood, 4*(3), pp. 161–167. doi:10.1177/2167696815579826

Shulman, S., & Connolly, J. (2013). The challenge of romantic relationships in emerging adulthood: Reconceptualization of the field. *Emerging Adulthood, 1*(1), pp. 27–39. doi:10.1177/2167696812467330

Shulman, S., Seiffge-Krenke, I., Scharf, M., Boiangiu, S. B., & Tregubenko, V. (2016). The diversity of romantic pathways during emerging adulthood and their developmental antecedents. *International Journal of Behavioral Development,* doi:0165025416673474

Shweder, R. A. (1998). *Welcome to middle age!: (And other cultural fictions).* Chicago, IL: University of Chicago Press.

Willoughby, B. J., & James, S. L. (2017). *The marriage paradox: Why emerging adults love marriage yet push it aside.* New York, NY: Oxford University Press.

2 ▲

Identity
Becoming an I, *Becoming a* We

> *We are not the same in all regions of our lives, and*
> *how we make meaning may change across situations*
> *or over time. Identity is what integrates our own*
> *diversity, gives meaning to the disparate parts of*
> *ourselves, and relates them to one another. Identity*
> *is how we interpret parts of ourselves, and relate*
> *them to one another. Identity is how we interpret*
> *our own existence and understand who we are in*
> *our world.*
>
> —Josselson, 1996, p. 30

Developing and refining a sense of self—an identity—is a central task of emerging adulthood. It is difficult to understand either the nature of emerging adulthood or the romantic challenges emerging adults face without considering identity. First and foremost a sense of self, an *I* develops, followed by a *we* identity if the individual is in a long-term committed romantic relationship. Identity construction is strongly influenced by the diversity of one's past and current experiences as well as one's ability to acknowledge, challenge, and integrate those experiences. It is not a unified event, but rather a negotiated, on-going process during which emerging adults respond dynamically to the ever-changing and sometimes contradictory world around them (Chappell, Rhodes, Solomon, Tennant, & Yates, 2003, as cited in Stokes & Wyn, 2007).

In the 21st century, emerging adults must exhibit greater fluidity and nimbleness in all domains of identity than they have in the past (Savickas, 1997; Porfeli & Savickas, 2012). Rules are in flux and are more contextual than ever before. At the same time, there is less institutional guidance pointing to clear and fixed developmental pathways (Konstam, 2015; Schwartz, 2016). Given the absence of reliable guidance in navigating these new waters, key questions such as "Who am I, and where am I going?" (Cote, 2000, p. 127) and "Whom do I want to go there with?" (Manning, Giordano, Longmore, & Hocevar, 2011, p. 319) seem overwhelming to many emerging adults. The onerous burden is now on them to discover their own answers (Cote, 2000).

Making the quest more bearable is the fact that many emerging adults feel a freedom to judge themselves by a different standard from those of previous generations (Cote, 2000). The menu of identity options is larger. The romantic landscape is changing, too: there is greater acceptance of premarital sex, cohabitation, and the delay of marriage, all of which have created the space to explore identity not only in emerging adults' romantic lives but also in their religious, ethnic, professional, and political lives (Kroger & Marcia, 2011; McNamara, Abo-Zena, & Abo-Zena; 2014; Schwartz, 2016).

Identity development is not a fixed or stable process; it is changeable and affected by external circumstances (Arnett, 2006; Zunker, 2006). A change in one's profession or social network, for example, can force an acceleration (or delay) in identity development during emerging adulthood. Identity is multidimensional and shifts along with one's sense of self (Aron & Aron, 1986; 1996). It does not necessarily remain stable across times and settings (McCarn & Fassinger, 1996; Schwartz, Luyckx, & Vignoles, 2011; Tanner, 2006). Furthermore, changes in one's sense of identity do not always represent departures from fundamental values; rather they are viewed as appropriate responses to the shifting expectations of various environments (Hays, 2008) and the roles one plays within those environments. For example, many emerging adults are living with their parents because of financial considerations, often on a revolving-door basis. They in turn report alternating periods of increasing and decreasing dependency during these shifts that can be understood as largely environmentally driven (Konstam, 2015).

In the current chapter, the theoretical constructs of Marcia, Josselson, and Schwartz, as they pertain to individual identity, will be presented, followed by a discussion of issues related to individual identity formation, such as group identification, the concept of agency, and the role of commitment. We will then examine the challenges of forming a couple identity, citing several prevalent theories and models, such as interdependence theory and the self-expansion model. We will discuss some of the common hallmarks and struggles of transitioning from an *I* perspective to a *we*. The experiences of 29 emerging adults will then be presented and discussed, highlighting their reflections on becoming a couple. Finally, we will take a closer look at Yasmine, one of the participants, who illustrates some of the struggles today's emerging adults face in laying claim to both an individual and a couple identity.

▲ Identity: Theoretical Considerations

Expanding on the seminal contributions of Erikson (1956), Josselson (1996) presents a cogent summary of identity that seems fitting for opening our discussion. She posits that we are not consistent in the way we make meaning across the various domains and situations in our lives. How we "integrate our diversity" and "relate them to one another" is central to how we construct our identities and define ourselves (p. 30).

James Marcia, one of the most prominent theorists in identity formation, delineated four identity groups. Marcia's four "identity statuses" (1966) include *diffusion* (absence of commitments, coupled with lack of interest in exploration); *foreclosure* (commitment to certain roles and values without prior exploration); *moratorium* (a state of active exploration with few commitments); and *achievement* (a set of commitments embraced following a period of exploration and identity crisis). These four identity statuses function within a wide range of domains: political preference, religious affiliation, gender, sexuality, values and morality, and family relationships, to name a few. The literature is somewhat ambivalent as to how identity should be operationalized—as a global construct or as specific to each of the domains (Schwartz, 2016). Studies that have focused on each of these domains separately suggest that identity develops unevenly across domains (Goossens, 2001; Pastorino, Dunham, Kidwell, Baccho, & Lamborn, 1997, as cited in Schwartz, 2016).

In order to make these four identity statuses "more descriptive" and "less evaluative," Josselson (1996) changed the names of these four groups to *drifters, guardians, searchers*, and *pathmakers*, respectively. Although Josselson's findings (1996) are based solely on research with female participants, she concludes that "extensive research with both males and females, over close to thirty years, reveals that these four groups can be reliably assessed" across gender and "share predictable personality characteristics and ways of behaving" (p. 36).

Drifters (diffusion) are, as their name suggests, noncommittal and delayed in forming their identity. They are often anxious, their choices capricious. Drifters have low self-esteem and often struggle to identify their own dreams and desires, which tend to shift frequently. Though they may function as prominent players in the plans of others, they have difficulty integrating a sense of self (Josselson, 1996). They don't generally have a lot of support from others. They tend to delay and postpone commitment and fulfillment. They don't know what they really believe or what they want to do with their lives, and they don't think it really matters, at least for the time being.

Guardians (foreclosure) tend to make life choices based on their parents' beliefs. They make these choices easily and without hesitation, evidencing a lack of exploration and consideration of other options. They are comfortable with tradition and embody the mindset, "This is how I am because it's how I was raised, or how I've always been" (Josselson, 1996, p. 35). They exhibit high levels of obedience to authority and respect for rules, and they seek out others who share their beliefs and reinforce their choices. They have lower levels of anxiety than the other groups (Josselson, 1996) and are untrammeled by introspection.

Searchers (moratorium) are, like drifters, uncommitted in many areas of their lives. But, unlike drifters, their reluctance to commit stems from exploration. They are actively evaluating their options. They are often idealistic and aspire to do great things but they may also feel unsure as to how to execute meaningful choices. They often feel trapped between their desires and the expectations of others. "I'm not sure about who I am or want to be, but I'm trying to figure it out" is their motto (Josselson, 1996, p. 35). After a period of self-examination and experimentation, most searchers do commit to a firmer identity, though they remain aware of their inner conflict.

Pathmakers (achievement) are the trailblazers, the pavers of the road for others. They are able to break away from their childhood patterns and parental influences. They make conscious decisions about how they want to contribute to the lives of others. They prefer action to endless introspection. They love to explore, but do so with the goal of reaching a resolution. When they form an identity, it is congruent with the values they have worked to develop (Josselson, 1996). After experimenting with options, they make their choices, although with less conviction than guardians—probably because they are more aware of the options that exist and are, by nature and experience, more open-minded than guardians.

The four groups should be viewed as on a continuum, not in fixed boxes. There is overlap amongst the four identity groups and many emerging adults fit into more than one group. Some emerging adults tend to remain in one group, while others may switch categories over time (Waterman, 1999). Belsky (2010) and other critics of this model have pointed out that membership in any of these groups may be domain-specific. A person might be a drifter when it comes to romantic relationships, but a pathfinder in the career or religion domain. To insist on placing individuals within one fixed, permanent group does not serve either the model itself or the individuals being described by the model (Kroger, 2000). Recent research efforts have produced empirical clusters in support of Marcia's four identity statuses (Crocetti, Rubini, Luyckx, & Meeus, 2008; Luyckx, Goosens, Soenens, Beyers, & Vansteenkiste, 2005). In addition, based on empirical findings, the models of Luyckx and Meeus suggest that identity statuses, for some adolescents and emerging adults, represent semi-permanent personality profiles, as originally hypothesized by Marcia (1966).

More expanded identity status models have emerged in recent years. Building on existing identity models, two new concepts were added: exploration in breadth and exploration in depth (Luyckx, Goossens, & Soenens, 2006; Crocetti et al., 2008). With respect to breadth, the individual sorts through various potential identity alternatives that are likely to result in commitment to a set of values, goals, and belief. After this commitment occurs, the individual engages in an in-depth exploration of these areas of commitment and over time integrates those aspects that "fit" as part of the self (Luyckx et al., 2006).

Understanding the theoretical underpinnings of identity formation allows us to appreciate the diversity of trajectories that unfold during emerging adulthood. These trajectories are likely to influence romantic attachments and romantic choices emerging adults make. For example, a study by Berman, Weems, Rodriguez, and Zamora (2006) found that college-aged guardians were less likely to avoid relationships than drifters, and were also less anxious about entering and sustaining relationships in comparison to searchers or pathmakers. Emerging adults who fit the drifter profile are likely to avoid romantic commitments, while searchers might engage in a series of experimental relationships, and guardians might seek a life partner who fit with a preconceived model consistent with parental or religious requirements.

In Chapter 11 of this text, devoted to the topic of divorce, we have an opportunity to observe directly how the premature foreclosure of the search for a coherent synthesized identity may inform the choices of emerging adults during the marrying process and later in divorce. When making their decision to marry, these emerging adults spoke of being without anchor, in transition, and seeking a safe harbor. Their underdeveloped selves left them vulnerable within the relationship. Most of the participants interviewed reported that after their divorce they revisited the work they had averted during adolescence and the early and middle phases of emerging adulthood, and recommitted to exploring their beliefs, values, and goals. In other words, they revisited the unfinished business of identity formation that they had "put on pause." Individual identity issues powerfully inform romantic choices. Who we believe ourselves to be informs who we believe we should be with.

▲ Self-Identity and Group Membership

The process of identity formation is also informed by group identity (Phinney, 2006). The influences of gender, race, ethnicity, social class, sexual orientation, religious and spiritual orientation, and disability—and how these influences intersect and interact—must be part of any meaningful discussion of identity. Thus far, these factors have not been given due consideration by researchers. While *some* progress has lately been made in developing the literature in this area (Schwartz, Cote, & Arnett, 2005; Schwartz et al., 2013; Syed et al., 2013), much work remains to be done. Author bell hooks (as cited in Phan, Torres Rivera, & Roberts-Wilbur, 2005), for example, points out that the current models do not *sufficiently* take cultural influences into account, including the effects of oppression and discrimination.

Exploration of one's group identity may not be a primary concern when one is in a homogenous social context (Phinney, 2006). However, individuals in more heterogeneous and global contexts have a stronger tendency to be concerned with group identity issues and with negotiating the self in relation to social groups—especially if these individuals have experienced oppression, stigmatization, or discrimination, any of which can restrict one's access to resources and/or limit one's personal and political power. Phinney (2006) also finds that factors such as personality, temperamental style, education level, and phenotype can help determine the likelihood that an individual will become concerned with group identity issues.

With regard to ethnic identity, some people feel a strong need to belong to a group; they may seek out people who share their ethnic background and obtain information about their ethnic heritage as a way of developing a place to belong. Others feel less need to belong or else fulfill the need within a different context, such as family or friends. Experiences of being treated stereotypically or discriminated against, or being asked to label oneself ethnically, can be strong motivators of exploration, regardless of the larger context. (p. 130)

Whether one identifies strongly with a cultural group or not, nearly all individuals seek a specific and unique identity (Harrison, 1995), which includes an "idiosyncratic constellation of qualities . . . that persists over time" (p.379). For those who belong to marginalized social groups that have suffered stigmatization and discrimination, the individual's identity is likely to incorporate a response to such transgressions. In other words, the individual's identity may develop in opposition to the bigotry and persecution the larger group has experienced. In considering such factors, it is important to recognize that individuals have multiple, overlapping group memberships, such as ethnicity, gender, race, education level, religion, environment, and socioeconomic class. The individual's responses to these various group memberships intersect and interact in rich and complex ways to affect the formation of individual identity, particularly for those who belong to multiple oppressed groups (Constantine, 2002).

When considering the powerful effect of such cultural influences, including bigotry and oppression, one must take care not to overgeneralize, or restrict, or stereotype the narrative. For example, bell hooks (1996) states, "There is no one story of African American girlhood," and points out that more work needs to be done in order to appreciate that particular reality in all of its richness, variation, and complexity (p. 13). When viewing "the other," one needs to try to see him or her as part of an idiosyncratic cultural context that includes a convergence of meaning systems that may be substantially different from one's own. It is important not to project meaning onto the other, but rather to try to understand the other's native meaning system. "Everyone sees what they want to see," reports one black female study participant. "But no one seems to want to see me" (Williams, 2005, p. 279).

The extent to which an individual identifies with a given group or groups—whether that identity is ethnic, racial, religious, or based on gender, education, and/or social class—the nature of that identification is likely to have a profound effect on the romantic choices that person makes. An individual with a strong positive identification with an ethnic or religious group, for example, would be more likely to choose a romantic partner from within that group, and vice versa. And the degree to which an emerging adult derives a sense of belonging and acceptance from a group can influence the degree to which that individual would be motivated to seek those qualities from a romantic relationship. Given that emerging adults are delaying romantic commitment, are they focusing more on group identity than past generations did? If so, how is that identification affecting the romantic choices they make? These seem like ripe questions for future research.

▲ Agency and Identity

How does identity affect one's functioning in the world, and vice versa? What is the relationship between identity and *agency*, or the ability to act on one's own power and make autonomous choices? Schwartz et al. (2005) investigated the correlation of agency and identity across three American ethnic groups (non-Hispanic Whites, non-Hispanic Blacks, and Hispanics). They evaluated differences in identity indices between clusters of participants organized according to agentic personality scores. The results revealed few mean differences along ethnic lines in the indices of agency and identity. However, agency *is* correlated with exploration and with varying degrees of commitment and choice, but, according to the authors, not with closure and conformity. Predictably, agency is negatively correlated with avoidant and aimless behavior. The authors conclude:

> These results support the cross-ethnic generalizability of Erikson's (1968) theory of identity as well as that of neo-Eriksonian identity theories proposed by Berzonsky (1989), Cote and Levine (2002) and Marcia (1966). More specifically, this finding supports Cote's (2000; Cote & Levine, 2002) contention that agentic functioning is an important component of individualized identity development and, hence, of effective adaptation to postindustrial societies, in emerging adulthood. (p. 222)

▲ The Role of Commitment

What appears to be critical is one's ability to work within the relative lack of structure emerging adults contend with when attempting to form an identity in today's society (Schwartz et al., 2005). Although the range of career, romantic, and "worldview" alternatives available to today's emerging adults is wider than ever, the support systems needed for identity formation is vanishing. Schwartz et al. found that regardless of ethnic group, it was those emerging adults who *committed to goals, values, and beliefs* who were able to "counteract" this pervasive lack of structural support (Schwartz et al., 2005, p. 223). The commitment itself seemed to be the key "ingredient" that enabled a successful transition to adulthood. The authors' findings, however, were based on a sample of students attending a private high school, and it is unknown to what degree these findings might be applicable to other settings, populations, or age groups.

If emerging adults are to make meaningful *life* commitments (e.g., romantic commitments), it seems they must first embrace the task of forming a stable and enduring individual identity that can nurture and sustain such commitments. This is especially true in an era in which community-oriented social protocols and production-based lifestyles have been supplanted by market-based social guidelines and consumption-based lifestyles. Those emerging adults who actively navigate the identity-formation process, and who exhibit high levels of agency, are more likely to successfully negotiate for social resources and position in such a market-driven world (Schwartz et al., 2005).

In summary, today's emerging adults experience and exhibit multiple discrete and overlapping "selves"; there is not a single, unidimensional identity. And yet there does appear to be a constellation of unique qualities that endures across time and social settings. Each of us is represented by a complex of interwoven narratives, and, according to Josselson (1996), growth entails "rewriting, revising, and interweaving these narratives." (p. 256). This is no easy task in an era when ideologies compete so openly with one another and when so many models of identity are presented to emerging adults and so many technologies for expressing identity are readily available to them.

Computer-mediated communication (CMC) is discussed in Chapter 5, but it is worth mentioning that cyberspace affords emerging adults access to realms of experience and socializing that otherwise might be closed to them. Through the use of online "avatars," emerging adults can instantly communicate any aspect of identity that becomes relevant at the moment, and can generate considerable visibility and notoriety by doing so. "Massively multiplayer" games such as World of Warcraft allow players to create "alternative" identities and to build substantial reputations based on these cyber-identities. Many emerging adults spend more of their leisure time "inhabiting" fantasy-world identities than they do their "real-world" counterparts. When it comes to cyber-identities, sheer presence seems more important than consistency or fine-tuned self-expression. Images play a powerful part in the establishment of online identities. Whereas in the past, publication of images related to the self was connected to events, talents, and achievements, today "self" images are made public via social media and constitute part of the identity formation process itself. How all of these factors influence the depth and endurance of identity over time is as yet unknown.

One thing seems certain, however. The role of individual identity is critical to the success of long-term romantic relationships. The intimacy of a close relationship, the constancy of the companionships, and the desire to bond with a romantic partner can present immense challenges to one's sense of identity, especially if the latter has not been sufficiently developed or is still fairly fragile. In an individualistic society such as ours, many individuals, of all ages, come to realize at some point that their sense of self has been lost in a relationship. The question, "Who am I outside of this relationship?" begins to loom large. That is partly because they have failed to adequately nurture and preserve their own interest, values, decision-making processes, personal world views, and sense of individual agency. The danger of this happening is particularly relevant during the years of identity formation, which for many individuals spans much of emerging adulthood. A strong identity is the foundation on which healthy and successful relationships are built. Therefore, taking this developmental process seriously during emerging adulthood is paramount.

▲ Couple Identity

As if forming a viable *I* were not challenging enough amidst today's unguided range of options, many emerging adults are also learning to form a *we* identity as part of a romantic couple. As noted in Chapter 1, emerging adults follow a variety of pathways toward sustained romantic commitment—short-term relationships of varying stability, steady long-term relationship(s), postponement of romance, and/or experimentation with casual sexual encounters—and there is no uniform or "recommended" path toward a *we* identity. Developing and maintaining a romantic identity is not likely to be a linear process. Thelen and Smith's (1996) Developmental Systems Theory asserts that new structures may emerge after a period exploration and mastery of new skills. Change occurs after a reorganization of skills, resulting in newly emerging integrated abilities.

In the next section, we will explore the transition from an individual identity to a couple identity, a process that requires a shift from an *I* to a *we* perspective. An important caveat: this focus on "couplehood" does not imply that developing and maintaining a couple identity— nor participating in the associated milestones, such as long-term relationships, marriage, and/or parenting—is the only normative path toward a satisfying and productive life.

▲ On Becoming a *We*

In the United States, partners in romantic relationships are likely to both seek connection and maintain autonomous selves (Baumeister & Leary, 1995). Baxter (1988) posits that a central feature of close relationships includes the negotiation of tensions related to the need for autonomy as well as connection. Both partners seek to develop and preserve an iden- tifiable *I* as well as an identifiable "we."

Initially, in most couple formations, each partner functions inde- pendently. Over time, the couple transitions to a core position of inter- dependence, a joint partnership that relies on coordinating efforts and working toward mutually agreed-upon goals (Knobloch & Solomon, 2004). The level of intimacy the couple enjoys serves as a marker of inter- dependence between the romantic partners. Becoming a *we* is facilitated by in-depth self-disclosure. Individuals have the desire to achieve close- ness with their romantic partner; however, desired closeness is based on the individual needs of the dyad members and therefore requires ongoing negotiation.

Interdependence theory (Kelley & Thibault, 1978) focuses on the "needs and interests" aspect of being an individual and a couple. It emphasizes a process in which members of the couple move from a perspective of self-interest to one of concern for both the self and the partner. Each partner becomes increasingly focused on the other's wel- fare and needs. Whitton, Stanley, and Markman (2002), based on the work of Stanley and Markman (1992), elaborate on this shift from self- identity to couple identity. They distinguish couple identity by the extent to which the partners view the relationship as a team rather than two separate individuals trying to maximize their individual gains and optimize their own positioning.

Within the relationship, romantic partners strive to find equilibrium, a balance that typically requires a process of negotiation so that one's own needs, the other's needs, and the collective needs of the relationship are all met to the greatest extent possible (Slotter et al., 2014). Communication skills are essential. Both partners have opportunities to learn to express their needs and wants and ensure that they are known and respected, while at the same time learning to genuinely listen to accommodate the needs of another. Emerging adults who are able to maintain a balance between these conflicting and often competing needs report greater life and personal satisfaction (Kumashiro, Rusbult, & Finkel, 2008) than those concerned with only a single set of needs. In fact, perceived similarity in *needs*, more than objective similarity of the partners, predicts positive individual *and* relationship outcomes, such as self-esteem and relationship satisfaction (Slotter & Gardner, 2009).

Investment in a romantic relationship flows from a greater commitment to the relationship. Greater commitment is associated with "an interdependent mental process" that includes transitioning from an *I* orientation to a *we* orientation (Agnew, Van Lange, Rusbult, & Langston, 1998, p. 428, as cited in Monk, Vennum, Ogolsky, & Fincham, 2014). Interdependence theory supports the perspective that with growing interdependence, the couple shifts from a self-interested perspective to a relationship-focused perspective.

As the couple transitions to a *we* identity with a long-term view of the relationship, each member of the couple increasingly shifts their attention toward the couple as an entity and away from the notion of separate individuals trying to do the best for themselves (e.g., Kelley & Thibaut, 1978; Stanley & Markman, 1992). Whereas in the initial stages of couple identity, each partner is more likely to focus on individual gains when competing needs arise, over time partners tend to focus on the well-being of the couple instead (Stanley & Markman, 1992). Losses and gains are viewed differently; losses are no longer perceived as giving up a core part of one's self. One hallmark of a couple that is strongly identified as a unit is that a circumstance that benefits the partner more than the self is not experienced as a personal loss (Whitton et al., 2002). Even though the members of the couple may actually *perform* greater sacrifices than they did before, they do not perceive those acts as sacrificial or as detrimental to their own self-interest.

Similarly, individuals who take a *long-term view* of the relationship are less likely to view the forgoing of self-interest as sacrificial because they understand that their "unselfish" actions will be reciprocated in the future and will lead to a happier relationship in the present (Whitton et al., 2002, p. 174). We will discuss the concept of sacrifice within a romantic relationship in greater depth in Chapter 4.

Slotter and colleagues (2014) outline two distinct tensions that arise when a couple simultaneously negotiates the needs of *I* and *we*. The first tension, well researched, addresses the negotiation of "my needs versus your needs," needs that often compete and conflict due to limited time and resources. The second identified tension, an underdeveloped area of research focus, emphasizes the conflicting desires to be part of a romantic dyad *and* to remain an autonomous self. Both of these identified tensions have the potential to create disequilibrium in a romantic relationship.

The research efforts of Slotter et al. (2014), grounded in Optimal Distinctiveness Theory (ODT), shed light on the negotiation of these identified tensions. According to ODT, individuals who perceive that they are "highly assimilated" within a group or a romantic relationship tend to try to emphasize their uniqueness when they see assimilation as a threat to their individuality. Conversely, when individuals assess that they are not sufficiently assimilated within a relationship or group, they will try to downplay their uniqueness in order to better fit into the relationship or group. In attempting to achieve balance within the romantic relationship, negotiating the need to be assimilated versus the need to remain autonomous is an ongoing, fluid process.

The skills required to engage with this emotional work do not emerge in a vacuum. During adolescence, opportunities abound to learn about the self in relationship. Adolescents become increasingly adept at forging deeper and more intimate relationships. They begin to develop the foundations necessary for negotiating conflict. Through experiences with friends and romantic partners, they learn about pursuing their needs in relationship, including how to negotiate tensions between the need for autonomy/independence and the need for affiliation/connection (Seiffge-Krenke & Shulman 2012, as cited in Shulman & Connolly, 2016). In addition, developmental precursors for long-term, satisfying relationships are put into place. Emerging adults who have had positive, secure experiences with friends (Dhariwal, Connolly, Paciello, & Caprara, 2009; Simpson, Collins, Tran, & Haydon, 2007 as cited in Shulman & Connolly, 2016) and romantic partners (Madsen & Collins,

2011, as cited in Shulman & Connolly, 2016) during adolescence are more likely to have positive romantic experiences as emerging adults.

▲ Expanding the *I* Through the *We*

Becoming part of a *we* can actually enhance the *I*. The self-expansion model, developed by Aron and Aron (1996), examines how initiating and developing a romantic relationship is associated with self-expansion in the romantic partners. According to Aron and Aron, romantic relationships allow for expansion of the self by providing access to new interests, resources, and opportunities. Individuals are motivated to grow, and in the process, expand their sense of self, by (a) integrating aspects of the partner into their own identity, and (b) gaining access to social resources that expand and redefine the self. The self continues to expand as the relationship grows closer. As intimacy increases between the partners, the likelihood of including the partner as part of the self also increases (Carpenter & Spottswood, 2013). As the partners become more inclined to see themselves as a single unit, they are more likely to share their network of friends, which, in turn, serves to further expand the sense of self for each.

Although individuals may *feel* as if they have lost a part of themselves after ending a romantic relationship, they usually, in fact, experience a net gain. Interests and resources gained as a couple tend to persist even after the relationship has ended (Lewandowski, Aron, Bassis, & Kunak, 2006), as cited in Carpenter and Spottswood, 2013). Slotter and Gardner (2009), building on the tenets of the self-expansion model, posit that integration of the attributes of the other person—attributes that were not part of the self before the relationship—is typically achieved through shared experiences. The interests of the other partner outlive the breakup because they are incorporated as part of the self (Carpenter & Spottswood, 2013). Emerging adults are also likely to increase their social networks after a breakup, since those networks have now been expanded to include the family, friends, and work contacts of the former partner. These findings suggest that forming a *we* can be one of the most powerful vehicles for the growth of the *I*.

The process of transitioning from an *I* identity to a *we* identity entails developing a care and concern for the other such that the individual no longer strives constantly to protect his or her own self-interests, but rather works to further the interests of the couple as a unit. When this stage is reached, sacrifices are no longer perceived as losses, but rather as investments in the long-term "success" of the relationship, which in itself is experienced as a reward.

Becoming a *we* is about much more than negotiating needs and interests, however. It is about learning to think and act in new ways—developing mutual interests, learning a shared vocabulary of words and behaviors, solidifying shared values, learning new levels of intimacy, and planning a future that includes another person. Ideally, developing a *we* develops the *I* as well. The self-expansion model points to the idea that each of the partners gains an expanded sense of self through being intimately exposed to the interests, ideas, passions, and social networks of a romantic mate. And both partners grow as a result of this, not only collectively, but also individually.

Paradoxically, however, this growth occurs only when both partners work to retain a robust sense of *I*. This *I* identity must be protected and developed even as the couple is becoming a more solidified *we*. Individual interests, values, and opinions must be preserved. Each member of the couple must learn to negotiate for their individual needs and to navigate the perennial tension between their own desires and what is best for the couple. The two individuals must speak up for themselves and make their preferences and needs known. In the process of these negotiations, the two must take care not to become so *we*-oriented as to lose the *I*, nor so *I*-oriented as to lose the *we*. In the next section, participants' thoughts about becoming a *we* are presented. The 29 emerging adult participants share their experiences of forming a couple identity, as well as their thoughts on what constitutes a couple, what it takes to become a *we*, and the challenges of balancing the needs of the *I* with the needs of the *we*.

▲ Participant Responses

Each of the 29 participants spoke about the challenges of developing an identity as a couple while continuing to develop an individual identity. After the individuals responded to the question, "How do you know if and when you have become a *we*, as opposed to two *I*s?" the collected data was analyzed and two domains emerged: (a) developing and maintaining an *I*, and (b) becoming a *we*.

Developing and Maintaining an I

Participants spoke extensively about the need to preserve an *I* even while working on a *we*. Three categories were further identified within this domain: (a) developing the self, pursuing one's own interests and goals; (b) having your say, standing up for yourself; and (c) fear of losing yourself, creating a balance.

Developing the self, pursuing one's own interests and goals

Reflecting on their romantic relationships, five participants spoke to the importance of the ongoing process of developing the self and pursuing one's own passions and interests. Their responses yielded a *variant* category. These five participants emphasized the idea that each individual within a relationship is enriched by bringing an independent self to the relationship. They focused on the importance of being one's "own person," and continuing to develop and maintain one's autonomy, as expressed through individual goals and interests. In developing an independent self, according to the participants, each individual enriches the relationship by bringing greater complexity, confidence, self-knowledge, and value to the union.

Alana (21) asserted that having individual interests and goals "keeps you as *you* and sharing your experiences [with your partner] as *us*." Andrea (24) emphasized the importance of maintaining an *I* and stated that this strengthens the couple relationship rather than weakens it.

> You need to be you and they need to be them. And honestly that strengthens your relationship because it builds trust, it builds confidence, and [in the process you come to] like yourself . . . and if you are . . . a *we* all the time, it's not going to work.

Rita (26) spoke of feeling threatened and insecure in past relationships, of always having to present her best self to a potential romantic partner, an insecurity she attributes to youth and to failing to know herself. In developing and maintaining an *I*, as she does now, Rita believes that she is continuing to grow emotionally and, in the process, is enriching the relationship:

In prior relationships, I was self-conscious of having to be my best self all the time and remain[ed] conscious of it in order to keep their attention. . . . I always knew that the commitment was threatened. Maybe because we were young, because we didn't know really what we were working toward individually.

By bringing self-knowledge and individual goals to the relationship, Rita now believes that she is more comfortable being herself. Knowing who she is and what she is working toward individually serves as a buffer against feelings of insecurity. Rita suggests that this self-knowledge diminishes the pressure to always be the best version of herself in relationship, a stance that in the past has felt onerous to her.

Standing up for yourself, having your say

Four of the participants described a process in which they learned to be able to identify their likes and dislikes, to be their own person, and to remain authentic while simultaneously standing up for themselves within the relationship. This yielded a *variant* category, indicating that this topic, in keeping with CQR terminology, was reported by at least two participants, but fewer than half. Michael (27), initially insecure in his relationship and afraid to upset the tenuous equilibrium that had been established, states:

Make sure you are still your own person. You still have to be honest with [the other] person and make your own decisions, even though it might disappoint them. . . . It is important in the long run to establish what you like, and what you are into. That is very important. . . . You will kind of get somebody upset and it is going to be okay and you are going to survive it.

Sandra (26), in the process of building a romantic relationship, has learned that she needs to stand up for herself, assert her voice, and work toward securing and solidifying her own identity. She explains:

Standing up for myself as opposed to just going with whatever he says [is important]. . . . Speaking up for myself and having the mind of my own as opposed to feeding off everything he says and just going with it [is an important lesson I have learned].

Fear of losing yourself, creating balance

In discussing the importance of maintaining an individual identity, four of the participants spoke about creating balance so as not to "lose yourself" in a relationship, yielding a *variant* category. Yasmine (22) experienced a tumultuous beginning with her current partner. Working through the tensions and fears of losing herself in the relationship, she has come to a new understanding of herself. She states:

> We appreciate each other as individuals. We are a couple and we are proud of it; people see that. Maintaining your individuality is a crucial thing. You won't want to lose yourself, where you are no longer happy.

Similarly, Becky (24) used the terms "being yourself" and "get[ting] lost in the relationship." "Awareness," she noted, is critical to the process of being yourself.

> You don't want to get lost in the relationship and lose yourself, your identity. But you also do not want to be so absorbed in your own identity that you can't experience what a relationship can offer, like the *we*ness or togetherness. . . . And I definitely think that you need to be aware of a lot and to try to have some sort of equal balance.

Although Becky said she was sensitive to the experience of being a *we*, and the potential richness that that experience brings, she stressed the importance of being self-aware and balanced within the relationship.

Though adults of all ages can experience the fear of "getting lost" in a relationship, these fears tend to be more acute in emerging adulthood. That is likely due to multiple factors, including the possibility that an individual identity has not yet been fully solidified or that other aspects of the individual's life are unstable, leaving the emerging adult vulnerable to over-reliance on the relationship.

On Becoming a We

The second domain, *on becoming a we*, generated three categories: (a) external validation, (b) it takes time to become a *we*, and (c) finding a balance; "it's hard."

External validation

Ten participants spoke of a time in the relationship when they realized that a shift in identity had occurred, a time when they no longer viewed themselves as an *I* exclusively. This yielded a *variant* category. External markers, such as sharing personal space together, served as cues to the participants that a shift toward becoming a *we* was occurring. For example, Alana (21) knew that she had started to think of herself as a couple, a *we*, by observing, "I can just go out when my phone battery dies because someone will worry about me. When you start to consider someone else's reaction on par with your own, [you know you are a *we*]."

With respect to this first category, external validation, responses were organized into the following three subcategories: (1) sharing space and resources, (2) social embeddedness, and (3) *we* narratives in everyday conversations.

Sharing space and/or resources. Participants spoke of sharing living space and/or resources (e.g., finances) together as concrete evidence that a shift from an *I* identity to a *we* identity had occurred. Sandra (26) states that it is no longer, "You respect my space, I'll respect your space. . . . You start to share space; that's when it's like a 'we' thing, to me."

Cam (23), in speaking about his same-sex romantic relationship, refers to the significance of taking on "financial burdens together." He is now cohabiting with his partner, a change that also symbolizes to Cam that a serious commitment has been made.

> I would say one of the things that goes into that is sharing
> finances. Or not sharing finances, but taking on financial burdens
> together. And not just like your bills and my bills, they become *our*
> bills because we live together. . . . It does definitely make you a *we*,
> part of a *we*.

Tina (27) mentioned the significance of sharing schedules with her partner on Google Calendar, an activity that represents a shift toward becoming a *we*. She stated that she is no longer exclusively responsible for herself and the way she manages her time. She and her partner are always "in the know" about the way the other is spending time outside of the relationship and the about commitments they have made to each other in the way they manage their time.

The shift from a sense of "territoriality" to one of shared space, whether literal or conceptual, seemed to be an essential hallmark of becoming a *we* for this group.

Social embeddedness. Acknowledgment and validation by one's social network was noted as a marker that the couple has transitioned to a *we* relationship. Leslie (27) shared that when invited to a social gathering, it is now assumed by their respective friends that both she and her partner are included in the invitation. Leslie stated, "I think it becomes a *we* when people kind of start seeing you as one, like when they ask you to do something, they are also asking the other person; you don't have to ask to include them."

Tina (27) spoke of the negative implications of her social network's providing *premature* validation of a shift toward a *we* relationship. When this occurs, according to Tina, there is "pressure on the relationship . . . to be something that it is not."

> You realize that other people saw us that way, and there is some degree of pressure that comes with that. I've experienced that in other relationships as well. As soon as other people hear about it, there becomes a sense of pressure and expectation. That sounds negative. There's good things about it too. It's exciting and fun. But I have seen it play out negatively, where the pressure of other people . . . to view [us as a] *we* or *us* can put pressure on the relationship so that you have to have a commitment, or be something that [you're not].

Alison (28) similarly captures the dynamic of others assuming that the couple has become a *we*: "Even if you have not moved in together . . . when your family is always including the other, your partner, to be at events."

The perception of "couplehood" by one's social/family circle helped reinforce the couple's own sense of same in ways that were positive and negative, for this group.

We narratives in everyday conversation. Four of the participants reported becoming aware of identifying as a *we* when they began incorporating their respective partners in their everyday narratives to friends, family, and work colleagues. The subject of their sentences became a plural *we*, whereas in the past it had been a singular *I*.

Rhonda (22) noted that this *we* shift was automatic on her part, without deliberation and intentionality. "I feel like people see us as a *we* by how we interact with each other or the fact that we tell stories with each other in [them]. . . . They know we are somehow together. I know because I included him in my story."

It takes time to become a *we*

This *variant* category reflects participants' beliefs that the passage of time plays an important role in a couple's becoming a *we*. While forming a couple identity happened "naturally" in many cases for participants ("when you feel comfortable with the person"), there was also a sense that relationships require building something together, such as trust and intimacy, which, according to seven of the participants, takes time. Joseph (25) states, "You build up your relationship, you build up your trust, you build up your intimacy, you build up supportiveness of each other, and then it comes to be [a *we*]."

Mateo (27), in reviewing his past same-sex relationships, states, "It takes time to tell if you become a we or not." In evaluating whether or not one is in a *we* relationship, Mateo said that a key measure is the willingness of the partners to "do a lot of sacrifices." If the two people "are on the same track, and aren't selfish, they won't be like me me me me—no, like they will be more about the partner and each other and both, both, both. Then, with time, they become a *we*."

> It takes time. I think in this situation it's about time, and to know each other, and that will happen after time, after you spend time, after you have done different sacrifices, and if you have done a lot of stuff because you want to be with this person. And then it's very emotional . . . having that connection. That . . . will take time.

Rhonda (22) and Rachel (22) reinforce the ideas that becoming a *we* takes time. For Rhonda (22) the process may occur "without even noticing."

> For me it took some building up. I had to have lived with him for a while and have been around his stuff for a while . . . enough time to call it *our* bed and house. . . . It took a few . . . times to be able to get to the word "we" . . . . I had to get there.

Similarly, Rachel asserts that "it just happens over time, like eventually, some people do it without even noticing, like they transform from a me-you to an *us* or a *we*."

Finding a balance; "it's hard."

Seven participants spoke of how "hard" it is to find a balance between satisfying the needs of the *I* and the *we*, yielding another *variant* category. These participants described two parallel processes, each with its own ongoing struggles. In referring to the level of difficulty, six of the seven participants describe the challenge of finding a balance as "hard," while the seventh participant used the term "difficult." Having the same interests and friends brought its own unique challenges to a few of the participants. Becky (24) states:

> Working on both [identities] at the same time, I think it's a lot. You kinda need to be aware of both, [of] doing too much of one [rather] than the other. . . . You need to be aware of a lot and try to have some sort of equal balance.

Joseph (25) spoke of the difficulties inherent in allocating time for his relationship, and in respecting the needs of both the *I* and the *we*, particularly since he viewed his romantic partner as someone he could "spend the rest of [his] life with."

> It's hard [to maintain your own identity], because it's like when you're a *we*, and you're with somebody that you, like, feel like you could spend the rest of your life with, you *want* to spend a lot . . . you end up spending a lot of time with them.

Leslie (27) spoke to the influence of social media in maintaining an *I* and a *we*, which presented issues for her:

> I think it's really hard for me. It's really hard to maintain my own identity. . . . Especially in my social media, I'm very just like, I'm open with a lot of things about my relationships and so people are seeing not just Leslie as Leslie but as Leslie-and-so-and-so, and I think it's really, really hard for me to maintain my own identity.

Finding a balance between the *I* and the *we* is a challenge for partners of all ages, but it is a particularly difficult challenge for emerging adults, who are often working on establishing an individual identity. Even for those who have "mastered" this developmental task, a relationship puts the fledgling *I* to the test, as the *we* is defined and established.

▲ Analysis of Findings

Participants openly shared their thoughts and expectations relative to identity and to their collective experiences of *becoming an I, becoming a we*. These emerging adults tended to regard their romantic relationships as central to their identity. They recognized the effect that becoming a *we* played in everyday encounters.

Our participants also stressed the importance of maintaining and developing one's individual identity when in a couple relationship. They noted that the *I* must be acknowledged, honored, and heard. Maintaining one's own interests and goals was viewed as a major way of preserving the *I* in the midst of a *we*. Speaking up for one's own desires, even if this causes friction in the relationship, was noted as another way of honoring the *I*. The participants did not directly address the core nature of the *I* identity—that sense of knowing who one is in regard to work, relationships, worldviews—but spoke of it indirectly by pointing out that individuals must actively preserve their interests, desires, goals, and opinions, even as they are working on becoming part of a thriving couple.

Preserving the *I* is not just for oneself; participants expressed the belief that maintaining a strong individual identity was likely to enrich the relationship as well, by adding complexity, confidence, and value to the mix. Conversely, individuals who entered committed relationships without knowing and maintaining the personal self were viewed as courting feelings of insecurity. Participants felt it was important not to lose the self in the relationship, but at the same time not to be so self-absorbed as to miss out on the benefits of togetherness.

Both autonomy and connection were reported to be highly valued by the majority of the participants; protecting both was viewed as a dynamic process, requiring adjustments and revisions along the way. Successfully navigating the need for autonomy and connection was regarded as potentially fulfilling and enriching, strengthening the couple both individually and collectively, building trust and confidence along the way. Interdependence theory was strongly in evidence, with both members of the couple learning to function as a team and not to view gains for the couple as losses for the individual. However, continued negotiation to preserve the *I* was seen as vitally important. Thus, we might describe the desired equation as "independence + interdependence." Ideally, there is a feedback loop in which growth of the couple contributes to individual growth, which, in turn, feeds back into further growth for the couple.

Negotiating the needs of both the *I* and the *we*, however, is a process that many of the participants found "hard." The difficulty was accentuated, rather than alleviated, when the couple shared many of the same interests and friends, and when the relationship was perceived as a highly desirable one. The theoretical paradigm presented by Slotter et al. (2014) emphasizes the importance of nurturing two simultaneous desires: the desire to be part of a romantic relationship and the desire to grow and develop as an autonomous self. Mishandling these tensions can upset the equilibrium within a relationship. Too much focus on the *I* can result in the partners being little more "roommates with benefits"; too much focus on the *we* can lead to enmeshment and codependency. However, successful negotiation of these dual tensions can mitigate periods of perceived threat, particularly when individuals are feeling overly assimilated within the relationship and in danger of "losing themselves." The paradox born of the need to be connected and also to maintain one's independence creates a constant tension, a "push and pull" (Loving, 2011) that needs to be acknowledged and appreciated in Western cultures.

The self-expansion model points to the idea that each of the partners gains an expanded sense of self through being intimately exposed to the interests, ideas, passions, and social networks of a romantic mate. And both partners grow as a result of this, not only collectively, but also individually. The relationship itself, however, can be the partners' greatest resource. In a mutually supportive, respectful, and nurturing relationship, both parties can learn to become better versions of the *I* at the same time they are learning together to become a better *we*. The relationship can serve as a buffer against a sometimes hostile and unsupportive world and can give the individual the confidence and clarity to pursue further self-knowledge, self-definition, and self-acceptance.

The individual case of Yasmine, a participant in the study, speaks poignantly to the struggles of developing and maintaining both a strong individual identity and a strong couple identity, especially when cultural and familial stressors are added to an already challenging set of societal pressures and influences.

Yasmine: In Search of a Coherent Self

Yasmine, a heterosexual 22-year-old woman of Middle Eastern descent, the eldest of three siblings, has attempted to develop an identity that remains true to who she is, individually and within a *we* relationship.

For 3.5 years, she has been in a long-term relationship with her romantic partner, a man she hopes to marry when she receives her academic degree in engineering. In response to strong parental disapproval of her romantic choice, however, Yasmine has established a relationship with her parents based on duplicity: she presents a nonauthentic self to them on a day-to-day basis, a stance that prevents her from having the freedom to give voice to an authentic identity informed by both an *I* and a *we*. As a result, she senses herself as fragmented, not whole.

> I want his name when I get my degree. I have been living such
> a strong double life. My family knows me as a different person,
> my boyfriend [knows me] as my real self. I don't want my life
> separated. I want to reach [a point in] my life where I have
> wholeness. I am ripped apart and I am just tired.

This quotation eloquently summarizes Yasmine's struggles and her yearnings for a time in the future when she will be able to feel "whole." Yasmine anticipates that she will take her future husband's name on the *same day* she completes her engineering degree. (Yasmine rejects the idea of using a hyphenated name that includes her parents' surname; that would symbolize the lack of identity integration she is feeling. Conversely, taking on one name—her partner's—signifies the adoption of a single identity that incorporates who she is and who she yearns to be). Yasmine aspires to live with her partner as a married couple, under one roof. Although she anticipates that her parents will disown her when she marries her partner, Yasmine views the relinquishment of her current duplicitous existence as potentially freeing and as critical to moving forward with her life. She relishes the idea of dropping the facade that has become so entrenched in her daily life.

Yasmine's parents are immigrants from Egypt who endorse traditional notions about how Yasmine should conduct her life both professionally and romantically. Both of her parents strongly object to her choice of partner, a man she met as a freshman and who has since dropped out of school to pursue a career as a boxing coach. They view her boyfriend as "beneath her," not her intellectual, economic, or social equal. They have forbidden Yasmine to see him. Her adaptation has been to assume a "double life" vis-à-vis her parents. In contemplating how to navigate her dilemma with her parents, who have threatened to withdraw payment for her education and disown her if she continues her relationship with her boyfriend, Yasmine has concluded that she cannot move out of their home, in part due to the cultural expectations for a young woman of her age and status. Yasmine reveals that the degree of subterfuge and duplicity is taking an onerous emotional toll on her. She did not anticipate how "hard" it would be to live a nonauthentic life, lying and pretending so much of the time.

In reflecting on her relationship with her boyfriend, Yasmine emphasizes the importance of "being yourself," being your "own person" within a romantic relationship:

> We are a couple and we are proud of it. Maintaining your individuality is a crucial thing. You won't want to lose yourself [to the point] where you are no longer happy. . . . We complete each other. He goes after what he genuinely wants to do. . . . We have passions in different ways. I have to take [his passions] into account to meet certain standards, and have determination [to meet my standards], and he respects that.

Yasmine is enjoying her studies, and her educational accomplishments are a source of pride. She is invested in her career choice of an engineer, a choice modeled after her parents, both of whom trained as engineers. Her mother functioned at a more senior level than her father, mirroring Yasmine's current relationship. When Yasmine's mother became a parent, she elected to quit her job and became exclusively responsible for the home. Yasmine is planning to pursue a graduate degree in engineering. Given adequate financial resources, however, Yasmine would prefer to stay at home in the role of wife and mother, not unlike the choice her mother made. (Her mother's choice occurred at a very different time and in a very cultural context in terms of freedom of choice for women).

While Yasmine's romantic relationship was initially tumultuous and unstable, a defining moment altered ongoing and seemingly unresolvable tensions between Yasmine and her partner. Despite wishing to remain a virgin before marriage, Yasmine felt pressured by her boyfriend to have a sexual life: "He almost broke up with me when he was sexually frustrated. I was still a virgin and I was being too 'naggy.'" She did not make a deliberative choice to have sex with her boyfriend; rather it "just happened." She became pregnant, claiming that she could not afford birth control pills, and elected to have an abortion. This was a tumultuous and emotionally wrenching time for Yasmine, filled with shame and sadness, due in part to her religious beliefs about the sanctity of human life. Yasmine became depressed and riddled with shame. She experienced her boyfriend as nurturing, caring, and supportive during this crisis, and, as a result, the relationship was cemented. The couple transitioned to a long-term view of the relationship and made plans to marry when Yasmine completes her education.

During this time of turbulence in her relationship, Yasmine was unable to garner support from her most significant, and only, female friendship. She describes her friend as traditional and judgmental, deeply steeped in the values of their cultural heritage. She no longer seeks advice from her friend because she has found that the worldview her friend espouses is restrictive, predictable, and unhelpful to Yasmine's particular circumstances. Yasmine's social network is extremely limited; she has not developed further friendships since this critical incident.

Yasmine seems vulnerable as she has not yet successfully negotiated new social resources that will be supportive to her, particularly if her family elects to reject her when she follows through on her choice to marry. Currently her long-term romantic partner is her only source of social support. Once married, and feeling more "whole," perhaps Yasmine will have the emotional energy, strength, and resilience to connect with a more extensive social network that will be supportive of her. The impact of "breaking off" with her parents remains an unknown.

Yasmine's narrative illustrates some of the theoretical points made earlier in the chapter. Her experiences support the notion that identity status can differ across life domains (Belsky, 2010; Goossens, 2001; Pastorino, Dunham, Kidwell, Baccho, & Lamborn, 1977, as cited in Schwartz, 2016). Yasmine's selection of a career, for example, is consistent with the guardian identity group. She has had a career life plan mapped out since an early age and has followed a path devoid of experimentation. However, with respect to her romantic life, she has not followed a path of "obedience to authority" (Josselson, 1996, p. 35). Rather, her path suggests that she fits more readily into the pathmaker identity; she has made her decision about a mate, and she intends to stick with it despite anticipated rejection by her family.

It seems that cultural influences have been internalized by Yasmine and inform her major decisions around work, family, and the meaning of home, while others have not. In terms of her group identity (as a middle Eastern woman) we see the dynamic that Phinney (2006) described at play. Had she been raised in a more homogenous cultural environment, it is reasonable to hypothesize that Yasmine would not be experiencing as many identity struggles. She is trying to straddle the line between her traditional upbringing and the more modern values she sees around her at school, at work, and in American society.

Yasmine is in a great deal of conflict. We see this conflict play out in her romantic relationship. Though her "traditional side" was not comfortable with premarital sex, she eventually relinquished to her partner. Though Yasmine's "modern side" wants an independent career, she expresses preference for the traditional role of wife and mother. These conflicts are clearly more pronounced when there are overtly clashing cultures at play. However, all emerging adults are likely to experience some form of identity-related conflicts. *I* and *we* identity tensions are further complicated by religious, cultural, political, educational, and social class considerations.

▲ Summary and Conclusions

In sum, identity development is an ongoing process, multifaceted and informed by environmental expectations and contingencies. It is a process that involves both "chang[ing]" and "stay[ing] the same" (Josselson, 1996, p. 256). It also involves choosing which aspects of our past experience we wish to integrate into our enduring self-concept and which we wish to jettison. Though this process extends across a lifetime, it is a central task of emerging adulthood.

When emerging adults enter committed romantic relationships, their identity-formation tasks become more difficult. Emerging adults must constantly negotiate the inherent tensions between becoming more of an *I* and more of a *we*. Our 29 research participants spoke to these tensions at length. They endorsed the need to continue developing the *I* within the parameters of a couple relationship, but they also spoke of the inherent difficulty of trying to faithfully serve both identities. The struggles emerging adults face in balancing these twin priorities are understandable when one considers how difficult it is for them to find an *individual* identity that fits. In a world where identity options abound but reliable guidance is largely absent, it is not surprising that emerging adults are taking longer than their parents did to solidify a sense of who they are as individuals. Many of them are working these tensions out even as they find themselves mired in intimate couple relationships. The challenges of trying to forge both an *I* and *we* identity simultaneously, without a roadmap, are likely to be daunting.

The relationship itself, however, can be the partners' greatest resource. In a mutually supportive, respectful, and nurturing relationship, both parties can learn to become better versions of the *I* at the same time they are learning together to become a better *we*. The relationship can serve as a buffer against a sometimes hostile and unsupportive world and can give the individual the confidence and clarity to pursue further self-knowledge, self-definition, and self-acceptance. The self-expansion model points to the idea that each of the partners gains an expanded sense of self through being intimately exposed to the interests, ideas, passions, and social networks of a romantic mate. And both partners grow as a result of this, not only collectively, but also individually. The relationship can serve as a buffer against a sometimes hostile and unsupportive world and can give the individual the confidence and clarity to pursue further self-knowledge, self-definition, and self-acceptance.

It remains uncertain whether this will happen for Yasmine as she strives, from within a couple relationship, to decide which parts of her cultural heritage she will adopt and which she will reject, which parts of herself she will preserve and which parts she will change. Identity and its nurturance is not a one-time task; identity is a dynamic, evolving process.

▲ References

Agnew, C. R., Van Lange, P. M., Rusbult, C. E., & Langston, C. A. (1998). Cognitive interdependence: Commitment and the mental representation of close relationships. *Journal of Personality and Social Psychology, 74*(4), 939–954. doi:10.1037/0022-3514.74.4.939

Arnett, J. (2006). Emerging adulthood: Understanding the new way of coming of age. In J. Arnett & J. Tanner (Eds.), *Emerging adults in America: Coming of age in the 21st century* (pp. 3–19). Washington, DC: American Psychological Association.

Aron, A., & Aron, E. N. (1986). *Love and the expansion of self: Understanding attraction and satisfaction.* New York, NY: Hemisphere/Harper & Row.

Aron, A., & Aron, E. N. (1996). Self and self-expansion in relationships. In G. O. Fletcher & J. Fitness (Eds.), *Knowledge structures in close relationships: A social psychological approach* (pp. 325–344). Hillsdale, NJ: Lawrence Erlbaum.

Baumeister, R. F., & Leary, M. R. (1995). The need to belong: Desire for interpersonal attachments as a fundamental human motivation. *Psychological Bulletin, 117*(3), 497–529. doi:10.1037/0033-2909.117.3.497

Baxter, L. A. (1988). A dialectical perspective on communication strategies in relationship development. In S. Duck, D. F. Hay, S. E. Hobfoll, W. Ickes, & B.

M. (Eds.), *Handbook of personal relationships: Theory, research and interventions* (pp. 257–273). Oxford, UK: Wiley.

Belsky, J. (2010). *Experiencing the lifespan* (2nd ed.). New York: Worth.

Berman, S. L., Weems, C. F., Rodriguez, E. Z., & Zamora, I. J. (2006). The relation between identity status and romantic attachment style in middle and late adolescence. *Journal of Adolescence, 29*(5), 737–748.

Carpenter, C. J., & Spottswood, E. L. (2013). Exploring romantic relationships on social networking sites using the self-expansion model. *Computers in Human Behavior, 29*(4), 1531–1537. doi:10.1016/j.chb.2013.01.021

Constantine, M. G. (2002). The intersection of race, ethnicity, gender and social class in counseling: Examining selves in cultural contexts. *Journal of Multicultural Counseling and Development, 30*(4), 210–215. doi:10.1002/j.2161-1912. 2002.tb00520.x

Cote, J. (2000). *Arrested adulthood: The changing nature of maturity and identity— What does it mean to grow up?* New York, NY: New York University Press.

Crocetti, E., Rubini, M., Luyckx, K., & Meeus, W. (2008). Identity formation in early and middle adolescents from various ethnic groups: From three dimensions to five statuses. *Journal of Youth and Adolescence, 37*(8), 983–996. doi:10.1007/s10964-007-9222-2

Erikson, E. H. (1956). The problem of ego identity. *Journal of the American Psychoanalytic Association, 4*, 56–121. doi:10.1177/000306515600400104

Harrison, J. (1995). Roles, identities, and sexual orientation: Homosexuality, heterosexuality, and bisexuality. In R. F. Levant & W. S. Pollack (Eds.), *A new psychology of men* (pp. 359–382). New York, NY: Basic Books.

Hays, P. (2008) *Addressing cultural complexities in practice: Assessment, diagnosis and therapy.* Washington, DC: American Psychological Association.

hooks, b. (1996). *Born African-American: Memoirs of childhood.* Boston: South End Press.

Josselson, R. (1996). *Revising herself: The story of women's identity from college to midlife.* New York, NY: Oxford University Press.

Kelley, H. H., & Thibault, J. W. (1978). *Interpersonal relations: A theory of interdependence.* Indianapolis, IN: Wiley.

Knobloch, L. K., & Solomon, D. H. (2004). Interference and facilitation from partners in the development of interdependence within romantic relationships. *Personal Relationships, 11*(1), 115–130. doi:10.1111/j.1475-6811.2004. 00074.x

Konstam, V. (2015). *Emerging and young adulthood: Multiple perspectives, diverse narratives* (2nd ed.). Cham, Switzerland: Springer International.

Kroger, J. (2000). *Identity development. Adolescence through adulthood.* Thousand Oaks, CA: Sage.

Kroger, J., & Marcia, J. E. (2011). The identity statuses: Origins, meanings, and interpretations. In S. J. Schwartz, K. Luyckx, V. L. Vignoles, S. J. Schwartz, K. Luyckx, & V. L. Vignoles (Eds.), *Handbook of identity theory and research, Vols. 1 and 2* (pp. 31–53). New York, NY: Springer Science & Business Media. doi:10.1007/978-1-4419-7988-9_2

Kumashiro, M., Rusbult, C. E., & Finkel, E. J. (2008). Navigating personal and relationship concerns: The quest for equilibrium. *Journal of Personality and Social Psychology, 95*(1), 94–110. doi:1037/0022-3514.95.1.94

Loving, T. J. (2011). Is distance bad for relationships? In G. W. Lewandowski, T. J. Loving, B. Le, & M. E. J. Gleason, *The science of relationships: Answers to your questions about dating, marriage, and family* (pp. 67–73). Dubuque, IA: Kendall Hunt.

Luyckx, K., Goossens, L., & Soenens, B. (2006). A developmental contextual perspective on identity construction in emerging adulthood: Change dynamics in commitment formation and commitment evaluation. *Developmental Psychology, 42*, 366–380.

Luyckx, K., Goosens, L., Soenens, B., Beyers, W., & Vansteenkiste, M. (2005). Identity statuses based on 4 rather than 2 identity dimensions: Extending and refining Marcia's paradigm. *Journal of Youth and Adolescence, 34*(6), 605–618. doi:10.1007/s10964-005-8949-x

Manning, W. D., Giordano, P. C., Longmore, M. A., & Hocevar, A. (2011). Romantic relationships and academic/career trajectories in emerging adulthood. In F. D. Fincham & M. Cui (Eds.), *Romantic relationships in emerging adulthood* (pp. 317–333). New York, NY: Cambridge University Press.

Marcia, J. E. (1966). Development and validation of ego identity status. *Journal of Personality and Social Psychology, 3*(5), 551–558. doi:10.1037/h0023281

McCarn, S., & Fassinger, R. E. (1996). Revisioning sexual minority identity formation: A new model of lesbian identity and its implications for counseling and research. *The Counseling Psychologist, 24*(3), 508–534. doi:10.1177/0011000096243011

McNamara, C. B., Abo-Zena, B., & Abo-Zena, M. M. (Eds.). (2014). *Emerging adults' religiousness and spirituality: Meaning making in an age of transition.* New York, NY: Oxford University Press.

Monk, J. K., Vennum, A. V., Ogolsky, B. G., & Fincham, F. D. (2014). Commitment and sacrifice in emerging adult romantic relationships. *Marriage & Family Review, 50*(5), 416–434. doi:10.1080/01494929.2014.896304 doi:10.1177/0743558404273118

Phan, L. T, Torres Rivera, E., & Roberts-Wilbur, J. (2005). Understanding Vietnamese refugee women's identity development from a sociopolitical and historical perspective. *Journal of Counseling and Development, 83*(3), 305–312.

Phinney, J. (2006). Ethnic identity exploration in emerging adulthood. In J. Arnett & J. Tanner (Eds.), *Emerging adults in America: Coming of age in the 21st century* (pp. 25–36). Washington, DC: American Psychological Association.

Porfeli, E. J., & Savickas, M. L. (2012). Career Adapt-Abilities Scale-USA Form: Psychometric properties and relation to vocational identity. *Journal of Vocational Behavior, 80*(3), 748–753. doi:10.1016/j.jvb.2012.01.009

Savickas, M. L. (1997). Adaptability: An integrative construct for life span, life space theory. *Career Development Quarterly, 45*, 247–259. doi:10.1002/j.2161-0045. 1997.tb00469.x

Schwartz, S. J. (2016). Turning point for a turning point: Advancing emerging adulthood theory and research. *Emerging Adulthood, 4*(5), 307–317.

Schwartz, S. J., Cote, J. E., Arnett, J. J. (2005). Identity and agency in emerging adulthood: Two developmental routes in the individualization process. *Youth and Society, 37*(2), 201–229. doi:10.1177/0044118X05275965

Schwartz, S. J., Luyckx, K., & Vignoles, V. L. (2011). *Handbook of identity theory and research* (Vols. 1 & 2). New York, NY: Springer Science & Business Media. doi:10.1007/978-1-4419-7988-9

Schwartz, S. J., Zamboanga, B. L., Luyckx, K., Meca, A., & Ritchie, R. A. (2013). Identity in emerging adulthood: Reviewing the field and looking forward. *Emerging Adulthood, 1,* 96–113.

Shulman, S., & Connolly, J. (2016). The challenge of romantic relationships in emerging adulthood. In J. J. Arnett (Ed.), *The Oxford handbook of emerging adulthood* (pp. 230–244). New York, NY: Oxford University Press.

Slotter, E. B., Duffy, C. W., & Gardner, W. L. (2014). Balancing the need to be "me" with the need to be "we": Applying Optimal Distinctiveness Theory to the understanding of multiple motives within romantic relationships. *Journal of Experimental Social Psychology, 5271–5281.* doi:10.1016/j.jesp.2014.01.001

Slotter, E. B., & Gardner, W. L. (2009). Where do you end and I begin? Evidence for anticipatory, motivated self–other integration between relationship partners. *Journal of Personality and Social Psychology, 96*(6), 1137–1151. doi:10.1037/a0013882

Stanley, S. M., & Markman, H. J. (1992). Assessing commitment in personal relationships. *Journal of Marriage and Family, 54,* 595–608. doi:10.2307/353245

Stokes, H., & Wyn, J. (2007). Constructing identities and making careers: Young people's perspectives on work and learning. *International Journal of Lifelong Education, 26*(5), 495–511. doi:10.1080/02601370701559573

Syed, M., Walker, L. H. M., Lee, R. M., Umaña-Taylor, A. J., Zamboanga, B. L., Schwartz, S. J., . . . Huynh, Q.-L. (2013). A two-factor model of ethnic identity exploration: Implications for identity coherence and well-being. *Cultural Diversity and Ethnic Minority Psychology, 19,* 143–154.

Thelen, E., & Smith, L. B. (1996). *A dynamic systems approach to the development of cognition and action.* Boston, MA: MIT Press.

Waterman, A. (1999). Identity, the identity statuses, and identity status development: A contemporary statement. *Developmental Review, 19*(4), 591–621. doi:10.1006/drev.1999.0493

Williams, C. (2005). Counseling African American women: Multiple identities—multiple constraints. *Journal of Counseling and Development, 83*(3), 278–283.

Whitton, S., Stanley, S., & Markman, H. (2002). Sacrifice in romantic relationships: An exploration of relevant research and theory. In A. L. Vangelisti, H. T. Reis, M. A. Fitzpatrick, A. L. Vangelisti, H. T. Reis, & M. A. Fitzpatrick (Eds.), *Stability and change in relationships* (pp. 156–181). New York, NY: Cambridge University Press. doi:10.1017/CBO9780511499876.010

Zunker, H. (2006). *Career counseling: A holistic approach.* Belmont, CA: Thompson/Brooks/Cole.

3 ▲
Premarital Romantic Commitment

Increased societal risks and uncertainties that
characterize the current lives of young people
lead to the postponement of taking on relational
commitments and societal responsibilities. . . . This
postponement and intentional refrain from
commitment might then be not an indicator of
confusion and aimless exploration, but rather
a calculated response to the realities and recent
complexities of young people's lives.
—Shulman & Connolly, 2013, p. 35

Commitment is a dynamic, multifaceted construct at the heart of romantic relationships. Most emerging adults engage in several romantic relationships of varying commitment levels during this stage of development (Jamison & Proulx, 2013). Commitment is associated with a range of positive outcomes: relationship satisfaction and attachment (Ruppel & Curran, 2012), improved couple functioning, and lower rates of couple dissolution (Corkery, Curran, & Parkman, 2011).

Definitions of commitment vary, emphasizing different aspects of the commitment process and the nature of commitment. Context matters, as does the individuals' cognitive and affective appraisals of the issues and challenges they are navigating (Joel, MacDonald, & Shimotomai, 2011). During emerging adulthood, romantic commitments are variable and tend to be characterized by instability, confusion, and internal conflict. Emerging adulthood is a time of learning not only what commitment means in general, but also what it means to oneself.

The focus of this chapter is to gain greater understanding of premarital romantic commitment and how it unfolds and is sustained during emerging adulthood. Two prevalent theories about commitment will be presented (interdependence theory and investment theory; Kelley & Thibaut, 1978; Rusbult, 1983). The voices of 29 participants will be heard—their thoughts about romantic commitment, what they are looking for in committed romantic relationships, and how they live commitment in their day-to-day lives. The commitment talk in which the partners discuss their relationship status and desire for a future together (Aldrich & Morrison, 2010) will be examined, including its meaning and possible significance in the trajectory of emerging adult romantic relationships.

▲ Commitment and Its Meaning

How does romantic commitment unfold between emerging adults, and what are the drivers of this dynamic construct? A clarifying definition of commitment is provided by Van Lange, Rusbult, Drigotas, Arriaga, Witcher, and Cox (1997). It includes the following components: "(1) a long-term orientation toward the relationship; (2) intent to persist through both 'good and lean times'; (3) feelings of psychological attachment; and (4) implicit recognition that one 'needs' the relationship" (Van Lange et al., 1997, p. 1374).

According to Stanley and Markman (1992), romantic commitment is comprised of two interrelated elements: (a) personal dedication (the desire to continue the relationship and improve its quality for the mutual benefit of its participants), and (b) commitment constraint (factors within the relationship that induce the parties to feel either trapped and/or obligated to remain, irrespective of their personal dedication to the relationship). Constraints serve to raise the cost of leaving the relationship, either financially or personally.

In summary, dedication to the relationship is associated with the desire to continue the relationship into the future, and to invest in it and make sacrifices for it. Dedication is also linked to personal goals. Some people, for example, place a high value on being in a committed relationship and see it as central to their happiness and/or success; others do not. Constraints contribute greatly to the stability of the relationship by causing the participants to feel that there is a high cost for terminating the relationship. That cost may be economic, emotional, social, and/or psychological. A noteworthy finding is that factors contributing to feelings of constraint or obligation are better predictors of relationship *stability* than measures related to satisfaction. By contrast, variables related to personal dedication are better predictors of relationship *quality* (Givertz, Woszidlo, Segrin, & Jia, 2016).

What are some of the underlying dynamics that contribute to the strengthening or weakening of commitment in a relationship? In the next section, two prevalent theories are presented.

▲ Interdependence and Investment Theory

Two models that ground the literature on romantic commitment are interdependence theory (Thibaut & Kelley, 1959) and investment theory (Rusbult, 1983; Rusbult & Buunk, 1993). According to interdependence theory, commitment is influenced by the personal attributes of each partner and the interdependence that develops between them (Thibaut & Kelley, 1959). There are rewards and costs in romantic relationships, and each partner works toward maximizing benefits and minimizing costs.

Within this theory, two main factors contribute to the growth of commitment: (1) high satisfaction—high levels of positive affect and low levels of negative affect in the relationship, and (2) the quality of alternatives available to the individual—the degree to which an individual's important needs can be met outside of the relationship, either through friends, family members, or one's own personal resources (Rusbult, Martz, & Agnew, 1998). Interdependence is at its highest when (a) the emerging adult has a strong desire to persist in the romantic relationship, and (b) alternatives to the relationship are perceived as poor. An increase in interdependence tends to increase commitment to the relationship.

The investment model (Rusbult, 1983; Rusbult & Buunk, 1993) provides a theoretical framework for understanding how individuals decide to persist in a romantic relationship. Commitment involves both "behavioral intent" and "psychological attachment" (Rusbult, 1983, p. 102). The tendency to feel psychologically attached to a relationship and to wish to continue in it, is strengthened through increasing *investment* in the relationship.

Investments can be emotional (e.g., self-disclosure) and/or structural (e.g., financial investments, possessions; Johnson, 1973; Stanley & Markman, 1992). The result of the investment is that resources become tied to the relationship—resources whose value would diminish if the relationship were to end. The more invested the participants are in the relationship, the less likely they are to voluntarily end it. Dependence on the relationship is also based on the individual's satisfaction with the relationship, and the quality of available alternatives.

Both of these theories view commitment in a somewhat one-dimensional way. Johnson (1991), however, proposes a three-part model that reflects the multidimensional aspects of commitment, both internal (e.g., values, self-concept, attitudes) and external (e.g., social and financial constraints). Emerging adults choose to stay in relationships because they *want to* (personal commitment), because they feel they *ought to* (moral commitment), or because they perceive that they *have to* (structural commitment). Factors such as the degree of satisfaction in the relationship, the perceived alternatives, and the couple's investment in the relationship have an important influence, but commitment remains the strongest predictor of persistence in romantic relationships (Van Lange et al., 1997; Rusbult et al., 1998).

In sum, commitment among emerging adults is experienced and expressed in a variety of ways; while there is common ground, there is also a substantial amount of variance, specifically with respect to subjective experiences (Surra & Hughes, 1997; Marston, Hecht, Manke, McDaniel & Reeder, 1998; Galambos, Barker, & Krahn, 2006). To add a further dimension, Sahlstein and Baxter (2001) have re-conceptualized commitment using a relational dialectics approach. In their model, commitment is not so much a fixed outcome of the desire to be in a relationship or the positive feelings the partners have toward the relationship; it is a fluid, dynamic construct, a negotiation of contradictions between the partners (e.g., connection-autonomy, openness-closedness, and/or predictability-novelty). Thus, the nature and quality of commitment in a relationship can and does change over time.

How relationship partners define commitment informs their daily interactions, including the ways they spend time together and the future goals they set for themselves (Weigel, Bennett, & Ballard-Reisch, 2003). Because commitment between partners is dynamic and fluid, meanings and experiences of commitment can shift over the course of the relationship, both for the individual and the partnership.

In the next section, participants' thoughts about commitment are presented. The 29 emerging adults in this study share their meanings and expectations of commitment, followed by their revelations about a particular time in their relationship life when the commitment talk—an attempt to verbally define the relationship and the partners' goals for it and commitment to it—occurred.

▲ Participant Responses

Each of the 29 participants spoke about commitment in various contexts that reflected their experiences and expectations. Four domains of commitment emerged from the data: (a) meaning of commitment; (b) expectations of a committed romantic relationship; (c) considerations made prior to commitment; and (d) experiences of commitment talk.

Meaning of Commitment

All of the participants were asked to provide a response to the question "When you think of romantic commitment, what comes to mind?" Twenty-nine participants provided their eclectic thoughts about commitment and what it meant to them, yielding the domain *meaning of commitment*. Three categories were further determined: (a) monogamy; (b) working as a team: being there for each other; and (c) loyalty, trust, and respect.

Monogamy

Twenty-one of the participants included sexual and emotional exclusivity between two partners, or monogamy, in their definition of romantic commitment, yielding a *typical* category, which, according to CQR reporting standards, means that more than half of the participants spoke of this topic. For 12 of the 21 participants, monogamy was associated with a desire to be with no one else but one's partner, in action *and* in thought. Romantic and/or sexual thoughts/fantasies about another were viewed as a betrayal. Leslie (27), for example, represents this point of view in stating: "Commitment is not only not cheating, but also not wanting to or not having desire to be with anybody else because you are happy."

Of this group, some participants focused on the need for both partners to be explicit and clear about defining monogamy. Rhonda (22), for example, clarified that monogamy in a romantic commitment means "no cheating: cheating includes sleeping with somebody else, kissing, hugging to an extent, saying sexually inappropriate things to others, and longing for someone who is not your partner." Similarly, Daniel (21) recognized that each couple might define monogamy differently; however, the critical component involved the *rules* established between the partners around monogamy. The rules needed to be mutually defined and agreed upon according to Daniel:

> Commitment means that both parties understand that they are going to be monogamous to whatever level they agree on. It's about coming to an agreement about what monogamy means and sticking to the rules of their relationship.

An overall theme that emerged was that exclusivity is essential to a committed relationship for emerging adults and should be defined and agreed upon by the partners.

Working as a team: being there for each other

Thirteen of the participants emphasized *working as a team* and *being there for each other* when considering what commitment means to them, yielding a *variant* category. For these participants, commitment meant working together toward shared goals, being supportive, giving time to each other and the relationship even when physically apart, communicating openly, shared decision making, and staying together even when times are hard. Becky (24) highlighted the interdependent nature of working as a team while remaining "your own person": "[you are] working as a team as well as being your own person . . . being like support systems; being compassionate." Greta (26) conceptualized working as a team in terms of communication and involvement: "I'm involved in the other person's life . . . I would be more or less aware . . . of what they're doing with their life . . . if someone had a big review or something special, I would know about those things and we would be in close communication."

Honesty, trust, and respect

In a committed relationship, six participants attached importance to personal qualities such as honesty, trust, and respect, yielding a variant category. Honesty and openness to one's partner were considered critical components of a committed romantic relationship. Sam (25) emphasized being able to trust the other person unconditionally, while Mark (24) noted honesty and transparency as being important when one is in a committed romantic relationship. Jessica (also 24) thought that "being open with someone and being true to them and honest with them" were critical components of a committed romantic relationship. For this group, transparency was critical.

Expectations of a Committed Romantic Relationship

Participants also expressed specific *expectations* of a committed romantic relationship. A second domain, *expectations of a committed romantic relationship*, was thus generated to capture their expectations. Three categories were determined: (a) having a future together: "shooting for the long run"; (b) marriage and family; and (c) physical presence.

Having a future together: "shooting for the long run."

In speaking about their expectations of a committed romantic relationship, 10 participants were oriented toward a future life with a partner. They expected to be in the relationship for the long term. For them, the relationship existed beyond the immediate present: they would be "shooting for the long run." Each partner would work toward individual and common goals, grounded in similar values and aspirations, yielding a *variant* category.

Having a future orientation, according to the participants, involved both a formal declaration and a less formal understanding of the relationship between the partners. Mark (24), for example, stated that his expectation would be that "both people in the relationship very candidly and clearly declare for each other that they have every intention, you know, of staying in the relationship with each other for the foreseeable future." Yasmine (22) expressed the expectation that she would have "a feeling, you trust each other enough, you can see you guys are going to be together for a long time." Daniel (21) eloquently summarizes that his expectation would be that in a committed relationship between two romantic partners: "I guess, between two people that they are shooting for the long run, like marriage and living together forever. And the goal would be to sort of bring each other up." Long-term thinking about the relationship, for this group, was a hallmark of commitment.

Marriage/long term commitment and family

Seven of the participants discussed having the expectation that they would *foresee a future* together with a partner that would include marriage. Analysis of their responses yielded a *variant* category. Rita (26) said: "I'd like someone who believes family is important. . . . I'm always considering the person as a father because I know I want kid.". A minority of these participants tended to associate marriage with a legal document and a costly wedding, both of which they viewed as not critical to the viability and success of being a family, and/or having children.

Some of the participants considered how their partners would assume the role of spouse or long-term partner and parent. Participants thought about the type and quality of parenting their respective partners received. In the process of evaluating a potential marital partner, Mahesh (23) expected that his partner would be a good mother and that the two of them together would have similar values and orientations toward raising their child[ren]:

I look at like, how their family is, that's pretty big to me because, um, knowing how you were raised is pretty big to me. Because I feel like quality like that is going to determine how they're going to be as a mother, or how they're going to be as when dealing with kids and stuff.

The idea of marriage and family was seen by these participants not only as an expected future goal for a committed relationship but also as a criterion for assessing a partner's qualities in the present.

Physical presence

Five participants expressed the expectation that their romantic partners be physically present in their lives, yielding a *variant* category. As committed partners, they expected that they would be spending a significant amount of time together. Physical presence was considered a necessary ingredient, as was consistent communication between the partners. Approximately half of these participants emphasized that spending time with a partner should feel good and be pleasurable. Kris (25) said: "So I think just wanting to be around them . . . and feeling if I hung out with them, them being a very uplifting person in your life. You want them to be a positive and not another burden for you to carry." Rachel (22) shared that talking with the person, including willingness to "take time out of your days to text them and call them, and go see them" was important. Cam (23) summarized that if "you don't see yourself being able to say *I would like to spend large amounts of time with you long term* then I don't think that you should be entering into a commitment with that person." Frequent shared presence was seen by this group as an essential component of commitment.

Considerations Made Prior to Commitment

Participants spoke of a time in the trajectory of their relationships when each or one of the partners considered romantic commitment, yielding the domain *considerations made prior to commitment*. Many spoke to the importance of being candid in the process of knowing and being known in the relationship, and readiness and motivation to be exclusive, while at the same time acknowledging the relinquishment of a single life. Two categories emerged: (a) am I ready, what am I giving up? and (b) knowing and being known.

Am I ready, what am I giving up?

In their consideration regarding whether to commit to another, five participants questioned whether they were ready and/or motivated to commit, emotionally capable of committing, and to a lesser extent whether their partners were ready to commit to them, yielding a *variant* category. There was a range of attitudes and feelings. For example, Kris (25) stated: "I think you need to consider what you're emotionally capable of handling," whereas in contrast, Daniel (21) described for-going self-assessment and "going with your gut feeling."

Four of the participants acknowledged that commitment included recognition of loss, and the relinquishment of a "single life" and its benefits. For example, Mateo (26) stated: "You must be conscious of, or have an idea of a relationship, [what it] is, and know if you're really willing to put yourself in a relationship, to lose your single life." Ellen (24) highlighted the costs and benefits of being in relationship and being single. In evaluating her current relationship, she concluded that the benefits outweighed the costs: "Basically [the relationship] just needs to be worth not being with another person." For these participants, it was vital to consider the costs of committing to a relationship.

Knowing and being known

Before considering commitment, knowing yourself and knowing the other were critical considerations for six of the participants, yielding a *variant* category. Rachel (22) spoke of the importance of not "jumping into things" and not "fantasizing about the other." She stated that she needed to assess whether "the person . . . [she was] with doesn't care as strongly about me as I do about them."

To guard against impulsivity and not knowing, these participants spoke to the importance of taking it slow, engaging in self-disclosure, and being candid with their partners. In stressing the importance of the passage of time in terms of knowing and being known, Michelle, (26) stated:

> When you're first with someone . . . they paint that picture that they're that perfect person, they're there for you, they paint that picture so you really don't know what you're in for . . . you don't know who they really are until the shit hits the fan. Until you let them in and slowly they get comfortable that their true colors show.

Similarly, Mahesh (23) spoke about initially being "on your best behavior" in the relationship, which does not allow for getting to know your partner; he asserted that taking the time to get to know the person, at least a year, was necessary to "figure out what both people want in the relationship."

Leslie (27) currently in a long-term relationship, reminisced about the importance of being honest with yourself and your partner before making a romantic commitment:

> I think it is important to be able to know that you can be yourself with that person and you can be honest with that person . . . if it is someone that really makes you feel like you can be yourself, and that you can talk with, and that accepts you for like who you are.

These participants viewed honest self-revelation as a defining characteristic of a committed relationship.

Commitment Talk

Participants discussed the decision to commit to another and whether *commitment talk* occurred to acknowledge that decision. This resulted in our final domain. All of the participants reflected on a point in a relationship experience in which an *opportunity* to engage in commitment talk occurred. The talk involved a conversation in which the status of the relationship was discussed and the results would lead to further clarity including the decision to commit (or not) and possibilities for a future together. Participants in this study were both initiators and receivers of the talk. Responses to the commitment talk generated three categories: (a) intentional commitment talk; (b) casual commitment talk; and (c) no commitment talk.

Intentional commitment talk

Eight participants described an *intentional* conversation focused on themes such as a future together and an in-depth understanding of their relationship status, yielding a *variant* category. Participants spoke of a process that was anxiety provoking and "scary," but the results of the conversation were often clarifying. For example, Chantal (23) stated:

> Honestly, I think that talk is probably like one of the most scariest conversations. Especially if you're not like 100% sure. . . . I just feel like it's this, like you have to put your pride aside and you have to like I guess open up and tell the person exactly like what you want and how you're feeling and you're just hoping that they'll say the exact same to you.

Half of the eight participants described the circumstances around an intentional talk as tumultuous; they also felt vulnerable. Brian (24), for example, described that the urgency for an intentional commitment talk may not be reciprocal: "[With] my first boyfriend and my most recent person I was in a relationship with . . . I would bring it up continually and they would be not only unwilling to talk about it, but upset at me for bringing up with conversation." Mateo (26) also spoke to the lack of reciprocity that he has endured in his most recent relationship, and described being "frustrated" that his partner didn't follow through with being committed in the ways that they agreed to during their talk. Katherine (25) described that she and her partner had an intentional commitment talk, only because her partner had become "very irrationally jealous." It is revealing that while most of the 29 participants said they valued honest communication in a relationship, only a minority (8) described having an intentional talk about commitment levels.

Casual commitment talk

Eight participants described a casual conversation about "what are we and where are we going?" yielding a *variant* category. They spoke of longing for clarity regarding their relationship, but noted that they did not necessarily see the need for a formal conversation. Rather, they described a process that was somewhat spontaneous and casual. For example, Becky (24) stated:

> At least in [my relationship] there has been some sort of talk, just like an understanding, like this is where we are. There haven't always been like these explicit talks or long talks but usually it's some sort of statement.

A brief discussion regarding commitment was sufficient for some, and signified that a commitment had occurred: for example, "I love you and I wanna be with you." Monica (22) stated, "so far what I have had is just spontaneous like the guy would be like 'hey be my girl' and I am like 'ok.'" For these participants, the commitment talk was more implied than explicit.

Absence of commitment talk. Five participants did not engage in a talk about their relationship yielding a *variant* category; four of these participants described that commitment was enacted regardless. For example, after traveling long distances to see his partner, Michael (27) stated he knew they were exclusive: "I do not think we ever had a conversation about [whether] we are going to be exclusive, I think it just kind of at a certain point, it just came like an accepted thing, like a nonverbal kind of, hey this is we are clearly going to be with each other." Cassandra (22) shared a similar experience: "there wasn't really a talk, or anything, it was more like . . . we had been dating awhile, and then we were just like, oh, it kind of just morphed into a relationship."

▲ Analysis of Findings

Participants explored the meanings and patterns of commitment in their romantic relationships. Collectively, the findings support the existing body of knowledge on commitment and uncover new understandings related to committed relationships among emerging adults. Results suggest a complexity that, with few exceptions, has not been captured in the literature (Stanley, Rhoades, & Markman, 2006). While their understanding of commitment as well as their expectations of committed relationships and romantic partners were clear and differentiated, their behaviors related to the enactment of the commitment talk belied their expectations. For that reason, we will explore "the talk" in additional detail.

Participants revealed a view of monogamy as an essential feature of a committed relationship, and defined monogamy as including emotional and sexual exclusivity, built on trust and teamwork. Emerging adults were specific in their views as to what constitutes betrayal and described their own suitability for monogamy in terms of their "readiness" to not be with anyone else. For a minority of the participants, even having fantasies about another person was considered a violation of monogamy. Emerging adults in our sample endorsed traditional values of family and home, findings that are supported in the literature (e.g., Sahlstein & Baxter, 2001; Konstam, 2015).

Expectations of a committed relationship were consistent with the meanings and values these emerging adults attached to commitment. For example, the category of loyalty and emotional fidelity mirrored the view of commitment as monogamy. Despite the heterogeneity of the sample with respect to demographics, most emerging adults wished to find partners who were in it for the long run, and viewed themselves as being part of a unit—interdependent, while at the same time maintaining a sense of individuality. These emerging adults expressed the expectation that in a committed relationship, decisions would be made together, and that the time spent together would be both valued and pleasurable. They sought partners who would raise them up, offer respect, and demonstrate reciprocity in communication.

Some of the participants emphasized that although they envisioned communicating with their partners by texting and other electronic means, physical presence was believed to be necessary for a committed relationship. In describing the workings of a committed romantic relationship, they stated that trust, honesty, and candidness should serve as a foundation or a template for current and future interactions. Incorporation of parents and extended family members into the couple's day-to-day lives was also a stated expectation and consideration.

When asked about the commitment talk—the verbal formalization of a couple's commitment considerations—participants were able to identify a juncture in their relationship in which commitment talk did or did not occur. For close to two thirds of the participants, the commitment talk was either casual, often captured in one or two sentences, with no further specifics and discussion of the change in status, or did not occur. Only one third of the participants described the commitment talk as planned and intentional.

The findings of our study confirm that while emerging adults have very clear and concrete images of what commitment means to them and what they expect of a committed relationship, they are hesitant and anxious about discussing their feelings in the form of a talk about commitment. A previous research study (Nelms, Knox, & Easterling, 2012) reveals that 14.7% of participants, after having the talk, terminated their relationships. In our sample, participants reported that talk triggered fears and feelings of vulnerability related to saving face, risk, and potential loss of the relationship. These fears often took precedence; possibilities for allaying the fears and for learning new skills and insights that might lead to emotional growth were thus foreclosed. Unlike the study by Nelms and colleagues (2012), in which only participants who *initiated* the talk were included, participants in the current study were both initiators and receivers of the talk.

Participants' views on the talk and its actualization varied. Reasons given for initiating the talk included "just a feeling," "the guy is ready to ask you," and "jealousy." For some, attitudes about "the talk" were shaped by previous experiences in which the talk did not take place and by the ensuing desire to avoid repeating past patterns. For example, Rachel, while recognizing the ominous nature of the commitment talk, stated, "[I was] cheated on due to lack of *the talk*." Helen suggested a gender divide, stating, "Guys don't want to do it." There was also an assumption on Ellen's part that the male would be the initiator of the talk when he was ready, and that she, subscribing to traditional notions of gender, would respond accordingly.

Declaration of one's commitment to a partner is an important juncture in the evolution of a romantic relationship. It provides an opportunity for each member of the couple to make a choice. However, by having a concrete talk about the status of the relationship and its future, other choices are necessarily foreclosed (Stanley, 2009; Rhoades, Stanley, & Markman, 2009). There is potential loss. On the positive side, a clear, focused discussion, including expectations of the self, the other, and the relationship, increases the likelihood of "deciding" to enter a committed relationship, rather than "sliding" into one (Rhoades et al., 2009; Stanley, 2009). The danger of sliding into commitment is that the opportunity to clarify expectations and understandings and to make clear, conscious choices is lost.

Rhoades and colleagues (2009) suggest that having a clear and focused talk prior to cohabiting may "may more fully support the motivations to follow-through during the inevitable tougher times that many, if not most, relationships will experience" (Stanley & Rhoades, 2009; Rhoades et al., 2009, p. 101). Future research is needed to ascertain whether this is also the case for the commitment talk. Based on related research (on cohabitation and marriage, for example), acknowledgment of ambiguity in the relationship's "rules" and pursuit of greater clarity enables each member of the couple to make better, more informed decisions. Commitment talk provides an opportunity to become more self-aware and emotionally attuned to one another, as well as to understand personal goals and expectations. Contextual implications with respect to commitment talk (e.g., gender and power dynamics within the couple) merit further investigation.

Learning about the self in relationship is a key developmental task of emerging adulthood. Taking risks, dealing with uncertainty, and navigating interpersonal conflict are experiences that have important implications for future well-being and behavioral adjustment (Braithwaite, Delevi, & Fincham, 2010). The ability to engage in honest clarifying dialogue is an important skill that can help emerging adults actualize relationship potential as they navigate this period of transition and growth.

Commitment talk can serve a protective function by keeping emerging adults aligned with their future aspirations and goals (Rhoades et al., 2009). Clear communication around commitment is associated with moving the relationship forward toward greater intimacy (Nelms et al., 2012) and relationship satisfaction (Knobloch & Theiss, 2011). Yet, participants in the present study were not inclined to view the talk in these terms. Rather, it appears that for many of the participants, commitment talk was experienced as a potential threat or risk, a finding that is consistent with previous research (Aldrich & Morrison, 2010; Knobloch & Solomon, 2005). Even when intentionally initiated, the talk about commitment often emerged from a tumultuous space within the relationship and did not always result in improved stability and satisfaction. Clarifying discussions with helping professionals and/or trusted friends and colleagues about commitment and how it is lived in relationship may be helpful for emerging adults, even in the absence of the talk.

We have heard the voices of emerging adults, their meanings and expectations related to commitment, and their experiences at an important juncture in their relationship: the decision to have (or not have) the commitment talk. We next examine another important juncture in the romantic lives of emerging adults and how it may relate to commitment: the decision to cohabit.

▲ Cohabitation: Committed or Not?

The decision to enter premarital cohabitation is a major juncture that can seriously impact the future of the relationship. The number of couples living together outside of marriage has increased significantly (Guzzo, 2014): an estimated 50–60% of couples in the United States cohabit before marriage, with fewer of these cohabitations leading to marriage (Stanley et al., 2006). The increase in cohabitation rates, in fact, seems to be associated with the de-linking of cohabitation from marriage. Today's couples attach a wide variety of meanings to premarital cohabitation; some see it as a step or trial before marriage, others as a source of convenience, a form of dating, and/or an economic convenience (Thornton, Axinn, & Xie, 2008, as cited in Stanley, Rhoades, & Whitton, 2010).

From 1995 to 2010, there was an 18% drop in the number of couples who were married within 3 years of cohabiting (a decrease from 58% to 40%), a finding that is attributed to (a) a change in attitudes toward marriage, and (b) economic changes related to the perceived costs and incentives of getting married (Guzzo, 2014). Given the range of meanings and reasons for premarital cohabitation and the increasing number of emerging adults who are electing to cohabit, opportunities to study commitment within this context abound.

Stanley et al. (2010) draw from rich and multidisciplinary literatures to study how decisions to cohabit are made. They investigate the decision-making processes of 18- to 34-year-old emerging and young adults who are currently cohabitating. How does this population approach the decision to cohabit—with intention and planning, or do they slide into cohabiting without much forethought or deliberation? What are the consequences of these different approaches? Specifically, Stanley et al. (2010) asked participants to indicate which of the three following options best described how they came to the decision to cohabit: (a) "We talked about it, planned it, and then made a decision together to do it";

(b) "We didn't think about it or plan it. We slid into it"; or (c) "We talked about it but then it just sort of happened."

Approximately one third of the participants in the Stanley et al. study reported that they came to cohabit via a pathway that was planned and intentional; two thirds reported that they "slid" into cohabiting without deliberation and forethought, a finding that mirrors the commitment talk results reported in this chapter.

Gender differences emerge when considering cohabiting relationships (Stanley, Whitton & Markman, 2004, as cited in Stanley et al., 2010). Men who engage in cohabiting relationships prior to marriage report lower dedication scores than men who do not cohabit. Stanley and colleagues posit that men who cohabit, in comparison to women, are less committed and motivated to enter marriage; they are more inclined to enter cohabiting relationships due to "inertia" or "premature entanglement" (p. 252).

The authors hypothesize that constraints imposed by the relationship may interfere with the search to find a good partner fit. These constraints derive from the fact that members of the cohabiting couple, regardless of whether they are suitable for one another, tend to take actions toward continuing the relationship before they become fully aware of the decrease in alternatives. Burke, Woszidlo, and Segrin (2013) also found a correlation between feelings of constraint in a committed relationship and feelings of loneliness. By contrast, committed relationships that are less constraining are associated with less loneliness and greater relational satisfaction.

▲ In Defense of Clarifying Conversations

Opportunities to declare one's commitment to a romantic partner emerge during important relationship junctures (e.g., the initial decision to commit to another; the decision to cohabit and/or marry). These junctures beckon the emerging adult to make a choice and declare, typically in a public forum, his or her level of investment in the relationship. The results reported in this chapter support an emerging literature that focuses on one point in the trajectory of a romantic relationship: the initial decision to commit to another. Our findings suggest that a large contingency of emerging adults encounter difficulties with conversations related to commitment talk. They appear to be guided by fears related to emotional vulnerability, saving face, risk, and potential loss of the relationship (Aldrich & Morrison, 2010; Knobloch & Solomon, 2005). The possibility of divorce is also a concern voiced by many of our participants.

An incomplete literature suggests that clarifying conversations are associated with diminished risk. For example, during the period of transitioning to cohabitation, the greater the expressed clarity between partners in terms of their respective commitment levels, the lower the risk of the relationship's dissolving (Lichter & Qian, 2008). Clarifying conversations—including discussion of the meaning of cohabiting for each member of the couple, as well as their understandings of commitment and how it is enacted—*before the transition occurs* can help to offset risk. Where there is ambiguity, there is greater risk of dissolution. In other words, clear conversations are associated with preserving the integrity of the couple.

It follows, therefore, that couples who cohabit *after making the decision to marry* are at lower risk than couples who do not, a finding that is borne out in the literature. Perhaps this is because entering a cohabiting relationship without conscious deliberation and choice tends to increase one's *perceptions* of constraints and limits (Stanley et al., 2010). By contrast, when couples deliberately decide to commit to another and/or cohabit after making a formal declaration of commitment (e.g., getting engaged), constraints are chosen and therefore do not feel so onerous. This pattern, according to the authors, applies to other "sliding" behaviors between romantic partners, including the decision to have sex and the decision to have children.

Clear decisions generally build the most "resilient intentions" (Stanley et al., 2010, p. 253). Sliding transitions, on the other hand, can undermine dedication in romantic relationships, even in those relationships that continue. Partners may feel constrained because they never made a clear intention to *choose* the very situation responsible for limiting their options.

Stanley et al. (2010) further assert, "There has been a decided shift in recent decades in the direction of individuals entering constrained pathways in romantic relationships before the development of dedication" (p. 254). Part of the reason for this may be that there is an increasing number of emerging adults who have grown up with family instability (Bumpass & Lu, 2000) and have been exposed to multiple romantic partners in their parents' lives (Cherlin, 2009). Whatever the reason, the authors predict that this shift toward "leaping" into constrained relationships without dedication will result in "increasing numbers of couples with weakened commitment dynamics at the base of their romantic relationships" (p. 254). If they are correct about this, and if our present data is also correct in showing that emerging adults still desire and value strong commitment, (a finding that has been consistently reported in the literature), then some frustration seems inevitable. It seems we will be looking at a generation of adults who *want* strong commitment but who aren't finding it or living it in their actual relationships. The authors suggest that "the need for well-formed clear commitment that can secure romantic attachments may be increasing, even as this becomes harder to achieve" (p. 254). Understanding the differing views of commitment held by emerging adults, as evidenced by our participant group, is an essential ingredient in understanding these dynamics, and in understanding the various trajectories that emerging adults relationships take.

These findings, while interesting, are speculative at this juncture. Future research is needed that captures the romantic lives of emerging adults during key decision points (e.g., the decision to initially commit to one another) and focuses on the processes related to how these decisions unfold and evolve over time and their consequences. Research efforts that identify the role of clarifying conversations in mitigating risk and enhancing relationship quality and persistence have the potential to be illuminating; they can inform clinicians and other related support personnel in the service of improving the lives of emerging adults.

▲ Summary and Conclusions

Relational skills gained through forming committed romantic partnerships in emerging adults provide the foundation for sustained intimacy in later adult relationships. Commitment is a crucial factor in the quality and longevity of romantic relationships. Examining the subjective experience of the individual adds much to our understanding of the shifting commitment patterns among emerging adults.

Though emerging adults' concepts of commitment mirrors traditional ideals—in that they expect to have sexual and emotional exclusivity and to work together toward shared goals and interests in a long-term partnership—many emerging adults are hesitant about discussing their expectations with partners in the form of an intentional talk about commitment, as clearly evidenced in the responses of our research participants. This intriguing finding invites further research efforts to examine the larger contextual and sociopolitical factors that influence this hesitance (for example, gender expectations or the prioritizing of career development). Individual factors such as avoidance of emotional vulnerability, tolerance for risk taking, and ability to deal openly with ambiguity in romantic relationships merit further exploration. Such research will provide a broader understanding about the potential impact of these factors on relational well-being.

▲ Author's Note

The content of this chapter will be published as Konstam, V., Curran, T., Celen-Demirtas, S., Karwin, S., Bryant, K., Andrews, B., & Duffy, R. (in press). Commitment among unmarried emerging adults: Meaning, expectations and formation of relationships. *Journal of Social and Personal Relationships.*

▲ References

Aldrich, R. S., & Morrison, K. (2010). Exploring why college students discuss commitment in dating relationships. *Florida Communication Journal, 38*(2), 113–122.

Braithwaite, S. R., Delevi, R., & Fincham, F. D. (2010). Romantic relationships and the physical and mental health of college students. *Personal Relationships, 17*(1), 1–12. doi:10.1111/j.1475-6811.2010.01248.x

Bumpass, L., & Lu, H. H. (2000). Trends in cohabitation and implications for children s family contexts in the United States. *Population studies, 54*(1), 29–41. doi:10.1080/713779060

Burke, T. J., Woszidlo, A., & Segrin, C. (2013). The intergenerational transmission of social skills and psychosocial problems among parents and their young adult children. *Journal of Family Communication, 13*(2), 77–91. doi:10.1080/15267431.2013.768247

Cherlin, A. (2009). Marriage, divorce, remarriage. Cambridge, MA: Harvard University Press.

Corkery, S. A., Curran, M. A., & Parkman, A. (2011). Spirituality, sacrifice, and relationship quality for expectant cohabitors. *Marriage & Family Review, 47*(6), 345–362. doi:10.1080/01494929.2011.594213

Galambos, N. L., Barker, E. T., & Krahn, H. J. (2006). Depression, self-esteem, and anger in emerging adulthood: Seven-year trajectories. *Developmental Psychology, 42*(2), 350–365. doi:10.1037/0012-1649.42.2.350

Givertz, M., Woszidlo, A., Segrin, C., & Jia, Q. (2016). Direct and indirect effects of attachment orientation on relationship quality and constraint commitment in married couples. *Journal of Family Studies*, online first. http://dx.doi.org/10.1080/13229400.2016.1211548

Guzzo, K. B. (2014). Trends in cohabitation outcomes: Compositional changes and engagement among never-married young adults. *Journal of Marriage and Family*, 76(4), 826–842. doi:10.1111/jomf.12123

Jamison, T. B., & Proulx, C. M. (2013). Stayovers in emerging adulthood: Who stays over and why? *Personal Relationships*, 20(1), 155–169. doi:10.1111/j.1475-6811.2012.01407.x

Joel, S., MacDonald, G., & Shimotomai, A. (2011). Conflicting pressures on romantic relationship commitment for anxiously attached individuals. *Journal of Personality*, 79(1), 51–74. doi:10.1111/j.1467-6494.2010.00680.x

Johnson, M. P. (1973). Commitment: A conceptual structure and empirical application. *Sociological Quarterly*, 14(3), 395–406. doi:10.1111/j.1533-8525.1973.tb00868.x

Johnson, M. P. (1991). Commitment to personal relationships. In W. H. Jones & D. W. Perlman (Eds.), *Advances in personal relationships* (pp. 117–143). London: Jessica Kingsley.

Kelley, H. H., & Thibaut, J. W. (1978). *Interpersonal relations: A theory of interdependence*. New York, NY: Wiley.

Konstam, V. (2015). *Emerging and young adulthood: Multiple perspectives, diverse narratives* (2nd ed.). Cham, Switzerland: Springer International.

Knobloch, L. K., & Solomon, D. H. (2005). Relational uncertainty and relational information processing questions without answers? *Communication Research*, 32(3), 349–388. doi:10.1177/0093650205275384

Knobloch, L. K., & Theiss, J. A. (2011). Depressive symptoms and mechanisms of relational turbulence as predictors of relationship satisfaction among returning service members. *Journal of Family Psychology*, 25(4), 470–478. doi:10.1037/a0024063

Lichter, D. T., & Qian, Z. (2008). Serial cohabitation and the marital life course. *Journal of Marriage and Family*, 70(4), 861–878. doi:10.1111/j.1741-3737.2008.00532.x

Marston, P. J., Hecht, M. L., Manke, M. L., McDaniel, S., & Reeder, H. (1998). The subjective experience of intimacy, passion, and commitment in heterosexual loving relationships. *Personal Relationships*, 5(1), 15–30. doi:10.1111/j.1475-6811.1998.tb00157.x

Nelms, B. J., Knox, D., & Easterling, B. (2012). The relationship talk: Assessing partner commitment. *College Student Journal*, 46(1), 178–182.

Rhoades, G. K., Stanley, S. M., & Markman, H. J. (2009). Working with cohabitation in relationship education and therapy. *Journal of Couple & Relationship Therapy*, 8(2), 95–112. doi:10.1080/15332690902813794

Ruppel, E. K., & Curran, M. A. (2012). Relational sacrifices in romantic relationships: Satisfaction and the moderating role of attachment. *Journal of Social and Personal Relationships*, 29(4), 508–529. doi:10.1177/0265407511431190

Rusbult, C. E. (1983). A longitudinal test of the investment model: The development (and deterioration) of satisfaction and commitment in heterosexual involvements. *Journal of Personality and Social Psychology, 45*(1), 101–117. doi:10.1037/0022-3514.45.1.101

Rusbult, C. E., & Buunk, B. P. (1993). Commitment processes in close relationships: An interdependence analysis. *Journal of Social and Personal Relationships, 10*(2), 175–204. doi:10.1177/026540759301000202

Rusbult, C. E., Martz, J. M., & Agnew, C. R. (1998). The investment model scale: Measuring commitment level, satisfaction level, quality of alternatives, and investment size. *Personal Relationships, 5*(4), 357–387. doi:10.1111/j.1475-6811.1998.tb00177.x

Sahlstein, E., & Baxter, L. A. (2001). Improvising commitment in close relationships: A relational dialectics perspective. In J. H. Harvey & A. E. Wenzel (Eds.), *Close romantic relationships: Maintenance and enhancement* (pp. 115–132). Mahwah, NJ: Lawrence Erlbaum. doi:10.4324/9781410600462

Shulman, S., & Connolly, J. (2013). The challenge of romantic relationships in emerging adulthood reconceptualization of the field. *Emerging Adulthood, 1*(1), 27–39.

Stanley, S. M. (2009, May 9). The DTR dance: Avoiding the talk [Blog post]. Retrieved from http://slidingvsdeciding.blogspot.com/2009/05/dtr-dance-avoiding-talk-i-wrote-in.html

Stanley, S. M., & Markman, H. J. (1992). Assessing commitment in personal relationships. *Journal of Marriage and the Family, 54*(3), 595–608. doi:10.2307/353245

Stanley, S., & Rhoades, G. (2009). Marriages at risk: Relationship formation and opportunities for relationship education. In H. Benson & S. Callan (Eds.), *What works in relationship education: Lessons from academics and service deliverers in the United States and Europe* (pp. 21–44). Doha, Qatar: Doha International Institute for Family Studies and Development.

Stanley, S. M., Rhoades, G. K., & Markman, H. J. (2006). Sliding versus deciding: Inertia and the premarital cohabitation effect. *Family Relations, 55*(4), 499–509. doi:10.1111/j.1741-3729.2006.00418.x

Stanley, S. M., Rhoades, G. K., & Whitton, S. W. (2010). Commitment: Functions, formation, and the securing of romantic attachment. *Journal of Family Theory & Review, 2*(4), 243–257. doi:10.1111/j.1756-2589.2010.00060.x

Surra, C. A., & Hughes, D. K. (1997). Commitment processes in accounts of the development of premarital relationships. *Journal of Marriage and the Family, 59*(1), 5–21. doi:10.2307/353658

Thibaut, J. W., & Kelley, H. H. (1959). *The social psychology of groups.* New York, NY: Wiley.

Van Lange, P. M., Rusbult, C. E., Drigotas, S. M., Arriaga, X. B., Witcher, B. S., & Cox, C. L. (1997). Willingness to sacrifice in close relationships. *Journal of Personality and Social Psychology, 72*(6), 1373–1395. doi:10.1037/0022-3514.72.6.1373

Weigel, D. J., Bennett, K. K., & Ballard-Reisch, S. (2003). Family influences on commitment: Examining the family of origin correlates of relationship commitment attitudes. *Personal Relationships, 10*(4), 453–474. http://dx.doi.org/10.1046/j.1475-6811.2003.00060.x

4 ▲

Sacrifice
An Unfolding Narrative

> *I only understood why someone would sacrifice a lot*
> *[when] I found someone I really liked.*
> —Kris, 25, a research participant

> *Sacrifice is not a burden.*
> —Angela, 27, a research participant

Sacrifice is an important, though sometimes overlooked, component of romantic relationships. It has been shown to be associated with beneficial outcomes such as personal well-being (Impett, Gable, & Peplau, 2005), positive affect (Kogan, Impett, Oveis, Hui, Goron, & Keltner, 2010), relational satisfaction (Stanley & Markman, 1992), and lower rates of relationship dissolution (Van Lange, Rusbult, et al., 1997). Critical to intimate relationships—along with caring, trust, respect, and loyalty (Noller, 1996, as cited in Stanley, Whitton, Sadberry, Clements, & Markman, 2006)—sacrifice has often been identified as a major aspect of love. Yet, the construct has received relatively scant attention in the literature.

Because early romantic relationships formed during emerging adulthood inform future relationship functioning (Donnellan, Larsen-Rife, & Conger, 2005; Overbeek, Stattin, Vermulst, Ha, & Engels, 2007), studying sacrifice in emerging adult relationships provides us with an opportunity to gain greater understanding of how romantic relationships develop and thrive throughout adulthood (Stanley et al., 2006). For that reason, sacrifice will be the focus of this chapter.

Sacrifice tends to be presented in the literature as *either* a theoretical sub-construct of commitment *or* a closely related but distinctive construct that stands on its own (Stanley et al., 2006). Commitment and sacrifice are closely related. Individuals who are highly committed in a relationship are more likely to sacrifice for one another, as compared to those who are not highly committed (Van Lange, Agnew, Harinck, & Steemers, 1997; Van Lange, Rusbult et al.,1997; Wieselquist, Rusbult,

Foster, & Agnew, 1999). However, sacrifice also uniquely accounts for some of the variance in couple functioning not shared with commitment (Corkery, Curran, & Parkman, 2011). The two constructs overlap but remain distinct.

Definitions of sacrifice in the literature emphasize two components: giving up something beneficial to the self *and* benefiting the romantic partner and/or the relationship. For example, according to Whitton, Stanley, and Markman (2007), sacrifice is an act that involves forgoing the satisfaction of an immediate personal desire for the purpose of improving the relationship or benefiting the partner. Similarly, Kogan et al. (2010) define sacrifice as "actions in which an individual forgoes his or her immediate self-interest to promote the well-being of a partner or a relationship" (p. 1918).

As partners identify more strongly as a committed couple, they begin to focus increasingly on the needs of the couple and less on the personal needs of two separate individuals trying to maximize their own gain and comfort (Agnew, Van Lange, Rusbult, & Langston, 1998; Kelley & Thibaut, 1978; Stanley & Markman, 1992, as cited in Stanley et al, 2006). The greater the willingness of romantic partners to sacrifice, the higher the likelihood that their relationship will continue (Van Lange, Agnew, et al., 1997; Van Lange, Rusbult et al., 1997). Some of the factors believed to contribute to a higher likelihood of sacrificing between committed individuals include long-term orientation toward the relationship (Van Lange et al., 1997; Van Lange, Rusbult, et al., 1997), feelings of dependence on the partner (Van Lange et al., 1997), psychological attachment to the partner (Aron & Aron, 1986), and a desire to reciprocate a partner's perceived kindness and sacrifice (Wieselquist, Rusbult, Foster, & Agnew,1999). Not all of these are healthy relationship markers, and it should be noted that feminist researchers tend to assume a somewhat critical approach toward sacrifice and its definition, partly because of its potential for contributing to codependency, relationship dissatisfaction, and depression (e.g., Jack & Dill, 1992; Jordan, 1991; Lerner & Lerner, 1985).

Myriad types of sacrifice have been identified: *active* and *passive* sacrifice, and *major* and *daily* sacrifice (Van Lange, Rusbult et al., 1997). Active sacrifice involves affirmatively taking an action step that is viewed by the self as undesirable (e.g., moving to a location that is not beneficial to the individual in order to support the relationship; Impett & Gordon, 2008). Passive sacrifice involves forgoing something desirable in the interest of serving one's partner or the relationship (e.g., turning down a good job offer or giving up a friendship). Some sacrifices are *major* while others involve daily exchanges, typically of less import to the individual (Van Lange, Agnew et al., 1997; Impett et al., 2005). The assessment of whether a particular act is a sacrifice, and what type of sacrifice it constitutes, depends entirely on the appraisal of the individual doing the act. One partner may experience a sacrifice as major, another may not. Sacrifice is a subjective experience; only the doer knows the felt cost.

Acts that are genuinely self-harmful do not typically fall within the bounds of healthy relationship sacrifice. The perception of sacrifice as harmful is, in fact, negatively correlated with relationship commitment and couple functioning (Whitton et al., 2007). Sacrifices that are harmful to the self can be motivated in part by fear of physical and/or verbal abuse by the partner, or fear of relationship dissolution and are associated with depression and physical danger, not relationship building (Stanley et al., 2006). Sacrifice is *not* the same as martyrdom, which can be defined as an attempt by an individual to benefit the self by "put[ting] the other in debt" to her/him (Whitton, Stanley, & Markman, 2002, p. 159).

This chapter describes two types of relationships with respect to sacrifice—communal and exchange—and why some emerging adults are more likely to enjoy the emotional benefits from sacrifice than others. We explore the mechanisms that are thought to underlie the association between commitment, sacrifice, interdependence, and couple adjustment. The experiences and reflections of our 29 study participants with regard to sacrifice are examined: their understandings of sacrifice and their perceptions of how sacrifice unfolds in relationships during the dynamic period of emerging adulthood. Finally, we explore risk, commitment, and how these dynamics are navigated in a population that has been consistently disappointed by the significant people in their lives and by failing institutions. The narrative of Tina highlights her thoughts on sacrifice that are representative of many of our study participants.

▲ Communal Relationships Versus Exchange Relationships

Kogan and colleagues (2010) have brought their research expertise to bear on the following two questions: (1) Who is likely to receive the benefits of sacrifice—the receiver of the sacrifice or the individual doing the sacrificing? and (2) Why do some individuals receive greater joy than others when sacrificing in communal relationships? (A *communal relationship* is one in which sacrifices are made in response to the perceived needs of the partner(ship) and are not contingent upon a return of the favor; Clark & Mills, 1979, as cited in Kogan et al., 2010). Kogan and colleagues hypothesize that individuals who are most likely to sacrifice are those who evidence more communal strength. Such individuals are more likely to intrinsically enjoy the relational and emotional benefits of sacrifice (Mills, Clark, Ford, & Johnson, 2004). As to why some individuals reap more benefits from sacrifice than others, Kogan et al. posit that authenticity mediates the relationship between sacrifice and relational satisfaction: Is the act performed in a genuinely "giving" way or with expectations of returned benefits? To the extent that the latter is predominantly the case, the relationship can be defined as an *exchange relationship* (Clark & Mills, 1979) or an *equality-matching relational model* (Fisk, 1992). Such relationships are organized around the expectation that benefits given will be directly reciprocated. Conversely, in communal relationships, expectation of reciprocation does not inform the act of sacrifice; partners express little concern about whether their prosocial acts have been reciprocated.

Relationships vary in the degree to which they are communal or exchange-oriented, and each of the partners may exhibit these two orientations to different extents (Clark & Mills, 1993, as cited in Kogan et al., 2010). Greater communal strength is correlated with being more satisfied with one's romantic relationships and having partners who are more satisfied (Mills et al., 2004; Impett et al., 2005); it is also associated with being more emotionally expressive (Clark & Finkel, 2005, as cited in Kogan et al., 2010).

In a study of 69 couples, ages 18–60, after controlling for relationship duration, Kogan et al. found that communal strength was correlated with positive emotions and relationship satisfaction during those days in which participants engaged in acts of sacrifice. The greater the level of communal strength, the more authentic the individuals felt when making their daily sacrifices for their partner, and the likelier they were to experience feelings of being appreciated. It is important to note that this study was correlational and therefore causality cannot be assumed. Kogan and colleagues did not measure self-identity perceptions, but they do suggest that individuals high in communal strength may internalize ideas of being caring, responsive partners as part of their identities (Cross, Bacon, & Morris, 2000, as cited in Kogan et al, 2010).

In sum, the findings of Kogan et al. suggest that acting communally is beneficial to romantic relationships. Individuals who are motivated to respond to their partners in a noncontingent fashion receive a sense of personal satisfaction as well. Such benefits may not be limited to romantic partnerships; there is a growing body of work suggesting that acting communally is associated with greater relational satisfaction in friendships as well (Clark & Aragon, 2013).

What are some patterns that promote a healthy mutual process of sacrifice both on the level of individual commitment ("I am more committed so I am willing to sacrifice more") and as an interdependent dynamic between partners ("My partner has given up so much to show their commitment, I want to reciprocate"; Monk, Vennum, Ogolksy, & Fincham, 2014, p. 429)? The next section addresses this question and describes the mechanisms that are thought to underlie the association between commitment, sacrifice, interdependence, and couple adjustment.

▲ Interdependence, Commitment, and Sacrifice

Emerging adults who are committed to their partners are more likely to invest in their relationships and in their futures than those who are not. They believe in the long-term viability of the relationship (Monk et al., 2014). Commitment to a romantic relationship induces pro-relationship behavior, including communication of the committed individuals' long-term orientation. The members of the couple understand that cycles of reciprocity are likely to yield direct self-benefit over the long run, and each individual sacrifices his/her short-term needs for the long-term stability of the relationship (Stanley, Rhoades, & Whitton, 2010).

Sacrifice contributes to investment in the relationship and maintenance of the relationship (Monk et al., 2014). Investment in a romantic relationship is associated with greater commitment to the relationship. Greater commitment, in turn, is associated with "an interdependent mental process" (p. 428). As suggested by interdependence theory (elaborated in Chapter 2), with growing interdependence, the couple transitions from an *I*/self-interested orientation to a *we*/other-directed orientation. The transition represents a shift toward a long-term view of the relationship (Stanley et al., 2006).

An interdependence explanation assumes that commitment promotes willingness to sacrifice and that sacrifice strengthens couple functioning. Partners engage in sacrifice because they are committed to the continuation of the relationship. Maintenance of a well-functioning relationship *requires* sacrifice (i.e., willingness to set aside personal interests that conflict with the well-being of the couple), but it is the way in which the individual *views* sacrifice, more than the act itself, that is critical (e.g., satisfaction with the sacrifice as opposed to resentful feelings that one is giving up more than one's partner). Better relationship functioning has been found in partners who did not view sacrifice as detrimental to themselves (Whitton et al., 2007). Rather, they saw themselves as engaging in maintenance behaviors that were critical to the long-term functioning of the couple. By contrast, when a relationship deteriorates and commitment is declining, the individual becomes increasingly self-interested and exerts less effort toward relationship maintenance goals.

Emerging adults seem to understand the importance of sacrifice in relationship and view the learned ability to make adult sacrifices as a developmental milestone. Carroll, Badger, Willoughby, Nelson, Madsen, and Barry (2009), in a study of 788 college students from across the country with a mean age of 20.0 (*SD*=1.8), reported that emerging adults are endorsing a new philosophy regarding marriage readiness. They believe they will be ready for marriage when they have accomplished tasks as a single person that include developing interpersonal competencies, such as the ability to shift emphasis from self-care to caring for others. In the process of being able to self-identify as an "adult," the "self" can then shift its focus toward preparing for marriage. The authors' findings suggest that for many emerging adults, it is only when they have accomplished what they hoped for as a single person, including the ability to view oneself as an "adult," that they will be ready to shift their orientation from *intra*personal competencies toward *inter*personal competencies and become less self-oriented.

The study suggests that transitioning from an *I* to a *we* needs to occur sequentially. Only after sufficiently developing the self, and learning that one can rely on the adult self, can one authentically shift to a couple orientation. For those marriages that prioritize self-actualization for each of the partners, however, marital outcomes and the implications for sacrifice are not well known. There are competing points of view. While higher levels of exploration during the emerging adulthood years may be associated with better marital relationships, they may be associated with worse marital relationship outcomes. For example, Tanner (2006) has pointed out that a greater number of partners and an extended time frame to experiment and establish romantic preferences may be associated with difficulties in compromising for the other, key to a successful long-term romantic relationship or healthy marriage.

It may be that both positions are correct. Emerging adults may need to have satisfied many of their important individual development goals before they feel ready to sacrifice meaningfully for another person. On the other hand, if they become too focused on self-development, for too long a period of time, they may be less willing to make the sacrifices that are essential to successful long-term relationships. The perspective of Tanner (2006) merits further investigation.

The next section presents the experiences and reflections of our 29 study participants with regard to sacrifice. We will examine their understandings of sacrifice and their perceptions of how sacrifice unfolds during the dynamic period of emerging adulthood.

▲ Participant Responses

All 29 of the participants were asked the question, "What comes to mind when you think about sacrifice in a romantic relationship?" Each of the participants provided unique responses about sacrifice and what it meant to him or her, yielding the domain *meaning and experience of sacrifice*.

A second domain, *sacrifice: changes over time* represented the participants' responses to the question, "Have you changed your thinking about sacrifice since your early 20s? If so, how have you changed?"

Meaning and Experience of Sacrifice

Within the first domain, five categories were further established to capture the range of meanings and experiences associated with sacrifice: (a) sacrifice and compromise, (b) giving something up: volitional or obligatory, (c) sacrifice, large and small, (d) sacrifice and parity, and (e) sacrifice, loss, and friendships.

Sacrifice and compromise

Twelve of the participants used the terms *sacrifice* and *compromise* interchangeably, yielding a *variant* category. For these participants, sacrifice involved a process of adjustment and calibration, a meeting in the middle for the partners.

For Becky (24) sacrifice is associated with mutual compromise:

> A sacrifice means, I guess, doing things that you may not necessarily want, or chang[ing] things about you [that you] like [and changing] what's going on in your life to help the relationship. I don't really see it as much sacrifice as I do compromise.

Andrea (24) has similar views. She suggests that when both parties compromise, equity and/or fairness is a likely outcome.

> I think that a real relationship is about compromise. There is no way that it could work without compromise, because you know [you] are different creatures, [you] do different things, and [you] may not like something that the other person is doing—or the other person may not like something that you are doing . . . but you do need to meet each other halfway, you do need to meet in the middle. . . . You have to.

Rita (26) suggests that in the process of compromising—meeting the other person halfway—you introduce the element of possibility. New options may emerge. For Rita, meeting in the middle is not simply a matter of a transactional exchange between two individuals:

> Sometimes the compromise leads you to totally new things . . . like new things that you two created or decided to do, and that's the beauty of compromise.

Sacrifice and compromise are not interchangeable concepts. Sacrifice refers to a unilateral action, while compromise entails mutual adjustment. Research participants spoke mainly of compromise and its power to make couples "recalibrate" the relationship.

Giving something up: volitional or obligatory?

Eleven of the participants associated sacrifice with "giving something up" for the sake of the other person and/or the relationship, yielding a *variant* category. Sacrifice, for the majority of the participants, was seen as an organic process, part and parcel of being in a romantic relationship. While the majority of the participants expressed a willingness to sacrifice and viewed their actions as serving to make the other person feel "special," "loved," and/or "cared about," the remaining five participants spoke of not wanting to sacrifice, yet feeling obliged to do so ("I need to do this, but I don't want to") in order to maintain the relationship.

For the six participants in the majority group who viewed sacrifice as a volitional act, they sacrificed for their partner because they felt it was something one just does when one is in a loving relationship; it is "part of love." Alana (21) states, "When something is hard, you still do it because you really love the person."

Mahesh (23) and Angela (27) suggested that while sacrifice means giving some things up, it is part of being in a loving relationship. Although Mahesh is not currently in a relationship and Angela is in a nine-year relationship, both noted that when sacrifice is part of love, the losses do not seem as pronounced as involuntary losses; there is an acceptance of the notion that when you love another, you will give up things that are "valued."

> MAHESH: You're going to have to give up something that. . . you either value or you just really love doing. . . . Giving up things or just sacrificing for your partner is. . . all a part of love.
>
> ANGELA: I think we do sacrifice for each other but . . . I do *not* think it is a huge burden to do things for him, because I want to do things for him.

Sacrifice is not a "burden" for Angela because she "wants to do things" for her romantic partner. Six of the participants expressed similar views; they did not feel "burdened" by the act of sacrifice.

A minority of the participants (5), however, felt obliged to sacrifice; they viewed sacrifice as necessary. They emphasized loss and obligation. Sacrifice was described as something one has to do in order to be in a romantic relationship and make it work. These five participants stated that they wanted to stay in their respective relationships and, in their view, that involved sacrificing, giving some things up for the other.

Mark (24) and Ronda (22) focused on what they had to do, either to keep the relationship going or to keep the partner in the relationship "happy":

MARK: Sacrifice means either doing something that I don't want to do, or *not* doing something that I otherwise want to, for the sake of the person I'm with, or for the sake of keeping the relationship.

RONDA: Sacrifices mean giving something that you obviously do not want [to give], but it is for the benefit of, or happiness of, somebody else.

Sacrifice was seen by these emerging adults as the price one pays for being in a relationship, rather than as a positive investment in the long-term vitality of the partnership—a subtle difference, but one that may have important day-to-day implications.

Sacrifices, large and small

Not all sacrifices are the same; some are major and some are minor. Eight of the participants made that distinction, yielding a *variant* category. The assessment of the scope and size of the sacrifice was viewed as subjective and as impacting one's attitude toward the "sacrificial" actions. For example, while Tina (27) recognizes that there are small and large sacrifices, Alana (21) states that small sacrifices are not sacrifices at all; rather, they are just part of being in a relationship when you "like the person."

TINA: In any given situation, it might be something different— whether it's something small, like let's go do something you want to do instead of something I want to do, or something big, like we're going to move to where you have a job versus where I get the chance to have a job.

ALANA: I guess it should not really seem like a sacrifice if it is for the person you like. And I mean little things—if you have to drive over 20 minutes to see someone, some people, I guess, would consider that a sacrifice . . . but I don't really feel like that.

Daniel (21) notes that sacrifices can be of different types:

> [Sacrifice] can range. . . . Sometimes that would be small goals that you . . . might sacrifice to help with your significant other's larger goals. Or sometimes it could be just something small like doing the dishes.

Katherine (25) and Alison (28) noted that some sacrifices are "lofty" and some are "smaller," such as taking days off from work for your partner, and going to social events. They both acknowledged, however, that they have never had to make a large sacrifice:

> KATHERINE: I think there are definite levels [of sacrifice] that I've had to make. . . . I don't feel like I've had to make a big sacrifice, but, um . . . I think maybe it can come down to the little things.
> ALISON: I think the sacrifices that I have [made] are more on a day-to-day basis, and they are small; there have not really been huge sacrifices.

In general, this group expressed the point of view that small sacrifices are a "routine" aspect of any relationship, while large sacrifices are reserved for more serious relationships and can put the partners' commitment to the test.

Sacrifice and parity

Parity in the relationship—who does more sacrificing, who does less—was an important consideration for six of the participants. Net gains and/or losses were considered; participants made judgments about the likelihood of reciprocation by their respective partners.

Parity was an expressed concern for Alison (28) who spoke of the importance and necessity of the two partners mutually giving to one another.

> I think that sacrifices are inevitable and [it is] really important in all relationships, but there either needs to be a mutual giving or mutual sacrifice on both parts.

In speaking about parity in relationship to changes each partner has to make for the sake of the other, Becky (24) asserts: "I feel like if you're . . . [making changes], you should be asking the other person to do it too."

The participants who expressed concern about parity tended to view themselves as more willing to sacrifice, and as giving more to the relationship, than their partners. They tended to feel that they were being taken advantage of by their partners and consequently were dissatisfied with the lack of parity in the relationship. This was a dynamic they wished they could change but did not feel optimistic about changing.

Sacrifice, loss, and friendships

Six participants acknowledged sadness and/or loss about sacrificing friendships for the sake of the relationship, thus yielding a *variant* category. In these cases, tensions existed regarding how certain friends would be integrated with the romantic relationship. Sometimes the tensions came from within the romantic relationship; other times they came from within the friendship. In situations where a friend might be viewed as a potential cause for jealousy within the relationship, the decision to end the friendship was perceived as an easier one.

The friendship-related constraints experienced by these six participants revolved around two factors primarily: (a) not having enough time in the day to attend to both their partners and friends, and (b) disapproval by the friends and/or the partner of the other party. When making the decision to give up their friend(s) in favor of the romantic relationship, participants stressed that they did not perceive they had a choice; it was an either/or scenario. The decision continues to be a source of pain for some of them.

Leslie (27) states:

> You give them up (friends). . . . You stop investing in other
> relationships for this one person. I've made a lot of sacrifices. . . .
> I would end friendships with males, other males, [so that] my
> boyfriend never felt uncomfortable—or even females too. And
> then, sometimes even family, you know . . . [I would] not really
> invest in relationships with other people for [the sake of] this one
> person.

In the words of Katherine (25):

> My boyfriend didn't get along with my friends. . . . I remember
> they told me, we don't like him, and you won't listen to us, so you

either break up with him now or we won't be your friends. And
I didn't break up with him, and I haven't spoken to them since
I was 19.

In contrast, Angela (27), an outlier, says of friends: "Friends come with
you. I mean, romantically you do not sacrifice friends."

The willingness or unwillingness of emerging adults to sacrifice
friendships for a relationship must be weighed against the fact that for
many emerging adults, friendships are more central to their lives in
comparison to past generations, in part because of the growing trend to
delay long-term romantic relationships. Friendships take on more importance and therefore sacrificing friendships might be deemed a more
meaningful act, in many cases, than it would have been in the past.

Sacrifice: Changes Over Time

For the second domain, participants were asked whether and how
their views and experiences of sacrifice had changed since their early
20s. Many of the emerging adult participants relayed that in their
early 20s, they tended to view sacrifice as something that one needs
to do in order to stay with a partner, something that one does *only* as
part of maintaining a relationship. Shifts in viewpoint occurred over
time. While some of the participants became focused on the other or
on making the relationship work, others came to emphasize the importance of knowing oneself and setting boundaries. Three categories were
generated: (a) making the relationship "work," (b) sacrifice and parity,
and (c) knowing yourself, setting boundaries.

Making the relationship "work."

Six participants stated that they had revisited their understanding
of sacrifice since their early 20s and, in the process, had revised their
construct of sacrifice and the way they lived sacrifice. Their combined
responses yielded a *variant* category.

Joseph (25) described his attempts at making meaning of sacrifice
in his early 20s. Whereas he initially equated sacrifice with compromise, over time he revised his understanding of the two, adding a more
nuanced caveat: "Now I see compromise as something that you give
up . . . *to make your relationship work.*" For Joseph, making a relationship

work is "hard." Whereas in his early 20s, he prioritized what *he needed* from the relationship, with the passage of time he has become less focused on his own needs and more on what needs to be given up in order for relationships to "work."

> I was not fully developed and I used to consider [certain things] compromises when they were not really compromises. Now compromises are giving up things to make the relationship work.

Similarly, Cam (26) says "sacrificing [to me] now is to make things work with each other as a team." Both Joseph and Cam seemed to increasingly understand that making things "better" in the relationship involves the perspectives of both partners, both of whom are motivated to make "things work."

Chantal (23) said that in her early 20s she thought it was the male's responsibility to "win her over" by sacrificing, but that she now associates sacrifice with two-way compromise: each partner must meet the other person halfway in order to make the relationship work:

> Making the relationship work, what do I have to do? I never really used to make sacrifices, honestly. . . . I never really felt like making sacrifices for guys that I was dating. I used to always think if he's interested in me, then he should be the one that's trying to win me over. I never really used to like . . . meet the guy halfway.

Chantal views her new willingness to make sacrifices and compromises for the sake of the relationship as a sign of her unfolding maturity. In sum, these responses suggest that the 20s are a crucial decade for deepening and revising one's understanding of sacrifice and one's willingness to engage in it.

Sacrifice and parity

For four of the participants, learning about the self and sacrifice over time resulted in a modification of their expectations of their partner and/or themselves with respect to whether they viewed themselves as sacrificing too much or too little. Their responses yielded a *variant* category. All four participants in this group spoke about learning over time that sacrifice was a worthwhile endeavor.

Leslie (27) states:

In my early 20s, I felt like [my partner] should also sacrifice
a lot for me. . . . But now I've lessened my expectations and
I don't expect [my partner] to make sacrifices for me if they
don't want to. For myself, I don't think it has changed much;
I'm willing to sacrifice, you know, a lot. Whatever it's worth to
get the partner.

Leslie has matured in some ways but perhaps not in others. Lessening
one's expectations of others can be part of the journey toward maturity,
but Leslie seems to be developmentally "stuck" in terms of her expectations of herself. Her willingness to do whatever it takes to "get" the
partner, at any cost to herself, may be leaving her vulnerable.

In contrast to Leslie, the three other participants in this category—
Andrea, Sandra, and Mark—found that, with maturity, they had
changed in the direction of sacrificing *less*. They had learned to expect
more from their partners with respect to sacrifice.

Andrea (24) who noted that she identifies as a "natural giver,"
states:

I feel like I was open to a lot more things . . . I feel like I have a
big heart, and I think people can take advantage of that, so my
compromise now is that things need to come for me too. I can't
just give and give and give.

Sandra (26) has been hurt in several relationships and feels that she has
been taken advantage of as a result of her giving nature. She has decided to rely exclusively on her judgment and put herself first.

[I] have stopped doing for others, I don't do what I used to do
anymore, and I'm more " tuned" to myself. I take care of me first
before anything else. In the past, I would take care of other people
first and then worry about me.

Mark (24) who previously had "ridiculous romantic values about self-
sacrificing . . . for your love," says, "One of the good things I've learned
is that I really will be happier if I sacrifice less of myself just for my
boyfriend."

As a result of becoming clearer about sacrifice, these four emerging
adults have changed their behavior accordingly, either by *making*
or by *expecting* fewer sacrifices in their relationships. This suggests a

continued evolving and reevaluation of individual needs as emerging adults learn how to "live in relationship" with a romantic partner.

Knowing yourself, setting boundaries

Learning to set boundaries for themselves and their partners was an important area of growth for eight of the participants, whose responses generated a *variant* category. Issues related to both parity and clarity were in the foreground for many of the participants; they spoke of the necessity of knowing oneself and being "in tune" with oneself in the process of boundary-setting.

Participants acknowledged that it was a difficult to establish a common relationship space that felt comfortable to both partners. In the process of setting boundaries, several participants were concerned about feeling "pressure[d] to not disappoint" their partners.

Michael (27) in describing his struggle to set boundaries that worked for him, suggested that disappointing one's partner—and being disappointed by one's partner—was inevitable. However, he concludes:

It is more important in the long run to establish what you like, and what you are into. [You] have to stand up for yourself and, you know . . . make sacrifices for yourself too.

Michael reported that he is struggling to find balance around sacrifice and that he uses the lens of "in the long run" to try to assert his needs while at the same time recognizing the needs of his partner. He says, "You have to have faith that the relationship will last, and that the two people in the relationship have it within their repertoire to negotiate difference[s]."

Rita (26) asserted that one cannot be in a relationship and work exclusively from one's own construct of sacrifice. In her efforts to establish a common space in her relationship, she tries to ensure that the perspectives of both partners are acknowledged and heard:

Not just that I'm loved the way I want to be loved, but that I'm loving him and I can care for him in the way that he needs, not just the way that I think someone should be.

In reflecting how she has changed since her early 20s, Rita said that she has incorporated a process that involves conversations between the two partners in which each is able to express how he/she wants to be loved and cared for. Each partner acknowledges and addresses the needs of the other, without imposing an agenda on the other. In considering how much or little to sacrifice for another, it is both partners' responsibility to state what they want and expect from each other.

Amelia (24) asserts that one has to remain true to oneself, a process that requires self-knowledge: "You cannot sacrifice yourself, you need to love yourself. . . . You need to take care of yourself. At the end of the day, you have to be yourself always." She concluded that she had "matured" and become more "realistic" over the past few years: "For sacrifice, you have to know what you are willing to give and he has to know what he is willing to give."

Both Amelia and Rita recalled that they initially viewed sacrifice through the lens of you-versus-me, an orientation that required prioritizing the self over the other. Both women revised their stances such that they are now able to meet their partners in a space that acknowledges the other. Knowing themselves helped them learn to communicate openly with their partners in a two-way exchange. Sacrifice was no longer a matter of you-versus-me—it became one of you *and* me.

▲ Analysis of Findings

Participants relayed that they experience sacrifice as an evolving process that carries important implications for how they live their day-to-day romantic lives. Collectively, the findings of this study, while supportive of the sacrifice literature (e.g., meanings attached to sacrifice, degrees of sacrifice, etc.), also suggest the need for a more nuanced and complete understanding of sacrifice during emerging adulthood. Our analysis suggests that during this period of experimentation and instability, emerging adults' beliefs about sacrifice are unfolding and incomplete, and are likely to be revisited and revised at later points in their lives. Emerging adulthood is a time of self-focus, when issues of developing the self are in the foreground and likely to compete with development of a relationship. Hence, issues related to parity and loss of the self are likely to be more pronounced. As emerging adults develop a stronger sense of "self," and view themselves as "adults" with clearer boundaries, they are less likely to view sacrifice as taking something away from themselves and their personal development.

Our 29 emerging adult participants continue to wrestle with the meaning of sacrifice in their romantic relationships. However, with time and increasing self-knowledge, they have adjusted their orientations toward sacrifice. A minority of the participants shared that to date they had never been called upon to make a large sacrifice. This implies that their current attitudes toward sacrifice have not yet been fully "tested." For many, the concepts of sacrifice and compromise were virtually indistinguishable.

Kogan's description of communal sacrifice did not tend to resonate with the descriptions and experiences of our study group. There was an implicit expectation of reciprocity in most of their accounts. These results are consistent with Arnett's characterization of this period as one of self-focus and self-development. There were some exceptions however, as exemplified by two of the participants, both of whom were comparatively older and had been in longer and more stable relationships. These two participants appeared to have made the transition from an *I* to a *we* orientation in their respective relationships.

Evolving from an individual to an interdependent perspective—from an *I* to a *we*—requires that each member of the couple shift from prioritizing self-interest to prioritizing the *good of the relationship*. This shift typically requires a corresponding shift in identity as discussed in Chapter 2. It is when the relationship is given priority that commitment and sacrifice are linked in a virtuous cycle. One's commitment to the relationship increases because one has a more positive attitude toward sacrifice; in turn, one's attitude toward sacrifice grows more positive because one is more committed to the relationship. More than half of the participants were either not in current relationships or were struggling to assess whether they wanted to be in long-term committed relationships with their current partners. For example, Tina is currently in a relationship but is trying to decide whether she is ready for the level of sacrifice that will be required if she transitions to a long-term commitment. She is able to envision how hard it is to be in a sacrificing relationship, yet she can also see how "worthwhile" it can be.

Sibley (2015) suggests that the process of romantic sacrifice is not exclusively cerebral. It needs to be *experienced* in relationship with others. With an accumulation of experiences, emotional growth is more likely to occur. This was reflected in our participants. Through romantic experiences, they had learned about what they needed for themselves, what they expected from themselves, and what they needed from their partners in terms of sacrifice. They had become more efficacious in negotiating their needs with their partners (despite the fact that as, as noted in Chapter 2, the majority reported being reluctant to have the "commitment talk"). Based on the seminal work of Bandura (1986) on self-efficacy, Sibley suggests that in the process of living sacrifice, emerging adults learn more about themselves and their respective partners, as well as how to "perform" sacrifice.

In learning through doing, emerging adults revisit their assumptions about sacrifice and adjust their constructs and behaviors accordingly. They begin to work toward mastery of sacrifice, which comes only with experience. Sibley's findings on commitment in emerging adults suggest that with experience, emerging adults come to believe that the goal—a happier, healthier long-term relationship—is "worthwhile," "attainable," and "sustainable" (Sibley, 2015, p. 41).

Based on the theoretical work of Kelley and Thibaut (1978), Monk et al. (2014) posit that "transformation of motivation" to a communal attitude is more likely to occur when there is commitment in the relationship and satisfaction with sacrifice. Intentionality and hard work better position the emerging adult to make such a transition possible, according to Sibley (2015).

The attitudes of the five study participants who associated sacrifice with obligation spark a noteworthy observation. Although they viewed sacrifice as necessary for relationship maintenance, they did not view sacrifice as a process that was open to negotiation and mutual redefinition. They did not speak of actual or hoped-for opportunities to work through differences in understandings about sacrifice between themselves and their partners. They seemed to be functioning from a closed, you-versus-me orientation; there was a winner and a loser and no opportunity for learning to reinterpret sacrifice itself. By comparison, those who viewed sacrifice as a volitional act were more inclined to engage in an evolving process vis a vis sacrifice, one that unfolded over time. Their understanding of sacrifice was an ongoing work-in-progress.

For the latter group, their evolving attempts at sacrifice in service of making the relationship "work" required that they increasingly take their partners' needs into account. These participants observed that over time they became more focused on what the partner and/or the relationship needed, while at the same time remaining cognizant of their own needs in the relationship.

Perhaps at some point in the future many of the participants will shift their orientation to a communal understanding of sacrifice and develop their own sense of *I* and *we* as a couple, particularly as they become increasingly invested as couples and/or families with child[ren]. Their ability to make this shift will likely hinge, to a large extent, on whether they view sacrifice as less or more harmful to themselves (Whitton et al., 2007). It is not the act of sacrifice itself but rather the way the individual personally interprets sacrifice—e.g., as an obligation, as a gift, as an investment, etc.—that is critical.

An important caveat regarding research studies on sacrifice need to be mentioned. Sacrifice is typically assessed using self-report questionnaires that measure participants' perceived attitudes toward sacrifice and that make no distinctions between levels and types of sacrifice, such as communal and exchange-oriented sacrifice. Extant studies for the most part have not adequately controlled for important factors such as religious and cultural orientation.

Application of a cultural lens would enrich our understanding. For example, the literature on sacrifice has not sufficiently explored the implications of living in collectivistic societies versus individualistic societies. Sacrifice in romantic relationships is likely to be experienced and lived differently in these respective societies. Even within our dominant culture, there are cultural considerations. Cultural shifts have led some emerging adults to evaluate relationships based on their ability to satisfy their personal needs for self-actualization. Other couples, however, have chosen to make a commitment to mutual growth in which the two individuals focus on the overall well-being of the relationship. What transpires when each of the partners increasingly identify as a couple, but also want to serve the needs of two separate individuals trying to self-actualize (Stanley et al., 2006), particularly when children become part of the family structure, remains an unknown. There is a need for longitudinal studies that involve both partners and that rely on a diversity of methods, including the use of diaries.

Our participants made the distinction between small and large sacrifices. Many had never made large sacrifices, although all had been in romantic relationships during their emerging adulthood years. Future research studies are needed to further elaborate on these important distinctions.

Many of the participants viewed sacrifice through the lens of parity: who is giving more and who is giving less in the relationship. Some became more entrenched in their orientation over time, while others shifted to an "other" orientation, wanting to make their partner "happy." What are the dynamics and contingencies that allow some to make the shift while other become increasingly frustrated and less inclined to sacrifice within a romantic relationship? Future research is needed to elaborate on and answer such questions.

In the next section, we explore risk, commitment, and sacrifice and how they are navigated among emerging and young adults. The focus is on an understudied population that has been consistently disappointed by significant others and the systems in which they are embedded.

Sacrifice, Commitment, and Risk: Cultural and Economic Considerations

There is a paucity of narratives that address the experiences of emerging adults who have encountered substantial individual and systemic challenges on the way to adulthood. A notable exception is the work of Silva (2012, 2013), who captures an important segment of emerging and young adults underrepresented in the literature. Silva interviewed participants who grew up in Lowell, Massachusetts and Richmond, Virginia, cities that were hit hard by changing economic conditions in the early 2000s. In response to these new economic realities, uncertainty and insecurity prevailed in the day-to-day lives of the individuals Silva interviewed. They grew up learning some hard truths: people disappoint you and the only person you can count on is yourself.

Silva asks the question: "When your family life and your past experiences with significant others have been filled with disappointments and little hope for a satisfying future, how can you risk and sacrifice for another?" Silva's research efforts shed some light on this question.

Based on extensive interviews with 93 emerging and young adults in their 20s and 30s, Silva asserts that the youth she interviewed had learned early in life that sacrifice in the service of relational commitment was not an investment that typically paid off. Rather, it seemed like one more demand in a world that was already asking too much of them. Having grown up in turbulent family and parental situations, many of them avoided pursuing romantic relationships from a place of fear of spending time and energy into something that was likely to fall apart or cause them pain. The prospect of losing what little they already had, made the idea of romantic commitment seem too risky. They did have a desire for an enduring connection and hoped to anchor their lives with a partner. However, they encountered too many obstacles to make such connections happen.

How can one risk and sacrifice for a romantic partner when past experiences strongly suggest that you will be disappointed? According to Silva (2013), experiences of instability, chaos, betrayal, and loneliness, alongside failing institutions, results in an inability to see connections between one's "labors to a life that has the potential to be economically rewarding" (p. 149). Similarly, it is difficult to see how mainstream cultural prescriptions for romantic behaviors will lead them to stable and rewarding long-term relationships.

Sacrificing for the future is a behavior whose logic often eludes emerging and young adults who have repeatedly observed and experienced that the future is likely to disappoint them. The majority were struggling with the realization that traditional life pathways were not available to them. They could not count on traditional rites of passage such as leaving home, finding a stable job, and getting married (with the exception of some men who relied on public sector jobs). They had come to believe that they were incapable of affecting their unfolding destiny.

Silva (2013) observes that the creation of marriages based on distinct gender roles and obligations conflict with the structure of the economy. Men often cannot find stable jobs and, if they do find employment, it does not typically pay sufficient wages to support a family. "Couples who want to create relationships that foster the growth of their deepest selves find that self-realization requires resources that they do not have, and they must decide whether commitment is worth sacrificing their own interests and desires" (p. 149). Women, especially, fear the loss of self. They feel too fragile to risk being in a relationship and often choose to be alone.

Silva (2013) observed that in order to give meaning to their lives, participants made use of a therapeutic model to help them navigate and narrate their experiences. They redefined competent adulthood as overcoming a painful past and constructing a self that was autonomous. Silva describes a process whereby many of these emerging and young adults numb the ache of betrayal and the hunger for connection by embracing ideals of self-reliance, individualism, and personal responsibility. In the process, they become "hardened" to the world around them (p. 149) and many are "lost in transition" (Brinton, 2010; Furedi, 2004, as cited in Silva, 2013). Unable to find jobs and assume traditional adult roles, these emerging and young adults begin to inhabit the "mood economy," which defines growth in terms of emotional self-management rather than traditional accomplishments such as marriage or work. The mood economy provides a vehicle for making meaning in the face of a lack of access to traditional life pathways. "Through the therapeutic narrative, young people 'employ' their adult selves in a forward-moving narrative of suffering and self-transformation (Illouz, 2008), whether through the overcoming of an alcohol addiction . . . coming out and claiming one's sexuality . . . or struggling to not become one's own mother" (pp. 150–151).

Silva (2013) argues that therapeutic discourse has become ingrained in our institutions (through popular cultural icons such as Oprah, meet-up groups, Narcotics Anonymous, etc.) and that it shapes the lives of working-class emerging adults by reinforcing self-reliance and responsibility for one's own emotional well-being. She argues that this generation of working-class emerging adults "draws swift and unforgiving boundaries against those who cannot achieve self-change and contentment through sheer emotional resolve" (p. 151).

But with such resolve, one also needs to have the tools or resources to attain one's vision of healthy selfhood. Without the necessary resources—which many emerging and young adults lack—they become stuck in the mood economy. For such individuals, who feel they are fighting for every inch of emotional ground they are able to claim, the idea of sacrificing for another person seems untenable. Any hopes of having traditional, long-term, mutually satisfying romantic relationships are likely to be met with frustration. Silva (2013) proposes alternative narratives that depend on shifts in the current cultural model.

> In order to tell a different kind of coming of age story—one that promises hope, dignity, and coaction—they must begin their journeys to adulthood with a living wage, a basic floor of social protection, and the skills and knowledge to confront the future. . . . As they search for intimacy, they need cultural models that do not force them to sacrifice egalitarian gender ideals for the promise of lasting commitment or self-fulfillment for trust and certainty. Finally, young working-class men and women need new definitions of dignity and progress that do not reduce their coming of age stories to a quest to manage their emotions and will themselves to be content with insecurity and loss. The health and vibrancy of all our communities depend on the creation and nurturance of notions of dignity that foster connection and interdependence rather than hardened selves. (pp. 156–157)

However, such interdependence must be built on a willingness of emerging and young adults to forgo or delay the fulfillment of some of their own desires for the sake of a relationship that is stronger than the sum of its parts. And that suggests sacrifice, a price under the current exigencies that may be too high to pay.

For a closer look at what sacrifice means to one emerging adult, we will highlight the narrative of Tina, one of the 29 study participants. Her thoughts on sacrifice are uniquely her own, but they also echo the themes of many emerging adults.

Tina: To Sacrifice or Not

Sacrifice is something I have been taught about for
a long time, how sacrifice is part of the course of a
relationship. Just seeing this play out in relationships
around me, seeing how hard it is, but also how
worthwhile it is—how can I convert that in my own
heart, if it came to that for me? Would I be able to do
that? And so, I am wrestling through that . . . and
asking OK, do I really want to be in a relationship?
I always thought I did, but do I?
　　　　　　　　　　—Tina, 27, a research participant

Tina is a 27-year-old Christian woman who has spent the past 5 years in China, teaching English to high school students. She is currently back in the United States working towards a master's degree in international business.

While in China, Tina was in a relationship with a fellow American teacher, a relationship that left her feeling somewhat regretful. She now sees that a romantic partner cannot be a "hobby." "I know that there were times that I acted really selfishly and did not consider his feelings." She states, for example, that when she feels overwhelmed emotionally, she has a tendency to shut down and become emotionally unavailable to her partner. She relays that prior to this relationship she was experiencing internal pressure to marry, as many of her friends were marrying or becoming engaged. Partly in response to that pressure, she "slid" into the relationship with her colleague.

She states that although the two had similar goals for their lives, this was not enough to sustain her interest and investment in the relationship. She concludes that "you also have to have that chemistry. . . . He didn't give me butterflies most of the time."

Tina states that the decision to end the relationship was a "tortured" one. "It was a very hard decision. I had a lot of anxiety, and mild panic attacks." Tina wondered if and when she would break up with him, and if she did, would she "regret it?" She concludes that ending the relationship was the right decision. She entered a new relationship when she returned to the United States, a more satisfying relationship in which she shares similar goals with her partner and where there is also the chemistry she yearned for in her previous relationship. Her current relationship, she says, does give her "butterflies."

Tina views relationships as needing a foundation that is based on commitment and trust. "When I was 18, 20, 22, I thought I could just find someone who just makes me feel happy all the time. I wore kind of rose-colored glasses." She describes her current relationship in these terms:

> We are a couple . . . there's an us. . . . Right now in the relationship, we make decisions together. . . . We are moving toward marriage but we're not there yet. That's where we are at right now. . . . We become more of a *we* when we make more decisions together and when other people start noticing that we are a couple.

With respect to sacrifice, Tina makes a distinction between being in a committed relationship and being married. A couple works towards marriage, according to Tina, and once married, the degree of sacrifice needs to be greater:

> I don't think a dating couple should be required to make very large sacrifices for each other. In marriage, they absolutely do. You sacrifice whatever is necessary to stay together, up to a point—not for an extreme case like abuse. With marriage, there is greater commitment, greater intimacy, and greater sacrifice.

For Tina, sacrifice means "putting somebody else in front of me, putting his needs before mine." She emphasizes that this must occur in small, everyday matters, but also in large, important matters, such as deciding where you are going to live as a couple. But sacrifice must be "a two-way street." For Tina, sacrifice has to be "unconditional":

> Not like, well, I'm going to sacrifice this if you'll sacrifice that—because then that makes it just a business agreement and I don't want a business agreement for a relationship. I want a willing sacrifice from me to him and from him to me. . . . The bottom line is putting someone else in front of my desires.

Despite Tina's understanding of sacrifice that suggests communality, she states that she has never made a large sacrifice to date. Thus, as with many of the other study participants, her ideas and ideals about sacrifice remain somewhat theoretical at this point.

Tina seems aware that she has not really been tested in terms of sacrifice and is wrestling with the question of whether she is truly ready to make substantive sacrifices for another person. While she views marriage as a possibility with the current man in her life, she openly wonders at the same time, "Do I really want to be in a relationship. I always thought I did, but do I?"

Her seeming ambivalence might be viewed as a mark of immaturity, an unwillingness to give up some of the "selfishness" of early emerging adulthood—which she acknowledged was an issue for her in her first serious relationship. On the other hand, it can also be viewed as evidence of maturation: she is soberly taking stock of what it truly means to sacrifice for another. Should she decide to make a romantic commitment, she will now be doing so with full cognizance of what is required.

Tina seems to understand what a communal relationship is and seems to desire one, as indicated by her statement that she doesn't want "a business agreement" (an exchange relationship) but rather "a willing sacrifice from me to him and from him to me." But at this point, this is more of an aspirational goal for Tina than a lived one. She knows the kind of relationship, and the attendant type of sacrifice, she would *like* to have, eventually, and is struggling with whether she is ready or not for such a relationship now. Tina is an example of how the decade of the 20s serves as a "relationship laboratory" for emerging adults, in which they use their accumulated experiences to refine and develop their ideas about sacrifice and to prepare themselves for the larger sacrifices they associate with long-term committed relationships.

▲ Summary and Conclusions

Sacrifice has been shown to correlate with several positive aspects of relationship, such as satisfaction and longevity, and it has been considered a major component of love, but it remains a construct that has been underexamined in the literature. It entails forgoing the satisfaction of individual goals and desires for the benefit of a partner or a relationship. Sacrifices can be major or minor, active or passive. Only the person performing the action (or giving up the benefit) can determine whether a sacrifice has been made and what level of sacrifice it represents. Sacrifice is closely related to commitment. The greater the commitment, the greater the likelihood that the partners will willingly make sacrifices, and vice versa. As partners begin to identify more as a couple, they are increasingly likely to sacrifice for the good of the relationship.

As Kogan et al. (2010) have posited, those who experience sacrifice in a more positive way are typically those who have greater communal strength. Their sacrifices tend to be made without expectation of direct reciprocation and they tend to have higher levels of relationship satisfaction than those whose sacrificing is done on a quid pro quo basis. Making the transition to a communal mindset requires shifting from an *I* orientation to an *I* and *we* orientation.

This shift appears to be an important and evolving developmental task of emerging adulthood, and many emerging adults recognize it as such. They view their readiness for marriage—and the sacrifice marriage entails—in terms of whether they have completed their developmental goals as a single person and are prepared to begin making the shift from independence to independence *and* interdependence should they wish to make the choice to partner with another.

The 29 emerging adults in our present study seemed to recognize sacrifice as part and parcel of a successful long-term romantic relationship. They generally spoke of sacrifice and compromise as similar, if not identical, concepts. Differences among the participants emerged in their interpretation of sacrifice as an obligation versus a volitional act. Some participants described sacrifice as the price one must pay for being in a relationship. For them, sacrifice took on a static and somewhat negative quality. Others saw sacrifice more as a voluntary investment in the health of the relationship. These participants tended to have a continually evolving view of sacrifice and their relationship with it.

Many of the participants described a change of perspective over the course of their 20s, a shift from viewing sacrifice primarily as an obligation to viewing it as something one does voluntarily in order to make a relationship work. Others reported a shift from being taken advantage of in their early 20s to being more careful about what and how much they choose to sacrifice. Two of the participants seemed to have acquired a communal perspective in which they now try to sacrifice in a balanced way, but without a sense of expected reciprocity.

Some emerging adults—particularly those who have lived with significant economic, systemic, and familial challenges—may not have the inclination or skills to sacrifice for a relationship. These emerging and young adults, as Silva's study suggests, have grown up amidst failed relationships and have no credible reason to believe that sacrifice will result in happy and secure long-term relationships. Many have opted into a "mood economy," in which self-reliance, individualism, and personal responsibility are honored and growth is measured in terms of emotional self-management. For those who are struggling to overcome obstacles and find a sense of self-definition in the process, sacrificing for another person may seem too high a price to pay for the tenuous hope of an enduring connection with a partner.

With contextual considerations in mind, emerging adults may well benefit from an understanding of sacrifice that does not focus on loss but rather on the gains to be had when one forgoes the immediate gratification of some of one's needs in favor of a supportive, loving, and committed relationship. Toward that end, further studies are needed in order to better understand the dynamics of sacrifice and how its costs and benefits can be communicated effectively to emerging adults in ways that respect their contemporary values and their cultural, economic, religious, and ethnic backgrounds.

▲ References

Agnew, C. R., Van Lange, P. A. M, Rusbult, C. E., & Langston, C. A. (1998). Cognitive interdependence: Commitment and the mental representation of close relationships. *Journal of Personality and Social Psychology, 74*, 939–954.

Aron, A., & Aron, E. N. (1986). *Love and the expansion of self: Understanding attraction and satisfaction.* New York, NY: Hemisphere /Harper & Row.

Bandura, A. (1986). *Social foundations of thought and action: A social cognitive theory.* Englewood Cliffs, NJ: Prentice-Hall.

Carroll, J. S., Badger, S., Willoughby, B. J., Nelson, L. J., Madsen, S. D., & Barry, C. M. (2009). Ready or not? Criteria for marriage readiness among emerging adults. *Journal of adolescent research*, 24(3), 349–375.

Clark, M. S., & Aragón, O. R. (2013). Communal (and other) relationships: History, theory development, recent findings, and future directions. In J. A. Simpson & L. Campbell (Eds.), *The Oxford handbook of close relationships* (pp. 255–280). New York, NY: Oxford University Press.

Clark, M. S., & Mills, J. (1979). Interperssonal attraction in exchange and communal relationships. *Journal of Personality and Social Psychology*, 37(1), 12–24.

Corkery, S. A., Curran, M., & Parkman, A. (2011). Spirituality, sacrifice and relationship quality for expectant cohabitors. *Marriage and Family Review*, 47(6), 345–362. doi:10.1080/01494929.2011.594213

Donnellan, M. B., Larsen-Rife, D., & Conger, R. D. (2005). Personality, family history, and competence in early adult romantic relationships. *Journal of Personality and Social Psychology*, 88(3), 562–576. doi:10.1037/0022-3514.88.3.562

Fiske, A. P. (1992). The four elementary forms of sociality: Framework for a unified theory of social relations. *Psychological Review*, 99(4), 689.

Impett, E. A., Gable, S. L., & Peplau, L. A. (2005). Giving up and giving in: The costs and benefits of daily sacrifice in intimate relationships. *Journal of Personality and Social Psychology*, 89(3), 327–344. doi:10.1037/0022-3514.89.3.327

Impett, E. A., & Gordon, A. M. (2008). For the good of others: Toward a positive psychology of sacrifice. In S. J. Lopez (Ed.), *Positive psychology: Exploring the best in people, Vol 2: Capitalizing on emotional experiences* (pp. 79–100). Westport, CT: Praeger/Greenwood.

Jack, D. C., & Dill, D. (1992). The Silencing the Self Scale: Schemas of intimacy associated with depression in women. *Psychology of Women Quarterly*, 16(1), 97–106. doi:10.1111/j.1471-6402. 1992.tb00242.x

Jordan, J. V. (Ed.). (1991). *Women's growth in connection: Writings from the Stone Center*. New York, NY: Guilford Press.

Kelley, H. H., & Thibaut, J. W. (1978). *Interpersonal relations: A theory of interdependence*. New York, NY: Wiley.

Kogan, A., Impett, E. A., Oveis, C., Hui, B., Gordon, A. M., & Keltner, D. (2010). When giving feels good: The intrinsic benefits of sacrifice in romantic relationships for the communally motivated. *Psychological Science*, 21(12), 1918–1924. doi:10.1177/0956797610388815

Lerner, H. G. (1985). *The dance of anger: A woman's guide to changing the patterns of intimate relationships*. New York, NY: Harper & Row.

Mills, J., Clark, M. S., Ford, T. E., & Johnson, M. (2004). Measurement of communal strength. *Personal Relationships*, 11(2), 213–230. doi:10.1111/j.1475-6811.2004. 00079.x

Monk, J. K., Vennum, A. V., Ogolsky, B. G., & Fincham, F. D. (2014). Commitment and sacrifice in emerging adult romantic relationships. *Marriage & Family Review*, 50(5), 416–434. doi:10.1080/01494929.2014.896304

Overbeek, G., Stattin, H., Vermulst, A., Ha, T., & Engels, R. E. (2007). Parent-child relationships, partner relationships, and emotional adjustment: A birth-to-maturity prospective study. *Developmental Psychology, 43*(2), 429–437. doi:10.1037/0012-1649.43.2.429

Sibley, D. S. (2015). Exploring the theory of resilient commitment in emerging adulthood: A qualitative inquiry (Doctoral dissertation). Retrieved from PsyINFO. (Accession No. 201617129129)

Silva, J. M. (2012). Constructing adulthood in an age of uncertainty. *American Sociological Review, 77*(4), 505–522. doi:10.1177/0003122412449014

Silva, J. M. (2013). *Coming up short: Working-class adulthood in an age of uncertainty.* New York, NY: Oxford University Press.

Stanley, S. M., & Markman, H. J. (1992). Assessing commitment in personal relationships. *Journal of Marriage and the Family, 54*(3), 595–608. doi:10.2307/353245

Stanley, S. M., Rhoades, G. K., & Whitton, S. W. (2010). Commitment: Functions, formation, and the securing of romantic attachment. *Journal of Family Theory & Review, 2*(4), 243–257. doi:10.1111/j.1756-2589.2010. 00060.x

Stanley, S. M., Whitton, S. W., Sadberry, S. L., Clements, M. L., & Markman, H. J. (2006). Sacrifice as a predictor of marital outcomes. *Family Process, 45*(3), 289–303. doi:10.1111/j.1545-5300.2006. 00171.x

Tanner, J. L. (2006). Recentering during emerging adulthood: A critical turning point in life span development. In. J. J. Arnett & J. L. Tanner (Eds.), *Emerging adults in America: Coming of Age in the 21st century* (pp. 21–55). Washington, DC: American Psychological Association.

Van Lange, P. M., Agnew, C. R., Harinck, F., & Steemers, G. M. (1997). From game theory to real life: How social value orientation affects willingness to sacrifice in ongoing close relationships. *Journal of Personality and Social Psychology, 73*(6), 1330–1344. doi:10.1037/0022-3514.73.6.1330

Van Lange, P. M., Rusbult, C. E., Drigotas, S. M., Arriaga, X. B., Witcher, B. S., & Cox, C. L. (1997). Willingness to sacrifice in close relationships. *Journal of Personality and Social Psychology, 72*(6), 1373–1395. doi:10.1037/0022-3514.72.6.1373

Whitton, S., Stanley, S., & Markman, H. (2002). Sacrifice in romantic relationships: An exploration of relevant research and theory. In A. L. Vangelisti, H. T. Reis, & M. A. Fitzpatrick (Eds.), *Stability and change in relationships* (pp. 156–181). New York, NY: Cambridge University Press. doi:10.1017/CBO9780511499876.010

Whitton, S. W., Stanley, S. M., & Markman, H. J. (2007). If I help my partner, will it hurt me? Perceptions of sacrifice in romantic relationships. *Journal of Social and Clinical Psychology, 26*(1), 64–92. doi:10.1521/jscp.2007.26.1.64

Wieselquist, J., Rusbult, C. E., Foster, C. A., & Agnew, C. R. (1999). Commitment, pro-relationship behavior, and trust in close relationships. *Journal of Personality and Social Psychology, 77*(5), 942–966. doi:10.1037/0022-3514.77.5.94

5 ▲

Techno-Romance and Emerging Adulthood

Do we expect more from technology and less from each other?
                              —Turkle, 2016, p. 29

When your social media persona takes over your life it can be hard to break character.
                              —Dollar, May 5, 2017

Emerging adults live in cyberspace a good part of each day. Because they spend a daily average of 3.5 hours using computer-mediated communication (CMC), approximately 52 minutes of which are dedicated to social networking sites (SNS)—as well as an additional 45 minutes on cell phones—the function, quality, and consequences of these interactions as related to their romantic lives merit critical examination (Coyne, Padilla-Walker, & Howard, 2013).

CMC has the ability to influence and define romantic relationships (Fox & Warber, 2013). The number and variety of CMC venues where possible versions of the self can be developed, honed, and given a trial run is ever-expanding. SNS are used by approximately 79% of adults who go online, and of that group 88% are 18 to 29 years old (Greenwood, Perrin, & Duggan, 2016). The selecting of CMC venues, the navigation of dating apps, and the management of risk and rejection are just a few of the issues emerging adults grapple with in cyberspace.

Although younger users are encountering "Facebook fatigue" and are spending less time on this site, Facebook remains the most popular site, with over 1.25 billion worldwide users (fb.com, 2017). On average, individuals unlock their phones 100 times per day in order to view texts, read emails, and check in on sites such as Facebook and Instagram (Hu, 2013). Declaring oneself "In a Relationship" and "Facebook Official" on Facebook represents a formal declaration of relationship status for most emerging adults. However, perceptions of the meaning of this status may differ; women are more likely to attach meanings of commitment and intensity to these digital declarations; men are less inclined to do so (a difference that has important implications for relationship satisfaction).

Gender differences have been observed in other areas of cyberspace as well. Based on survey data collected from 1,003 emerging adults 18 to 25 years of age, Rappleyea, Taylor, and Fang (2014) found that women prefer more relational communication technologies (e.g., phone, texting) while men prefer more web-based communication (e.g. Facebook, Twitter). In some cases, sex role stereotypes tend to prevail in cyberspace; for example, men are still more likely to initiate first dates (Ansari, 2015).

In cyberspace, there are no time boundaries. Similarly, constraints imposed by geographical location are no longer absolute barriers to the unfolding of a romantic relationship. Nearly 35% of all couples who married between 2005 and 2012 met online (Hall, 2014). Faced with an unprecedented array of options, many emerging adults are searching online for ideal romantic partners—soul mates—who will enter relationships with them as equals, based on love and irrespective of ethnicity, religion, sex, or race (Smith & Duggan, 2013). However, conversations that are occurring concurrently such as phoning are phasing out, and more informal, pithy, and superficial text-based communication is on the rise. Ansari (2015) suggests that spontaneous, in-person encounters are in danger of becoming a thing of the past, a development that seems likely to lead to an increase in alienation.

The romantic environment on SNS tends to objectify users and to lack social etiquette rules (Colier, 2016). For example, it is now possible to cancel a date or an in-person meeting a few minutes before the meeting time, simply because the technology (texting) allows it. Emerging adults are turning to SNS to help navigate their breakups as well as their romantic connections. Mend, an app designed for those coping with a romantic breakup, offers "training" and support in breakup-related issues. It provides access to peers who are also dealing with breakups, which helps to normalize the experience and provide a sense of community.

How does CMC enhance or detract from the romantic relationships experiences of emerging adults? How do emerging adults satisfy their needs for deeper connections in a romantic environment where interactions are becoming more and more digitized? In this chapter, CMC and its influence on the romantic lives of emerging adults will be discussed, followed by an exploration of topics such as "technoference," cyber-choice, dating apps, and sexting—and lastly an analysis of geographically close versus LD relationships and how CMC may influence the outcomes of such relationships. The 29 emerging-adult study participants introduced in earlier chapters will share their thoughts and experiences about CMC in relation to their romantic lives.

But first, a brief clarification of terms seems advised. Social media and SNS have assumed increasingly important roles in the romantic lives of emerging adults. The terms, although often used interchangeably, are distinctly different. Social media, the more general term, refers to any CMC application that makes possible the exchange of user-generated content (Kaplan & Haenlein, 2010). Included under the heading are video-sharing platforms such as YouTube, message boards, blogs, and SNS. SNS are web-based services that allow for the maintenance of social relationships within one's publicly visible social network (Ellison, 2007). Among emerging adults, SNS have become common cyber-locations for meeting romantic partners as well as for managing existing relationships.

▲ Theoretical Framework

Although CMC, including social media and more specifically SNS, has played an extremely important role in the romantic lives of emerging adults (Hall, 2014), there has been little to no unifying theoretical framework to ground a body of work on this topic. Our understanding of the influence of CMC on romantic relationships is incomplete and evolving. A good part of the reason for this is that the technology itself is changing rapidly, and the attendant behavior is changing with it. Longitudinal work is therefore difficult to do, and any conclusions we might draw today might be obsolete two years from now. Furthermore, it is important to note that most studies focus on college-age students, and the full range of diversity in terms of age, socioeconomic status, ethnicity, race, and sexual orientation within emerging adulthood is lacking. Attachment theory and self-expansion theory, however, are two theoretical perspectives that can help ground us in understanding the influence of CMC on emerging adults and their romantic lives.

Attachment Theory

The emergence of SNS has resulted in increased opportunities for observing and monitoring public displays of emotions and how they are regulated and managed online (Nitzburg & Farber, 2013). When a couple enters a romantic relationship, they are faced with making decisions as to how they wish to portray their relationships in the public and/or semi-public sphere of SNS. Sites such as Facebook have become preferred locations for couples to display aspects of themselves and their relationship's progress. As a result, it is common for couples to have discussions about whether to make their relationship Facebook Official (FBO), as well as what constitutes appropriate displays of affection on such sites (Fox & Warber, 2013).

SNS can intensify feelings of connection between romantic partners, but can also intensify feelings of jealousy and envy, as well as surveillance behaviors (Nitzburb & Farber, 2013). Attachment theory is discussed in the context of understanding and predicting CMC behaviors on SNS. (Research to date tends to be specific to Facebook, as it has been the most popular site used by emerging adults.)

Decisions related to couples' self-presentation on SNS can influence and skew relationship perceptions, feelings, and behaviors (Bowe, 2010; Fox, Osborn, & Warber, 2014). Actions taken, or *not* taken, on SNS can trigger obsessive qualities in a partner who is feeling jealous. In turn, such a partner is more likely to engage in surveillance behaviors that can exacerbate potential relationship conflict. (For further discussion of attachment theory, kindly refer to Chapter 7.)

When certain SNS-related behaviors of emerging adults are viewed against a backdrop of attachment theory, the findings have been consistent with theory. Surveillance behaviors and jealous feelings are correlated with attachment styles. As might be expected, higher rates of surveillance behaviors are linked to anxious attachment styles and lower rates of surveillance behaviors tend to coincide with avoidant attachment styles (Marshall, Bejanyan, Castro, & Lee, 2013, as cited in Nitzburg & Farber, 2013). In terms of specific behaviors, Emery, Muise, Dix, and Le (2014) found that emerging adults with anxious attachment styles were more inclined to post photos of themselves together with their partners on Facebook, thus creating visibility for the couple *as* a couple, and validation for the partnership. This type of public posting is more likely to occur in cases where the individual doing the posting believes that others in the social network perceive the relationship to be of poor quality. Individuals with an avoidant attachment style tend to prefer low "couple visibility" and are thus less likely to seek public validation of their relationships.

Jealousy, an emotion aroused in response to a partner's suspected or actual infidelity (Muise, Christofides, & Desmarais, 2014), has received considerable attention in the literature, specifically with respect to SNS use. The relationship between jealousy and surveillance behaviors tends to be cyclical: jealousy motivates surveillance behaviors, and surveillance behaviors are, in turn, associated with a greater degree of jealousy (Nitzburg & Farber, 2013). Jealousy, too, correlates with an anxious attachment style.

Gender differences are consistently reported with respect to jealousy and SNS (e.g., Fleuriet, Cole, & Guerrero, 2014; Muise et al., 2014). Facebook-related jealousy is associated with attachment anxiety in females only: females with higher attachment anxiety are more likely to engage in SNS partner monitoring. Females who spend more time on their partners' sites generally report higher jealousy scores (Muise et al., 2014). It is important to note that while attachment styles inform behaviors on SNS as discussed above, attachment styles also inform face-to-face (FtF) behaviors, each mutually informing the other (Collins & Allard, 2001).

Irrespective of attachment style, gender differences related to feelings of jealousy have been found on SNS. The way in which emerging adults reveal their relationships on SNS and the choices they make about providing access to their profile information influence jealousy in a gender-related way, according to Muscanell, Guadagno, Rice, and Murphy (2013). In a study they conducted, differing conditions of access were provided to the participants, each of whom was asked to imagine that their partner posted a photograph of him- or herself with a member of the opposite sex on his or her Facebook wall. Results revealed that the most stringent privacy settings for these posts were associated with the highest jealousy scores, irrespective of gender. However, females were notably more jealous under the privacy settings set to "all Facebook friends" or "all Facebook users" in comparison to those set to only the user. Self-esteem also moderated the relationship between SNS use and jealousy; those participants with lower self-esteem tended to experience greater degrees of jealousy (Utz & Beukeboom, 2011).

Self-Expansion Theory

The self-expansion model of Aron and Aron (1986, 1996), which is covered in Chapter 2, endorses the notion that romantic relationships lead to the expansion of the self. Some of the ways this occurs is through the partners' introducing new interests, social contacts, resources, and opportunities to each other. Individuals tend to incorporate aspects of the romantic partner into their own sense of self, and this expanded version of the self tends to endure even if the relationship ends.

In applying the self-expansion model, Carpenter and Spottswood (2013) hypothesized that self-expansion gained in present and previous romantic contexts should be reflected in the couple's SNS behavior. As emerging adults engage in an increasing number and duration of romantic relationships and begin to share their partners' interests and expand their sense of self, their accrued interests should theoretically be reflected in their Facebook profiles. And indeed, findings do show that participants add interests to their Facebook profiles as they develop their romantic relationships. The greater the number of romantic relationships, the greater the accumulation of interests and self-expansion-related activities on users' Facebook profiles. These accumulated interests survive relationship termination, according to the findings of Carpenter and Spottswood. In that regard, SNS such as Facebook serve as an electronic record reflecting how emerging adults have expanded via their past romantic relationships.

▲ CMC and Its Influence on Romantic Relationships: A Positive or Negative Force?

> Leaving ourselves endlessly available results in
> our being unavailable to another and to life. When
> you close the door to what else there is, then what
> actually is becomes valuable.
> —Colier, 2016

CMC offers emerging adults increased opportunities and freedom to pursue and maintain their romantic relationships. However, they may also feel fractured, distracted, alienated, overwhelmed, and anxious in response to the sheer number and range of communication options available to them (McDaniel & Coyne, 2016).

CMC certainly has the potential to help new romantic partners connect with each other; partners tend to rate their CMC interactions as positive overall. CMC also provides emerging adults with opportunities to stay connected with romantic partners on an ongoing basis, including during times of stress (Dietmar, 2005; Pettigrew, 2009, as cited in McDaniel & Coyne, 2016). Research suggests that CMC can increase relationship commitment and satisfaction (Sidelinger, Avash, Godorhazy, & Tibbles, 2008, as cited in McDaniel & Coyne, 2016).

However, it is fair to ask: Do we "expect more from technology and less from each other?" as Turkle (2016, p. 29) suggests? While experiences with CMC may be exhilarating and rewarding on a short-term, "quick fix" basis, they may also be limiting our opportunities for open-ended, spontaneous, person-to-person communication that can lead to deeper levels of mutual understanding (Turkle, p. 32). Many emerging adults struggle to maintain control over the powerful pull of CMC on their lives. Thirty-eight percent of romantic partners report that they send texts or emails while having conversations with their romantic partners (Czechowsky, 2008, as cited in McDaniel & Coyne, 2016). The next section focuses on the pull of CMC in the lives of emerging adults and how it may impact their romantic relationships.

▲ Technoference

"Technoference," defined as everyday intrusions and interruptions due to CMC, is a term that was created to capture the influence of technology on individuals' and couples' day-to-day lives (McDaniel & Coyne, 2016). CMC use appears to be associated with an increase in relationship conflict and poor relationship satisfaction (Schade, Sandberg, Bean, Busby, & Coyne, 2013). The two partners often place differing expectations and/or demands on CMC use, both within and outside the relationship, and may not always clarify these expectations with their partners.

McDaniel and Coyne (2016) studied "technoference" in 143 married/cohabiting women (mean age = 30.37 years old) to learn more about its frequency of occurrence and capacity to interfere with their day-to-day lives. The majority of the female participants (70%) reported that technology devices such as computers, smartphones, tablets, or TV, interfered with their romantic relationships. More specifically, they reported that these mediums of communication interfered with couple leisure time at least once a day (62%), with conversations between themselves and their partners at least once a day (35%), and with shared mealtimes at least once a day (33%). These interruptions were reported to contribute to conflicts around technology use. Participants who reported a greater amount of "technoference" were also more likely to report lower relationship satisfaction, greater depressive symptoms, and lower life satisfaction with their partners.

CMC is capable of interrupting in-person interactions at any time due to its omnipresent, "24/7" nature. When members of a couple give precedence to their techno-communications over their FtF "live" interactions with their partner, they may be sending subtle messages as to where their priorities lie, and this can lead to deterioration of intimate relationships.

▲ Autonomy Versus Connectedness

As discussed in a previous chapter, relationships are characterized by the sometimes-opposing needs for autonomy and connection (Baxter & Montgomery, 1996). Emerging adults who are in romantic relationships cherish both the freedom to act independently of the partner and the freedom to turn to the partner in times of need and want (Rawlins, 1992, as cited in Duran, Kelly, & Rotaru, 2011). CMC is capable of bringing this conflict into sharp focus.

Duran et al. (2011) studied the impact of cell phones, vital tools for modern communication, and their use among romantic partners. The authors suggest that the use of mobile phones has important implications for the autonomy-versus-connection dialectic. Cell phones can be a source of uncertainty, jealousy, and conflict in romantic relationships, but can also help romantic partners stay connected. The authors argued that since cell phones/smartphones provide emerging adults opportunities to "be" with each other, potentially 24 hours a day, these devices are likely to play a strong role in the way romantic couples negotiate needs for autonomy and connection.

Duran and colleagues questioned 210 undergraduate students from a small, private Eastern university who were involved in a relationship (mean age = 20.62, SD = 1.29). Participants self-reported on factors such as (a) whether rules for cell phone usage had been established between the members of couple, (b) conflicts related to cell phone use and how those conflicts were managed, and (c) the way the partners perceived issues of autonomy versus connectedness. Participants' answers revealed that higher tensions related to "autonomy versus connection" in couples were linked to increased conflicts over cell phone interactions. These conflicts included perceptions of insufficient calling and/or texting by the partner. Dissatisfaction around cell phone usage was associated with increased dissatisfaction over the amount of time spent with the partner, feelings of freedom constriction, and a greater desire to control the partner.

Although specific phone rules were viewed as unnecessary by the greatest number of the participants, over a third of them indicated that they do have rules about the timing of calls and texts and about the level of availability and frequency of contact to be expected. While most participants stated they did not believe rules were necessary to resolve autonomy-versus-connectedness conflicts related to CMC usage, they did feel some rules were needed simply to set limits on mutual expectations for ongoing contact and availability. Time, place, and frequency of contact needed to be taken into consideration. Duran and colleagues concluded that autonomy-versus-connection tensions within emerging adult relationships can only be expected to increase with the continually increasing presence of CMC in our lives.

The authors also reported strong correlations between "technoference" and levels of depression, and posited that these effects were bidirectional: depressed individuals tend to use technology as a means of coping with problems; however, increased reliance on technology can increase feelings of depression when the technology not only fails to solve personal problems but also interferes with and weakens FtF interactions. In sum, "technoference" is a complex phenomenon and interruptions can be due to a multiplicity of factors (e.g., individual characteristics such as romantic attachment style).

The question of how much "technoference" emerging adult couples allow into their lives leads naturally to a more general discussion about the exercising of choice with regard to SNS, and how such choices affect romantic relationships.

▲ Choice in CMC and SNS, and How It Affects the Romantic Lives of Emerging Adults

The thing is, with all these new possibilities, the process of finding that [special] person can be

seriously stressful. And, unlike the days when most
everyone got married by their midtwenties, today the
search for love can go on for decades.

—Ansari, 2015

My peers and I have all these exes, in part
because . . . the digital age enables us to never
truly break up. We don't have to shut the door on
anything. Which is good, because shutting the door
on something is not something we ever want to do.

—O'Connor, July 13, 2013

The above two quotations capture some of the essence of how CMC affects the relationship functioning of emerging adults. Because so much choice is available—choice as to whom we "pursue" romantically, whom we stay in contact with, *how* we stay in contact, and whom we wish to give our attention to in the moment—many emerging adults are reluctant to close any doors. At the same time, the overwhelming amount of apparent choice available to them often makes it harder, not easier, to make meaningful choices. Some emerging adults may perceive choice as promise, others may see it as anxiety provoking; others might experience a lack of actual choice and feel poorly as a result (Sheena & Lepper, 2000; Arnett, 2006; Konstam, 2014).

With so many computer-mediated tools available to assist us in the pursuit of romance, sex, love, and the quest for a perfect mate, evaluating our potential choices can become a time-intensive pursuit. A byproduct of this seemingly endless pursuit can be a bypassing of the work needed to invest in a relationship. Instead of giving deep and thoughtful consideration to a small handful of "love candidates," many emerging adults seem to be giving superficial consideration to a multiplicity of possibilities. Wishing to avoid "buyer's remorse," they are driven to keep considering potential mates.

With the advent of SNS, the viewing patterns of emerging adults reinforce their belief in the possibility of limitless "on demand" choice. For those interested in a long-term relationship, this belief may manifest in a seemingly endless quest to find a perfect partner. The "good enough" romantic relationship is anathema to many emerging adults.

The paradox of choice selection within a context of abundance was explored intriguingly by Schwartz (2004). He argued that distress is the ultimate end-product of an overabundance of choice. Factors that contribute to this choice-making distress are social comparison, status concerns, fear of "buyer's remorse," and a drive to have the best of everything and to make the best possible choices (p. 221). Faced with apparent abundance, choice is often harder, not easier.

Schwartz described two approaches to making choices, "maximizing" and "satisficing." Maximizers seek to always make the best possible choice, a strategy that becomes increasingly daunting as the menu of options grows larger via newer and better technologies (p. 78). "Satisficers," on the other hand, are content with making a choice that is "good enough." Satisficers have standards, but they stop their search when those standards have been met. Maximizers, however, are not satisfied with mere excellence; they want to believe they have made the *absolute best* choice.

One dynamic that occurs in a context of abundance is that we tend to seek out choices that are inherently scarce. The greater the perceived competition for these inherently scarce resources, the less the strategy of "good enough" seems sufficient. In situations of abundant choice, the tendency toward maximization increases. This can create a felt sense of pressure. Also, standards shift. For example, a user of a dating app, once made aware of all the available options, is likely to adopt a higher set of standards that are inherently more difficult to satisfy.

When the menu of choices is abundant, the likelihood of making mistakes increases, according to Schwartz. There emerges a tendency to focus on the available options, rather than on one's internal needs and desires. One can become a "picker" rather than a "chooser." Pickers review the external options presented to them and then make what they believe to be the best choice from the menu, hoping for the best outcome. Choosers, conversely, make choices based on what is important to *them* (their values, etc.). As CMC becomes more menu-driven, it is easy to shift to a "picking" style of choice-making, which can often deliver unsatisfying results.

Schwartz suggests that we subscribe to several faulty assumptions regarding choice:

1. The more choices people have the better off they are.
2. The best way to get good results is to have very high standards.
3. It is always better to have a way to back out of a decision than not. (p. 4)

In response to these faulty assumptions, he presents the following counterintuitive prescriptions. We would be better off, he says:

1. If we *embraced* certain voluntary constraints on our freedom of choice, instead of rebelling against them.
2. If we sought what was "good enough" instead of what was best.
3. If we lowered our expectations about the results of decisions.
4. If the decisions we made were nonreversible.
5. If we paid less attention to what others around us were doing.
   (p. 4).

Although Schwartz does not specifically address the developmental period of emerging adulthood, he does provide a framework for understanding choice and how it may apply to emerging adults in their romantic lives. Schwartz argues that in a context of abundance, creating "fishbowls" that allow us the freedom to explore and experiment with choices within safe, confined boundaries, may be a strategy that best serves us when we are barraged with choice.

Another effect of the "shopping" mentality that CMC encourages is the tendency to objectify and superficialize potential romantic partners. There is an interesting disconnect here: while emerging adults state that they value authenticity, deep connections, and "being heard," CMC, their preferred mode of communication, relies on pithy, perfunctory conversations lacking in complexity of thought and feelings, and fails to provide the space for intimate communications in which deeper, more authentic connections can take place (Turkle, 2016). Digital interactions, such as clicking preference buttons, "swiping," and even texting are lacking in human inflection, such as voice, body language, touch, and facial expressions, where the bulk of meaning and sincerity is conveyed. The more digitized the communication, the less nuanced and personal it is.

Comedian and social observer Aziz Ansari (2015) points out that most text messages are generic and uninspiring, and, because they are so easily and hastily written, tend to make the recipient feel "not special"—which further contributes to a general romantic atmosphere of objectification. The ease of choice that technology affords also tends to encourage impulsive choosing, based on temporary and fleeting desires. Colier (2016), though not addressing romance specifically, points out, "We mature when we exercise the discipline and discernment that it takes to move beyond our momentary desires. Technology, sadly, is leading us away from choosing such opportunities for growth" (p. 64). In sum, the seeming ease and abundance of choice made possible by technology has made meaningful romantic choice more difficult to enact on a day-to-day, moment-to-moment basis.

One of the biggest changes technology has brought to the romantic lives of emerging adults is online dating, the subject of the next section.

▲ Dating Apps: Exercise in Choice

> *Dating apps are the courtship equivalent of next-day shipping, where you don't have to twiddle your thumbs and wait for an adequate romantic prospect to drift by. They release a flood of potential suitors, your inbox notifications flashing red with heartbeats of their own.*
>
> —Lauren Petersen, *New York Times*,
> May 26, 2017

Two generations ago, individuals of marrying age did not typically explore beyond their immediate neighborhoods when selecting a mate. Today's generation of emerging adults is not constrained by geographical location; with the aid of SNS, they have access to seemingly unlimited choices, a situation that can be both liberating and overwhelming. Dating apps now make it possible to easily connect with strangers from distant geographic locations and from "specialized" groups connected by traits such as religion, politics, and sexual preference. Dating apps also remove much of the risk and guesswork that was formerly part of the dating scene.

Emerging adults who self-identify as LGBTQ, and are in geographical locales that offer fewer choices for potential partners, are even more likely to meet partners using SNS. They are able to find "matches" in a safe and targeted way, as opposed to the riskier and far less efficient means previous generations had at their disposal. Partnership rates for same-sex couples have increased, a finding that is in part attributed to increased availability of CMC and SNS (Frost, Meyer, & Hammack, 2015).

Although sex-role stereotypes persist on SNS (men are still more inclined to initiate the first encounter), what is true for both sexes is that emerging adults are marrying half a decade later, on average, than people did in 1980 (http://wtop.com/living/2016/01/how-the-age-people-marry-has-changed-over-time). With the aid of CMC, more experimentation is taking place, with seemingly unlimited possibilities for exploration.

Emerging adults understand the importance of the decision to commit to a long-term relationship (Konstam, 2015). However, they tend to be attracted to superficial features of the other (e.g., physical appearance, taste in music, etc.). A relationship based on love and deeply held values and preferences requires a much richer and more complex understanding of the other person, which takes time and effort to develop and unfold (Eastwick & Hunt, 2014; Finkel Eastwick, Karney, Reis, & Sprecher, 2012). There is a disconnect here in the way many emerging adults make their initial decisions regarding their dating selections: while their stated goals may focus on internal traits and values of potential mates, their actual choices, assisted by SNS, perpetuate behavior not in keeping with deeper appreciation of the other.

Emerging adults tend to be well aware of the risk of divorce and are fiercely determined not to replicate the divorce rates of their parents' generation (Konstam, 2015). This may be one of the reasons they are so focused on "optimizing" their romantic matches. However, exposure to a greater number of options does not always yield positive benefits, as the research of Schwartz suggests. More is not always better. In using an optimization-of-choice strategy, it is very easy to exclude a person who might, in fact, make an outstanding partner if a more holistic choice process were employed.

Lauren Petersen, an emerging adult writer and winner of a writing competition in "Modern Love," a New York Times weekly column, reflects on her experiences with dating apps:

> They tempt you to keep swiping, and as you whiz through
> tens, hundreds or even thousands of profiles, you can only infer
> the obvious. Out of all these people, there's got to be someone
> better than the person I'm seeing right now. Which means that
> monogamy requires more sacrifice than ever. If offered free travel,
> why would anyone settle for one place when it's possible to tour
> the entire world?

Schwartz (as cited in Stanley, 2016), poses a thoughtful question: "How many potential partners do you need to 'vet' before feeling confident that you've made the best choice?" He suggests that the entire "search for the best" strategy is doomed to failure. The notion that a perfect match is waiting predisposes one to believe that there is always someone better out there. This makes searchers frustrated during the search process and also less satisfied with any romantic choice they finally make. There is always the nagging suspicion that if they had only searched a little longer and a little harder, they might have found the perfect partner (Stanley, 2016).

Dating apps *can* be powerful and time-saving tools, provided users understand that they are merely a starting point, not a way to instantly "order" a new relationship as soon as the old one becomes challenging or boring. It is by working through the challenging times that relationships are seasoned and deepened.

CMC presents many methods of communicating and staying in touch in a way that romantic partners no longer have to participate in each other's lives in an exclusively physical way. We can enjoy shared presence in a new, hybrid way—partly virtual, partly physical. Yet, however much time one spends connecting with others in a "pancake" or surface way, there will always be a need to connect on a deeper level. CMC can help or hinder that experience, depending on how it is used.

We will now explore the literature as it relates to LD relationships in order to shed light on how CMC may be a help or a hindrance.

▲ Romantic Relationships and CMC Across Distance

Because of educational demands, dual-career pursuits, military deployment, and increased societal mobility, maintaining romantic relationships across geographic distance has become a common practice among emerging adults in the United States (Stafford 2005, as cited in Jiang & Hancock, 2013). Approximately 25–50% of college students are "dating" across long distances, and 75% have been in LD relationships at some point in their college careers. With respect to marital partners, approximately three million Americans are living apart from their spouses through circumstances that are not divorce- or discord-related (Berge, Kirby & McBride 2007, as cited in Jiang & Hancock, 2013).

The prevalence of LD relationships provides an opportunity to gain greater understanding of how physical distance is managed in emerging-adult relationships, the ways in which CMC is used to help and/or hinder these relationships, and the outcomes associated with these relationships.

Research to date suggests that relationship stability, satisfaction, and trust are not compromised in LD relationships; on average, couples in LD relationships report scores that are equal to or better than geographically close (GC) couples on three outcome variables: relationship stability, satisfaction, and trust. Loving (2011) argues that LD relationships address the paradoxical need in many Western cultures to be in connection with one's partner and at the same time to maintain a sense of independence. The push and pull between the need for independence and connection is actually made easier in LD relationships. Emerging adults in LD relationships have opportunities to take care of their individual needs and use their time and resources as they wish.

Jiang and Hancock (2013) focused their research efforts on intimacy: how it is sustained and/or enhanced in LD versus GC heterosexual romantic relationships. They recruited members of 63 couples from communication and psychology classes at a large university in the northeastern United States, some of whom were in LD and some of whom were in GC relationships. On average, the LD couples had been separated for 17.03 months. In addition to FtF encounters, a total of 1,986 techno-interactions was reported by the LD partners—1,090 were texts, 557 were phone calls, 101 were video chats, 202 were instant messages, and 36 were emails (http://news.cornell.edu/stories/2013/08/new-media-allows-requited-love-know-no-distance).

Analysis of the findings indicated that LD couples, in order to mitigate lack of FtF intimacy, engage in adaptive behaviors such as frequent self-disclosures and idealization (viewing their partner and the relationship in unrealistically positive terms). LD partners strategically tailor their communications to include a greater number of self-disclosures. Idealization, in turn, is driven by "over-interpretation of the selective self-presentations" (Loving, 2011, p. 69). Loving (2011) argues that distance, in essence, allows one to wear rose-colored glasses for longer periods of time: "It is easy to overlook the annoying things about your partner if you only have to experience them every now and then" (p. 69). The restricted amount of communication makes it possible to ignore the aspects of the partner that might be annoying.

The findings reported by Jiang and Hancock have important implications. Emerging adults in LD relationships, in comparison to GC relationships, tend to be more self-disclosing with their romantic partners, which leads to idealization. And these two processes, self-disclosure and idealization of one's partner, are associated with greater relationship intimacy.

CMC facilitates many aspects of LD relationships and offers unprecedented ways for LD couples to remain close. These choices are limited only by the imagination. Partners can watch a movie or TV show together while texting or talking about it; go on walks "together," each using the FaceTime app to show their respective surroundings; schedule Skype "dates" once or twice a week; send special content to each other via private or public settings on SNS; play games together; or engage in "sexting." There is even technology that allows them to give one another a LD massage. Sending short text messages or instant messages throughout the day is a way that many LD partners remain present with one another during times apart. If there is commitment and intention to stay connected, CMC offers unprecedented options for doing so.

▲ Sexting

A chapter on CMC and romantic relationships would not be complete without at least a brief examination of a widespread practice that did not exist two decades ago: sexting. Sexting is the exchange of sexually explicit photographs, images, videos, and/or messages via cell phone or an internet-enabled device. Klettke, Hallford, and Mellor (2014) conducted a systematic literature review of 31 studies and reported the following sexting prevalence rates: 10.2% for adolescents and 53.31% for adults, including emerging adults. With respect to emerging adults, sexting is fairly common among all types of romantic relationships (committed, casual sex, and cheating). Females of all age groups were reported to be slightly more active sexters than males (Doring, 2014; Klettke et al., 2014).

Doring reviewed 50 sexting-research manuscripts that appeared between 2009 and 2013 on *PsychINFO* and *PubMed* databases in order to assess the risks and opportunities of consensual sexting. Within the context of romantic relationships between adolescents, emerging adults, and adults, consensual sexting can be viewed as an expression of intimate communication that may lead to emotional growth. On the other hand, sexting is also associated with risky behaviors, particularly among adolescents: promiscuity, unsafe sex, sexual infidelity, bad judgment, sensation seeking, problematic alcohol and drug use, objectification of the other, and bullying.

However, given that sexting between consenting adults is now often viewed as a mainstream way of adding interest and variety to romantic relationships, the question arises as to whether sexting between consenting adolescents and emerging adults ought to be depicted in presumptively negative terms, as it typically is (e.g., Livingstone, 2008; Livingstone, Haddon, Gorzig, & Olafsson, 2011). Perhaps instead the focus should be on individual and societal conditions for "appropriate" sexting, and on guidelines for ethical sexting behavior.

Doring argues that there is a need to progress towards a nuanced, evidence-based understanding of sexting, with a focus on risk prevention that acknowledges both the "vulnerability" and "sexual agency" associated with sexting. A more comprehensive theoretical elaboration of the risks and opportunities associated with sexting behaviors in varying populations is just beginning to emerge and needs to be further developed (e.g., Livingstone, 2008; Livingstone et al., 2011).

Consensual sexting offers couples opportunities for expressing sexual desire and affection, engaging with one another playfully, giving each other mutual pleasure, building trust, and experiencing closeness (e.g., Hasinoff, 2013; Karaian, 2012). There are claims that sexting is dangerous because private sexts have a tendency to go viral. Most sexters, however—both adult and adolescent—exercise great care, discretion, and confidentiality in their sexting. In fact, only 3% of adolescent sexters have reported a private sext being shared in an unwanted way (Cox Communications, 2009). Despite some popular portrayals of adolescents and emerging adults as being reckless with sexual content, trust is regarded by most adolescents and emerging adults as a cornerstone of romantic relationships and is typically preserved (Gala & Kapadia, 2013).

The need for trust was emphasized in the responses of our 29 emerging adults when they spoke about romantic commitment in Chapter 3. They all tended to view trust as a non-negotiable element of successful romantic relationships. With that in mind, and knowing some of the other qualities emerging adults value in relationships, we will explore participants' thoughts and experiences regarding the role and effect of CMC on emerging-adult romantic life.

▲ Participant Responses

An omnipresent element in the lives of the 29 participants, CMC presented interesting choices at important junctures of their romantic relationships. Participants shared their experiences with CMC, including both the opportunities and the stressors. The 29 participants reported having engaged with a range of CMC options including dating/hookup apps such as Bumble, Grindr, and OkCupid, SNS such as Facebook and Snapchat, and direct person-to-person communication technologies such as video chat and mobile phones. They shared their assessments of the overall impact of CMC, including how it both detracted from and enhanced their romantic lives.

Two domains emerged from the data: (a) social networking: making choices, and (b) CMC and its influence, positive and negative.

Social Networking: Making Choices

Four categories were identified within this first domain: (a) online dating, (b) doing your homework; using online resources to research someone, (c) becoming "Facebook official" and changing one's relationship status, and (d) techno-breakups, the ins and outs.

Online dating

Participants were asked the following two questions, "Have you ever used an online dating site?" and "If so, can you describe your experiences?" In their responses, 22 of the 29 participants shared their varied experiences with dating apps, yielding a *typical* category. Six of the remaining seven participants said they chose not to experiment with dating apps, and one participant chose not to participate in SNS at all.

The 22 emerging adults who engaged with online dating sites identified features of these sites that enhanced and/or detracted from their overall dating experiences. The majority of these participants provided both positive and negative features of the sites. Access to a wider network of potential romantic partners was identified as a key positive feature, while the potential for deception and lurking "creepers" was viewed as a negative.

Rita (26) likened the experience of online dating to meeting someone at a bar. Both settings provided her with access, the ability to talk with men, and the freedom to "go home" whenever she felt like doing so. She states:

> Everyone's kind of, like, you know, just testing the waters, seeking to fulfill that need just to feel attractive and playful, without really having to engage with a lot of people. So I think I ended up just chatting with some people, casually, which I guess, it kind of would have been the same as if I were just sitting at a bar and . . . met a few people, talked to them, [and] went home.

Like Rita, Mark (24), a gay male, emphasized that access was a key feature when considering whether to experiment with dating sites. Motivated to increase his pool of potential dating partners, Mark made the decision to experiment with SNS. The process of meeting others was "easy" and "helpful" and provided him with choices he might not have had otherwise.

Ellen (24) spoke to the issue of being shy when meeting people, particularly initially. For her, the process of meeting a potential dating partner online feels less intimidating, less anxiety provoking, and less onerous than FtF encounters. She states that she has used online dating as a stepping stone to FtF "dating."

> Both of my previous boyfriends—this one and the other recent one—they were both, he was OkCupid and then this one was Tinder . . . which helped me because I'm a shy person. . . . Waiting for somebody to approach you and then talk to you in a bar is not going to work for me.

Chantal (23) enjoys the choices that online dating affords her. "You have this freedom to be suggestive, or to put your best self forward, or to edit what you're saying while you're saying it." She welcomes the opportunity to experiment with various facets of her personality.

Speaking to the downside of online dating, participants emphasized that some of the people they met on dating sites were "creepers," who say "crazy random things." Andrea (24) states, "I had to put up a lot of filters to filter out the crazies." Andrea has also had negative experiences related to being Asian-American on dating sites: "It hasn't been very good. I think as an Asian-American female, I get a lot of weird racial messages." Rachel (22) similarly states, "It was weird. I met a lot of weirdoes (laughter). . . . I have never been in a relationship from anyone online."

Participants identified concerns about dishonesty. They acknowledged that it was difficult to get to "know" the other person on this medium, since "truth" was often in short supply. An incomplete picture of potential partners emerged for the participants, especially initially. Participants felt they were not in an optimal position to assess the intentionality and potential character flaws of the individuals. The remedy, as suggested by some of the participants, was to "proceed with great caution."

Joseph (25) noted that people act differently when they are on these sites, and, as a result, "It is hard to know if you can trust what people post, you have to be careful." Similarly, Becky (24) states:

It's so hard to know if you can trust what people write about themselves. . . . You are just not getting a good picture of who the person is, even if they are being very honest. You are not getting a whole picture of what they are, until you meet them. . . . You don't know all of their life experiences and baggage, and that's what you need to know too.

Rachel also speaks to the issue of people lying on dating apps: "Everybody lies online, I guess. . . . like their picture was from ten years ago."

Monica (22) acknowledges that although dating sites provide her with access to potential dating partners, they are not a panacea, in that she "end[s] up picking bad guys." However, she is working on being less "blinded" by the process.

Sandra (26), offering a different perspective, talked about a previous partner being *more* honest on social media than he was with her in person. She didn't understand why he wouldn't express himself in person as he had online and said it was a "slap in the face." He was a completely different person on social media, more open and expressive.

The participants, in general, reflected the ambivalence toward online dating that is evidenced in much of the literature on this topic. The ease of meeting potential partners is offset by the ease with which people can lie or mislead online.

Doing your homework; using online resources to research someone

Participants were asked, "Has social media ever influenced your decision to advance a relationship or end it? If so, please describe." Eleven of the participants stated that they had tried to use social media and other online resources to help them make a decision about whether or not to take the next step—in other words, to "see" an individual in person. These responses yielded a *variant* category. Participants explained that all of the dating sites were different and that the people they met on these sites were diverse. Online dating was seen as something to be careful about—you meet "nice" people and "weird" people and, therefore, you need to do your homework.

Andrea said she strongly believes in researching a potential date. She googles him before deciding how to proceed. "You have to nowadays. The juicy stuff is on the internet, and you can't really run away from that."

Leslie (27) approaches the process of learning about others on dating sites carefully and deliberately. She tries to get to "know the person" and is "influenced through their photos and what they post. . . . I get to see who they really are and decide whether I like them or not."

Rita (26) describes a positive scenario that occurred after doing some research on a potential "date":

> Oh, I find him attractive, and I think he is kind of cute, and [he] makes me laugh, [but then] we became friends on Facebook and I saw the things that he posted and they were inspiring to me. I felt myself compelled to connect or share, knowing that we have similar perspectives.

Rita adds, "I have been exposed to nice guys and weird guys [on dating sites]. . . . [Researching them], I see it as more of an entertaining thing to go through than anything."

Ellen (24) and Joseph (25) assume a cautionary stance regarding doing prior "homework" on someone, since the information may not fairly represent the individual. Ellen uses herself as an example of how one can arrive at the wrong conclusions based on old posts:

> You can go back through my Facebook from right after the breakup in college, and you will find morbid, depressing lyrics, poem lines and lyrics from songs, and [you'll be], like, "Oh my God, this girl is, like, passive aggressive and looking for attention. . . ." But that is not how I am now. . . . So you can take things out of context from the internet that I think is really dangerous and can hurt people.

In general, the participants recognized that online dating offers many benefits and conveniences, but also entails a responsibility not to accept that information at face value. Emerging adults perceive that they need to exercise an added level of caution in the "courting" process that previous generations did not.

Becoming "Facebook official" and changing one's relationship status

In response to the question, "How important is it to you to share your relationship status on social media?" 26 of the participants described their experiences, or lack thereof, of sharing their status on social media, yielding a *typical* category. Of the 26, 19 participants said they weren't necessarily against sharing status, but it was definitely not important to them either; four participants said it was important to share status and/or they are actively thinking about sharing status when relationships begin; and three participants expressed that they were "against" sharing their status for reasons that were idiosyncratic to their particular circumstances. Eight of the participants spoke about issues related to breakups and status-sharing. Responses represented the spectrum of possibilities, ranging from, "I am totally against that (sharing relationship status)" to "not important to share status, but not necessarily against it" to "I've done that (shared status)."

Chantal (23) thought carefully about what she did *not* want to share with respect to her current relationship status. There were boundaries to consider. "If you guys get into a fight, the whole world knows, what for? But I do think that you should post on your profile that you do have a significant other. . . . I think that's a message . . . that you're taken."

Mark (24), although ambivalent about his motivation to post his relationship status, concludes that his desire to share his relationship with others overrides his concerns.

> I guess because there's definitely a part of me, I feel like if I want to share it on social media. . . . Because of the part of me that wants to have a boyfriend for the sake of having a boyfriend and . . . [is] using it to validate myself . . .

Leslie (27) admits to posting her relationship when she initially enters a romantic relationship, but when the relationship breaks up, "I actually try to hide it, I don't share that."

Of the three participants who elected *not* to share their relationship status on social media, a variety of reasons particular to their social contexts were given. One of the participants, Mahesh (23), for example, made it a practice not to participate in SNS at all because of concerns about people in his religious and ethnic community passing judgment.

Tina (27) takes the perspective that relationship status changes over time and that posting one's status may lead to later regret and embarrassment. "I've seen other people put [a status] up and then have to take it down. . . . So it's just my policy . . . you don't have to declare anything until you're engaged."

Michael (27), currently in a long-term relationship, provides his rationale for not posting his relationship status: "It is trivial to do it and it is kind of like we are trying to tell other people how great we are together. . . . [It is as if] we need to say that to other people, just to feel like we are."

The temptation may exist—based on popular media portrayals of emerging adults—to conclude that the majority of emerging adults are heavily invested in status-sharing on SNS; however, emerging adults clearly represent a wide range of opinions and approaches. The majority of the participants stated, perhaps surprisingly, that they did not care strongly about the issue.

Techno-breakups, the ins and outs

In dissolving a romantic relationship with a partner, regardless of who initiates the dissolution, important decisions must often be made online to reflect on and accommodate to the relationship change. Considerations such as filtering (what information to hold onto and let go of in the relationship), whether to block one's former partner, whether to unfriend a former partner, whether to untag oneself from photos or delete them completely, and whether to block a former partner from Skype or email must be entertained by each member of the couple. Some do this in a thoughtful fashion, others from a place of anger, hurt, retaliation, or resentment.

Participants' decisions were heavily informed by the desire to put closure on the relationship and to avoid the temptation to reconnect with their ex-partners. Maintaining distance was an important concern for the majority of the participants. Only three of the participants elected *not* to filter information about the relationship, and thus the majority response yielded a *typical* category.

In describing the process of changing one's online status, Tina (27) says, "It feels weird, like you're cutting out, to some degree, a record of part of your life. But it also brings a degree of closure—I don't need to keep this around. . . . It's done.

Greta (26) states:

I like the slow taper[ing] of letting go of someone, if possible, even though I [have] made the dramatic decision to block someone—but that was because I felt that I really needed to move on.

Alison (28) says, "I usually block the people that I have broken up with so that I specifically do not put myself in a position where I'm maybe tempted to go back," while Ellen (24) notes, "When I want to end something, I . . . remove them from my newsfeed and things like that. . . . I make sure I don't see them within my normal social media vision."
According to Mark (24), however:

I'm usually very wary about unfriending someone or blocking someone because I feel like I'll regret it. So I guess the most I would do is unfollow them on Facebook, so I don't see their posts. I try to limit the amount of time I will see them on social media, without preventing them from reconnecting with me if they so choose.

Three of the participants elected not to filter at all—no blocking of the former romantic partner occurred. Alana (21) explains, "It's just kind of over. Like, when it's done . . . we're Facebook friends, whatever. . . . It doesn't really matter."
Within the category of techno-breakups; the ins and outs, a subcategory emerged: reverting to single status after a breakup.

Reverting to single status after a breakup

While the majority of the participants embraced the act of announcing that their relationship had become "official," participants were more hesitant with regard to ending their relationships. Of the 26 who posted their relationship status when it became "official," approximately 8 participants were disinclined to share that they were no longer in a relationship. The remaining 18, although they did post the dissolution of their relationship, tended to experience the process as painful.
As described by Ellen (24), the act of sharing her breakup on social media was gut-wrenching: "When we broke up, I had to come home and change my profile picture, change my relationship status, and that was

just like another punch." Leslie (27) similarly states: "Breaking up, I actually try to hide it, I don't share that. But when I get into a relationship, I get really excited and I *will* share that." The participants' online behavior tends to reflect that emerging adults experience pleasure and pride in starting a relationship, but pain and a measure of shame in ending one.

Influence of CMC, Positive and Negative

To determine the influence of technology on emerging adults' romantic lives, participants were asked the question: "How has technology influenced your romantic life?" Their responses generated this second domain, influence of CMC, positive and negative. This domain was further broken down into the two categories implied by the domain name: (a) positive aspects, and (b) negative aspects.

About half (14) of the 29 emerging adults spoke about the positive aspects of CMC in their lives, while the other half (15) spoke exclusively of the negative aspects. Even those who acknowledged the pitfalls of CMC generally acknowledged that CMC provides important functions, access, and possibilities for connection.

Positive aspects. Because fewer than half of the participants (14) emphasized the positive aspects of CMC, a *variant* category was established. Among this group, access to present and potential romantic partners was viewed as a critical aspect of CMC; the ever-expanding options for connection on CMC offered possibilities for developing and cementing the participants' romantic relationships.

Alison (28) notes that with the emergence of Skype, Facetime, and Instagram—in addition to her current communication staple, texting—she spends more time connected to her romantic partner, and the quality of their relationship has greatly improved. As a result, relationship satisfaction has increased for Alison. Similarly, Chantal (23) states, "If you both have iPhones, then you can FaceTime all you want, and see each other, even if you're not next to each other, so that's a good thing." Kris (25) echoes Alison's delight with the range of CMC options available to him. He identifies "Google Calendar, cell phones, Instagram, Snapchat, social media, and sharing photos" as his preferred methods of getting in touch with his partner "instantly." Alana (21) states that technology makes it "easier" to maintain contact and "see" each other every day. The ability to exchange pictures makes it easier to communicate and also increases the amount of communication.

Three of the participants focused on LD relationships and how CMC allowed for the relationship to continue and thrive. Tina (27), for example, used technology to sustain a relationship with her partner while she was away in China for a year:

> I . . . would not have been able to really have a relationship without technology, email, Skype, and instant message. . . . We didn't like meeting online, but our relationship was basically only maintained because of [using online] technology so we could communicate.

Putting in long hours at work, Amelia (24) notes that CMC provides the continuity and a sense of "presence" that is very much appreciated. Michael (27) adds, "It helps us when you work long hours in that you can check in with the person, you are connected to them and talk with them throughout the day."

Angela (27) shares that texting and talking on the phone as well as Facebook and Myspace were useful forms of communication when she and her partner first started their long-term relationship, but now that they spend more time together, they tend to use texting and talking on the phone.

Negative aspects. Fifteen participants spoke of the negative aspects of CMC, yielding a *typical* category. Some were wistful about the lack of opportunity for in-depth, meaningful conversations. Becky (24) states:

> I feel like there is less emphasis on having real, open, communicative relationships when you are just doing 150 characters or less. . . . I want to have those real open meaningful conversations and in the technology age I think we are less challenged to have them.

Joseph (25) focuses on the sheer number of people who are involved in your social network and how they can interfere with the relationship.

> There's all these people out there that could potentially just drop out of nowhere into someone's relationship. . . . It's because people put their relationship out there. So . . . then it's open for all these other people to comment, and I guess . . . wreak havoc, if they want.

Alison (28) talks about how technology has "caused problems in my relationship . . . just the misunderstanding what the other person was saying, or what I was saying, and that leading to arguments."

Greta (26) offers many insights about how it is difficult to "read" a potential partner's intentions, particularly when texting:

> You never know how serious a guy is because everybody texts so the guy who just wants to sleep with you will text you, and the guy who really wants to . . . take you out on a beautiful date will also just text you. So it's like really hard to decipher who really means it and who really doesn't. . . . [Also, you] don't know what the tone of their voice is behind what they're saying.

Ellen (24) adds her concerns and insights related to expectations around texting:

> Before cell phones [and texting], if you were interested in a person, you would call that person every night and talk. And that's how you'd know that person was interested. In today's world, most people have their phones on them *the entire time*. If they're not texting you, you feel like they don't *want* to be texting you. But they could also be feeling the same way. . . . And then everyone's, like, "You're not texting me. But *you're* not texting *me.* . . ."

Daniel (21) echoes the notion that management of expectations around techno-communications can be an issue:

> I am not very good at texting to begin with, and then I was going to some conferences this year so we had quite a few arguments about my frequency of texting back. Apparently, I was not texting back enough or well enough. They weren't quality text messages.

Three of the women and two of the men (both of whom self-identified as gay) expressed concern about the way CMC can enable cheating to happen. Becky (24) asserts:

> I think there is extra paranoia . . . because it's easy for people to connect online and . . . I think it makes the idea of monogamy and commitment a lot harder . . . because people are a lot more paranoid, I think. *I* am a lot more paranoid!

Participants generally indicated that thoughtful and deliberative use of CMC can enhance relationships, while an overreliance on technology can detract from them.

▲ Analysis of Findings

Participants' responses reflected attitudes toward, and experiences with, technology that might be expected from a generation that grew up with cell phones and the internet. CMC is an integral part of emerging adults' romantic lives, in both positive and negative ways. Omnipresent forces in the lives of most of the participants, CMC and SNS presented a range of choices at important junctures of their relationships. Participants described their attempts to negotiate the many challenges CMC presented in their romantic lives. Key activities such as online dating and the use of technology to maintain relationships were discussed, as were important junctures such as becoming "Facebook official" and managing breakups through CMC.

While cognizant of the general benefits of CMC, more than half of the participants failed to extol any particular virtues of CMC and focused exclusively on the downsides. Such responses are consistent with the findings of McDaniel and Coyne (2016). For example, more than half of the participants concluded that dishonesty was rampant on SNS and that "doing one's homework" was necessary to ensure a safe and salutary dating experience. There was a sense, for many, that truth is a commodity in short supply where CMC is involved. Many of the participants felt it was important to try to learn more about the intentions of potential romantic partners in a CMC environment, but overall felt unsure and uneasy about the process. More than one half of the participants reported a tendency to research the person they dated. Trying to discern whether others are simply presenting themselves in the best possible light or lying outright was viewed as a difficult, nuanced process, and participants felt ill equipped to make such determinations. Managing the onslaught of issues presented by dating apps was reported as time-consuming.

Those participants who honed in on the shadow side of CMC also spoke about the social pressures that CMC triggers and the steady barrage of information that needs to be managed. They reported that differing expectations related to CMC sometimes arose between romantic partners, creating conflict. One partner's desire for frequent

CMC on a day-to-day basis, and even throughout each day, emerged as a potential trigger for conflict within relationships, a finding supported in the literature (e.g., Fox & Moreland, 2015). CMC can lead to miscommunication as well; the tone and intent of text messages, for example, are sometimes difficult to decipher.

The autonomy-versus-connection tension that romantic partners are trying to keep in balance, especially in Western nations, is often brought to a head by new technology. As noted early in the chapter, autonomy-versus-connection tensions are higher in couples where there are disagreements around cell phone usage (Duran, et al., 2011). On the one hand, CMC offers a wide array of opportunities for couples to stay meaningfully connected. On the other hand, the ease of connectivity often raises the expectation that connection will occur continually. For this reason, about one third of couples establish explicit rules around cell phone usage, and most other couples presumably develop implicit understandings about phone usage, so that some autonomy can be preserved.

Participants spoke about texting and its impact on couples; they opined that it can both "help" and "hurt" communication. As with cell phone usage, expectations related to texting can differ between partners and may lead to conflict and relationship dissatisfaction. One partner may feel ignored or minimized by inadequate texting, while the other may feel criticized for being a poor texter, an experience Daniel, a participant reported. Texting also brought up concerns regarding how couples relate to one another. One participant Becky expressed belief that the bar has been lowered in terms of quality of conversations, owing to text-based CMC. Participants who were in LD relationships spoke of the advantages that CMC brought to the relationship.

In sum, technology, as one participant noted is, "a huge part of a relationship"; it provides multiple avenues for relationship management and in turn presents critical challenges and necessitates new types of negotiations. Various technology mediums offer various features and drawbacks, and romantic partners use them differently at different junctures of their relationship.

In terms of exercising choice online, emerging adults are using technology in ways that may not serve them well. For example, exposure to online profiles deprives emerging adults of some of the enjoyable and important process of interpersonal discovery.

A limitation of the present study is that participants were not asked about specific tools such as Facebook or categories of CMC. The questions were broad in scope. Specificity with regard to the wide range of technologies was not possible given the scope of this study.

▲ Summary and Conclusions

Technology is redefining relationships, especially for emerging adults. Smartphones, texting, Facebook, Instagram, and other types of CMC have added a cyber dimension to romance. Romantic partners can use technology to stay present in one another's lives, even when physical presence is not possible. LD relationships, sometimes necessitated when a romantic partner takes a job or goes to school in a faraway location, can be maintained in creative and effective new ways. When properly managed, communication technology can help emerging adults negotiate the tension between autonomy and connectedness that most romantic couples seek to balance.

Emerging adults can also use technology to find new romantic partners. Dating apps and other SNS allow users to quickly comb through hundreds, even thousands, of potential partners and look for the qualities and values they desire. Members of minority groups who might have a hard time meeting potential partners in their local neighborhoods can especially benefit from the targeted offerings these sites provide.

Technology has a dark side. "Technoference" keeps many emerging adults distracted from giving full attention to their FtF relationships. The ease of techno-communication has destroyed etiquette in many areas of romance, allowing users to break dates and even end relationships without any direct communication with the other person. Feelings of jealousy, regret, and inadequacy can all be triggered by online behaviors and expectations. SNS and dating sites tend to objectify their participants. Lying is commonplace online; thus it is difficult to begin relationships from a position of trust, which is a commodity that most emerging adults value. There is a jarring disconnect between the growth-driven and honest relationships most emerging adults say they desire and the superficial dating behavior that many of them engage in via CMC. The "tyranny of choice" that is perpetuated online has many emerging adults stymied into making no choice at all.

Emerging adults have a challenge before them that past generations have not faced: an onslaught of technology that makes dating far easier and less risky (in terms of potential rejection), but also, by virtue of its ease and its endless array of offerings, can keep emerging adults locked in a perpetual "shopper's" mentality—looking for a more perfect choice, rather than getting to know a person in greater depth. The issue at hand is learning how to use CMC wisely, how to use it as a tool that facilitates choice rather than dictates it.

▲ Author's Note

Because of the length of this chapter and other editorial considerations, an in-depth presentation of a participant was not included in this chapter.

▲ References

Ansari, A. (2015). *Modern Romance*. New York, NY: Penguin Press.

Arnett, J. (2006). Emerging adulthood: Understanding the new way of coming of age. In J. Arnett & J. Tanner (Eds.), *Emerging adults in America: Coming of age in the 21st century* (pp. 3–19). Washington, DC: American Psychological Association.

Aron, A., & Aron, E. N. (1986). *Love and the expansion of self: Understanding attraction and satisfaction*. New York, NY: Hemisphere/Harper & Row.

Aron, A., & Aron, E. N. (1996). Self and self-expansion in relationships. In G. J. O. Fletcher & J. Fitness (Eds.), *Knowledge structures in close relationships: A social psychological approach* (pp. 325–344). Mahwah, NJ: Lawrence Erlbaum.

Baxter, L. A., & Montgomery, B. M. (1996). *Relating: Dialogues and dialectics*. New York, NY: Guilford Press.

Bowe, G. (2010). Reading romance: The impact Facebook rituals can have on a romantic relationship. *Journal of Comparative Research in Anthropology and Sociology, 1*(2), 61–77.

Carpenter, C. J., & Spottswood, E. L. (2013). Exploring romantic relationships on social networking sites using the self-expansion model. *Computers in Human Behavior, 29*(4), doi:1531-1537.doi:10.1016/j.ch.b.2013.01.021

Colier, N. (2016). *The power of off: The mindful way to stay sane in a virtual world*. Louisville, CO: Sounds True.

Collins, N. L., & Allard, L. M. (2001). Cognitive representations of attachment: The content and function of working models. *Blackwell handbook of social psychology: Interpersonal processes, 2*, 60–85.

Cox Communications. (2009). *Teen online & wireless safety survey. Cyberbullying, sexting, and parental controls*. Retrieved from http://ww2.cox.com/wcm/en/aboutus/datasheet/takecharge/2009-teen-survey.pdf

Coyne, S. M., Padilla-Walker, L. M., & Howard, E. (2013). Emerging in a digital world: A decade review of media use, effects, and gratifications in emerging adulthood. *Emerging Adulthood, 1*(2), 125–137. doi:10.1177/2167696813479782

Dollar, C. (2017, May 5). My so-called (Instagram) life. *The New York Times.* Retrieved from https://www.nytimes.com

Döring, N. (2014). Consensual sexting among adolescents: Risk prevention through abstinence education or safer sexting? *Cyberpsychology: Journal of Psychosocial Research on Cyberspace, 8*(1), article 9. doi:10.5817/CP2014-1-9

Duran, R. L., Kelly, L., & Rotaru, T. (2011). Mobile phones in romantic relationships and the dialectic of autonomy versus connection. *Communication Quarterly, 59*(1), 19–36.

Eastwick, P. W., & Hunt, L. L. (2014). Relational mate value: Consensus and uniqueness in romantic evaluations. *Journal of Personality and Social Psychology, 106*(5), 728–751. doi:10.1037/a0035884

Ellison, N. B. (2007). Social network sites: Definition, history, and scholarship. *Journal of Computer-Mediated Communication, 13*(1), 210–230.

Emery, L. F., Muise, A., Dix, E.L., & Le, B. (2014). Can you tell that I'm in a relationship? Attachment and relationship visibility on Facebook. *Personality and Social Psychology Bulletin, 40,* 1466–1479. http://dx.doi.org/10.1177/0146167214549944

Finkel, E. J., Eastwick, P. W., Karney, B. R., Reis, H. T., & Sprecher, S. (2012). Online dating: A critical analysis from the perspective of psychological science. *Psychological Science in the Public Interest, 13*(1), 3–66. doi:10.1177/1529100612436522

Fleuriet, C., Cole, M., & Guerrero, L. K. (2014). Exploring Facebook: Attachment style and nonverbal message characteristics as predictors of anticipated emotional reactions to Facebook postings. *Journal of Nonverbal Behavior, 38*(4), 429–450. doi:10.1007/s10919-014-0189-x

Fox, J., & Moreland, J. J. (2015). The dark side of social networking sites: An exploration of the relational and psychological stressors associated with Facebook use and affordances. *Computers In Human Behavior, 45,* 168–176. doi:10.1016/j.chb.2014.11.083

Fox, J., Osborn, J. L., & Warber, K. M. (2014). Relational dialectics and social networking sites: The role of Facebook in romantic relationship escalation, maintenance, conflict, and dissolution. *Computers in Human Behavior, 35,* 527–534. doi:10.1016/j.chb.2014.02.031

Fox, J., & Warber, K. M. (2013). Romantic relationship development in the age of Facebook: An exploratory study of emerging adults' perceptions, motives, and behaviors. *Cyberpsychology, Behavior, and Social Networking, 16*(1), 3–7. doi:10.1089/cyber.2012.0288

Frost, D. M., Meyer, I. H., & Hammack, P. L. (2015). Health and well-being in emerging adults' same-sex relationships: Critical questions and directions for research in developmental science. *Emerging Adulthood, 3*(1), 3–13. doi:10.1177/2167696814535915

Gala, J., & Kapadia, S. (2013). Romantic relationships in emerging adulthood: A developmental perspective. *Psychological Studies, 58,* 406–418. doi:10.1007/s12646-013-0219-5

Greenwood, S., Perrin, A., & Duggan, M. (2016). Social media update 2016. *Pew Research Center*. Retrieved from http://www.pewinternet.org/2016/11/11/social-media-update-2016/

Hall, J. A. (2014). First comes social networking, then comes marriage? Characteristics of Americans married 2005–2012 who met through social networking sites. *Cyberpsychology, Behavior, and Social Networking*, 17(5), 322–326.

Hasinoff, A. (2013). Sexting as media production: Rethinking social media and sexuality. *New Media & Society*, 15, 449–465. doi:10.1177/1461444812459171

Hu, E. (2013, October 10). New numbers back up our obsession with phones. *National Public Radio*. Retrieved from http://www.npr.org

Jiang, L. C., & Hancock, J. T. (2013). Absence makes the communication grow fonder: Geographic separation, interpersonal media, and intimacy in dating relationships. *Journal of Communication*, 63(3), 556–577. doi:10.1111/jcom.12029

Kaplan, A. M., & Haenlein, M. (2010). Users of the world, unite! The challenges and opportunities of social media. *Business Horizons*, 53(1), 59–68.

Karaian, L. (2012). Lolita speaks: "Sexting," teenage girls and the law. *Crime, Media, Culture*, 8, 57–73. doi:10.1177/1741659011429868

Klettke, B., Hallford, D. J., & Mellor, D. J. (2014). Sexting prevalence and correlates: A systematic literature review. *Clinical Psychology Review*, 34(1), 44–53. doi:10.1016/j.cpr.2013.10.007

Konstam, V. (2015). *Emerging and young adulthood: Multiple perspectives, diverse narratives* (2nd ed.). Cham, Switzerland: Springer International.

Livingstone, S. (2008). Taking risky opportunities in youthful content creation: Teenagers' use of social networking sites for intimacy, privacy, and self-expression. *New Media & Society*, 10, 393–411. doi:10.1177/1461444808089415

Livingstone, S., Haddon, L., Görzig, A., & Ólafsson, K. (2011). Risks and safety on the internet: The perspective of European children: full findings and policy implications from the EU Kids Online survey of 9-16 year olds and their parents in 25 countries. *EU Kids Online*, Deliverable D4. EU Kids Online Network, London, UK. Retrieved from: http://eprints.lse.ac.uk/33731/1/Risks%20and%20safety%20on%20the%20internet%28lsero%29.pdf

Loving, T. J. (2011). Long-term relationship processes. In G. W. Lewandowski Jr., T. J. Loving, B. Le, & M. Gleason (Eds.), *The science of relationships: Answers to your questions about dating, marriage, and family*. Dubuque, IA: Kendall Hunt.

McDaniel, B. T., & Coyne, S. M. (2016). "Technoference": The interference of technology in couple relationships and implications for women's personal and relational well-being. *Psychology of Popular Media Culture*, 5(1), 85–98. doi:10.1037/ppm0000065

Muscanell, N. L., Guadagno, R. E., Rice, L., & Murphy, S. (2013). Don't it make my brown eyes green? An analysis of Facebook use and romantic jealousy. *Cyberpsychology, Behavior, and Social Networking*, 16(4), 237–242. doi:10.1089/cyber.2012.0411

Nitzburg, G. C., & Farber, B. A. (2013). Putting up emotional (Facebook) walls? Attachment status and emerging adults' experiences of social networking sites. *Journal of Clinical Psychology*, 69(11), 1183–1190.

O'Connor, M. (2013, July 13). All my exes live in texts: Why the social media generation never really breaks up. *The Cut*. Retrieved from https://www.thecut.com/2013/07/texting-exes-social-media-generation.html

Petersen, L. (2017, 26 May). Wanting monogamy as 1,946 men await my swipe. *The New York Times*. Retrieved from https://www.nytimes.com

Rappleyea, D.L., Taylor, A.C., & Fang, X. (2014). Gender differences and communication technology use among emerging adults in the initiation of dating relationships. *Marriage & Family Review, 50*(3), 269–284. doi:10.1080/01494929.2013.879552

Schade, L. C., Sandberg, J., Bean, R., Busby, D., & Coyne, S. (2013). Using technology to connect in romantic relationships: Effects on attachment, relationship satisfaction, and stability in emerging adults. *Journal of Couple & Relationship Therapy, 12*(4), 314–338. doi:10.1080/15332691.2013.836051

Schwartz, B. (2004). *The paradox of choice: Why more is less*. New York, NY: Harper Collins.

Sheena, S. I., & Lepper, M. (2000). When choice is demotivating: Can one desire too much of a good thing? *Journal of Personality and Social Psychology, 79*, 995–1006.

Smith, A., & Duggan, M. (2013). Online dating and relationships. *Pew Research Center*. Retrieved from http://www.pewinternet.org/2013/10/21/online-dating-relationships/

Stanley, S. M. (2016, November 5). What happens when partners aren't equally committed. New study examines relationships where one is just not that into the other. *Psychology Today*. Retrieved from https://www.psychologytoday.com/blog/sliding-vs-deciding/201611/what-happens-when-partners-arent-equally-committed

Turkle, S. (2016). The empathy gap: Digital culture needs what talk therapy offers. *Psychotherapy Networker*, 29–33.

Utz, S., & Beukeboom, C. J. (2011). The role of social network sites in romantic relationships: Effects on jealousy and relationship happiness. *Journal of Computer-Mediated Communication, 16*(4), 511–527. doi:10.1111/j.1083-6101.2011.01552.

6 ▲
Casual Sexual Relationships and Experiences

> *I feel like . . . [friends with benefits] were actually*
> *the sexual experiences where I was able to*
> *experiment more with ideas of what I like—where*
> *I felt a little more free to own myself as a sexual*
> *being. . . . Previously in a relationship, I was worried*
> *about performance, or maintaining sexual attraction,*
> *or something like that, whereas someone who is*
> *a friend with benefits, that I wasn't expecting to*
> *build a romantic relationship with, that I wasn't as*
> *worried about maintaining interest, where I felt a*
> *little more freer in the moment.*
>
> —Rita, 26, a research participant

Friends with benefits? Hookups? One-night stands? Booty calls? Although casual sexual relationships and experiences (CSREs) have not been consistently operationalized in the literature, and meanings attached to CSREs are often idiosyncratic among emerging adults (Williams & Adams, 2013), the main defining element of these sexual relationships is that they take place outside of "formal romantic relationships" (Claxton & van Dulmen, 2013, p. 138). Approximately 50–84% of emerging adults engage in these nonromantic sexual encounters (Knight, 2014), which are emblematic of the period of sexual identity exploration (Morgan, 2013).

CSREs provide *alternatives* to traditional dating relationships; they have not *taken the place* of committed relationships (Armstrong, Hamilton, & England, 2010). These largely attachment-free sexual relationships arose during the 60s, primarily as an outgrowth of the women's movement, the availability of birth control, and the decline of *in loco parentis* on college campuses. Emerging adults, particularly those who are economically advantaged, are investing in careers that require education and training that extends into their 20s; consequently, they are delaying romantic commitment and marriage. Thus, CSREs are filling a vacuum by providing flexible alternatives to formal romantic relationships. The likelihood of involvement in CSREs is increased by factors such as sexual desire, peer pressure within one's social sphere, and the physical attractiveness of a potential partner (Claxton & van Dulmen, 2013). Intoxication, normalization of CSREs, and an individual's previous number of hookups are additional factors that influence the likelihood of CSRE engagement (Fielder & Carey, 2010, as cited in Claxton & van Dulmen, 2013).

The current literature on CSREs is not inclusive across a diversity of backgrounds with respect to ethnicity, sexual orientation, religious orientation, and educational level. What is known and represented in the literature relates primarily to the experiences of heterosexual middle-class college students. As Claxton and van Dulmen (2013) suggest, engagement in CSREs is likely to be informed by cultural values, and future research efforts are needed in order to appreciate the variability and nuance that can be assumed to exist across a diversity of cultural contexts.

One view of CSREs is that they offer a path toward "relational identity exploration" (Arnett, 2000, 2004, as cited in Knight, 2014, p. 277). CSREs provide opportunities for emerging adults to gain greater understanding of themselves in relationship, including assessing their readiness for a committed relationship. According to this point of view, the cumulative insights from these sexual experiences can better inform emerging adults' choice of more "serious" partners. Not all researchers agree. Some suggest that CSREs, rather than helping emerging adults develop a relational identity and explore what they are looking for in a long-term partner, can actually reinforce behaviors that work against the development of healthy reciprocal romantic relationships (Cote, 2000, 2006). According to this view, CSREs represent meaningless engagements that bear little resemblance to the romantic relationships emerging adults will experience in their roles as long-term committed partners (Haber & Burgess, 2012).

In this chapter we will explore meanings associated with CSREs represented in the literature, including the contexts in which CSREs occur. Gender, as well as inequality and how it may be enacted across CSREs, will be explored, followed by an in-depth discussion of friends with benefits relationships (FWBRs), including communication patterns that have been identified in these relationships. Greta, a research participant who is struggling with the ambiguities of navigating a romantic life that includes CSREs, will be presented for a closer look.

Specific questions that will be addressed in this chapter include: (a) do CSREs represent a cultural shift specific to this new generation of emerging adults, and, if so, how are we to understand the shift? and (b) do CSREs serve as points of entry into the more enduring committed relationships that are formed during one's late 20s, or do they carry more negative consequences, including predisposition toward low self-esteem, lack of trust, depression, and/or anxiety?

First, a brief description of CSREs and their various types.

▲ Casual Sexual Relationships and Experiences

Casual sexual relationships and experiences (CSREs), also sometimes referred to as *casual relationships, casual sex,* and *romantic experiences,* are noncommittal sexual relationships that meet the following criteria: (a) they occur outside of a committed romantic relationship, (b) they involve sexual connotations and/or conduct, and (c) they include, but are not limited to, discrete experiences—they can also bear some characteristics of a relationship (Claxton & van Dulmen, 2013). CSREs include hookups, one-night stands, friends with benefits, and booty calls.

Interestingly, emerging adults are *not* having more sex than their parents' generation. In fact, some are not having sex at all. A recent government survey revealed that in Japan, for example, 42% of men and 44.2% of women between the ages of 18–34 are virgins, a statistic that has been attributed to a variety of economic, social, and psychological factors, such as stagnation in the economy and a possible growing preference toward sexual fantasy over sexual reality. An additional factor may be the loss of self-esteem and romantic confidence among men, whose salaries have decreased dramatically as women's economic strength and independence has been on the rise (http://www.cnn.com/2016/09/20/asia/japanese-millennials-virgins).

During their college years, approximately 80% of emerging adults have experienced at least one CSRE (Armstrong et al., 2010). Fun is very much on the radar screen of many emerging adults (Konstam, 2015). CSREs allow for sexual exploration, avoidance of intense committed relationships, and a "way of balancing fun and risk" (Armstrong et al., 2010, p. 24). Although CSREs have been normalized among emerging adults, they are not risk-free, as evidenced by the increased risk of sexually transmitted infections (STIs) and pregnancies (Ashenhurst, Wilhite, Harden, & Fromme, 2016).

In the process of assuming roles associated with adulthood (e.g., full-time employment, having a child), adolescents and emerging adults over time are less inclined to participate in CSREs (Lyon, Manning, Longmore, & Giordano, 2015). For both male and female adolescents and emerging adults, dating relationships, and the behavior of peers, served as important social contexts that informed the likelihood of engagement in CSREs. Although alcohol use was positively associated with the number of CSREs, it did not significantly increase the number of CSREs (Lyons, Giordano, Manning, and Longmore, 2011, as cited by Lyon et al., 2015). Parental relationship quality did not predict number of CSREs. Further research efforts are needed to determine whether and how parents may change their approach in speaking with their emerging adult children about sexual behaviors, including CSREs.

Hookups

By senior year of college, approximately 40% of college students report having engaged in three or fewer hookups, 40% in four to nine hookups, and 20% in 10 or more hookups (Armstrong et al., 2010). "Hookup," however, is an ambiguous term. It is used to describe a range of behaviors including kissing, intercourse, and anything in between (Claxton & van Dulmen, 2013). The nomenclature leaves the specific sexual behavior open to interpretation (Manning, Giordano, & Longmore, 2006). There is also ambiguity as to the length of these experiences, the degree of closeness of the individuals involved (e.g., friends, acquaintances, strangers), and the question of whether or not these experiences occur independently from other CSREs. Research efforts are hampered due to the wide breadth of definitions and the wide range of behaviors associated with the term "hookup."

One-Night Stands

A one-night stand is traditionally defined as a sexual encounter that occurs singularly (Claxton & van Dulmen, 2013). In this regard, it is similar to a hookup; also in the fact that these encounters typically take place between strangers and/or acquaintances and are likely to be more focused on the sexual versus the emotional component when compared to booty calls or committed relationships (Jonason, Li, & Richardson, 2011). However, "Emotion-based sexual acts such as hand-holding and kissing are more common than explicitly sexual acts (i.e., oral and vaginal sex) within one-night stands, suggesting that emotional acts may be used to bring the encounter quickly to sex" (Jonason et al., 2011, as cited in Claxton and van Dulmen, 2016, p. 248).

A common understanding of one-night stands is that they are primarily sexual, with little emotional investment and little or no intention on the part of the participants to repeat the experience. Hookups, on the other hand, may happen more than once and may contain an emotional component.

Friends With Benefits Relationships

Friends with benefits relationships (FWBRs), studied more frequently in the literature than other CSREs, refer to sexual relationships between friends who do not consider themselves to be in a committed relationship with each other (Stafford, Price, & Reynolds, 2014). A FWBR can arise from a variety of arrangements, including a former committed relationship or a previous CSRE between the two parties. Mongeau, Knight, Williams, Eden, and Shaw (2013) describe seven types of FWBRs: (a) a "true" friendship, (b) a sexual relationship, (c) an opportunistic networking relationship, (d) a transition from another relationship, (e) an unintentional transition to a romantic relationship, (f) a successful transition to a romantic relationship, and (g) a failed transition to a romantic relationship. A "true" FWBR is the most frequently reported FWBR (Claxton & van Dulmen, 2013). "True friends" are close friends who have "gotten together" sexually on one or more occasion, but whose friendship extends beyond the romantic/sexual and contains features of a nonsexual friendship. When compared to other CSREs, FWBRs, although characterized by ambiguity in communication and understanding, tend to be the most stable and include a greater degree of emotional involvement and mutual respect.

Booty Calls

A booty call may be defined as a noncommittal, short-term sexual encounter used to fulfill an urgent desire that is either stated or implied at the time of communication. (Claxton & van Dulmen, 2013). Booty calls are new to research efforts. They embrace the new advantages of technology (e.g., cell phones, texting, social media). Booty calls typically reoccur, but tend to be characterized by less emotional investment than other CSREs, and, when compared to FWBRs, are viewed as less emotionally satisfying. Claxton and van Dulmen (2013) suggest that booty calls offer little affection and that those involved in these relationships tend not to engage in activities with one another outside of the sexual relationship.

The next section examines gender and inequality across CSREs, followed by an in-depth discussion of FWBRs, a type of CSRE that provides a lens to understanding communication patterns among emerging adults.

▲ Gender and CSREs

CSREs are "riddled" with gender inequality, according to Armstrong et al. (2010). The sexual double standards persist. Men still tend to be socially lauded for having casual sexual experiences, while women may be stigmatized. The following statement effectively captures the terrain: "Guys can have sex with all the girls and it makes them more of a man, but if a girl does then all of a sudden she's a 'ho' and she's not as quality of a person" (Armstrong et al., 2010, p. 24). It has been argued that CSREs are more psychologically damaging for women than for men and reinforce societal power imbalances (Manning, Giordano, & Longmore, 2006; Stinson, 2010). Sexual assault is also believed to be facilitated by these encounters and is exacerbated when alcohol is at play (Owen & Fincham, 2012).

Many emerging adult women believe that CSREs are normative, and that compliance with these norms is their only viable choice if they are to remain "in the game." Men, for their part, may be pressuring women to have casual sexual encounters because *they* "feel at ease with the behavior and over-estimate women's comfort level" (Claxton & van Dulmen, 2013, p. 144).

When engaging in CSREs, men report more pleasure during the experience and less guilt and regret in the aftermath than women do (Fisher, Worth, Garcia, & Meredith, 2012). Overall, men are more comfortable than women with uncommitted sex (Reiber & Garcia, 2010). However, women are as invested in pleasing men during CSREs as they are in more romantic committed relationships, while men are more invested in providing sexual pleasure in committed romantic partnerships than in CSREs. Oral sex is more likely to be reciprocal between men and women in committed relationships (Armstrong, et al., 2010), but in CSREs, men are more likely to receive fellatio than women are to receive cunnilingus.

A caveat when considering gender differences: it is important not to overgeneralize. A great deal of variability exists within the population that engages in CSREs. Women, not just men, may enjoy the process of sexual experimentation and the rewards that experimentation provides, including validation of the self, personal empowerment, and increased self-efficacy, all of which can serve emotional growth (Armstrong et al., 2010; Hamilton & Armstrong, 2009). In addition, college women may view committed relationships as interfering with their school work and ability to meet new people, important developmental tasks associated with mastery of the college experience. Similarly, career-focused women may not feel they have the time for romantic commitment but may still wish to enjoy occasional sexual companionship.

In sum, although inequality is rampant in CSREs, the logical conclusion is not to assume that women's sexual activity is therefore ideally suited to committed romantic relationships. That perspective "reinforces the notion that women shouldn't want sex outside of relationships and stigmatizes the women who do" (Armstrong et al., 2010, p. 27). Gender inequality, however, does exist and can impact CSREs in pernicious ways that must be challenged:

> It is critical to attack the tenacious sexual double standard that leads men to disrespect their hookup partners. Ironically, this could improve relationships because women would be less likely to tolerate "greedy" or abusive relationships if they were treated better in hookups. Fostering relationships among young adults should go hand-in-hand with efforts to decrease intimate partner violence and to build egalitarian relationships that allow more space for other aspects of life—such as school, work, and friendship. (Armstrong et al., 2010, p. 27)

▲ Friends with Benefits: An Unfolding Narrative

FWBRs are defined as relationships between friends who engage in sexual activity on repeated occasions (Stafford et al., 2014), ranging from kissing and petting to oral sex and sexual intercourse (Furman & Shaffer, 2011). These relationships have some of the qualities of traditional friendships—such as trust, mutual reliance, and an enjoyment of shared, nonromantic activities—as well as some qualities of romantic relationships, such as sexual intimacy, but they also seem to possess a unique "flavor" all their own (Owen & Fincham, 2012). Approximately 50–60% of emerging adults in the United States have experienced a FWBR (Furman & Shaffer, 2011). Approximately 10–20% of emerging adults in FWBRs shift to an exclusive relationship (Eisenberg, Ackard, Resnick & Neumark-Sztainer, 2009). Emerging adults perceive little or no risk of sexually transmitted infections (STIs) when engaged in FWBRs, although 44% reported having additional sexual partners during their most recent FWBR, and 33% reported either no condom use or inconsistent condom use (Weaver, MacKeigan, & MacDonald, 2011).

Positive aspects of FWBRs include the potential for gaining confidence and experience, comfort, trust, closeness, companionship, safety, and freedom to have control of, and easy access to, sex. Negative aspects of FWBRs include the potential for getting emotionally hurt, ruining a friendship, and the relationship becoming complicated and/or awkward (Weaver et al., 2011). Also, a majority of young adults (77%) believe that a sexual double standard exists in FWBRs, with women being judged more negatively than men for participating in these relationships.

FWBRs are represented in the growing literature predominantly through the experiences of college students. A diversity of participants and experiences with regard to factors such as ethnicity, race, sexual orientation, and religious orientation, is not well represented in the literature, and therefore research findings must be viewed in that light (Williams & Adams, 2013). Also, when emerging adults are asked to identify a FWBR, it cannot be assumed that they are speaking within the exact definition provided in the academic literature; understandings of the term, as well as specifics as to how these relationships are carried out and experienced, vary among emerging adults. The seven types of FWBR identified by Mongeau et al. (2013) were differentiated by degree of commitment, investment, exclusivity, secrecy, and emotional closeness, a typology that has not largely been applied across the FWBR research literature. Perhaps the absence of clear definitions for these relationships is deliberate given the degree of ambiguity inherent in these relationships. It may serve to disguise unrequited romantic feelings or outside sexual affiliations.

The motivations that propel emerging adults to enter these relationships vary (Bisson & Levine, 2009). For some, FWBRs evolve from failed attempts to develop more intimate relationships. For others, this type of relationship is chosen specifically because it allows one or both partners to explore their sexuality and/or sexual identification without pressure. For others still, avoidance of more intimate committed relationships may be the primary motivator for choosing FWBRs. For this latter group of emerging adults, the relationship is likely to be viewed as nonthreatening and requiring minimal effort (Knight, 2014). Researchers need to acknowledge and address these motivational differences in future research designs.

FWBRs are characterized by limited direct communication between partners (Knight, 2014). This is not surprising given the nascent relational skills of emerging adults and the chronically undefined nature of these relationships. Feelings that accompany FWBRs are complex and confusing to process: some emerging adults in these relationships describe a lack of romantic passion toward the partner, while others seem to be disguising a desire for a more committed romantic relationship (Mongeau et al., 2013). Feelings and tensions related to relational uncertainty, emotional vulnerability, power struggles, and diverging goals and expectations for the relationship are likely to exist. Ambiguity in communication tends to sustain homeostasis in these relationships, however, and opportunities for working through unproductive communication patterns around relationship issues are typically not openly addressed (Knight, 2014).

In fact, part of what seems to *define* this type of casual sexual relationship is the avoidance of talking about it. Talking about a relationship is viewed as an aspect of a committed relationship as opposed to a FWBR. Those who avoid talking about FWBRs are often perceived as agreeable and easygoing, while those who want to talk about the relationship may be viewed as nagging, problematic, or "high-maintenance" (Knight, 2014, p. 274). Since the partners are not "in a relationship," feelings of jealousy are frequently suppressed, and discussion of such feelings may be viewed as "transgressive" (p. 274). Suppression of both talk and feelings serves to maintain the status quo; there is a fear that if feelings are openly discussed, the relationship might need to change or end. Knight (2014) concluded that "there is a mismatch between the expectations of openness and honesty in FWBRs and actual communication practice" (p. 271). Although honest and explicit relational talk exceeds the boundaries of FWBRs, Knight asserts that "the ability to engage in relational talk is important to the success of all relationships but may be especially salient in the management of FWBRs because of their ambiguous nature" and the complexity of feelings likely to be generated (Knight, 2014, p. 271).

Owen and Fincham (2012) conclude that emerging adults who engage in FWBRs employ less thoughtful relationship decision-making processes than those who have not engaged in these relationships. However, they point out that emerging adults who begin an *exclusive* romantic relationship within a FWBR "may not have some of the hallmark risk-factors that are typically reported in FWB relationships such as avoidant communication patterns and lack of clarity about commitment levels" (p. 992). Hookups typically involve "more isolated and decontextualized interactions" (p. 277) Communication behaviors in FWBRs require ongoing negotiations. Yet, there is little opportunity for the articulation of concerns and resolution of patterns of interactions that may have implications for future romantic relationships.

Paul, Wenzel, and Harvey (2008), on the other hand, suggest that casual relationships contain opportunities for moments of sense-making. These moments, according to the authors, may help clarify what one wants and doesn't want from future romantic relationships. Emerging adults can make sense of casual relationships by comparing and contrasting them with other known relationship scripts. "Struggling through or against overlapping relational scripts—and even tripping over problematic relational talk—may assist emerging adults in forming a preferred relational identity" (Stafford et al., 2014, as cited in Knight, 2014, p. 277).

The questions currently being asked by researchers are likely to be too global in scope. Analysis and discussion of responses of our 29 participants was not included in this chapter because the questions asked of the participants lacked sufficient specificity. Given the ambiguity and variability in terminology used by the participants, the research team concluded that the results obtained were hampered by the wide breadth of definitions and behaviors associated with such terms as "hookup" and "casual sexual relationships" as suggested by Claxton and van Dulmen (2013).

Future research could be improved by seeking insights with practical applications. What are the scripts and relational skill sets that emerging adults bring to this developmental period? What are the conditions that foster further growth and development? What are the factors that predispose emerging adults to moments of sense making and to periods of reflection that mobilize them into action? How does participation in CSREs inform these scripts and skill sets (Paul et al., 2008)? These are some of the questions that require further research development. Sexual harassment in the context of CSREs among emerging adults requires further exploration and understanding, particularly given the current political climate in the United States.

The next section presents Greta, a research participant in the study, who speaks eloquently to the struggles and ambiguities of navigating a romantic life that includes CSREs. For that reason, we will discuss her case in some detail. The striking aspect of Greta's case is that despite the insights she has garnered, she continues to be frustrated with herself, the choices she has made to date, and her CSRE partners. Her perceived inability to learn and change in response to these experiences seems to baffle Greta.

▲ Greta

Greta is a 26-year-old, single, nonpracticing Catholic female pursuing a Master's degree in teaching (her second graduate degree). She is currently working part-time at an urban university as an assistant to a department program director. Greta was born in the Netherlands and came to this country with both of her parents when she was 3 years of age. She lives with her mother, the breadwinner of the family, her father, a stay-at-home dad, and her 22-year-old sister, who is nearing completion of an undergraduate degree in nursing.

Greta reveals that since the age of 18 she has been in three short-term romantic relationships, each no longer than 1 year in duration. She has also engaged in CSREs for the past 8 years. Greta is clear about the qualities she is seeking in a man and asserts that she will not "settle just to be in a relationship." The individual must be respectful, financially stable, and intellectually capable (not unlike herself). She expects her potential partner to have a strong work ethic, an expectation that might be informed by her experiences with her father who has not been gainfully employed since he immigrated to the United States. While she desires to be in a relationship where each partner is an "equal," she speaks of a long-term romantic relationship with a man who "woos her and provides [her with] kind gestures." There is a wistfully traditional aspect to her relationship goals that stands in contrast to her present experiences.

In her most recent short-term relationship, Greta was frustrated with the relationship and describes the man as a "freeloader" (she makes no apparent association to her stay-at-home dad, who presumably has the capacity to generate income for the family now that his children have reached adulthood). In her two prior relationships, which occurred during college, Greta experienced both men as "inconsiderate" and "not very communicative." Neither of these relationships was sexually satisfying.

Greta has engaged in numerous CSREs. She describes, with some dismay, an incident related to a "booty call."

> I went over for a booty call with a former partner and . . . he made an assumption that I wanted more than just a physical relationship. He made it clear that we were not going to have any other kind of relationship, which made me feel hurt and offended, and emotionally exposed. . . . I felt horrible about myself, I realized I was in a destructive pattern.

Greta was genuinely puzzled by her former partner's behavior, specifically his need to set limits on the relationship. According to Greta, it was not necessary for him to "confront" her about relationship expectations:

> I was surprised to be confronted about my relationship expectation by a hookup partner, which is what hurt me. It is implied that two people who meet for sex are not looking for something serious. It's more typical for partners to discuss relationship expectations if they have hooked up several times, not right away. He took the [potential of] serious to the casual right away. Usually, that to me is something that would happen after several times of being with someone.

Greta felt diminished and shamed by her former partner's comments. Greta believed that the "confrontation"—as she characterized it—was premature and that the man should have waited to see what happened. Notably, she describes the hookup as if it was first-time encounter, apparently disregarding the fact that she had had a previous relationship with this person.

The "rules" and understandings in these encounters are no doubt unclear and complicated. Greta could not entertain the possibility that her previous partner might have been concerned about her misreading the cues, that his desire to make his intentions known might have been an attempt to decrease the ambiguity in the hope of minimizing possible misunderstandings and hurt feelings. Greta felt that the clarity was unnecessary and premature, and that she did not need to be "confronted."

Greta and her partner, unbeknownst to each other, seem to have been using different relationship scripts to navigate an inherently ambiguous situation. The shame on Greta's part appears to stem from the belief that her partner misinterpreted her script. (It is emblematic of women's changing sexual roles and identities that in previous generations a woman might have felt shame for being seen as wanting *only* sex; Greta's shame flows from being seen as possibly wanting *more* than sex.)

Before she turned 18, Greta anticipated that her first sexual encounter would be with someone whom she cared about and that the encounter would be "meaningful" and "special." With time, though, she began to doubt that she would find a "special relationship." She decided she did not want to turn 30 without having had sexual experiences.

> My regret is that I feel like I have been single my entire life and while I like to have fun and not be strict with myself, part of me wishes that I had not been so promiscuous because it makes me feel poorly about myself. I regret the kind of hooking up where I thought I was pregnant, had an STD [sexually transmitted disease], or felt especially bad about myself afterward. It's frustrating that I can't seem to translate what I've learned into meaningful future action. . . . I feel like if you're not hooking up then you are just waiting around for a romantic relationship with someone who cares. . . . I get really upset sometimes thinking about it because I feel like it's never going to happen for me. I'm never going to find "the one" so you know what's the use of waiting around?

Greta, in reflecting on her decision, is ridden with anxiety and regret. Although she is articulate and shows capacity for some reflection, she is not able to translate her self-knowledge to an action plan and follow through with it. For example, "nine out of ten times" when she engages in hook ups she is under the influence of alcohol. She describes a lack of confidence in her ability to make good decisions:

I know that certain things make me feel poorly about myself, but that doesn't prevent me from doing them again. I am frustrated with myself because I am aware of destructive patterns but I can't change my actions. So, I get frustrated with myself that I'm aware but that I can't put it into practice.

Greta asserts that she has never had a satisfying romantic relationship; while her relationships appear to start off well, they invariably end badly. She feels badly about herself, and a sense of regret pervades her narrative. Although she is able to identify a pattern of behavior that has led to less than optimal results, she is frustrated by her inability to change her behavior accordingly. She prizes actions over words, and is genuinely perplexed by her inability to mobilize her insights into changed behavior. Although intellectually able and somewhat reflective by nature, she has certain blind spots. She seems to be looking for "the one"—someone who will provide her with financial and emotional security—yet finds herself with men who are "freeloaders" and unable to be emotionally present for her.

Greta has difficulty "trying on" a relationship perspective that differs from her own. She is frustrated by her romantic prospects as well as her own behaviors, and has felt ashamed and diminished in both the CSREs and short-term relationships she has experienced. Her sense of self-efficacy with respect to her ability to impact her romantic environment is clearly compromised. It is not surprising that Greta has significant doubts about whether she will be able to experience a satisfying relationship in the future.

It is difficult to assess the full range of factors (e.g., family dynamics, influence of friends, temperamental style, biological factors) that contribute to Greta's feeling stuck and pessimistic about her future. One can't help but wonder, though, whether educational and public institutions could have helped Greta along the way, and, if so, how.

▲ Sociocultural Factors

Although Greta brings personal confusion and frustration to her romantic life, sociocultural factors are no doubt informing her actions and feelings as well. What are some of the societal influences that help shape women's behaviors and attitudes related to CSREs?

Orenstein (2016) compares the sexual environments of two geographical locales, Greta's native Netherlands and the United States. As a way of establishing contrast between the two, she notes that teen pregnancy rates in the Netherlands are among the lowest in the industrialized world, while the rates in the United States, are 8 times higher. Teens in the United States become sexually active at a younger age than Dutch teens, have greater experience with CSREs, are less likely to use birth control, and are more likely to regret the early timing of their first sexual experience. U.S. teens are also more likely to respond to social pressure from friends or partners relative to their first intercourse experience, and more likely to experience CSREs in which male pleasure is "prioritized" (p. 220). Dutch women, by comparison, are more likely to express a greater degree of comfort with their bodies and are more in "touch with their own pleasure," according to Orenstein.

What accounts for these differences? Acknowledging factors such as a greater degree of diversity, higher rates of poverty, and fewer social welfare guarantees in the United States compared to the Netherlands, we can also identify specific attitudes and actions that are different in the two countries. A salient factor appears to be whether systemic programs are in place that facilitate and empower professionals (e.g., teachers, physicians) and parents to talk candidly about sex and emphasize the importance of a loving sexual relationship. American adolescents, by contrast, are more likely to hear from their mothers about the *risks* of having sex, while fathers either withdraw from the conversation or provide inappropriate levity. Dutch parents are more likely to talk openly about both the pleasures and responsibilities of having sex (Orenstein, 2016).

During the late 1960s, when the sexual revolution took hold, both Dutch and American parents were concerned about adolescents having sex. The difference, according to Orenstein, was that the United States viewed this as a health crisis while the Dutch took the position that adolescent sexuality was a natural phenomenon that required adult guidance, backed by government policy. Teachers were encouraged to focus on the positive aspects of sex and relationships while openly and directly addressing issues such as masturbation, oral sex, same-sex relationships, and orgasm within the classroom setting. Interactional skills were emphasized, including the ability to express to the other person "what feels good," and the importance of setting boundaries.

Shalet, a researcher in the field, compares the two contexts and suggests that American parents consider their adolescents "innately rebellious" (as cited in Orenstein, p. 221) and in turn view their own parental role as one of setting restrictive limits. Perhaps partially in response to this, American adolescents tend to "sneak around" in sexual matters. Dutch parents, by contrast, tend to speak honestly and openly about sex, extolling the virtues of having sex from a place of love. They welcome the boyfriend or girlfriend into the house, negotiating with them the rules for sleepovers. Shalet characterizes the Dutch approach as "soft control": parents discourage promiscuity and take the opportunity to "exert influence, reinforce ethics and emphasize the need for protection" (Orenstein, p. 223), rather than setting hard limits.

Orenstein's study suggests that parental influence—reinforced by a cohesive societal approach—can go a long way toward shaping emerging adults' behavior around casual sex. By exposing teens to open talk about sex and its positive, loving features during their sexually formative years, the "rebellious" and "driven" aspects of sexual experimentation seem to be diminished. One can't help but wonder whether Greta would be experiencing her current struggles had she remained in the Netherlands instead of moving to Boston at age 3.

▲ Summary and Conclusions

In sum, the romantic lives of emerging adults do not follow clear linear pathways toward intimacy; they tend to be circuitous, fluid, flexible, and diverse. Research efforts related to CSREs have not incorporated or accounted for the nonlinear, uneven, and "messy" romantic paths that typify the romantic lives of emerging adults. The CSRE literature does not adequately address how emerging adults transition from CSRE relationships to long-term, committed relationships. Further studies are also needed to clarify the impact of CSREs on future patterns of romantic interactions. For example, it remains unclear how the types of FWBRs identified by Mongeau and Knight (2015) differ in terms of their impact on factors that can affect romantic relationships (e.g., uncertainty management, topic avoidance and suppression, and the management of negative emotion).

What *is* known, based primarily on cross-sectional studies, is that individuals who report "secure attachment styles, low levels of anxiety and high levels of intimacy goals are also more likely to report low levels of CSRE engagement" (Claxton & van Dulmen, 2016, p. 251). Gender differences are evident in this regard. The link between anxious attachment and casual sex is stronger for females than males, and sexual risk taking is more prevalent among males than females. Research findings suggest that, regardless of any positive impact that may be attributed to CSREs, these casual relationships do *not* seem to be contributing, overall, to more secure romantic attachments, especially among females.

Furthermore, there are inherent ambiguities in FWBRs that support continued ambiguous communication patterns between the partners. For some emerging adults, these relationships occur in response to failed attempts at developing more intimate relationships. For others, these relationships are chosen specifically because they allow for avoidance of the commitment and maintenance work associated with more intimate, long-term relationships. For the latter group, these relationships are likely to be viewed as convenient and nonthreatening, filling a vacuum. They do not require the emotional resources and hard work inherent in more intimate and committed relationships.

As to when, how, and if emerging adults begin to move away from CSRE behaviors to more committed behavior, Carroll, Badger, Willoughby, Nelson, Madsen, and Barry (2009) suggest that there are two distinct transitions for emerging adults. One is centered on becoming an adult and the other is centered on readiness for a more committed long-term relationship. In regard to the latter, marital horizon theory (covered in greater depth in Chapter 10) can help inform our understanding of emerging adults and their CSRE-related behaviors. The theory posits that the more ready for long-term commitment and marriage emerging adults view themselves, the more likely they are to engage in behaviors that are in keeping with norms associated with such committed relationships (Johnson, Anderson, & Stith, 2011), and the less likely they are to engage in casual sexual activities. In comparing emerging adults who have distant marital horizons (early 20s) to those with closer horizons (mid 20s and later), the latter group is less likely to take part in destructive drinking behavior and drug use. It may be that as emerging adults' marital horizons draw closer, they shift their views and behaviors toward CSREs as well.

According to marital horizon theory, perceptions regarding the preparatory work needed to enter and maintain long-term relationships inform the behaviors of emerging adults (e.g., shifts in commitment- and compromise-related behaviors). Hence, behaviors consistent with committed or marital relationships may be dormant for a period, only to be reawakened and refined at a time when emerging adults assess that they are actually ready to engage in such relationships (e.g., they have their vocational lives on track).

Longitudinal studies that address the complexity of casual relationships are needed. For example, transitions from casual relationships to more exclusive relationships are not well understood: Are they characterized by reflective work prior to making the transition, and is honest, open, clarifying communication part of the decision-making process? Are emerging adults *"sliding"* or *"deciding"* to transition from casual relationships into more exclusive relationships, and how do selection processes and prior romantic experiences inform these transitions?

The current literature does not address prior learning that has occurred nor does it address the fluidity of these relationships. For example, many emerging adults have experienced exclusive relationships, followed by CSREs, followed in turn by other exclusive relationships. What are the combined influences of these various relationships on one's romantic functioning and one's capacity for entering and maintaining satisfying long-term relationships?

Clearly, as Greta's narrative illustrates, these are confusing times for emerging adults as they try to navigate a challenging romantic terrain. Media and peer pressure may be telling them that CSREs are not only acceptable, but also desirable. Meanwhile, many emerging adults have internalized more traditional romantic ideals that clash with their CSRE behaviors and lead to feelings of guilt and low self-esteem. Reality often does not match the abstract ideas. Women, for example, are told that they are as free as men to engage in casual encounters, but are subjected to the traditional double standard when they actually participate in them. FWBRs are characterized in movies and television as open and communicative but in their lived experiences often suffer from lack of communication. "Rules" exist for hookups, booty calls, FWBRs, and one-night stands, and yet there are no universally accepted definitions for these various CSREs and their attendant behaviors and expectations.

Further efforts are needed to enhance our understanding of CSREs, including FWBRs and their effects on future committed relationships. The narratives of FWBRs and other CSREs as they are lived across contexts—socioeconomic status, ethnicity, race, religion, and sexual orientation—must also receive consideration and future examination. The present literature is biased towards self-reports by middle-class college students, overrepresented by females in many cases, many of whom are participating in these studies as part of their enrollment in college courses.

A better understanding of the definitions, meanings, and consequences of CSREs by those in the helping and educational professions should lead to the development of improved tools with which to help emerging adults make more informed decisions about their romantic lives and sexual behaviors.

▲ References

Armstrong, E. A., Hamilton L., & England P. (2010). Is hooking-up bad for young women? *Contexts, 9* (3), 22–27. doi:10.1525/ctx2010.9.3.22

Ashenhurst, J. R., Wilhite, E. R., Harden, K. P., & Fromme, K. (2016). Number of sexual partners and relationship status are associated with unprotected sex across emerging adulthood. *Archives of Sexual Behavior,* 1–14.

Bisson, M. A., & Levine, T. R. (2009). Negotiating a friends with benefits relationship. *Archives of Sexual Behavior, 38,* 66–73. doi:10.10007/s1058-007-92112

Carroll, J. S., Badger, S., Willoughby, B. J., Nelson, L. J. Madsen, S. D., & Barry, C. M. (2009). Ready or not? Criteria for marriage readiness among emerging adults. *Journal of Adolescent Research, 24*(3), 349–375.

Claxton, S. E., & van Dulmen, M. H. M. (2013). Casual sexual relationships and experiences in emerging adulthood. *Emerging Adulthood, 1*(2), 138–150. doi:10.1177/2167696813487181

Claxton, S. E., & van Dulmen, M. H. M. (2016). Casual sexual relationships and experiences in emerging adulthood. In J. J. Arnett. (Ed.), *The Oxford handbook of emerging adulthood* (pp. 245–261). New York, NY: Oxford University Press.

Cote, J. (2000). *Arrested adulthood: The changing nature of maturity and identity—What does it mean to grow up?* New York, NY: New York University Press.

Cote, J. (2006). Emerging adulthood as an institutionalized moratorium: Risks and benefits to identity formation. In J. Arnett & L. Tanner (Eds.), *Emerging adults in America: Coming of age in the 21st century* (pp. 85–116). Washington DC: American Psychological Association.

Eisenberg, M. E., Ackard, D. M., Resnick, M. D., & Neumark-Sztainer, D. (2009). Casual sex and psychological health among young adults: Is having "friends with benefits" emotionally damaging? *Perspectives on Sexual and Reproductive Health, 41*(4), 231–237. doi:10.1363/4123109

Fisher, M. L., Worth, K., Garcia, J. R., & Meredith, T. (2012). Feelings of regret following uncommitted sexual encounters in Canadian university students. *Culture, Health, & Sexuality, 14*(1), 45–57. doi:10.1080/13691058.2011.619579

Furman, W., & Shaffer, L. (2011). Romantic partners, friends, friends with benefits, and casual acquaintances as sexual partners. *Journal of Sex Research, 48*(6), 554–564. doi:10.1080/00224499.2010.535623

Haber, M. G., & Burgess, C. A. (2012). The developmental context of emerging adults' sexuality and intimate relationships: A critical perspective. *Sex in college: What they don't write home about, 2*(4), 65–89.

Hamilton, L., & Armstrong, E. A. (2009). Gendered sexuality in young adulthood: Double binds and flawed options. *Gender & Society, 23,* 589–616. doi:10.1177/0891243209345829

Johnson, M. D., Anderson, J. R., & Stith, S. M. (2011). An application of marital horizon theory to dating violence perpetration. *Family Science Review, 16*(2), 13–26.

Jonason, P. K., Li, N. P., & Richardson, J. (2011). Positioning the booty-call relationship on the spectrum of relationships: Sexual but more emotional than one-night stands. *Journal of Sex Research, 48*(5), 486–495.

Knight, K. (2014). Communicative dilemmas in emerging adults' friends with benefits relationships: Challenges to relational talk. *Emerging Adulthood, 2*(4), 270–279. doi:1177/2167696814549598

Konstam, V. (2015). *Emerging and young adulthood: Multiple perspectives, diverse narratives* (2nd ed.). Cham, Switzerland: Springer International.

Lyons, H. A., Manning, W. D., Longmore, M. A., & Giardano, P. C. (2015). Gender and casual sexual activity from adolescence to emerging adulthood: Social life course correlates. *Journal of Sex Research, 52*(5), 543–557.

Manning, W. D., Giordano, P. C., & Longmore, M. A. (2006). Hooking up the relationship contexts of "nonrelationship" sex. *Journal of Adolescent Research, 21*(5), 459–483. doi:10.1177/0743558406291692

Mongeau, P. A., Knight, K., Williams, J., Eden, J., & Shaw, C. (2013). Identifying and explicating variation among friends with benefits relationships. *Journal of Sex Research, 50* (1), 37–47. doi:10.1080/00224499.2011.623797

Mongeau, P. A., & Knight, K. (2015). Friends with benefits. *The International Encyclopedia of Interpersonal Communication,* 1–5. doi:10.1002/9781118540190

Morgan, E. M. (2013). Contemporary issues in sexual orientation and identity development in emerging adulthood. *Emerging Adulthood, 1*(1), 52–66.

Orenstein, P. (2016). *Girls and sex: Navigating the complicated new landscape.* New York, NY: Harper-Collins Publishers.

Owen, J., & Fincham, F. D. (2012). Friends with benefits relationships as a start to exclusive romantic relationships. *Journal of Social and Personal Relationships, 29*(7), 982–996. doi:10.1177/0265407512448275

Paul, E. L., Wenzel, A., & Harvey, J. (2008). Hookups: A facilitator or barrier to relationship initiation and intimacy development? In S. Sprecher, A. Wenzel & J. Harvey (Eds.), *Handbook of relationship initiation* (pp. 375–390). New York, NY: Psychology Press.

Reiber, C., & Garcia, J. R. (2010). Hooking up: Gender differences, evolution, and pluralistic ignorance. *Evolutionary Psychology, 8*(3). doi:147470491000800307.

Stafford, L., Price, R., & Reynolds, M. (2014). Adults' meanings of friends-with-benefits relationships: A romantic relationships-oriented study using focus groups and values coding. In J. Manning & A. Kunkel (Eds.), *Researching interpersonal relationships: Qualitative methods, studies, and analysis* (pp. 87–93). Thousand Oaks, CA: Sage.

Stinson, R. D. (2010). Hooking up in young adulthood: A review of factors influencing the sexual behavior of college students. *Journal of College Student Psychotherapy, 24*(2), 98–115. doi:10.1080/87568220903558596

Weaver, A. D., MacKeigan, K. L., & MacDonald, H. A. (2011). Experiences and perceptions of young adults in friends with benefits relationships: A qualitative study. *The Canadian Journal of Human Sexuality,20*(1), 41–53.

Williams, L. R., & Adams, H. L. (2013). Friends with benefits or "friends" with deficits? The meaning and contexts of uncommitted sexual relationships among Mexican American and European American adolescents. *Children and Youth Services Review, 35,* 110–1117.

7 ▲

The Breakup

Dissolution of Premarital Romantic Relationships

> *Few things in life are more traumatic than being*
> *rejected by someone who knows you well and then,*
> *with this insight, decides that she or he no longer*
> *cares for you or wants to be with you.*
> —Dweck, 2016, as cited in Parker, 2016

During emerging adulthood, a time when many individuals are already mired in developmental uncertainty, the emotional upheaval that accompanies a romantic breakup can feel overwhelming—particularly if the individual is invested, satisfied, and committed in the relationship (Frazier & Cook, 1993, as cited in Dailey, Jin, Pfiester, & Beck, 2011). Breakups are a painful but important part of maturing as a romantic partner and learning about the self.

Most emerging adults have experienced the dissolution of a romantic relationship: among college students, approximately 70% have undergone at least one breakup during their college years (Knox, Zusman, & Nieves, 1998). While breakups can be emotionally grueling— associated with symptoms of depression, anxiety (Field, Diego, Pelaez, Deeds, & Delgado, 2009), and posttraumatic stress (Samios, Henson, & Simpson, 2014)—they also represent opportunities for personal growth and development (Tashiro & Frazier, 2003).

Approximately one half of emerging adult romantic relationships feature at least one breakup and reconciliation, and approximately one quarter of emerging adults have had "sex with an ex" during their present or most recent relationship (Halpern-Meekin, Manning, Giordano, & Longmore, 2012). The complexity of such on/off relationships is difficult to capture in a literature that relies heavily on survey data (Halpern-Meekin et al., 2012), particularly when the relationship is undefined and fluid, as emerging adult relationships often are. Asking emerging adults "digital" questions, such as whether they are together or not, or the exact starting and ending dates of their romantic relationships, tends to produce an incomplete and often skewed narrative of the participants' experiences of the relationship.

Nonmarital romantic breakups are important to examine because of the influence they can exert on future relationship choices (Halpern-Meekin et al., 2012). In trying to understand relationship dissolutions among emerging adults, contextual considerations are critical. For example, individuals are less likely to reconcile when either or both partners are less committed to the relationship (Binstock & Thornton, 2003). Factors such as the length and quality of the relationship, the influence of past romantic relationships, and the availability of social supports contribute to shaping the course of a breakup and its ensuing fallout (Gilbert & Sifers, 2011). The gradual tapering off of relationships, as well as the possibility of continued contact and reconnection via social media, may make it more difficult to determine whether a breakup is indeed happening, and when the relationship is officially over. One study participant, for example, remarked that he once thought he was still in a relationship that had ended a month earlier in the partner's understanding.

This chapter explores how emerging adults make meaning of breakups and adapt to romantic loss. Both positive and negative outcomes of breakups are explored. An examination of on/off relationships (*churning* relationships), as well as of common sexual behaviors around breakups (e.g., sex with an ex, rebound sex, revenge sex), help inform our understanding of when and how relationships come to an end. We revisit the 29 emerging adult participants and capture their experiences and points of view with respect to romantic breakups. Attachment and narrative theories are presented to anchor our discussion.

▲ Attachment and Loss

In order to understand how emerging adults come together and break apart romantically, it is helpful to examine early experiences related to attachment, for these provide a foundation for the development of "internal working models" critical to understanding the self in relationship (Davis, Shaver, & Vernon, 2003, p. 872). Individuals, when distressed, will act in a manner that is syntonic with their attachment experiences. Experiences with caretakers during infancy inform attachment styles that carry into emerging adulthood (Bowlby, 1973, 180, as cited in Davis et al., 2003). Secure attachment develops when a caretaker or caretakers are able to provide a "safe haven" from which a thriving infant can explore and develop positive internal working models of the self in relationship (Davis et al., p. 872). Insecure attachments flow from caretakers who are either unresponsive, inconsistently sensitive, or emotionally unavailable to the infant.

Three main strategies associated with attachment styles are typically adopted during infancy: (a) secure strategy, (b) avoidant strategy, and (c) anxious strategy (Davis et al., 2003). In the context of a romantic breakup, a secure style predicts that individuals will express their feelings openly and seek comfort and support from their social networks (e.g., parents, friends). In contrast, individuals who have learned as infants that the expression of their needs will be ignored or punished are more likely to adopt an avoidant style, expressing their emotional needs indirectly and to reverting to self-reliance and nonsocial coping strategies (e.g., drinking and taking drugs). Finally, individuals who rely on an anxious style, born of inconsistent parenting in terms of emotional sensitivity and availability, are more likely to express their needs using aggressive and/or seductive behaviors in attempts toward reconciliation.

Further refinement of Bowlby's attachment model is provided by Bartholomew and Horowitz (1991). They describe four categories of attachment based on combinations of anxiety (negative view of the self) and avoidance (negative view of others). Securely attached individuals, low in both anxiety and avoidance, are likely to experience intimate romantic relationships that are rewarding. "Anxious-preoccupied" individuals, high in anxiety and low in avoidance, will typically seek closeness but are afraid of being abandoned. Those who are high in *both* anxiety and avoidance are more likely to avoid close relationships, relying on a defensive posture that is motivated by the desire to avoid being hurt. Those who are low in anxiety and high in avoidance may be inclined to avoid close relationships entirely.

▲ Narrative Theory and Loss

Emerging adults in the process of grieving a romantic loss find new meaning by revising their understandings of both themselves and the former romantic partner in such a way that they can make adjustments and move ahead with life (Davis et al., 2003). Those who are securely attached develop forward-looking, meaningful narratives that emphasize the *learning through experience* and *emotional growth* that occur in response to loss (Neimeyer, 2001, as cited in Davis et al., 2003). They are able to reconfigure their understanding of how they continue to relate to their (former) romantic partners and thus have the opportunity to retain changed, but healthy, emotional bonds with the person.

Narrative theory provides a theoretical grounding for understanding loss in the context of a relationship breakup. In the throes of a breakup, learning about loss, grief, and the self can lead to life-altering positive changes (Gilbert & Sifers, 2011), provided the individual is able to adopt a growth-oriented narrative. When two individuals decide to call an end to their romantic relationship, the creation of a narrative that enables the partners to see possibilities, risk romance again, and generate new scripts, is associated with positive adaptation (King & Hicks, 2007).

Finding meaning in loss is linked to positive adjustment outcomes (Helgeson, Reynolds, & Tomich, 2006, as cited in Samios et al., 2014). Positive changes can occur in a variety of ways: the changing of long-held assumptions (including philosophical orientation), an expanding of self-perception, and an increased capacity for empathy towards others (Gilbert & Sifers, 2011).

When a relationship ends, a version of the self is lost, along with a possible future self, and these losses need to be acknowledged and integrated. In the process of coming to terms with lost possible selves, emerging adults can begin to imagine and pursue new futures. Through a questioning of old assumptions and a re-examination of existing goals, they can begin constructing narratives that allow them to positively integrate the loss and adapt to it.

An important factor to consider when looking at the emerging adult population is that the narratives they initially tell themselves about their breakups are subject to error (Lewandowski & Bizzoco, 2007). In one study, for example, college freshmen substantially underestimated their resources and capacity to endure dissolution-related distress (Eastwick, Finkel, Krishnamurti, & Loewenstein, 2008, as cited in Lewandowski, 2011).

In creating a narrative about rejection and loss, one's beliefs about the self and personality come into play; such beliefs are the focus of the next section.

▲ Beliefs About the Self and Romantic Rejection

Howe and Dweck (2015) propose that beliefs about the self, in particular whether it is fixed (entity theory) or malleable (incremental theory), greatly influence one's adaptation to rejection. Emerging and young adults who accept entity theory are more likely to view events such as romantic rejection "as information about the self" and are more likely to experience "lingering negative affect toward the rejection experience" (p. 55). They then come to expect, and guard against, rejection in the future. By comparison, emerging and young adults who align with incremental theory are more likely to believe that changeable self-definitions play a positive role in recovery from rejection. A belief in one's ability to evolve and develop—even in the face of rejection—empowers one to imagine a brighter future and steer toward it.

Participants who endorsed entity theory tended to link rejection incidents to the core self and, 5 years after the breakup, were found to be carrying more negative emotions about the rejection, as well as stronger beliefs that others would view them negatively because of it. They were less likely to view rejections as opportunities for learning, growth, and development, and preferred instead to suppress memories of the rejection. They were also *more* likely to derive a sense of pessimism from reflecting upon the rejection experience. No gender differences were observed in relation to the these findings.

In working with emerging adults, the findings of Howe and Dweck (2015) suggest that the lingering influence of rejection may be diminished by examining the narratives emerging adults construct when in the throes of a breakup. By re-evaluating their past relationship behaviors and reframing their experiences with loss, emerging adults can create opportunities for increased understanding of the self and gain relationship competence and satisfaction. The *attributions* emerging adults make regarding the breakup can also play a crucial role in how quickly and effectively they recover from romantic dissolution.

In the next section, based on the work of Tashiro and Frazier (2003), we will examine how attributions can affect whether one is feeling stalled after the breakup or feeling as though one is progressing, moving forward, and learning to make better choices.

▲ Breakup Attributions

Attributions related to a past breakup are likely to inform relationship competence, personal growth, and satisfaction in future romantic relationships. A study conducted by Tashiro and Frazier (2003) with 92 undergraduates examined the attributions made by emerging adults and the emotional sequelae associated with these attributions.

Tashiro and Frazier hypothesized that the causes attributed to relationship breakups predict adaptation (e.g., blaming the ex-partner for the breakup, which is consistently associated with post-relationship distress). Four types of causal attributions for breakups were identified: *person* ("my mood," "my insensitivity"), *relational* ("communication problems," "value conflicts"), *environmental* ("work stress," "our friends were disruptive to the relationship") and *"other,"* referring to the ex-partner (e.g., "partner's mood," partner's insensitivity"). These types of causal attributions were examined in relationship to post-breakup growth. Participants who reported the most personal growth following breakup most frequently attributed this growth to specific (rather than general) traits and beliefs about the *person* (e.g., "I learned to admit when I am wrong;" Tashiro & Frazier, 2003, p. 120). The second most frequent attribution associated with positive growth tended to be *relational* in nature (e.g., "better communication," "I learned many relationship skills that I can apply in the future"). *Environmental* attributions were related to less distress *during* the relationship but more distress *after* the breakup, while, as noted previously, attributing the breakup chiefly to issues with the *other* person was linked to distress in the post-breakup period.

The authors found that the most adaptive attributions in response to relationship dissolution were those that were *external to the self* and *controllable*. When emerging adults were able to identify problems in their past romantic relationships and view them as solvable, their expectations for future relationships were positive. An ability to see the benefits of the breakup was associated with lower levels of depression, higher levels of life satisfaction, and higher levels of positive affect, excluding anxiety.

▲ Additional Post-Breakup Growth Factors

A few additional findings and considerations related to emerging adult breakups expand our understanding. In Tashiro and Frazier's study (2003), personality factors did not prove to be informative overall in explaining the variance in post-breakup growth. Neuroticism (especially as it gives rise to negative affect such as anger) was the only factor uniquely associated with greater post-breakup distress. Agreeableness (kindness, warmth, cooperativeness—qualities that enable the person to find social support following a breakup) was the only personality factor uniquely associated with greater growth.

Women reported greater emotional growth around breakups than men, a finding that was associated with women's greater attentiveness to relationship-oriented information (Cross & Madsen, 1997, as cited in Tashiro & Frazier, 2003). For example, Tashiro and Frazier hypothesized that greater attentional and observational skills enabled female participants to better assess relationship status and in turn make preparations for dissolution (Hill, Rubin, & Peplau, 1976, as cited in Tashiro & Frazier, 2003). Data for their study was based on self-report measures from individuals, not couples. Given the gender composition of the study (3/4 female), generalizability of the findings must be considered.

Learning to execute agency during a breakup is another factor that can be identified as a growth-enhancing experience. When a couple breaks up, there is usually an opportunity for one or both of the partners to learn to do things he or she formerly relied on the partner to do. Breakups also afford emerging adults the opportunity to learn about conflict and its resolution and the power of having clarifying conversations with their romantic partners, conversations that promote closure, integration, and maturity (Halpern-Meekin et al., 2012).

Breakups are "messy," and today's emerging adults engage in a number of behaviors related to breakups that inadvertently are likely to *magnify* the "messiness" rather than ameliorate it. Next, we will examine breakup-related behaviors, such as relationship churning and "remedy" and "statement" sex.

▲ Post-Breakup Sex With an Ex, Rebound Sex, and Revenge Sex

One way that emerging adults may deal with feelings of betrayal after a breakup is to employ sex as an emotional tool. Sex is often used to manage feelings and to gain a sense of control in a situation where one might feel like an emotional victim. Sex with an ex, rebound sex, and revenge sex are examples of behavioral adaptations made by some emerging adults in response to the dissolution of a romantic partnership.

In the case of sex with an ex, the couple has terminated the relationship but remains sexually connected. Sex with an ex has been described as a difficult or negative event (Koenig, Kellas, Bean, Cunningham & Cheng, 2008, as cited in Halpern-Meekin et al., 2012), because it contributes to the ambiguity of the relationship, and ambiguity is frequently associated with confusion, feelings of vulnerability, and a sense of being stuck or stalled.

Sex with an ex is also associated with increased risk of sexually transmitted infection (STI) or pregnancy if the couple reverts to the same contraceptive practices they were using toward the end of their relationship. That is because, as romantic partners get to know and trust each other over time, condom use, initially high early on in relationships, drops significantly (Civic, 2000; Manning, Giordano, & Longmore, 2006). Many people who would take careful precautions with a new or casual sex partner do not do so when having sex with a familiar ex. Adding to the STI risk factor is the possibility that one or both partners may be having sex with someone else at the time they reconnect with the ex. In fact, Halpern-Meekin et al. (2012) report that of their study participants who elected to have sex with an ex, only 37% were *not* having sex with other partners during the same time period.

Revenge sex—retaliatory sex with another person after the loss of a relationship partner—involves sexual encounters that are motivated primarily by the desire to make an ex-partner jealous or angry (Barber & Cooper, 2014). The actual sexual act may or may not ultimately be reported to the ex, but the motive has a vengeful aspect. By contrast, rebound sex—which also involves having sex with a new person shortly after a breakup—is typically motivated by feelings of low self-esteem and/or pain and loneliness associated with the loss (Barber & Cooper, 2014).

Using longitudinal data gathered over an 8-month period from diaries of 170 heterosexual students who recently broke up with their romantic partners, Barber and Cooper (2014) examined beliefs about whether and how the participants used sex as a way to get over, or get back at, their ex. These researchers found that emerging adults who reported having sex to cope with feelings of distress, anger, and low self-esteem continued to have sex with different partners during the duration of the study, suggesting that they were taking longer to get over the breakup than those who did not use sex in this manner. Participants who did not initiate the breakup were more likely to report feeling distressed and angry, and were more inclined to use sex as a way to deal with their loss.

A somewhat predictable pattern emerges with respect to the process of recovery (Barber & Cooper, 2014). On average, participants reported emotional distress during the first 6 months after breakup, but tended to recover after this 6-month period. Rebound and revenge motives stabilized between 13 and 16 weeks post-breakup. These patterns of recovery were observed in both men and women.

Should sex in response to relationship loss be regarded as risky, impulsive behavior to be avoided, or should it be viewed as a useful and potentially liberating step toward letting go and making room for moving forward in a positive direction? The answers to this question remain elusive; more research must be done and in all likelihood there is no "one size fits all" prescription.

To date, the limited research suggests that some emerging adults are able to use sex with a new partner as a healthy catalyst for "moving on." Others, however, seem to get drawn into the long-term habit of using sex to "treat" feelings of loneliness and anger toward the ex. When this behavior continues beyond approximately 8 months after breakup, it likely indicates the individual is having difficulty with the "moving on" process. A more complete theoretical picture is needed, one that incorporates the diversity of emerging adults and their sociocultural contexts. The public health implications must also be considered.

Relationship churning, the focus of the next section, is another topic ripe for further theoretical development and refinement.

▲ Churning Relationships

Churning relationships are defined by at least one breakup and reconciliation experience with a current dating partner. They occur in approximately 50% of emerging adulthood relationships (Dailey, McCracken, Jin, Rossetto, & Green, 2013), and on average last for no longer than a year (Halpern-Meekin et al., 2012). Couples in churning relationships typically reunite within 1 or 2 months after relationship stoppage (Dailey, Pfiester, Jin, Beck & Clark, 2009). Unlike in other romantic relationships of emerging adulthood, churning partners bring to the relationship their previous knowledge of the other, as well as their previous respective levels of relational commitment and their pre-established interactional patterns (Dailey, Hampel, & Roberts, 2010). The primary reason cited for terminating these relationships is ongoing and frequent conflict.

Why do emerging adults renew former romantic relationships, often repeatedly? Continued attachment to one's partner is a major reason (Dailey et al., 2010; Dailey et al., 2013). Close to 50% of the emerging-adult "relationship churners" interviewed spoke about missing their partners, still loving their partners, and/or feeling that they could not exist without their partners. Sprecher and Metts (1989) found that relationship churners were more likely to believe that love conquers all obstacles and that there was only one person for them: their ex-partner.

In an effort to better understand the types of churning relationships that emerging adults engage in, Dailey et al. (2013) asked 65 study participants (36 college students and 29 community members, mean age=24, 71% female) to describe communication patterns that characterized their interactions during each breakup and renewal. They also asked the participants to describe the level of explicitness the romantic partners used in defining, or redefining, their relationship during these transitions.

Dailey and colleagues identified five types of churning relationships among the study participants: *habitual, mismatched, capitalized-on-transitions, gradual separators,* and *controlling partner*.

Habitual participants fell back into previous relational patterns without resolving problematic issues. They showed apathy about the transition. The second type, mismatched, became cyclical in their relationship mainly because of misaligned needs, interests, or states of readiness (e.g., each partner was at a different life stage). The third type, capitalized-on-transitions, used the transitions as a way of managing problems or attempting to mobilize partners to change. The fourth type, gradual separators, gradually drifted apart, or with each subsequent transition became less interested in the relationship. The last type, controlling partner, was characterized by one partner's tendency to use manipulation or persistence to control and continue the relationship.

Capitalized-on-transitions and mismatched types engaged in more deliberate negotiation of transitions and reported the greatest relational quality in comparison to the other identified types. The capitalized-on-transitions types were most explicit in negotiating their breakups. The mismatched types were more explicit in their negotiations during transition and were most effective in negotiation of conflict.

Results revealed that churning relationships are more likely to end if: (a) both members of the couple perceive that the relationship has run its course, and/or (b) difficulties with the relationship are perceived as not likely to be resolved. It must be pointed out that the literature on churning relationships does not reflect the heterogeneity of emerging adults who enter these relationships. Emerging adults who engage in churning relationships differ from one another with respect to factors such as relational dynamics, structural considerations (such as length and number of previous on/off relationships), and stressors that impact their relationships (Dailey et al., 2013).

There is a lack of understanding about how to help emerging adults in the throes of churning relationships build more enduring resources. Vennum, Hardy, Sibley, and Fincham (2015) suggest that the lower dedication levels and greater relationship uncertainty reported in these relationships may be due to vague communication and nondeliberate decision making. The findings of Dailey et al. (2013) suggest that while some emerging adults view the reconciliations as temporary, others view them as more permanent, although this understanding might not be stated explicitly and thus might differ between partners. Each partner may have his/her own idea about where the relationship is going. Partners may also be more explicit with regard to defining the relationship, setting new terms or conditions, and/or agreeing upon the amount of contact they wish to have with one another after the breakup. Improved communication (e.g., more explicitness) around these issues, and a better mutual understanding of struggles the partners are having related to the transitions, can help emerging adults to more effectively negotiate their on again/off again relationships.

The churning relationship certainly cannot be held up as a model for long-term romantic satisfaction. However, the dynamics of these relationships have the potential to teach each of the partners important information about themselves—what they would like to seek or avoid in future relationships, for example—as well as important skills, such as establishing boundaries, negotiating breakups, listening, and advocating for oneself. Thus, transitional shifts may serve both positive and negative functions. While churning relationships can provide emerging adults with opportunities for clarity, growth, and mutual understanding, they can also trigger inertia, a pattern associated with sliding behaviors and a downward trajectory.

Breakups are difficult and untidy, and perhaps that is what is needed to help with their resolution. By engaging in behaviors that confuse and muddy the boundaries, emerging adults are testing their own tolerances and learning to find relational clarity from the inside out.

In the next section we will hear from our 29 study participants, whose thoughtful perspectives and life experiences will shed more light on the causes and outcomes of romantic breakups.

▲ Participant Responses

The 29 participants shared their experiences related to dissolving a previous romantic relationship. Participants were asked about reasons for their most recent breakup and anticipated breakup outcomes, both positive and negative. Two domains emerged from the data: (a) *reasons for breaking up*, and (b) *breakups, positive and negative sequelae*.

Reasons for Breaking Up

Participants were asked to provide a response to the question, "What are some of the reasons you or your partner ended a recent romantic relationship?" Their responses yielded five categories within the larger domain: (a) cheating, trust, and growth; (b) diminishing investment in the relationship; (c) inability to envision a happy future; (d) depression, anxiety, and regulating affect; and (e) physical and emotional abuse.

Cheating, trust, and growth

Nineteen of the participants identified "cheating" as a major reason for ending a romantic relationship, generating a *typical* category. Monogamy was considered sacred, and violations a definite "deal breaker" for 17 of the 19 participants. A few participants spoke of "forgiving and forgetting" and trying to work things out; however, Michael's (27) conclusion with respect to cheating represented a majority point of view: "If you cheat, it is over."

Cheating was considered an assault on participants' hopes for the possibility of building a future together. Trust was viewed by most participants as a necessary and non-negotiable relationship ingredient which, if in short supply, would end possibilities for growth as a couple. Growth, notably, was considered by most of the participants to be critical to the viability of the relationship.

Some of the participants grappled with the question: Can I envision a future with the person if there is no trust? They tended to conclude that they could not, and that ending the relationship was a logical and inevitable outcome of a major breach of trust. Cheating, trust, and possibilities for continued growth were critical considerations in making the decision to break up with a romantic partner. Rhonda (22) states, "I just think cheating . . . losing trust in your partner, if you don't see . . . any more room for growth in that relationship, then I think that that's a good time to break up." Angela (27) states: "You can no longer see a future with that person [if he cheats on you]. . . . If you feel you cannot trust them, that is a good reason [to break up]." Ellen (24) shares Angela's perspective: "Cheating is like the absolute betrayal of trust for me."

Diminishing investment in the relationship

Seventeen participants spoke about loss of investment in the relationship, "not feeling it anymore," and no longer being "emotionally on board," citing this as a major reason for ending a relationship. These responses yielded a *typical* category. Reasons for diminishing investment were diverse, including no longer being sexually attracted to the person; not "really knowing" the person; recognition that hopes of changing the person would end in frustration; differences in temperament, drive, and professional ambition; feeling it is "not the right time" for a relationship; not feeling understood and validated; and increased recognition that the two partners' interests and/or goals were not compatible (e.g., self-development versus building a foundation that includes a home and children).

Ellen (24) summarizes the rationale that her ex-partner provided at the time he elected to end their relationship, along with her reactions:

> He broke up with me and he was just like, I don't want to be in a relationship right now. [My reaction was], I'm not going to hold this grudge against you for breaking up with me. It hurts, but I'm not going to blame someone for not feeling it anymore.

Within this category of diminishing investment in the relationship, participants' responses were organized into two subcategories: (a) caring and personal growth, and (b) holding on.

Caring and personal growth. Within this group, five participants expressed the view that when you no longer care about the person, you no longer are invested in the relationship: "not feeling it anymore," "you are unhappy . . . with yourself and no longer happy seeing him walk through the door anymore," and it is time to "move on."

Becky (24) emphasized the importance of assessing the level of caring within the relationship as well as opportunities for personal growth. She concluded that "nothing positive can happen if the relationship is not a caring one." She also stated that she valued personal growth and that if those two core ingredients, caring and growth, were missing, disinvestment in the relationship would be a likely outcome.

> When you stop caring about the other person, being with them, and it is holding them back and yourself, nothing positive can happen . . . you've grown . . . to a point, like, where this person is not helping you grow anymore.

Holding on. Within this group, three participants spoke of having disinvested in the relationship, yet they were "holding on" and unable to let go of it in a timely way. They explained that they held on to something that "used to be there," "dragged it [on for] too long." All three of the participants in this subgroup concluded that ending the relationship at an earlier juncture would have been preferable. They felt that they prolonged their relationships when there were clear signs that it was time to disinvest. In the words of Tina (27):

> We both kind of dragged it on another couple of months when it should have been called off. I got very hurt when that happened to me, and I ended up hurting the guy when it happened to him because we didn't recognize, hey, this is a good reason to break up. I know our emotions go up and down and you don't want to just emotionally make some [impulsive decision] . . . [but] the person who didn't have those feelings anymore knew it, and knew it for a period of time, and still didn't call things off.

Angela (27) talked about holding on too long because of a reluctance to let go of the feeling of being loved by another.

> I think if you are really feeling like you are holding on because maybe that other person really likes you and loves you, you are not feeling it anymore and . . . holding on to something that used to be there, I think that is a reason to break up.

As Tina wisely points out, "emotions go up and down," so perhaps it is sometimes necessary to "hold on" to a relationship a bit longer than necessary, in order to assure oneself that the romantic feelings are *truly* gone and that one is not ending the partnership prematurely. Learning to recognize the difference between a relationship lull and an "it's over" is one of the key skills emerging adults are able to refine in their early relationships.

Inability to envision a happy future

Five participants spoke of entering relationships in the present and discovering that, as the relationship unfolded, they were imposing future-oriented evaluation criteria on it. In the process of getting to know the other person, they found themselves shifting toward evaluating the long-term potential of the relationship. A *variant* category was thus created to capture the shift that occurred for this group of participants.

In considering possibilities for a future life together, these five participants came to the conclusion that they could not envision themselves being happy with their partner in the long run. Their newly constructed narratives regarding how the relationship was likely to unfold revealed underlying problems to them. The disjuncture between the future they envisioned and the realities on the ground—especially as pertained to possibilities for growth—mobilized them to disinvest from the relationship: "If you're growing apart, you're not growing together, [and then it is time to end the relationship]." Greta and Tina shared a common perspective on romantic relationships: relationships need to move forward. Growing together for "the long term" was a necessary pre-condition for considering a future together. Stagnation was not an acceptable outcome and was viewed as a reason for ending the relationship.

GRETA: I broke up with my previous partner because I did not see a future with him and I felt like I was wasting both of our time. I was missing out on an opportunity to find someone better, and robbing him of the same opportunity.

TINA: There was some uncertainty about whether or not we would choose the same sort of lifestyle down the road. . . . We were both kind of hoping the other person would turn out to be a little bit different than we actually were . . . and not realizing that could have been really bad in the end.

There was an implied expectation among most of the participants that partners would grow and develop over time in ways that were compatible. If a relationship "is not going anywhere" and no longer provides meaning, happiness, and/or benefit to one or both parties, then it is time to end it.

Depression, anxiety, and regulating affect

Five of the participants spoke of having emotional struggles and, in some cases, also spoke of their partners' troubled reactions to those struggles, yielding a *variant* category. Mark (24) lamented his breakup with a previous partner:

> I scared him sometimes because I get so emotional and overreact to things so much that it . . . [got] scary [for him]. . . . I think that it's just [that] I get very insecure and vulnerable around him and that was always a "turn-off. . . ." And I think he was just never open with me about the fact that things about me, my personality, and my nature were starting to upset him.

Leslie (27) reported currently struggling with depression and said that she ended a previous relationship because she needed to be in a healthier place emotionally:

> What I'm going through is a really, really, tough, tough time. I [have been] dealing with depression these past two months, and I don't know if that vibe ended [the relationship] for me, but it just wasn't the right time.

For these participants, emotional issues were viewed as more acute than could be handled within the bounds of a relationship; thus a breakup was required.

Physical and/or emotional abuse

In discussing reasons for leaving a relationship, five participants identified abuse as a game changer, yielding a *variant* category. Cassandra (22) and Rhonda (22) spoke of being abused both emotionally and/or physically. Cassandra concludes, "A good reason to leave is if that person is just bad for you. Like you're constantly hurt, you're emotionally hurt or physically hurt or anything like that, those are good reasons." Rhonda asserts: "If they hit you in a way that you do not wanna be touched . . . [it] is a good reason, or if they abuse you mentally or emotionally."

Breakups, Positive and Negative Sequelae

Participants spoke of their breakups and the aftereffects thereof in both positive and negative terms, generating this second domain. Participants tended to link their breakups to reasons such as the style of entry into the relationship (not taking the time to get to know the person), the qualities they prioritized when initially selecting their partner, and changes in the individual(s) or in the relationship itself that had occurred over time.

Participants were asked to respond to the following two questions: (a) "Breakups can change you in positive and negative ways. Can you describe a recent negative outcome of a breakup that influenced your future relationship with a romantic partner?" and (b) "Can you describe a recent positive outcome of a breakup that influenced your future relationship with a romantic partner?" Two categories were thus generated: positive sequelae and negative sequelae.

Positive sequelae

Twenty-four participants spoke about their positive experiences after the breakup. They tended to view the process itself as painful, but necessary, for emotional growth. They learned about navigating loss, which allowed them to achieve greater clarity, perspective, and direction related to romantic relationships. Cam (23) sums up his experience with breaking up with a partner: "Breakups allow for growth. I learned about the process of recovery."

Some of the participants spoke of the importance of self-agency in response to loss. Amelia (24) became cognizant of her "personal strength":

> In losing the relationship, you lose your foundation. In the
> process, you find a new normalcy that does not involve the other,
> [as well as] your own source of strength and new paths that
> include new people and new relationships, finding your way.

Rhonda (22) acknowledges that she "did not realize what a good man was." She feels that she now has a better idea of what she needs in a relationship and has learned that breaking up "is a process" that leads to self-discovery.

> Even though [the breakup] was heartbreaking, I realized it will eventually be okay. Even though it is hard to break up, it will get easier. I realized I need to have power in a relationship . . . to cut off a relationship when it is not working out.

Rhonda feels that she now has a better sense of herself, increased confidence in her ability to exert her "power," and the strength to be who she wants to be within a relationship with a "good man."

Mateo (27) spoke about breaking up with his previous partner and what he has learned: "I have learned now when I break up with someone, I am clear and straightforward with my intentions. I don't try to salvage the relationship. I think the approach is better in the long run for both of us."

Participants provided a lens for seeing the value of narrative theory in action. They were able to frame their breakups within an overall narrative of growth and see them as learning experiences.

Negative sequelae

Twenty-one participants spoke of negative sequelae, yielding a *typical* category. Feelings of hurt and difficulty with trust were commonly reported issues. Reinvesting in another person who might hurt them again was a concern that led some of the participants to withdraw from serious relationships for a time and/or become "less open":

> MARK: I was so hurt. . . . For a long time, and even to this day, I was a little afraid of dating other people, to go on dates and have hooks-ups and meet people. . . . There's a part of me that is wary about dating because I'm afraid of getting hurt again.
>
> KATHERINE: I have a very serious trust issue . . . even as comfortable as I am with [my current boyfriend], [I] still [speculate] that he's texting some girl right now. That he's, like, flirting with someone, or talking to one of his ex-girlfriends. . . . I'm always suspicious. And that has caused problems for us at times.

Caution. Thirteen participants alluded to learning, through the breakup experience, to be more cautious in making relationship selections, hoping to stem their inclinations toward rushing into things.

> JOSEPH: I have pushed back, not getting involved in a relationship with somebody serious[ly] so quickly. I have been looking to see where things go and not get too serious about somebody that fast.
>
> MATEO: It's hard to trust in somebody. . . . I'm going to be more cautious, I will have judgement. . . . I will slow down a lot.

Many of these breakup sequelae could be viewed as either positive or negative, yet, interestingly enough, participants' interpretations of the outcomes tended to assume a negative tone, specifically in regard to becoming more cautious. For example, as participants revealed that they had become more "cautious" about potential future trust violations, they expressed concern that they would become more emotionally "closed."

▲ Analysis of Findings

Participants generously shared their experiences with romantic relationship breakups. Although the findings tended to support the existing literature, nuanced differences also became apparent, differences in emphasis, particularly regarding infractions such as cheating. The importance of nurturing emotional growth within the relationship, both individually and collectively, was also a prominent concern for our research participants. Many of the participants stated that lack of growth within a relationship was a strong reason for ending that partnership.

Participants were highly attuned to the negative sequelae of breakups: their narratives focused on the residual effects of "cheating" and violations of trust, experiences that made them hesitant, "cautious" and/or emotionally "closed." They were sensitive to past infractions and the possibility of the same infractions occurring again in their futures. Some, in turn, were wary of forming new attachments because of this.

The findings of Kluwer and Karremans (2009) suggest that infidelity is one of the "most serious forms of violating relationship norms" (p. 1299), a finding confirmed by our participants. When trust is violated, self-doubt, humiliation, jealousy, depression, and/or anxiety are likely sequelae, feelings that were reported by many of our participants. Barber and Cooper (2014) report that in the aftermath of a breakup, emerging adults often avoid their ex-partners and other romantic relationships for a time, or engage in time-limited behaviors such as revenge sex or rebound sex in an attempt to assuage feelings of betrayal and hurt.

Critical events such as cheating can change commitment levels within the relationship and serve as turning points in the development and dissolution of relationships (Dailey et al., 2013). While some problematic behaviors may be successfully negotiated during these critical periods, resulting in personal and relationship growth, others may be deemed more intractable. Fidelity infractions tended to be viewed by our participants as non-negotiable. Forgiveness was not seen as an option for most of the participants. As a developmental factor, however, research indicates that capacity for forgiveness increases with age and is, in fact, associated with longevity in marriages (Aalgaard, Bolen, & Nugent, 2016; Allemand, 2008).

The ability to deal with loss is another skill associated with maturity. The mature person is one who "acknowledge[s] loss," but is not defined by it (King & Hicks, 2007, p. 630). Emerging adults, in the process of adapting to loss, learn how to maintain focus and energy toward their current goals and also commit to new futures with new partners. Disengaging from former relationship goals and dreams, and constructing a renewed self that can focus on the good that is yet to come, become a priority. For some of the participants, the process of disengagement and the construction of new selves was incomplete. Past infractions served as a source of anxiety about the future, and participants had trouble engaging in a renewal process.

The predominantly negative interpretation of the sequelae to breakup was noteworthy. Perhaps this was because participants spoke mostly about their most recent breakups. They may have been too close emotionally to these experiences to view their relationships with distance and perspective. Periods of reflection and evaluation may not have occurred yet.

The participants were concerned and cautious about future betrayals and violations of trust, a caution that can either serve them well or close them off emotionally, depending upon how it is lived and interpreted. Narrative theory could be beneficial in this regard. A counselor or other helping professional working with emerging adults might find it fruitful to encourage them to reframe their narratives in a more growth-oriented way. Most of the participants did seem open to viewing their breakups as learning experiences, and many of them could perhaps benefit from creating more positive, forward-looking narratives, as opposed to narratives geared toward simply recovering or "bouncing back."

The woundedness and guardedness that some of the participants evidenced may be a sign that they are working from entity theory as opposed to incremental theory. That is, rather than seeing the self as a fluid, unfolding process capable of dynamic, ongoing redefinition, they may be viewing it as a fixed entity. They may, therefore, be experiencing rejection and/or relationship violations as attacks on their core selves. And to the extent that they are feeling stuck and reluctant to move on, they may be attributing the *cause* of the breakup to the other person and seeing that person as the source of their wounded trust. Shifting the attribution onto the self and/or the relationship dynamics would more likely serve to stir forward movement. With the passage of time, however, more nuanced narratives may naturally emerge among the participants (Kluwer & Karreman, 2009).

What was consistent in their narratives and emblematic of this transitional period of development, is the degree to which they emphasized the importance of growth within relationships. If a relationship was deemed to "not [be] going anywhere," it was time to end it. This prevailing sentiment was also consistent with an emerging literature that suggests that emerging adults—particularly those who are well resourced—are increasingly prioritizing growth in relationships, a topic that will be covered in greater depth in Chapter 10 on marriage. Howe and Dweck (2015) report that individuals who believe in growth and development can more easily recover from breakups and orient themselves toward a positive future.

This study did not control for variables such as time elapsed since breakup, duration of relationship, and current dating status, important considerations that are likely to influence participants' assessments of their breakups. Other factors that can contribute to positive adaptation include the quality of parental bonding and availability of social supports, factors that were not considered in this analysis. Commitment levels among the participants were also not assessed—however, a range was evident. Some of the participants, when talking about their respective breakups, were clearly committed to the relationship; others were less invested and tended to take a shorter view. Finally, we did not ask how many of the participants were on the receiving end of a breakup and how many did the initiating. Approximately one half of our participants were not in committed romantic relationships at the time of our study.

Loss is a dominant theme when discussing breakups. A history devoid of loss is an incomplete history (King & Raspin, 2004); nearly all adults, at one time or another, must deal with the loss of important people and relationships. Growth entails accepting loss, looking un-flinchingly at what might have been, and developing the capacity to reinvest and risk loss once again.

In the next section, we will look at two study participants who serve as examples of emerging adults who have endured relationship loss. Belissa, a 28-year-old heterosexual woman, is encountering difficulties with coming to terms with her loss and risking loss once again, while Mark, a 24-year-old gay male, has recently rewritten his narrative with renewed confidence in himself and his capacity to find a more satisfying relationship in the future.

▲ Belissa: A Struggle to Let Go

Belissa, a 28-year-old Latina American, is currently single and living with her parents. She is still reeling from the dissolution of a 5-year com-mitted romantic partnership that ended 4 years ago. Belissa's biggest regret in life is holding on to this relationship for so long, ignoring both her intuition and the advice of family and friends.

When asked what comes to mind when she thinks of a romantic re-lationship, Belissa's immediate response is brief and to the point: "mar-riage." When prompted to expand on this response, she includes happiness, joy, and being best friends. Her ideal relationship would in-clude being able to tell her partner "anything that I'm feeling, and that he will support me—and I will be the same for him." She expects her ideal partner to come to her first for advice and support. But most of all for Belissa, who is a practicing Catholic, a romantic relationship needs to move toward marriage and family.

Belissa's hopes for her next serious romantic relationship appear to be influenced by her assessment of her previous partner. In that re-lationship, Belissa mistook her partner's cavalier attitude and sarcastic comments about children and getting married for immature humor. Ultimately, however, their mismatched goals for the future led to the ending of the relationship and left Belissa wrestling with her expecta-tions for her romantic life.

He knew that I wanted to get married and he at first said yeah, he was also thinking about marriage and stuff, but later on, towards the end, he kept telling me that he wasn't ready. . . . [He] still wanted to be with me, but he wasn't ready to commit. And for me that was a big thing because I felt like, if you're not planning to get married then what are we doing here?

Belissa describes her relationship as a "roller coaster" in which at times she felt excited and optimistic that the relationship could work, and at other times felt sad and cried "a lot," unable to understand how her partner was apparently changing. When they met in college at age 18, they bonded over their shared faith. But as her partner began focusing on medical school and moving out of state to pursue his education, Belissa felt his priorities shift. He was no longer thinking about commitment, marriage, and starting a family, but rather was focusing on his career. He made mocking comments about her belief in God, which hurt her deeply. After they both graduated, Belissa recalls thinking that the relationship could not continue:

I decided that I wasn't going to pursue this anymore with him and he was on the same page [about that]. . . . I felt like I got hurt more than he did, and that made me feel really bad, because I felt like he didn't really care. . . . I felt like he just didn't love me enough, that's how I felt.

Despite knowing her ex was not a good fit, and that the relationship did not meet her expectations, Belissa continues to have difficulty "moving on."

I have this guard in my heart that I just don't allow anybody to come into my life. There have been other men at times, and I just think back to what happened with him and that makes me back off and not even try. . . . We had the same values in the beginning and they just changed, so I think I'm . . . fearful about that.

Belissa is also confused by the fact that her ex continues to reach out to her via Facebook and to inquire about how she's doing through her friends.

In the wake of her breakup, Belissa reassessed her priorities as well as the qualities she is looking for in a partner. She knows now that, above all, she wants someone who is "committed to his faith" and is able to balance his dedication to her and to his career. She remains optimistic that she can find a satisfying romantic partnership and achieve her dreams of marriage and family. And yet, after 4 years, she is still stinging from the disillusionment of her failed relationship. At this time, she prefers to stay "just friends" with new men she meets, in order to avoid vulnerability and developing "any emotional attachment to them."

▲ Mark: Forging a New Narrative

Mark, currently pursuing a degree in theater and creative writing, identifies himself as an "old fashioned romantic" who would "be surprised if [he] didn't get married." While Mark remains optimistic about finding a satisfying romantic commitment, two difficult breakups have left him wondering what he has to offer to a partner, and whether he should expect more from relationships. Although his first love is the arts and he tries to take freelance theater work whenever possible, Mark primarily works for his father, who owns a flooring company. Mark describes himself as ethnically Jewish, but does not affiliate with any organized religion. While Mark presently views himself as a "conventionally attractive" male, he was quite overweight as an adolescent, a factor that continues to contribute to feelings of low self-esteem and hesitation about dating. He reflects:

> I've kind of just let the [other] person take on so much of the
> power that I feel like there are actually very few times where . . .
> I've made a decision, except for the decision to just go with
> the flow.

A "go with the flow" attitude has put Mark in tumultuous territory. He describes his experience of losing his virginity at age 21 as questionably "date rape," but he also describes it as "beautiful." Mark has had two past romantic partnerships that he describes as "boyfriend" relationships. In both cases, his ex-partners were "critical" of him and unaffectionate at the end of the relationship. These experiences have left him feeling insecure and without control in his romantic relationships, and he reports feeling a need to reassess his romantic life.

In a "rebuilding" posture a year and a half after his most recent breakup, Mark is wary of "lies" that past partners have told, especially about their feelings toward him and their level of sexual satisfaction. He shares that while his most recent ex-partner came on strong at first, the relationship began to fade. Mark describes the unstable feeling when his partner began to withdraw:

> I would constantly want to talk about the state of the relationship and how he felt about me, and he would never want to talk about it. When I kept pressing him about it, he would get mad. . . .
> When he did talk about it—looking back—frequently he was just dishonest about how he felt about me. So, I just wish he was a lot more candid and honest with me.

Mark discloses that in his previous committed relationship, his partner believed they had broken up a full month before Mark was aware of this; perhaps this fact is contributing to his hypersensitivity about relationship status. In the second case, Mark was the one to initiate the breakup, as he became aware that the lack of affection between him and his partner was making him feel bad. Mark suspects that a combination of caution and insecurity has trapped him in a cycle of being needy, seeking too much reassurance, and pushing partners away:

> I regretted basically letting my insecurities show through so much to my ex because I felt like if he hadn't seen me as so insecure, he wouldn't have become so detached from me.

Following his breakup, low self-esteem and negative self-talk increasingly plagued Mark, and he questioned his desirability as a romantic partner. A string of casual encounters seemed to reinforce his feelings about himself as unworthy. He also reconnected with past casual partners and was surprised by what he learned:

> To this day—ever since *him* [referring to his previous partner]—almost every time that I have been in a romantic situation with someone I tend to assume the worst. . . . I had a lot of one-night stands and I spent a long time . . . wondering why was it that no one ever seemed to want to spend more than one night with me. . . . Is it about my body when I take off my clothes? Is it something to do with my personality? . . . I started going back and talking to people that I had what I thought were one-night stands a long time ago. I realized that there were lots and lots of

people who I had *thought* didn't want to see me again, and I was completely wrong!

Mark is aware of patterns of interactions that he wishes to change. He remains unsure about how to navigate the intersection of what he is looking for personally and the cultural expectations of dating in a "gay, metropolitan" scene. Still "curious" about what is "normal" in terms of dating, casual sex, and commitment, Mark states, "I don't know what I want. I almost feel like I'm at a point in my life where I want to start avoiding preconceived ideals that I create and try to just accept interactions as they come." At the same time, his ideal partner is not unlike what other emerging adults are looking for: someone who is "affectionate and supportive, gives a lot of positive reinforcement to me, and also wants us to work together to do various kinds of exciting life-development projects."

Mark continues to worry about being hurt in future relationships and is aware of his tendency to "oversacrifice" his own needs. He concludes, however, that "every breakup has been positive in the sense of dodging a bullet." He finds that his experiences of dating and breaking up have also been learning and growth opportunities. Shortly before his participation in the study, he experienced a sense of "release":

> I kind of woke up and I was very at peace with everything and was happy that it was over. And so I think this was the most meaningful breakup in the sense that I am now able to see there were a lot of . . . wonderful parts of this relationship. As much as [my ex] could be very critical and mean to me sometimes, he was also very encouraging. . . . At the end of the day I'm even more confident than I was six months ago, just because of the experience of dating him. It's kind of a wonderful double-edged sword, that I'm happy that it's over but I'm also able to look back and see [that I'm] a better person than I was when I met him.

The way we perceive and narrate the experience of loss is critical to our ability to move forward, as exemplified by these two narratives. Mark presents himself as somewhat more flexible and able to revise his narrative in a forward-looking way. Thus he would seem to be somewhat secure in his attachment style, despite his descriptions of himself as insecure. He is able to reflect on his experiences and reassess his beliefs and attitudes towards himself and his previous two relationships. He also seems to embrace what Howe and Dweck would term malleable beliefs about the self (incremental theory), as demonstrated by his description of himself evolving into a better person via his most recent, albeit failed, relationship. His final quotation suggests a discrete turning point for him, in which he took a deeper step toward this way of thinking.

Belissa, on the other hand, seems to represent a more fixed view of the self (entity theory). She seems to view her breakup quite personally; she has not "moved on" in the 4 years since the breakup occurred, and has become admittedly guarded. She fiercely holds on to her goal of marriage, but it is not clear, in the 4 years since her breakup, whether she has revised her narrative in ways that will help her disengage from her previous relationship, move on, and invest in expanded goals beyond seeking marriage. Her inability to rewrite her narrative in a more positive way, along with her prolonged avoidance of men and the possibility of a new relationship, would suggest an avoidant attachment style.

When Belissa and her romantic partner met at the age of 18 they were both in a period of transition, trying to establish themselves vocationally. Arnett (2004) asserts that few emerging adults at transitional junctures have clarity of focus across all domains. Belissa seems to have difficulty viewing herself and her ex-partner contextually; her partner was searching for meaning with respect to his religious life, whereas Belissa was, and continues to be, certain about her faith. Belissa tends to view her partner's changing point of view on spiritual matters as betrayal rather than as an evolution. Can she become flexible enough to incorporate the idea that the path that she chose was perhaps no longer a good fit for her partner?

What is common to Mark and Belissa is that they are both looking for partners who are more honest, clear, and steadfast in what they bring to the relationship. They are both looking for a partner who is upfront and does not leave them disillusioned. Both seem to have learned important lessons through their previous relationships and are trying, if haltingly and imperfectly, to apply those lessons to the next relationship.

▲ Summary and Conclusions

Breaking up a romantic relationship represents a substantial and painful loss. However, it also represents an almost unmatched opportunity for maturation and growth. Both the literature and the experiences of the 29 study participants strongly support the idea that *how* one processes loss, to a large extent, determines how productively and quickly one recovers from the loss and is ready to experience growth. A review of the literature suggests ways in which emerging adults can orient themselves toward growth, rather than stagnation, in the wake of a breakup: adopting an expanded narrative that views a breakup as an opportunity for self-discovery; learning to view the self as a malleable entity capable of constant reinvention; and avoiding fixating on the ex-partner as a source of pain and/or betrayal.

Maturity lies at the "intersection of happiness and complexity," and loss can help catalyze that convergence (King & Hicks, 2007, p. 634). The mature adult is informed by loss but not defined by it. When a loss is experienced fully, it forces one to rewrite one's internal scripts about happiness and to revise one's sense of self. While too much focus on lost possible selves can be maladaptive, as suggested by the case of Belissa, the full felt experience of loss *can* bring insight. By exploring what "might have been," along with all the related emotions that are triggered, opportunities unfold to clarify what one wants for one's future. The narrative can shift to one that privileges "what is" and "what will be," while recognizing the importance of "what has been."

Emerging adults are still developing during this transitional period. Perhaps some of the behaviors they engage related to breakups—such as rebound sex and relationship churning—are actually ways that enable growth. By inviting emotionally challenging experiences into their lives, they are giving themselves a "crash course" in relationship management. Provided they can maintain the belief that growth is the main goal for romantic relationships, as the 29 participants appear to be doing, then it may be that they will be able to use all aspects of the relationship process, including the breakups, as springboards for further self-development.

▲ References

Aalgaard, R. A., Bolen, R. M., & Nugent, W. R. (2016). A literature review of forgiveness as a beneficial intervention to increase relationship satisfaction in couples therapy. *Journal of Human Behavior in the Social Environment, 26*(1), 46–55. doi:10.1080/10911359.2015.1059166

Allemand, M. (2008). Age differences in forgivingness: The role of future time perspective. *Journal of Research in Personality, 42*(5), 1137–1147. doi:10.1016/j.jrp.2008.02.009

Arnett, J. J. (2004). *Emerging adulthood: The winding road from the late teens through the twenties*. New York, NY: Oxford University Press.

Barber, L. L., & Cooper, M. L. (2014). Rebound sex: Sexual motives and behaviors following a relationship breakup. *Archives of Sexual Behavior, 43*(2), 251–265. doi:10.1007/s10508-013-0200-3

Bartholomew, K., & and Horowitz, L. M. (1991). Attachment styles among young adults: A test of a four-category model. *Journal of Personality and Social Psychology, 61,* 226. http://dx.doi.org/101037/0022-3514.61.2.226

Binstock, G., & Thornton, A. (2003). Separations, reconciliations and living apart in cohabiting and marital unions. *Journal of Marriage and Family, 65*(2), 432–443. doi:10.1111/j.1741-3737.2003. 00432.x

Civic, D. (2000). College students' reasons for nonuse of condoms within dating relationships. *Journal of Sex and Marital Therapy, 26*(1), 95–105. doi:10.1080/009262300278678

Dailey, R. M., Hampel, A. D., & Roberts, J. (2010). Relational maintenance in on-again/off-again relationships: An assessment of how relational maintenance, uncertainty, and relational quality vary by relationship type and status. *Communication Monographs, 77,* 75–101. doi:10.1080=03637750903514292

Dailey, R. M., Jin, B., Pfiester, A., & Beck, G. (2011). On-again/off-again dating relationships: What keeps partners coming back? *The Journal of Social Psychology, 151*(4), 417–440. doi:10.1080/00224545.2010.503249

Dailey, R. M., McCracken, A. A., Jin, B., Rossetto, K. R., & Green, E. W. (2013). Negotiating breakups and renewals: Types of on-again/off-again dating relationships. *Western Journal of Communication, 77*(4), 382–410. doi:10.1080/10570314.2013.775325

Dailey, R. M., Pfiester, A., Jin, B., Beck, G., & Clark, G. (2009). On-again/off-again dating relationships: How are they different from other dating relationships? *Personal Relationships, 16,* 23–47. doi:10.1111=j.1475–6811.2009. 01208.x

Davis, D., Shaver, P. R., & Vernon, M. L. (2003). Physical, emotional, and behavioral reactions to breaking up: The roles of gender, age, emotional involvement and attachment style. *Journal of Personality and Social Psychology, 29*(7), 871–884. doi:10.1177/0146167203252884.

Field, T., Diego, M., Pelaez, M., Deeds, O., & Delgado, J. (2009). Breakup distress in university students. *Adolescence, 44*(176), 705–727.

Gilbert, S. P., & Sifers, S. K. (2011). Bouncing back from a breakup: Attachment, time perspective, mental health, and romantic loss. *Journal of College Student Psychotherapy, 25*(4), 295–310. doi:10.1080/87568225.2011.605693

Halpern-Meekin, S., Manning, W. D., Giordano, P. C., & Longmore, M. A. (2012). Relationship churning in emerging adulthood: On/off relationships and sex with an ex. *Journal of Adolescent Research, 28*(2), 166–188. doi:10.1177/0743558412464524

Howe, L. C., & Dweck, C. S. (2015). Changes in self-definition impede recovery from rejection. *Personality and Social Psychology Bulletin, 42*(1), 54–71. doi:10.1177/0146167215612743

King, L. A., & Hicks, J. A. (2007). Whatever happened to "What might have been"? Regrets, happiness, and maturity. *American Psychologist, 62*(7), 625–636.

King, L. A., & Raspin, C. (2004). Lost and found possible selves, subjective well-being, and ego development in divorced women. *Journal of Personality*, 72(3), 603–632. doi:10.1111/j.0022-3506.2004. 00274.x

Kluwer, E. S & Karremans, J. (2009). Unforgiving motivations following infidelity: Should we make peace with our past? *Journal of Social and Clinical Psychology*, 28(10), 1298–1325.

Knox, D., Zusman, M. E., & Nieves, W. (1998). Breaking away: How college students end love relationships. *College Student Journal*, 32(4), 482–484.

Lewandowski, G. J. (2011, August 17). Relationships 101: Having healthy relationships in your first year of college. *Science of relationships*. Retrieved from http://www.scienceofrelationships.com/home/2011/8/17/relationships-101-having-healthy-relationships-in-your-first.html

Lewandowski, G. J., & Bizzoco, N. M. (2007). Addition through subtraction: Growth following the dissolution of a low-quality relationship. *The Journal of Positive Psychology*, 2(1), 40–54. doi:10.1080/17439760601069234

Manning, W. D., Giordano, P. C., & Longmore, M. A. (2006). Adolescent dating relationships: Implications for understanding adult unions. *Center for family and demographic research*. Bowling Green State University. Bowling Green, Ohio.

Parker, C. B. (2016). Stanford research explains why some people have more difficulty recovering from romantic relationships. *Stanford News*. https://news.stanford.edu/2016/01/07/self-definition-breakups-010716

Samios, C., Henson, D. F., & Simpson, H. J. (2014). Benefit finding and psychological adjustment following a non-marital relationship breakup. *Journal of Relationships Research*, 5, 1–8. doi:http://dx.doi.org.ezproxy.lib.umb.edu/10.1017/jrr.2014.6

Sprecher, S., & Metts, S. (1989). Development of the 'Romantic Beliefs Scale' and examination of the effects of gender and gender-role orientation. *Journal of Social and Personal Relationships*, 6(4), 387–411. doi:10.1177/0265407589064001

Tashiro, T., & Frazier, P. (2003). "I'll never be in a relationship like that again": Personal growth following romantic relationship breakups. *Personal Relationships*, 10(1), 113–128. doi:10.1111/1475-6811.00039

Vennum, A., Hardy, N., Sibley, D. S., & Fincham, F. D. (2015). Dedication and sliding in emerging adult cyclical and non-cyclical romantic relationships. *Family Relations*, 64(3), 407–419. doi:10.1111/fare.12126

8 ▲

Pathways Toward Adulthood
Building Roads, Creating Detours in Work and Love

> *I know myself more now. I understand myself and*
> *I know who I am now as a person and I like sharing*
> *that with another person. And I know what I am*
> *looking for, [because] my education has helped me*
> *define my inner strength. I can see certain things.*
> *I know what to share and what not to share. And*
> *I know what to look for and what not to look for. . . .*
> *[If] I was not educated, I think I would have been*
> *insecure [in the relationship].*
>
> —Joseph, 25, a research participant

> *We owe so much money. . . . That has been a huge*
> *source of stress for us. And that is the part of the*
> *reason why I still live at home. I think if we had . . .*
> *started working after graduating from college, we*
> *would be further than where we are now, in terms*
> *of moving out. But he has hundreds of thousands*
> *of dollars still in debt and I had a lot when I first*
> *started working.*
>
> —Angela, 27, a research participant

Emerging adults face the daunting task of consolidating and integrating their work lives and their romantic lives at a time in history when both realms are in flux. Each of these domains, work and love, presents its own distinct challenges, and there is no one-size-fits-all approach to successfully coordinating and meshing these important life tasks. The integration of love and work is "uniquely expressed" for each individual and couple (Roisman, Masten, Coatsworth, & Tellegen, 2004, as cited in Mayseless & Keren, 2014, p. 64). Differences in expression frequently require individual solutions. Decisions made during this transitional period, however, are likely to leave their footprints and shape emerging adults' future behaviors and goals in both domains (Shulman & Connolly, 2013).

Emerging adults face a work environment that is global in scope, highly competitive, and in transition with significant disruptions in the marketplace (Carnevale, Hanson, & Fulish, 2017; Hettich, 2010). Fluidity, unpredictability, and uncertainty prevail, not unlike emerging adults' personal lives, which are also unstable, fluid, and in the process of sweeping rule revision. Cast adrift in the current of a labor market that is in constant turbulence, emerging adults must learn to adapt and be flexible (Fouad & Bynner, 2008). Rules that guided previous generations have broken down, and no clear alternative guidelines are in place (Konstam, 2015).

When and how emerging adults transition into their careers frequently informs how they negotiate other domains in their lives, such as romance (Settersten & Ray, 2010; Luyckx, Seiffge-Krenke, Schwartz, Crocetti, & Klimstra, 2014). The reverse is also the case, although for many emerging adults, work-related identity exploration and mastery takes precedence over the romantic domain (Luyckx et al., 2014). In the United States, a country that celebrates self-reliance, many emerging adults are embarking on committed relationships only when they reach the point where they feel ready—financially and emotionally—for the responsibilities associated with such relationships (Shulman, Seiffge-Krenke, Scharf, Boiangiu, & Tregubenko, 2016).

Top concerns on the minds of emerging adults are what they will do for work, whether they will find someone to love, and how they will successfully manage both a work and a love life (Luyckx et al., 2014). Although the literature on this topic is still nascent and evolving, the focus of this chapter will be on how emerging adults are coordinating and integrating these two crucial domains—work and romance.

First, we will explore the vocational and romantic contexts that emerging adults are encountering as they embark on their paths.

▲ The Work Context

While the previous boomer generation could depend on clearer divisions of labor at home and in the workplace (Peake & Harris, 2002), this approach no longer serves most emerging adults. Each couple must negotiate its own terms. Though emerging adults and their parents share similar work-related values, the importance accorded to finding meaning and passion in one's work is particular to this generation of emerging adults. Mayseless and Keren (2014) suggest that focus on the self, a defining feature of emerging adulthood, flows from a narrative of self-actualization, both at work and in one's romantic relationship. Overlaying this narrative is a larger meta-narrative, the search for a *meaningful and an authentic life*. Career is integral to this narrative.

The meaning of a career has changed. While educational achievements and credentials are increasingly important in gaining employment, there is substantial uncertainty as to whether emerging adults, even after investing in their education, will be able to enter their desired occupations, and at a livable pay level (Putnam, 2015). Defined pathways are no longer reliable. Maintaining flexibility and adaptability is key. Keeping one's options open and remaining nimble has become an overriding strategy in managing one's career (Stokes & Wyn, 2007). Rather than being locked into particular job positions or occupational preferences, emerging adults are viewing careers as personal pathways, with mobility *across* jobs in mind. Their various job choices and career activities are held together by a sense of personal narrative rather than by holding on to prescribed steps and patterns (Mayseless & Keren, 2014).

Forty-four percent of emerging adults do not expect to be in their current jobs within 2 years (Stokes & Wyn, 2007). Twenty percent of emerging adults change jobs at least five times within 6 years. Due to a competitive marketplace, employed emerging adults find themselves working in low-wage and low-skill jobs that do not match their interests and abilities; turnover intent is high. There is a trend of "degree inflation" whereby low-wage and low-skill jobs are increasingly requiring bachelors' degrees (Rampell, 2013). Many college graduates, while feeling lucky to have a job, are discovering they are unable to make a living wage. Given the current realities of the marketplace, the need for learning new work-related skills throughout one's life is an expectation that many emerging adults have internalized (Mayseless & Keren, 2014).

Since jobs are viewed as impermanent and career paths as uncertain, many emerging adults are navigating both their careers and romantic lives by relying on exploration and experimentation to guide them—sometimes systematically, other times haphazardly and seemingly without periods of reflection, assessment, and evaluation (Collins & van Dulmen, 2006). Figuring it all out on one's own may be the new norm.

In addition to the technical skills that are valued in the marketplace, adaptive skills (the ability to adjust to new jobs, new technologies, new management, new markets) and emotional intelligence are increasingly valued (Armstrong, Dedrick, & Greenbaum, 2003; Savickas, 1997, 2005). Lack of work permanence is creating an environment that sensitizes emerging adults to the importance of flexibility, adaptability, and openness to emerging options. Individuals with career adaptability are more likely to find employment and/or become re-employed (Koen, Klehe, Van Vianen, Zikic, & Nauta, 2010; Konstam, Tomek, Celen-Demirtas, & Sweeney, 2014).

Accrual of relevant and valued experiences at work frequently shapes and determines future opportunities for work-related learning (Shulman & Connolly, 2013). When faced with a lack of opportunity for employment and learning new skills, emerging adults tend to make decisive career choices at an earlier age than their parents did. At the same time, they are less likely to encounter opportunities and jobs that will propel them forward in their career trajectories (Shulman & Connolly, 2013; Karoly, 2009, as cited in Mayseless & Keren, 2014). Emerging adults without supports and sufficient educational training to help them compete in the workforce will experience greater and more frequent disruptions than those who have such support and training. Experience with part-time work, gap-year programs, and apprenticeships may serve as alternative options. For example, in a study of unemployed emerging adults, ages 21 to 29, Konstam and colleagues (2014) found that emerging adults who sought volunteer work while unemployed, in comparison to those who did not, were more likely to find future employment. It is not surprising that apprenticeship experiences are assuming increasing importance and popularity in the United States (Lerman, 2014).

Today's emerging adults are acting in ways that are different from their parents, career-wise. In comparison to the previous generation, emerging adults are more likely to relocate in search of new opportunities in the workplace, a finding that has been consistent for the past two decades (Arnett, 2006). Emerging adults are also less hampered by family and other responsibilities and more willing to assume work-related risk. However, emerging adults share many common work-related *values* with their parents' generation. Four major criteria guide the career decision-making processes of both emerging adults and their boomer parents (Pfau & Kay, 2002): feelings of pride related to the organization and its mission, opportunities for maximization of growth, fulfillment at work, and feeling that they are being treated well and that they are well compensated. Across race, gender, and age, individuals are seeking work environments that affirmatively address these four critical considerations.

As for what emerging adults are seeking in their romantic environments, we will address that question next.

▲ The Romantic Context

Since jobs are less permanent, and career trajectories less certain than in the past, many emerging adults are committing to developing their careers before their romantic lives. Work identity before romantic intimacy is a prevalent approach (Fouad & Bynner, 2008). Shulman and Connolly (2013) conclude that many emerging adults need to feel confident and secure about their career choices, and their mutual support for one another's careers, before moving forward with a long-term relationship. This has created the space for them to experiment romantically and sexually before launching long-term, committed relationships (Collins & van Dulmen, 2006). Investment in one's career provides a greater safety net from which to take steps toward greater romantic commitment.

Coordinating both partners' life and career plans in an unpredictable job world, with few guidelines to follow, is a hugely demanding task, especially when one is still developing as an individual. Shulman and Connolly (2013) suggest that emerging adults' postponement of long-term partnerships should not necessarily be viewed as aimlessness or immaturity, but rather as a healthy, adaptive response to today's complex realities. Uncommitted experimentation also provides a laboratory for learning about intimacy before investing in a long-term relationship. Periods of instability and regressions are part of the developmental reorganization, and are required to find and/or refine new forms of behavior that address the need and potential for change and growth (Knight, 2011, as cited in Shulman et al., 2016).

In addition to enhancing growth, these relationship fluctuations offer emerging adults the potential to reflect and learn from past and present romantic experiences. Opportunities for reflection and learning are thought to be the mechanism by which a new "structure" of relationship emerges (Fonagy & Target, 2005, as cited in Shulman et al., 2016). Seemingly contradictory behaviors and ideas can sometimes be woven into a new and original tapestry that works for the partners involved (Thelen & Smith, 1998, as cited in Shulman et al., 2016). However, it must be pointed out that many emerging adults do not engage in this type of conscious reflection and learning. For this group, the struggle to integrate work and romance may be more of an either/or proposition: "I can either have either a career or a committed relationship right now," in which case most emerging adults seem likely to choose work over relationships, at least for a period of years.

As noted in the introductory chapter, in the United States the average age of marriage occurs in the late 20s, and by the age of 30, 44% of men and 33% of women are unmarried (Settersten & Ray, 2010). This trend is not unique to the United States. Postponement of marriage is occurring across a majority of developed Western nations. A range of cultural and socioeconomic factors inform these findings. For example, data from the Pew Research Center reveals that education correlates with age at marriage. In states with higher percentages of college-educated adults, both men and women marry at later ages (http://www.pewresearch.org/2009/10/15/the-states-of-marriage-and-divorce). This supports the notion that for many emerging adults, marriage is viewed as a "capstone" achievement—something to be tackled only after one's financial/career track has been established—rather than as a "cornerstone" upon which the two partners can build their careers together (Willoughby & James, 2017).

Not only are emerging adults attempting to balance romantic relationships while *preparing* for careers (via education, internships, etc.), but they are also thinking about the future and how they will balance work and romance once they do have both careers and committed relationships such as marriage.

▲ Work and Romance: Walking the Line

Balancing a career and a romantic relationship, with or without children, can create tensions in both domains (Seiffge-Krenke & Luyckx, 2014). Work-family conflict is associated with negative career and family outcomes (e.g., family stress and job turnovers; Coyle, Van Leer, Schroeder, & Fulcher, 2015). Possible solutions are frequently fraught with complexity (Stokes & Wyn, 2007). Emerging adults are aware of the tensions that may arise, and the fear of divorce is ever-present (Konstam, 2015). These tensions are far reaching; in the United States, approximately 65% of two-parent families with children have both parents in the workforce (Pew Research Center, 2015).

Some emerging adults anticipate this potential conflict area and attempt to plan and accommodate to these circumstances; others do not. Females are more inclined to begin the planning process (Coyle et al., 2015). Anticipating and planning for the integration of a career and a romantic life is likely to be helpful; periods of reflection, as well as clarifying conversations with one's partner, may mitigate tensions, or at least clarify values, expectations, and understandings of what it means to be in a committed romantic relationship when both members of the couple are establishing themselves at work (Peake & Harris, 2002; Slaughter, 2015). However, despite changing beliefs and attitudes toward men and women in the workplace, gender-related norms remain deeply engrained in American culture. Coontz (2017), for example, reports that today's emerging adult men are retreating in their support of gender equality in their relationships (Coontz, 2017).

What discourses about career-family integration are emerging adults having, and are they consistent over time? Which discourses are attended to and which are ignored, and what informs these decisions? Coyle and colleagues (2015) surveyed the work and romantic attitudes and expectations of 121 undergraduate college-age students, 18 to 22 years of age, from two universities in the southeastern United States. Although the men in the study anticipated work-family tensions, nearly half reported no plans to address these tensions. They tended to view their role primarily as one of breadwinner. In comparison, women, viewing their roles as *both* providers *and* caretakers, experienced greater gender-related role pressures during their college years and made plans accordingly in the hopes of mitigating their concerns. In anticipation of multiple-role planning, college women endorsed established gendered templates in thinking about how to best address these competing demands, templates that may place them in confining spaces in terms of their ability to maneuver in both roles.

Common to *both* men and women was the expectation that men would assume the breadwinner/provider role primarily and that women would assume responsibility for dual roles, caregiver and breadwinner, and that these two roles would frequently be in conflict. Coyle and colleagues reported that men believed they would be able to simultaneously fulfill their family and work obligations through work. Women viewed themselves as responsible for both domains and tended to make premature career-related adjustments that reflected such expectations.

Career-wise, emerging adults tend to be in flux, moving in and out of employment and areas of study, embarking on multiple paths that reflect their changing personal and employment goals. Given that reality, might there be alternative templates that are less restrictive—templates that provide women and men with greater flexibility during the emerging adult years?

Sandberg (2013) presents a perspective that runs contrary to work-family solutions that have been promoted in the past. She posits that women are prematurely anticipating work-family tensions (corroborated by the findings of Coyle et al.), and suggests that they may benefit from bringing their "whole selves" to work (p. 89), particularly as they are establishing their careers. Her advice for women is that perhaps they should "lean in" and fully invest in their careers. The solutions women are presently generating, in variance with their male counterparts, may well prevent them from fully leaning in, however.

According to Sandberg (2013), women are shortchanging themselves and their careers by not fully investing in and accruing empowering skillsets along the way. Sandberg argues that careers do not need to be constructed in full, with every future detail in place; rather, she advocates that women entertain two plans simultaneously: (a) a long-term dream, and (b) an 18-month plan that might help prevent premature disinvestment at work (in part due to anticipation of future work-family tensions). It should be pointed out that Sandberg is coming from a privileged position; her solutions are targeted at women and men who have social capital at their disposal.

It is interesting to consider how the "capstone" versus "cornerstone" approach to work and marriage might be affecting the development of attitudes toward work-love balance for both men and women. When career is given priority, as it currently seems to be for many emerging adults, committed relationships are delayed, and women spend added years contemplating, in the abstract, how they will balance work and committed relationships once these two domains merge (Willoughby & James, 2017). This situation may be leading to skewed notions for both men and women. Were couples to prioritize relationship over career and marry at a younger age, it is possible that men would be more likely to begin addressing how they are going to balance these two domains at an earlier stage. Thus, they may not have the "luxury" of "retreating" in their support of gender equality (Coontz, 2017) and might have to make adjustments earlier in their development. This might help *both* men and women achieve better work/love balance, because women along with men would be giving thought and planning to this issue.

Future research efforts will be needed to understand how work and family roles may be renegotiated to offer more satisfying, flexible, and workable solutions to both men and women in the workforce (Slaughter, 2015). Coontz (2017) asserts that without better work-family policies in place on a societal level, most couples will not be able to adhere to aspired egalitarian values.

Policy notions aside, what are the actual factors that contribute to a satisfying balance of work and family life? In dual-earner families, relational satisfaction and stability are generally associated with the following factors: (a) partners holding less traditional views of gender; (b) partners discussing, during courtship, their plans for integrating careers and family life; (c) partners affirming each other's occupational pursuits; (d) partners viewing their mutual involvement in home roles as fair; (e) partners feeling supported for their lifestyle choices; (f) partners experiencing little discrimination based on gender, race, ethnicity, or sexual orientation in their workplace; (g) employers of both partners having benefits policies that are family-responsive; and (h) both partners actively participating in parenting, feeling comfortable sharing parenting with childcare personnel, and being satisfied with the childcare they are using (Gilbert & Rader, 2008; Gilbert, 2014).

Research to date reveals that although emerging adult couples are dealing with a level of work-family tensions higher than that of previous generations, they can mitigate these tensions by planning for them, communicating about them, and having flexible, respectful attitudes toward each other's roles both at home and at work.

▲ Clarifying Conversations

Slaughter, author of *Unfinished Business: Women Men Work Family* (2015) asks the question, "What if both members of the dyad want highly demanding, intense careers?" (p. 203). Although her insights are aimed specifically at women who are seeking prestigious professional positions while also having a family, they can also benefit women with more measured career goals. Slaughter suggests that women seeking highly demanding professional careers would in all likelihood need supportive spouses on the home front in the same way their male counterparts do.

In the past, according to Slaughter, romantic partners have not had conversations about such issues *before* being confronted with work-family tensions in their relationships. With the introduction of children, tensions build as couples realize that adjustments and accommodations are required. According to Slaughter, the choices couples end up making have typically disadvantaged women's careers. She advocates for honest conversations between romantic partners about their "deepest career aspirations" (p. 203) *prior* to committing to long-term intimate relationships and children. She recommends using conversation openers such as:

Regarding career:

> Who do you wish you could be?
> How ambitious are you?
> What will you consider a life well lived?
> What life goals do you have other than career success? (p. 203)

Regarding family plans:

> Do you want children?
> Do you assume you will have them someday?
> Do you imagine yourself caring for your parents when they are elderly? (p. 203)

Although the partners may not have all of the answers yet—including about whether to have children or not—it is "essential to have the conversation" (p. 205) in order to learn more about the self and each other.

Slaughter recommends revisiting these conversations on an ongoing basis. It is crucial for each partner to know what they and their partner will be gaining as well as giving up. It can also be helpful to discuss how the partners' respective roles might change or reverse in the future, under various conditions.

Presenting actual scenarios for discussion, in addition to questions, can be especially fruitful. For example:

> My boss has told me that he thinks I am leadership material and wants to promote me. My next job will certainly require a move.

Will you move with me? Even if that means taking a step down or sideways in your career? And when we move will you be willing to reweave the fabric of our own and our children's lives in terms of schools, friends, doctors, and activities while I try to get a handle on my new job?

If you move for my new job, you will not be able to accept the promotion you were offered and your boss really hates the idea of your working remotely. Will you defer your promotion so I can take mine?

If I take a job that requires lots of travel, will you be the available parent for everything from teacher conferences to snow and sick days to after-school activities requiring parental involvement? Will you still love and support me when the kids are crying and the house is a mess and I walk out the door to head for the airport?

Are you comfortable hiring outside help to raise our children? If not, are you willing to move to my family's hometown (or your family's) so that we will have grandparents and siblings nearby to help make it work?

Can you handle it if I earn more than you do and have a more conventionally successful career? Are you secure enough to handle any denigrating remarks about this from friends and family? (Slaughter, 2015, pp. 204–206)

Discussing specific scenarios frees up the imagination and often stimulates more conversation than asking abstract questions. Slaughter asserts that when couples discuss and anticipate potential tensions, they are more likely to manage such tensions successfully when they arise.

▲ Pathways Toward Adulthood: Three Studies

The lives of emerging adults—fluid, flexible, and complex—often defy predetermined, predictable pathways (Savin-Williams, 2011). In taking snapshots of romantic relationships—as is typically done via traditional quantitative assessments of romantic partners—the results are often incomplete and misleading (Manning, Giordano, Longmore, & Hocevar, 2011). The heterogeneity of these paths is often difficult to capture. For example, steady and exclusive relationships are not always synonymous with long-term commitment and shared goals for emerging adults; instead, these relationships may simply indicate a convenient arrangement or may even mask issues with genuine commitment (as suggested by Shulman et al. 2016). Carefully executed longitudinal studies, although not without limitations, may expand our understanding of the complexity of these relationships and their interplay with the domain of work.

Fortunately, some revealing longitudinal studies have been conducted. We examine three in particular, each of which sheds its own unique light on how exploration and commitment in two core domains, work and love, may unfold and intersect over time for today's generation of emerging adults. The studies took place in three geographic locales, the first in the United States, the second in Germany, and the third in Israel.

Manning and Colleagues (2011)

Manning and colleagues, drawing from quantitative (N=428) and qualitative (N=155) data of 428 emerging adults 18–24 years old from the Toledo Adolescent Relationship Study (TARS), examined the ways in which romantic partners influence their partners' education and career trajectories.

Results revealed that emerging adults value financial security in their romantic relationships. Although all of the study participants were only "dating"—not cohabiting or married—the majority cared about their partners' ability to provide for themselves economically and to have good, secure financial futures. For those participants who elected, at times, not to date, the most common reason offered (56%) was the desire to avoid the drama that may come along with dating, while the next most common reason (48%) was the need to focus on their work/ school life. Participants reported that educational attainment influenced their ability to engage in long-term commitments such as marriage. Similarly, Smock, Manning, and Porter (2005) found that both men and women tended to believe that being financially stable was a prerequisite for entry into marriage—evidence that today's emerging adults tend to view marriage as a "capstone" rather than a "cornerstone." Beliefs such as these have strong implications for the trajectories emerging adults take toward adulthood, including the timing and types of relationships formed.

Luyckx and Colleagues (2014)

Luyckx et al. designed and conducted a three-year longitudinal study with a sample of 1,873 German emerging adults (18–30 years old, 65.5% women), to examine the interplay of identity commitment and exploration processes across the domains of love and work. The research team was interested in answering the question, How firmly have emerging adults established identities in both their career lives and their love lives? The research team also studied how identity commitments influence mental health and psychosocial outcomes (work satisfaction, work stress, and work-family conflict). Using Marcia's identity status model (see Chapter 2 for further explication), the analysis revealed the following career and relational clusters for both identity-commitment domains: *achievement, foreclosure, moratorium, carefree diffusion*, and *undifferentiated*. For the relational domain only, a *troubled diffusion* cluster was identified (individuals not appearing to be strongly committed to their partner, and ruminating about the relationship and where it was going), and for the career domain only, a *searching moratorium* category was identified (individuals appearing committed to a career but also exploring and worrying about where their career paths would take them).

Findings revealed that only 18% of the participants were able to meet criteria for high-commitment status in both domains, results that suggest how difficult it is for emerging adults to maintain identity investments in both arenas at once. Emerging adults in the study tended to develop their identities in the two domains sequentially, "selecting," "focusing," and "sequencing" their life goals (p. 199). Thirty-seven percent of the participants were firmly committed in one domain only. The largest group of the participants had not firmly committed and consolidated either identity, suggesting that identity formation is a work-in-progress during emerging adulthood. While some emerging adults were worried about their lack of identity commitment in either of the domains, others seemed untroubled by this.

The researchers postulated that those participants who expressed lack of concern about their career-related identity choices (*carefree diffusion* status) did not appear to have the needed skills to manage their responsibilities in either domain. Previous studies have reported that carefree diffusion is associated with low levels of competence in dealing with the demands of everyday life (e.g., Schwartz, Beyers et al., 2011, as cited in Luyckx et al., 2014). Self-reported rates of hard drug use were more prevalent among those in the carefree diffusion status groups—2 to 3 times greater than in any other status. Luyckx et al. concluded that low interest in identity issues is associated with poor life outcomes as well as potentially self-destructive behaviors.

Individuals who met the criteria for high commitment in love and work scored most favorably on all outcomes measuring psychological functioning. They scored (a) lowest on psychological symptoms and conflict between family and work, and (b) highest on life satisfaction, work satisfaction, and work-family conflict self-efficacy. The authors concluded that the presence of identity commitment in the domains of love and work facilitated the balancing of tensions between these two domains. Those emerging adults with strong commitments in both domains were most likely to successfully tackle the myriad challenges of emerging adulthood. Findings illustrate, however, that high commitment in both domains is fairly rare during emerging adulthood; the majority of emerging adults tend to focus on one domain predominantly or else are not ready to consolidate an identity in either domain.

Gender differences were observed: men were more likely to be represented in the *achievement* or *foreclosure* status in the career commitment domain, but not in the relational commitment domain; women were more likely to be represented in the relational commitment domain. The women were less sure of the types of work they wished to commit to. The authors posit that this may be due to their searching for careers that would allow them to balance work and family—findings supported by the observations of Sandberg (2013), Slaughter (2015), and others.

Notably, results were somewhat different in a Swedish study conducted by Frisen and Wangqvist (2011): the women in this study were more likely to be associated with identity achievement in both the work and romance domains, whereas the men were more often associated with identity *diffusion* across all life domains. There were no significant gender differences in the occupational domain and thus it cannot be argued that the occupational domain is more important to men than to women. The authors attributed these findings to advances in gender equality in Sweden and a family ideal that promotes the notion that women and men have equal responsibility for supporting and taking care of the family (Bjornberg, 2000, as cited in Frisen & Wangqvist, 2011).

In the Luyckx et al study, married individuals were more likely to make progress toward identity commitments in love and work. This finding lends credence to the possibility that marriage or a long-term committed relationship as a "cornerstone" rather than a "capstone" might propel emerging adults to grapple with work/love tensions together and more directly (Willoughby & James, 2017), rather than in a hypothetical sense as the findings of Coyle and colleagues suggest. Further research efforts are needed to address assumptions held about these competing points of views and how they relate to existing work/love tensions.

In addition, Luyckx and colleagues posit that single individuals are likely to receive their social supports from friends and families of origin, while married individuals are more apt to receive their support from their spouses. However, the presence of a stable romantic partnership did not consistently help individuals to feel involved and satisfied with their work. A meta-analysis of 120 longitudinal studies conducted by Kroger, Martinussen, and Marcia (2009) involving adolescents and emerging adults reported similar results. The main aim of this study was to examine any developmental changes in identity status during adolescence and emerging and young adulthood. The percentage of participants in their mid-30s who met the criteria for identity achievement in both domains was relatively low. Consolidation of identities *both* in work and relational domains is an ongoing process that appears to continue well into the fourth decade. Studies that follow the lives of emerging adults further into adulthood are needed to elaborate on the processes of consolidating, coordinating, and integrating identity commitment in these two domains.

Shulman and Colleagues (2016)

The final of the three studies sets out to examine if and how patterns of romantic pathways unfold among emerging adults on their way to adulthood. In a 7-year longitudinal study, Shulman and his colleagues examined patterns of romantic pathways in 100 Israeli heterosexual emerging adults (54 males, 46 females) 22–29 years of age who were primarily from lower middle-class families and aspiring to obtain a college education. At the 7-year time point, the researchers found evidence of four distinctive pathways: (a) *sporadic short involvements and casual romantic encounters* (35.9% of the sample, 66% men and 33% women), (b) *lengthy relationships but absence of experiential learning* (10.9% of the sample, 80% women, 20% men), (c) *moving from casual to steady involvements* (32.6% of the sample, 70% men, 30% women), and (d) *steady relationships* (20.7% of the sample, 64.3% women and 34.7% men).

In the first pathway, emerging adults engaged in short-term relationships that were casual in nature. In the second, emerging adults were in long-lasting relationships but these relationships were neither intimate nor mutually respectful; rather, they were characterized by partner "appeasement" and, after dissolution, a lack of understanding as to why the relationship had ended. In the third pathway, characterized by instability and fluctuation, approximately 33% of emerging adults were moving toward more enduring relationships. This group was able to reflect on their previous relationships and to learn and grow emotionally as a function of having been in these relationships. In the fourth pathway, emerging adults tended to form long-lasting, stable relationships. In comparison to the second pathway, these emerging adults had learned how to negotiate romantic relationships based on past experiences either with their families of origin or with prior romantic relationships. Integrating intimacy and commitment appears to be a more important factor in relationship "success" than whether emerging adults are involved in a romantic relationship at a particular moment in time. Male and female participants were not equally represented in all four pathways. Males were more likely to be represented in the *moving from casual to steady involvements* and *sporadic short involvements and casual romantic encounters* pathways, whereas females were more likely to be represented in the *steady relationships* and *lengthy relationships but absence of experiential learning* pathways.

What accounts for females staying in steady relationships that stagnate in terms of growth and learning? Jordan (2010) suggests that women, as compared to men, tend to be more invested in their romantic relationships and are therefore more willing to forgo personal preferences in order to be in a relationship; they prefer to stay in continued connection.

Another question posed by the second pathway is, How does one become committed to a romantic relationship in the absence of experiential learning? Shulman and colleagues (2016) suggest the possibility that individuals in the second pathway may be "sliding" into relationships, without periods of reflection and deliberation, and in turn not acting with intentionality (as elaborated in the work of Stanley, Rhoades, & Markman, 2006). Partners who are unable to achieve more in-depth intimacy over time may be in these relationships because they perceive that they provide stability and security and meet their needs for dependency.

Those participants in unstable relationships were more likely to report lower levels of goal progress and more depressive symptoms compared to those in intimately committed relationships. However, Shulman and colleagues suggest that fluctuation in romantic and sexual experiences of emerging adults may not necessarily reflect confusion or immaturity, but rather may provide opportunities for learning and relationship growth.

These studies have helped to reveal some patterns in the ways emerging adults are thinking about work and relationships in an era when CMC and other factors are creating a highly fluid work context for many emerging adults, and when the rules of romance are under active revision. More longitudinal studies, asking probing questions from a variety of perspectives, will undoubtedly help flesh out and add dimension to this still-fragmentary and incomplete body of knowledge.

Before looking at our own research results, there is one additional topic related to work and romance that deserves attention. Because emerging adults are waiting longer to enter long-term relationships, they no longer enjoy the support system of marriage that previous generations had in their 20s. As a result, emerging adults are leaning more heavily for support on two sources: friends and parents. Thus, these two key relationships have taken on a different level of importance for emerging adults, partially as a result of emerging adults prioritizing career over marriage.

▲ The Role of Friends

Friends are central figures in the lives of emerging adults. During this transitional period to adulthood, today's emerging adults turn to friendships as sources of companionship and self-esteem (Collins & Laursen, 2004) and psychological well-being (Galambos, Barker, & Krahn, 2006). Friendships provide the stability and support that may be lacking in other domains of emerging adults' lives. It is not surprising that they accord a high priority to their friendships (Collins & van Dulmen, 2006; Konstam, 2015). Connecting with friends through social media is one of the major sources of intimacy among emerging adults (Coyne, Padilla-Walker, & Howard, 2013; Pew Research Center, 2015).

In interviews with emerging adults, Konstam (2007) reported that emerging adults considered friendships "key to living a balanced, meaningful, and enriching life" (p. 68). Emerging adults in committed long-term relationships find it difficult to balance their friendships and romantic partnerships. They also express regret that friends are sometimes sacrificed due to heavy work demands (Konstam, 2007, 2015), a finding that was replicated with our 29 research study participants.

Watters (2006) has observed a tribal element in the relationships of male emerging adults that is guided by unspoken roles and hierarchies. Tribal members make a distinction between who belongs in the tribe and who does not in order to create a more powerful sense of belonging. Each member is held accountable for his actions and, according to Watters, tribal behavior does not result in a loss of family values. Rather, it represents a fresh expression of family values.

Friends can serve as "anchors" during emerging adulthood and can help clarify values and goals. Friends may also help with periods of assessment and self-reflection. Watters notes an interesting twist: male tribal friends—who are traditionally viewed as stalwarts against marriage—may actually serve to support the very institution they have been seen as undermining. Because men value their tribes so highly, and do not wish to give them up, they are not likely to enter marriage casually or lightly, simply because it is the next prescribed step. Rather, according to Watters, they enter marriage with the full knowledge that they are losing something precious. By that act of sacrifice, they thereby accord marriage the seriousness of intent it deserves.

The increasing postponement of long-term romantic relationships for emerging adults also makes another relationship more central—for a longer period of time—than it was for the prior generation: the relationship with one's parents.

▲ The Role of Parents

Because emerging adults are not easily consolidating careers, and because they are launching committed relationships later in life, parents are being asked to fill a support vacuum. They are taking their responsibilities seriously, although most of them have not been prepared for the specifics of this task that is often associated with ambivalence

(Konstam, 2013). They did not anticipate the revolving door they are seeing as their emerging adult children enter and leave their homes repeatedly in the process of trying to launch into a career.

Aquilino (2006) observes:

> Tensions and contradictions in the parent-emerging adult relationship result from the child's having adult status in many domains while still dependent on parents in some ways. . . . Most still need some measure of parental support to thrive, which thus creates a contradiction between society's granting of [legal] adult status and autonomy while economic realities often necessitate a lingering dependency on parents (p. 195).

A support vacuum also exists in the workplace for emerging adults. Structural supports within the workplace are frequently lacking, and mentoring is not rewarded. Mentors, frequently overwhelmed by their own work demands, do not have the time or the institutional backing to provide effective guidance to younger employees. In addition, the financial rewards are not there (Konstam, 2015). This likely puts an added burden on parents to provide some of the vocational guidance that is lacking for emerging adults on the job.

Many parents believe that the appropriate response to the unanticipated needs of emerging adults is to either withdraw financial help or to coddle them (Konstam, 2013). Withdrawing help and support from emerging adults does not engender independence, nor does coddling. Given the fact that emerging adults have fewer support networks outside the family home, parents are engaging in the delicate dance of giving their emerging adult children both space and support simultaneously, a challenging and tension-ridden set of circumstances (Konstam, 2013). They must stand by in a supportive way, while accepting their children's choices and having faith that they will find their way to independence. Emerging adults often push back against the "help" their parents offer and judge themselves harshly for still needing their parents' support. A complex dynamic is often at play that requires patience and perseverance on the part of both emerging adults and their parents.

Below, the 29 participants in our present study make their contribution to a better understanding by answering questions about how they personally integrate the domains of work and love.

▲ Participant Responses

Participants were asked to reflect on how the two domains, work/education and romance, informed each other. In addition, in order to capture one representative decision point—the decision to relocate for professional reasons—participants were asked to share their thoughts about relocating professionally for their partners or themselves. One domain emerged from the data: interrelationships between work/education and romance. Four categories were generated within this domain: (a) work/education and its influence on romantic relationships, (b) romantic relationships and their influence on work and/or education, (c) relocating for the partner, and (d) relocating for the self.

Work/education and its influence on romantic relationships

Twenty participants endorsed the view that their work life influenced their romantic relationships, yielding a *typical* category. The remaining seven participants asserted that there was no relationship between these two domains. Two participants misunderstood the question.

Work or education-related distress and its influence on romantic relationships was identified as an ongoing struggle by many participants. Their need for support and/or acknowledgment of their work/educational accomplishments from their partners was also discussed as an influence on their relationships. Self-knowledge was identified as an important variable that helped them deal with relationships more effectively.

Alison (28) shared some of her concerns and insights:

> I would say [my being in school] affects my current
> relationship. . . . I think that when I get really stressed out, I tend
> to take that out on [my partner]. And that causes a great source
> of tension. So when there are papers due or there's tests, or finals,
> I have less patience and I snap at him—even though it's not fair,
> it's what I do. So he has to bear the brunt of it, and that causes
> problems in our relationship, obviously. . . . Also working as a
> waitress is very stressful, and he also works in the food industry,
> so I think we both kind of get really stressed out and kind of take
> it out on each other.

Alison was able to reflect on a pattern she observes with her partner and how she contributes to the escalation of stress between them. Both Alison and her partner, who is no longer a student, are aware of the dynamic and how its impacts their relationship. Because of their understanding, they are trying to address the issue preventatively in the hopes of minimizing tensions: "[Stress] kind of started to go away [as a result of their efforts]. I'm more aware of it now."

Joseph (25) talks about how education has helped him learn about himself, and how he uses that knowledge in service of the relationship.

I know myself more now. I understand myself and I know who
I am now as a person and I like sharing that with another person.
And I know what I am looking for, [because] my education has
helped me define my inner strength. I can see certain things.
I know what to share and what not to share. And I know what
to look for and what not to look for. . . . [If] I was not educated,
I think I would have been insecure [in the relationship].

For Angela (27), the financial costs associated with her and her partner's education have created stress in the relationship.

We owe so much money. . . . That has been a huge source of stress
for us. And that is the part of the reason why I still live at home.
I think if we had . . . started working after graduating from college,
we would be further than where we are now, in terms of moving
out. But he has hundreds of thousands of dollars still in debt and
I had a lot when I first started working. . . . I am trying to pay off
the college and grad school loans so it definitely does affect us.
That is how our education influenced our romantic life.

Ellen (24) shared the details of how a relationship ended because of the stress she carried over from work. Her ex-partner felt overwhelmed at work as well. Ellen's stress along with his work and family-related stress exceeded his capacities to deal effectively with the tensions. Ellen surmises that he ended their relationship because it was the easiest and most pragmatic choice he could make.

I think he was having issues with his family, he was feeling
overwhelmed at work, and then he felt like he needed to do the
committed thing and be present for me. And I think he felt pulled

by too many directions and had to cut one of them, and I was the one you could cut—you can't really cut your family or your job, but you can cut your relationship.

Participants encountered stress either at work or in school, or both, which influenced their romantic relationships. Self-knowledge and insights about the self and the relationship helped alleviate the stress for some of the participants. For others, the build-up of stress resulted in the ending of the relationship.

Romantic relationships and their influence on work and/or education

Twenty-two of the participants asserted that their romantic lives influenced their work/educational lives, yielding a *typical* category, while seven spoke only to the influence of their work/educational lives on their romantic lives.

The participants in this group talked about the choices they made in their work/educational lives as a function of being in a romantic relationship. Rhonda (22), for example, spoke about how being in a romantic relationship has influenced her in terms of how to manage work and parenthood:

> Not that we are engaged or considering marriage or anything, but we have talked about kids, and he is more the fan of me staying home with kids, not working. And I am more the fan of okay, I am gonna have kids, take my six weeks of leave, and go back to work.

Rhonda and her partner have had many discussions about how their lives might unfold with children. As of now, there is no resolution. Because her partner is clear about wanting children and wanting her "to stay home with the kids," she feels she needs to figure out how to integrate children and career *before* she takes any steps toward starting a family.

Leslie (27) shares that she has been strongly influenced by her partner with respect to her decision to go to college:

> When I was 21–24, he had advised me to go to college, so he really pushed for me to go back to school. So we knew that we wanted,

long-term, to be married and all that, and I didn't want to go back to school, so he really influenced me to go back.

Cassandra (26) is facing challenges in time management: balancing time between her studies and her relationship. Being in a relationship, she feels, has influenced the time she allocates to her studies. Cassandra has chosen to spend more time with her partner, and that, in turn, has created less time to spend on her studies. Balancing the dual demands has been difficult for Cassandra. She is conflicted about the choices she has made and what she is "supposed to be doing."

> I know that sometimes when I should be studying I'm not
> because . . . I'd rather hang out with him, or go out with him. . . .
> And that affects my schoolwork because I'm not doing what
> I'm supposed to be doing. . . . You know, it's just like a balance,
> I believe, because sometimes you study too much, you don't see
> them, and then they feel neglected because you don't see them
> as much.

While on the one hand, Cassandra wishes she could allocate more of her time to her studies, she is also concerned about the possibility of neglecting her partner.

Amelia (24) is currently cohabitating with her partner and focuses on how that relationship nourishes each of them. She states that the support the partners provide to one another helps both of them in their respective careers: "Our romantic life helped us support each other in our work lives. We both supported each other financially [and] emotionally."

While in the past, Chantal (23) allowed herself to be influenced by her romantic partner, she now prioritizes her education. She states that her romantic life would not influence her academic or career decisions, unless perhaps there was a formal commitment in place such as marriage.

> I would definitely not make a career decision or educational
> decision with somebody that I'm in a relationship with. Maybe
> if I was married, so it would be a different story, but just in a
> relationship, no.

Similarly, Mahesh (23) stated that his romantic life did not shape his educational/career life. His decision to change his major was informed by his personal interests exclusively. He was seeking a career for himself, and although parental influence was high, he stated that his career belonged to him and not his parents. Negotiating the competing demands of career and relationship was on the minds of the majority of participants, but the prioritizing of career was a dominant theme, albeit expressed in a variety of ways.

Relocating for the partner

Meanings associated with one particular decision point—job relocation on behalf of the partner or the self—were assessed. All 29 participants responded to, and expanded upon, the following two questions: "Would you relocate for your partner for professional reasons/opportunities?" and "Would you relocate for professional reasons/ opportunities for yourself?" In response to the first question, 25 of the 29 participants indicated that they would relocate for their partner, yielding a *typical* category.

Their responses, although affirmative, were varied. While some stated they would relocate unconditionally because they were without a present anchor in their work life ("Yeah, I really don't have any attachments at the moment; I don't have any really good paying jobs or anything so I'm kind of floating around"), most participants imposed conditions on their decision to relocate. Discussion of the issue with the partner was paramount, as was their own ability to find work opportunities for themselves at the new location. For two of the participants, marriage or engagement served as a prerequisite condition for relocating. Representative responses by Alison (28), Mateo (27), and Joseph (25) suggest that they would be open to such a move, but that it would need to be done thoughtfully, not impulsively. Alison states:

> The answer is yes, I would. But I think that we would have to really heavily discuss [this] between the both of us, and it would have to really mean a lot to me or my partner for us to move.

Mateo would move with his partner if he viewed it as a "great opportunity." However, he would need to create something for himself as well.

> I [would] highly think about it. I think honestly that I would be willing to do it to move if I know that that is a great opportunity for my partner and if I can see that I can move as well and do something professionally where he is moving to.

According to Joseph:

> I would do it and if it is, like . . . providing me the stability for my
> future and our relationship, I would relocate myself; yes, if I had
> to, I would.

Mark (24) would not consider relocating for his partner under any
conditions, given his commitment to the theater:

> No, not at all. I would never, ever, ever [relocate]. I'm married to
> the theater and everything else is just an affair. I would never put
> the relationship over my theater work.

Ellen (24) points out that she would need marriage or engagement first:

> Because . . . that shows the commitment. You would hope that
> they would do the same for me if I got this amazing job in a
> different state and it didn't happen to be where his job happened
> to be at that point in time. But I wouldn't do it for just . . .
> I wouldn't relocate unless we were at least engaged.

Relocating for a partner's career was clearly considered a major step
and one that would be entertained only in the context of a serious relationship, if at all.

Relocating for the self

Twenty-six participants would relocate for a work opportunity on behalf of the self, yielding another *typical* category. Again, there were
qualifying conditions for most, such as financial considerations and
completion of one's studies. Once their education was complete,
most of the participants said that they would be amenable to a move.
Consideration of where they would like to raise children and logistics
with respect to finances were also important qualifiers.

> ANDREA: I feel like if I didn't have any roots, like as of right now—
> what I mean by roots is if I don't have any kids . . . then yeah
> I think I would.
> RITA: I mean, ideally I'd like to finish my program. . . . Financially this
> city has become so crippling *(laughter)*.

TINA: I think, um, just in general, sure, I would consider it. But if I were—like I am—in a committed relationship, I would put the relationship above the promotion and would, um, prefer to stay with and nearby the person I'm dating versus pursuing my career.

ALANA: I guess, really, as long as we both could afford to live out there. Like if I could afford to leave with him, then yeah, I'd go.

Relocating for a job was considered by most to be a decision they expected to encounter at some point in their careers. They expected to balance that decision with considerations about family, finances, and other important life issues.

▲ Analysis of Findings

Participants shared their thoughts about how their work/educational lives and their romantic lives influenced one another. Although many of their responses were idiosyncratic and specific to their life circumstances, participants were able to articulate how these two domains inform their lives. The observations of Manning et al. were quite pertinent in that each of the domains had the potential to exert both positive and negative influences on the other domain and on the individuals themselves.

A prevalent concern for the participants was the amount of stress they experienced in relationship to both domains. Many of the participants encountered stress at work/school and were able to identify how the two domains—work and romance—intersected with one another and exacerbated stress levels. The demands of school were noted as a factor that often brought stress to the relationship. One participant, Angela, spoke about how academic decisions—specifically the accumulation of massive amounts of student loan debt—had affected her and her partner's ability to advance their relationship. Trying to balance the amount of attention to give to school and romance was also a reported source of stress.

Self-knowledge and insights about the self within a romantic relationship helped alleviate the stress, a finding supported by Shulman et al. (2013, 2016). For others, the build-up of stress resulted in the ending of the relationship. As one participant concluded, when a person is burdened by the complexity of adult demands and has the perception that his or her resources are inadequate to meet those demands, dissolution of the relationship is a likely outcome. Given a choice between relationship, family, and work, Ellen stated—with the sting of experience in her voice—that it's the relationship that has to go.

For a minority of the women, the question of how to best incorporate the desire to have children with developing and/or continuing a career was an important consideration. One research participant, Rhonda, stated that although she was ambivalent about having children prior to her current relationship, she is reassessing her priorities and the meaning of work in her life. Her partner is clear about his preferences and he has made those preferences known to her, and she is in the process considering alternatives (e.g., working part time).

As Sandberg's work suggests, the premature decision not to lean into one's career may hold women back from fully actualizing their abilities at work. In reconsidering her work commitments, for example, Rhonda seemed to be responding in part to pressure from her partner, although no firm commitments had been made by him. Embracing both short-term and longer-term goals may serve to mitigate women's need to disengage prematurely from the world of work.

For some, being in a relationship had a positive effect on their career/educational life because of the sense of support it gave them. Some of the participants were encouraged by their partners to pursue their education, which was viewed as a positive influence (others were not). Participants mentioned that they were proud of their educational and career accomplishments and were solicitous and appreciative of validation from their partners in that regard.

Results revealed that emerging adults are quite mobile in terms of the way they view their careers. Most of the participants were willing to relocate to advance either their own or their partners' careers. However, they tended to impose qualifiers on such a decision. These qualifiers were pragmatic in nature, such as financial considerations, the status of the relationship, and whether the new location would provide job-related opportunities for both partners. Meaningful discussions about any such moves were deemed important by many of the participants. Findings also support the idea that the present generation of emerging adults is less hampered by family and other responsibilities than previous generations, and more willing to assume work-related risk.

The importance of talking about critical decisions with one's partner was emphasized by many of the 29 participants. This can be viewed as a positive sign in that they are acknowledging the potential for work/romance tensions in the future and realizing that talking about them ahead of time is likely to be helpful. However, their ability to follow through on these insights has yet to be determined.

A fruitful area for future study would be to examine how career/educational goals and pursuits affect the four romantic pathways identified in the Shulman et al. study, and vice versa. For example, does career advancement influence one's movement from casual to more committed relationships? Do career issues, positive or negative, affect one's likelihood to remain in lengthy relationships that may be stagnant from an emotional-growth perspective? The present study, because of its general scope, was not able to address such questions, but we will examine three *unique and individual* pathways taken by our participants with respect to the sequencing and coordination of their romantic and work lives. These three diverse narratives may help to shed some light on the pressures and influences that are shaping romantic pathways for many emerging adults.

▲ Diverse Pathways: Daniel, Mahesh, and Rita

Daniel, Mahesh, and Rita represent three distinct pathways taken by our research participants, each of them trying to find his/her way to adulthood, some with more resources and social capital than others.

Daniel

Daniel is a single 21-year-old heterosexual Asian male, currently living with roommates near his university. He was born in South Korea and, as a young boy, migrated to the United States with his parents who were hoping to find greater economic opportunities. His parents furthered their education while raising their family and each in their own right forged a successful career. Daniel's father is the CEO of an IT company, while his mother, currently unemployed, is taking some time off from her career as a computer analyst.

Daniel relates that he has made two attempts at committed romantic relationships during his emerging adulthood, both of which he views as unsuccessful. He is taking some time off from romance now and putting all of his energies into his studies, a decision many other emerging adults are also making. Daniel states:

I subscribed to certain ideas that were given to me about what an ideal relationship is, and so I think I rushed them a lot and it turned out life does not really work that way.

Daniel is questioning long-held assumptions about romantic relationships. Specifically, he points to his parents' teaching him about the importance of being a "protector" and being "stoic."

[I am thinking about] what my role in a relationship should be. . . . Because of my Eastern Asian background, a lot of it was being a provider and also a caretaker in an emotional sense. I guess I should be the one who is level-headed, stoic almost.

In speaking about his last two relationships, he seems somewhat regretful about his approach and the outcomes.

I rushed in [to the relationships]. I do not think we were meant to be together at all because we were at two different places in our lives. [In a previous relationship] I think we did a good job of building each other up and we did have a lot of fun. We both liked outdoorsy stuff. [However], the relationship turned out badly.

Daniel is reflective about his past relationships and is trying to change. For now, though, he is driven to succeed in his career and envisions himself working in Silicon Valley in a position of leadership.

He has experienced friends-with-benefits relationships in the past and concludes, "It is hard not to make it messy. . . . It usually does not work out. Either feelings are involved or somebody finds a romantic relationship and . . . it is a little harder to be friends." Although Daniel has engaged in casual encounters, he has not enjoyed them and now chooses to refrain from participating. He concludes, "They're not very fun. . . . I think part of the fun of sex is figuring out the person and things like that." He states that in past romantic relationships he "works off of a gut feeling" and is ready to make a commitment when he sees the possibility of a "bigger long-term picture with the other person."

Daniel plans to reengage romantically when he feels he is ready. He has a strong desire to be a father at some point in his life. He states that in the future he will be looking for women who are independent and who bring with them "clarity" in terms of their professional and personal goals. He adds, "Personal goals are important for each partner to have in a committed relationship." This has become a paramount consideration for him, after his two failed attempts with women whom he considered dependent and insecure. Daniel has shifted his priorities, and at this point in time is seeking a partner who is also developing herself professionally and personally. It is only when he realizes his own ambitions that he would consider joining forces with another who has also realized her ambitions. Interestingly, however, Daniel does not speak of a "we"; he does not appear to have a clear template for how two independent individuals will function within a loving relationship.

Daniel terminated both of his previous relationships because he believed he got lost in these relationships and was not thinking of himself and his needs. He says that the relationships "anchored both people down." Power dynamics need to be considered, according to Daniel: "If, for example, one person is liking or loving the [other] person too much," or in a disproportionate way. "I think obviously you try to work things out . . . but then there are times where that is just not sustainable." Couples should break up when "things start becoming unfair." The only good reason that Daniel considers for getting back together is if both people have grown "past the issues they had."

In his previous relationship, Daniel was at a different place from his partner developmentally: she was 6 years older than he was and wanted "marriage," a "house," and "kids." Daniel assessed that the only solution was to break up. He states that in the process of learning about relationships, he has learned how to break up with a partner: he assumes a "straightforward" stance and tries to be clear in the way he communicates.

Daniel states that he will also be clearer at the onset about what he communicates to future potential partners regarding the importance of his career. When considering whether he would entertain moving if a partner was offered a work-related opportunity, he says, "It would depend on the situation but instinctively I would say no." Daniel clarifies that he would only consider relocating if the move "aligns with my [career] goals."

In describing how he has changed over time, Daniel states, "I used to think dependence was a good thing and now I am more for independence." Daniel does not seem to consider a relationship template that includes *inter*dependence as a possibility. He does not know how "feasible marriage and family are" for him. He used to think that he would be married by 25 and then, in 2 years' time, have a child. His current "goals and dreams" do not allow for that possibility. He is "opting out" of romantic relationships so that he will not be derailed from pursuing his dreams. Luyckx et al., in their 2014 study, point out that many emerging adults are doing the same: choosing to end relationships that do not support their career goals or to opt out of relationships entirely while in the career-building phase of their lives.

Daniel is evolving in both his career and his views toward romantic relationships. With two relationships behind him, he is hesitant about future relationships but reflective about his experiences. Although tunnel vision toward his career goals is guiding him at the moment, Daniel shows some capacity to change and adjust his behaviors based on his experiences.

Daniel is questioning his values. He has learned to be more honest with himself and his past partners. In response to his two romantic experiences, he is now taking an approach that might be described as counter-dependent. Singular focus on his career is the path he has chosen for himself. Daniel has shifted his priorities: at this point in time he is envisioning a partner who is also developing herself profession-ally and personally. Interestingly, however, Daniel does not speak of an interdependent "we." Perhaps in the future he will deepen his under-standing of himself, his family, and his cultural context, and modify his template of relationships and career accordingly. Currently he seems to be following a singular path, described by Luyckx et al. (2014), above.

Mahesh

Mahesh, 23 years of age, is a Roman Catholic belonging to a close-knit sect (Kanaan) with clear and longstanding traditions, rituals, and guidelines. Unlike many emerging adults who are searching for guidelines, Mahesh faces an abundance of prescriptions for how to conduct himself during his emerging adulthood years. For example, in selecting a spouse, Mahesh explains that she is not permitted to be taller or older than him by even a day. Mahesh is working with these guidelines, and is in an extensive process of negotiation with his parents, who function as advisors in all aspects of his life. While he has rejected their "advice" about the specific path he should follow vocationally, he is trying to work within their parameters in terms of selecting a spouse.

Mahesh shares that if you marry outside of your faith, you can never come back to the community and that your parents would be prohibited from attending the wedding. He is uncertain whether his parents would continue their relationship with him were he to marry out of his faith. Mahesh and his parents are committed to working with each other and within the constraints of the community. As a male and the oldest of his siblings, Mahesh has the responsibility of taking care of the family should anything happen to his father. Mahesh asserts that he will carry on the family name, an honor that the oldest male in the family assumes.

With respect to his career, Mahesh states that it is quite common for parents to suggest a career for their children ("parents love to tell us what we should be in life"). His parents' plans for Mahesh included going to pharmacy school, getting a "safe job," and making "good money," goals that are considered "golden." Mahesh states:

> I love my parents and I am doing a lot of things to please them, but that is one aspect that I wasn't going to let anybody else control. . . . So that is why in my second year I decided to switch out into pharmaceutical business.

Mahesh is forging a career path in business, an arena where he feels he can follow his strengths and his preference for managing risk.

> I chose this profession because I know happiness is a choice. . . . I don't want to go to work every day pissed off, not happy, not motivated about going to work. That is something I didn't want to deal with. . . . I hear [my parents] venting about their stresses a lot and, you know, my mom's a nurse and she always tells me how difficult and demanding the job could be. . . . I could see how the stress really affected their life. And that's why I truly wanted to make sure that I . . . lead the life that I'm happy with, despite the decision or the choices my parents want to make for me.

In terms of his romantic relationships, Mahesh believes that you need to situate yourself first in your career, and understand what you need to do to advance in that career.

> I always try to tell people, get yourself good first before you jump into a relationship. . . . A lot of complications are going to happen, in my opinion. . . . Have yourself grounded before you start talking to somebody else.

Mahesh opines that he has been "very cooperative" with the prescription to marry within his community. He has asserted his wishes and negotiated with his parents. They have agreed that he may marry a woman of his choosing within the community. Mahesh is working within the boundaries of what is considered acceptable and yet asserting his individual needs. He has rejected his parents' "help" in arranging a marriage for him.

Romantically, Mahesh upholds modern ideals: "It has to be love. Like if I cannot stop thinking about this person." But he believes that love takes time, and that many people who think they are in love are premature in their assessment. At age 23, he does not think that he has been in "complete love" with anyone.

If his wife were offered a desirable job, Mahesh states that he would move with her. "It would mean that I would sacrifice my life in the Northeast . . . where I was born. . . . Giving up things or just sacrificing for your partner . . . [it] is all a part of love. You are willing to give up [something] for the betterment of your relationship."

Mahesh has been in one committed relationship with a woman who did not identify with his religion. He states that he learned about himself within the relationship and has grown emotionally. For example, he learned that he is like his father, who can be authoritarian, and is trying to change that about himself. Mahesh feels some regret about the relationship ending; however, he could not envision marrying outside of his faith. He did engage in casual encounters during the period when he was grieving the loss of his relationship. Mahesh views this behavior as a stress reliever and a coping mechanism, "an outlet for your sexual drives," but believes he is "kind of past that point right now."

While Mahesh lives in a world guided by rules, he is striving to experience new perspectives. Pathways toward adulthood, in the work and romance domains, have been scripted for Mahesh by his family and his religious community. The expectations and rules are well defined. Yet Mahesh is trying to find his own path within these constrictions. He is trying to lead an "authentic" life by making a career choice that he perceives will provide him with meaning and happiness. A delicate balance has been established—while his parents have strong ideas for his life, they also recognize his need to express himself and live his preferences. The fact that Mahesh is more willing to please his parents in the romantic realm than in the career realm may be viewed as another example of how emerging adults are personally prioritizing career over relationship.

Rita

Rita has had a series of romantic relationships. Unlike Mahesh and Daniel, she has relied on experimentation to help her find her way toward integration in both the work and romance domains. A product of a working-class family—a fireman father and a mother who holds a teaching degree—Rita shares that her parents were in a loveless marriage. She is determined not to replicate the choices they made.

Rita is committed to having a career; she is excited about her career choice and the prospect of becoming a history teacher when she graduates this semester. At 26, she has made a commitment to a partner who will be "the one" she will marry. Her varied experiences have helped her achieve greater relationship clarity: "knowing and learning when something is unworkable, and to stop giving without getting, and figuring out when it's time . . . to move on." Rita summarizes: "I like to be able to define myself and then what a relationship should be for the self. It makes it easier then to communicate . . . what your expectations really are."

Rita has experimented with friends-with-benefits and casual encounters, much preferring the former to the latter. In friends-with-benefits relationships, Rita felt free to explore her sexuality: "I was not expecting to build a romantic relationship. I was not as worried about maintaining interest, I felt a little . . . freer in the moment." With time however, Rita concluded that this kind of relationship was not what she ultimately wanted. She says she was "wasting my time with someone who I'm not investing in, where really I would probably be better spending the time out in the world possibly meeting someone." Of casual encounters, Rita says:

> I'm not a huge fan of the idea; it definitely makes me feel awful afterward. . . . It just feels disjointed. It feels messy. It arises out of not a great context, you're both out getting drunk.

Rita describes a casual encounter with a friend, where they had both recently broken up with people and had had a few drinks:

> We had been hanging out together, and sometimes we would just cuddle a little bit or be close to each other. One time we took it further and it was intrinsically awkward . . . because we both knew it was not coming from a place of being sexual, it was

coming from a sadder place of just needing someone, maybe to hold each other. It wasn't natural, it wasn't fluid, and ultimately we just called it off.

Rita is now in a different place. She is in a committed relationship that she describes as "mutual." The two became friends on Facebook. She was attracted to his inspiring postings and found him physically attractive. They share similar values: they are both invested in having a family and children. Rita believes he is someone who will allow their children to express themselves, choose their own religion, and "identify with gender and sexuality the way they like."

Rita states her current relationship is about "surprising each other, continuing to get to know each other, sharing new experiences."

This is definitely the first relationship that I have felt very much a *we*. In the past . . . I was forcing a *we* on the guys who were not ready for it. I knew they were not ready for a commitment that I was looking for. . . . In my previous relationship I needed to be my best self all the time and remain conscious [of that] in order to keep their attention. . . . I'm free [in my current relationship] to be who I am, and he knows I am coming back.

Rita summarizes:

Over the course of three main relationships I have had before this one—the high school, the college, and the postgrad—I have gotten better at what to expect from myself. . . . I have come to realize . . . my expectations for being cared for were perhaps very high. [In the past] boyfriends were emotionally unavailable, and sometimes I would try to counter that with needing them to do something for me. Now I take more enjoyment in doing things for myself. . . . Because my life is fuller . . . the attention I give sex isn't as obsessive, ridden with emotion. . . . Whereas I was fighting for attention in other relationships, and using sex to get that attention, in this relationship sex can be sex.

[My partner and I] are pretty open-minded about the way things need to flow. . . . I think we both have a rough idea that we will pursue our education, that kids will come into play, and marriage will come into play. We are not positive in what order, and I think we are okay with that.

I'm 26 and I am not married and I am not freaking out. . . .
I definitely need to be building a partnership, to be building a life,
sharing in the adventure of the relationship. . . . I am okay with
the idea that things aren't predictable. . . . I think by the time I am
in my 30s that my purpose will be more of a given and less of a
search.

In many ways, the lives of these three emerging adults could not
be more dissimilar. Contrast Mahesh's strict religious upbringing
and cultural framework with Rita's free-form sexual experimentation, for example. And yet the three share many ideas about work
and relationships that are similar and reflective of the thinking of their
peers: they all put a high premium on finding the right career; they all
seem to believe that getting one's career in order is a primary step before entering a committed, long-term relationship; they have all learned
important lessons about love from past relationships, and are actively
applying those lessons in their lives; they all seem to feel that finding
the right person is essential for romantic happiness; and they have all
reached a place where they feel unhurried about starting a committed
romantic life. There are clear themes specific to the transitional period
of emerging adulthood, even though these themes have been arrived at
by very different routes.

Emerging adults in the study tended to develop their identities in
the two domains sequentially, "selecting," "focusing," and "sequencing"
their life goals (p. 199). Thirty-seven percent of the participants
were firmly committed in one domain only. The largest group of the
participants had not firmly committed and consolidated either identity, suggesting that identity formation is a work-in-progress during
emerging adulthood, not unlike the finding of Luyckx et al. (2014).
While some emerging adults were worried about their lack of identity
commitment in one or both of the domains, others seemed less troubled
by this.

▲ Summary and Conclusions

Emerging adulthood is challenging even in the simplest of times, but
it is especially daunting in the early 21st century where global volatility in the job market and a disintegration of the rules and mores of
romance have combined to make the path to adulthood more of an

off-road adventure than a paved throughway. In the domains of work and love, the lives of emerging adults have shifted from predictable and tradition-bound pathways toward more fluid, fragmented, and unpredictable possibilities. The two domains of work and love powerfully influence one another, in both gross and subtle ways. Tensions and pressures carry from one domain to the other, and decisions made in one domain can constrict the choices made in the other.

In comparison to previous generations, emerging adults are taking longer to develop firm identities in both career and romance, with only a small minority evidencing highly developed identities in both domains. Flexibility in both arenas can be adaptive, given the social and economic realities emerging adults are facing.

For those emerging adults who are relatively well resourced, one clear trend in today's generation of emerging adults is to put work identity ahead of romantic commitment. Whereas in the past, marriage was viewed as an *early* step in the adulthood journey—one that could help lend support to career development—our participants tended to view long term commitment as a *later* step, one that is undertaken only after solidifying a career. Perhaps this is because forging a career now requires more sustained effort—and more missteps and false starts—than it did a generation or two ago. Emerging adults seem to sense the enormity of the career challenge they face and feel a desire to make some substantial progress along that path before adding on the responsibilities of intimate relationships and family.

Partly because of the longer career trajectory many emerging adults are following, they are being afforded a longer period of time in which to experiment romantically. Thus, they are using their 20s as a relationship "laboratory" and are delaying long term commitments.

Lacking the support of a spouse for much, or all, of their 20s, many emerging adults are seeking support from their friends and parents. Friends can help them assess their lives and clarify their values, while parents can lend economic, emotional, and domestic support (i.e., a place to live). Tensions naturally arise as parents learn how to encourage independence while providing nurturance, and as emerging adults walk the difficult line between needing their parents and needing to be autonomous.

Emerging adults seem to be well aware of the potential difficulties they will face as they try to successfully establish both careers and long-term relationships. Many are putting a great deal of effort into anticipating future issues in this regard. Traditional gender roles remain embedded in their scripts: women tend to plan toward becoming both breadwinners and homemakers/caregivers, while men still seem to plan more exclusively for the breadwinner role, a dynamic both genders appear to endorse. Because women anticipate bearing the brunt of the domestic responsibility, many of them begin truncating their career options at a premature stage. Clarifying conversations can be essential tools for partners to learn about each other's attitudes and expectations regarding the balancing of romance and career, and can help head off the crises that may happen when expectations remain unvoiced.

Studies reveal that identity formation in the domains of work and love is difficult for both men and women. Not surprisingly, men tend to develop firm identities sooner in the career domain, while women develop earlier in the relationship domain. Also not surprisingly, women tend toward romantic pathways that include long-term and steady relationships, while men are more likely to lean toward pathways that involve casual relationships. Eventually, for many emerging adults there is a balancing out as both genders mature and come together around shared goals: satisfying careers for both partners, and a long-term, committed, and intimate relationship. It may be taking emerging adults longer to "get there" than it did their parents, but the road emerging adults walk appears to be more complicated and not well mapped.

▲ References

Aquilino, W. (2006). Family relationships and support systems in emerging adulthood. In J. J. Arnett & J. L. Tanner (Eds.), *Emerging adults in America: Coming of age in the 21st century* (pp. 193–217). Washington DC: American Psychological Association.

Armstrong, K. H., Dedrick, R. F., & Greenbaum, P. E. (2003). Factors associated with community adjustment of young adults with serious emotional disturbance: A longitudinal analysis. *Journal of Emotional and Behavioral Disorders, 11*(2), 66–77. doi:10.1177/106342660301100201

Arnett, J. J. (2006). Emerging adulthood: Understanding the new way of coming of age. In J. J. Arnett & J. L. Tanner (Eds.), *Emerging adults in America: Coming of age in the 21st century* (pp. 3–19). Washington, DC: American Psychological Association. doi:10.1037/11381-001

Carnevale, A. P., Hanson, A. R., & Artem, G. (2017). Failure to launch: Structural shift and the new lost generation. *Center on Education and the Workforce.* Washington, DC: Georgetown University. Retrieved from: https://cew.georgetown.edu/cew-reports/failure-to-launch/.

Collins, W. A., & Laursen, B. (2004). Changing relationships, changing youth: Interpersonal contexts of adolescent development. *The Journal of Early Adolescence*, 24(1), 55–62. doi:10.1177/0272431603260882

Collins, A., & van Dulmen, M. (2006). Friendships and romance in emerging adulthood: Assessing distinctiveness in close relationships. In J. J. Arnett & J. L. Tanner (Eds.), *Emerging adults in America: Coming of age in the 21st century* (pp. 219–234). Washington, DC: American Psychological Association. doi:10.1037/11381-009

Coontz, S. (March 31, 2017). Do Millennial men want stay-at-home wives? *The New York Times*. Retrieved from https://www.nytimes.com

Coyle, E. F., Van Leer, E., Schroeder, K. M., & Fulcher, M. (2015). Planning to have it all: Emerging adults' expectations of future work-family conflict. *Sex Roles*, 72(11–12), 547–557. doi:10.1007/s11199-015-0492-y

Coyne, S. M., Padilla-Walker, L. M., & Howard, E. (2013). Emerging in a digital world: A decade review of media use, effects, and gratifications in emerging adulthood. *Emerging Adulthood*, 1(2), 125–137. doi:10.1177/2167696813479782

Fouad, N. A., & Bynner, J. (2008). Work transitions. *American Psychologist*, 63(4), 241.

Frisén, A., & Wängqvist, M. (2011). Emerging adults in Sweden: Identity formation in the light of love, work, and family. *Journal of Adolescent Research*, 26(2), 200–221. doi:10.1177/0743558410376829

Galambos, N. L., Barker, E. T., & Krahn, H. J. (2006). Depression, self-esteem, and anger in emerging adulthood: Seven-year trajectories. *Developmental Psychology*, 42(2), 350–365. doi:10.1037/0012-1649.42.2.350

Gilbert, L. A. (2014). *Men in dual-career families: Current realities and future prospects*. New York, NY: Psychology Press.

Gilbert, L. A., & Rader, J. (2008). Work, family, and dual-earner couples: Implications for research and practice. In S. D. Brown & R. W. Lent (Eds.), *Handbook of counseling psychology* (4th ed.; pp. 426–443). Hoboken, NJ: John Wiley & Sons.

Hettich, P. I. (2010). College-to-workplace transitions: Becoming a freshman again. *Handbook of stressful transitions across the lifespan* (pp. 87–109). New York, NY: Springer Press.

Jordan, J. V. (2010) *Relational-cultural therapy*. Washington, DC: American Psychological Association Press.

Koen, J., Klehe, U., Van Vianen, A. E., Zikic, J., & Nauta, A. (2010). Job-search strategies and reemployment quality: The impact of career adaptability. *Journal of Vocational Behavior*, 77(1), 126–139. doi:10.1016/j.jvb.2010.02.004

Konstam, V. (2007). *Emerging and young adulthood: Multiple perspectives, diverse narratives*: New York, NY: Springer Press.

Konstam, V. (2013). *Parenting your emerging adult: Launching kids from 18 to 29*. Far Hills, NJ: New Horizon Press.

Konstam, V. (2015). *Emerging and young adulthood: Multiple perspectives, diverse narratives* (2nd ed.). Cham, Switzerland: Springer International. doi:10.1007/978-3-319-11301-2

Konstam, V., Tomek, S., Celen-Demirtas, S., & Sweeney, K. (2014). Volunteering and reemployment status in unemployed emerging adults: A time-worthy investment? *Journal of Career Assessment*, 23(1), 152–165. doi:10.1177/1069072714523248

Kroger, J., Martinussen, M., & Marcia, J. E. (2009). Identity status change during adolescence and young adulthood: A meta-analysis. *Journal of Adolescence*, 33(5), 683–698. doi:10.1016lj.adolescence.2009.11.002

Lerman, R. I. (2014). *Proposal 7: Expanding apprenticeship opportunities in the United States*. American University and the Urban Institute Center on Labor, Human Service, & Population. Washington, DC.

Luyckx, K., Seiffge-Krenke, I., Schwartz, S. J., Crocetti, E., & Klimstra, T. A. (2014). Identity configurations across love and work in emerging adults in romantic relationships. *Journal of Applied Developmental Psychology*, 35(3), 192–203. doi:10.1016/j.appdev.2014.03.007

Manning, W. D., Giordano, P. C., Longmore, M. A., & Hocevar, A. (2011). Romantic relationships and academic/career trajectories in emerging adulthood. In F. D. Fincham & M. Cui (Eds.), *Romantic relationships in emerging adulthood* (pp. 317–333). New York, NY: Cambridge University Press.

Mayseless, O., & Keren, E. (2014). Finding a meaningful life as a developmental task in emerging adulthood: The domains of love and work across cultures. *Emerging Adulthood*, 2(1), 63–73. doi:10.1177/2167696813515446

Peake, A., & Harris, K. L. (2002). Young adults' attitudes toward multiple role planning: The influence of gender, career traditionality and marriage plans. *Journal of Vocational Behavior*, 60(3), 405–421. doi:10.1006/jvbe.2001.1840

Pew Research Center. (November 4, 2015). *Raising kids and running a household: How working parents share the load*. Retrieved from http://www.pewsocialtrends.org

Pfau, B. N., & Kay, I. T. (2002). *The human capital edge*. New York, NY: McGraw-Hill.

Putnam, R. D. (2015). *Our kids: The American dream in crisis*. New York, NY: Simon & Schuster.

Rampell, C. (2013). It takes a BA to find a job as a file clerk. *The New York Times*, 19. https://www.nytimes.com/2013/02/20/business/college-degree

Sandberg, S. (2013). *Lean in: Women, work, and the will to lead*. New York, NY: Knopf.

Savickas, M. L. (1997). Career adaptability: An integrative construct for lifespan, life-space theory. *The Career Development Quarterly*, 45(3), 247–259.

Savickas, M. L. (2005). *Career construction theory and practice*. Paper presented at the annual conference of the American Counseling Association, Atlanta, GA.

Savin-Williams, R. C. (2011). Identity development among sexual-minority youth. In S. J. Schwartz, K. Luyckx, & V. L. Vignoles (Eds.), *Handbook of identity theory and research, Vols. 1 and 2* (pp. 671–689). New York, NY: Springer Science and Business Media. doi:10.1007/978-1-4419-7988-9_28

Seiffge-Krenke, I., & Luyckx, K. (2014). Competent in work and love? Emerging adults' trajectories in dealing with work–partnership conflicts and links to health functioning. *Emerging Adulthood*, 2(1), 48–58. doi:10.1177/2167696813516090

Settersten, R. J., & Ray, B. (2010). What's going on with young people today? The long and twisting path to adulthood. *The future of children, 20*(1), 19–41. doi:10.1353/foc.0.0044

Shulman, S., & Connolly, J. (2013). The challenge of romantic relationships in emerging adulthood: Reconceptualization of the field. *Emerging Adulthood, 1*(1), 27–39. doi:10.1177/2167696812467330

Shulman, S., Seiffge-Krenke, I., Scharf, M., Boiangiu, S. B., & Tregubenko, V. (2016). The diversity of romantic pathways during emerging adulthood and their developmental antecedents. *International Journal of Behavioral Development.* doi:0165025416673474

Slaughter, A. M. (2015). *Unfinished business.* New York, NY: Oneworld Publications.

Smock, P. J., Manning, W. D., & Porter, M. J. (2005). "Everything's there except money": How money shapes decision to marry among cohabitors. *Journal of Marriage and Family 67*(3), 680–696.

Stanley, S. M., Rhoades, G. K., & Markman, H. J. (2006). Sliding versus deciding: Inertia and the premarital cohabitation effect. *Family Relations, 55*(4), 499–509. doi:10.1111/j.1741-3729.2006.00418.x

Stokes, H., & Wyn, J. (2007). Constructing identities and making careers: Young people's perspectives on work and learning. *International Journal of Lifelong Education, 26*(5), 495–511.

Watters, E. (2006). In my tribe. In C. Amini & R. Hutton (Eds.), *Before the mortgage: Real stories of brazen loves, broken leases, and the perplexing pursuit of adulthood* (pp. 86–89). New York, NY: Simon Spotlight Entertainment.

Willoughby, B. J., & James, S. L. (2017). *The Marriage Paradox: Why emerging adults love marriage yet push it aside.* New York, NY: Oxford University Press.

9 ▲
Love and Living LGBTQ

A double life is exhausting and ultimately tragic,
because you can't ever be loved if you can never
be known.
The biggest change for me is not going from male
to female: It's going from someone who has a secret
to someone who doesn't have secrets anymore.
—Solomon, 2012, p. 624

Heterosexuality continues to be the worldwide social norm and re-mains a basic assumption about an individual (Savin-Williams, 2011; Morgan, 2013). However, history reveals that same-sex sexual behaviors and transgendered individuals have long existed across global cultures. Therefore, any progress made toward the social acceptance and vali-dation of LGBTQ-identified (lesbian, gay, bisexual, transgender, queer) individuals must be seen, not so much as social "progress," but as acknowledgement of what has always been the case (Diller, 2011; Sue & Sue, 2015). Nevertheless, heteronormativity is slowly being decentered as our society continues to evolve (Torkelson, 2012). Attitudes and behaviors are changing towards LGBTQ-identified individuals, partic-ularly among the current generation of emerging adults, who are recep-tive to diversity, including sexual diversity. According to 2017 data from the Pew Research Center, 79% percent of individuals 18 to 29 years of age support same-sex marriage (Pew Research Center, 2017).

In a heteronormative society such as ours, social conventions and structures present challenging scenarios for LGBTQ-identified emerging adults: legal barriers, second-class citizenship (Frost, 2011), social stigma, and explicit and implicit discrimination persist (Sue & Sue, 2015). Despite similarities and common concerns that LGBTQ-identified emerging adults share with their heterosexual peers, there are challenges that are specific to the LGBTQ community—challenges that are complex and multidimensional in scope (e.g., intersectionality of multiple identities; Fukuyama & Ferguson, 2000).

LGBTQ identification is not isolated to one's sexuality or gender. It is not limited to particular behaviors or sexual acts. Rather, it is a process that is layered with complexity and requires incorporation of psychological, emotional, romantic, and sexual-orientation considerations. Previous research has tended to focus entirely on sexual desires and behaviors within same-sex relationships, neglecting the importance of relational contexts (Frost, Meyer, & Hammack, 2015). Couples who identify as LGBTQ do not differ from heterosexual couples in their desires for commitment, intimacy, love, and trust. However, some differences do exist and will emerge more clearly over time as society continues to evolve and heteronormativity is no longer the yardstick (Torkelson, 2012). Given that emerging adulthood is a time of experimentation and exploration, it is not surprising that a significant number of emerging adults question heteronormativity. The intersection of multiple and sometimes competing sexual identities and orientations is likely to be experienced during this juncture of development.

Coming of age sexually and developing a nonheterosexual identity has received scant attention in the emerging adulthood literature, even though sexuality is considered a key component of identity development during emerging adulthood (Torkelson, 2012). In fact, as Torkelson astutely notes, "when sexuality has been explicated [in the emerging adult literature], it is the increasing banality of premarital sex practices like 'hooking up' in college and/or related risk-perspective considerations that tend to dominate the narrative" (Arnett, 2004; Bogle, 2008; Collins & van Dulmen, 2006; Lefkowitz & Gillen, 2006, as cited in Torkelson, 2012)" (p. 134).

To date, there is a paucity of research on the intersectionality of sexual/gender identity formation with a complexity of additional dimensions such as race, ethnicity, socioeconomic status, and religion, to name a few, and on the combined and interactional effects of these intersecting dimensions on emerging adults. This intersectionality has important implications for romantic relationships during emerging adulthood. Choices made are informed by these intersectional identities. Though these choices are subject to renegotiation and revision at later points in time, they often set the trajectory for an emerging adult's romantic journey. Thus, the better the understanding of the multidimensional complexities specific to emerging adults in the LGBTQ community, the better the support and communication that can be offered.

In recent years, there has been a blurring and condensing of timing of sexual identity milestones during adolescence and emerging adulthood (Morgan, 2016). Emerging adults and adolescents are using similar same-sex identity labels during these two developmental stages. Historically, it was thought that adolescence was a time in which recognition of same-sex attraction and same-sex identity labels occurred, whereas emerging adulthood was a period in which *consolidation* and refinement of same-sex identity took place, a division that no longer seems to apply (Glover, 2009, as cited in Morgan, 2016).

Diversity and fluidity have been observed among heterosexual emerging adult college students (Vrangalova & Savin-Williams, 2012). Fifty three percent of males and 67% of female students reported that they engaged in sexual identity questioning (Morgan, Steiner, & Thompson, 2010; Morgan & Thompson, 2011). Vrangalova and Savin-Williams (2010) reported that among college students, 79% of females and 43% of males experienced at least a small level of same-sex attraction, and that 53% of females and 22% of males engaged in some fantasizing about members of the same sex. These findings are culturally specific, however, and not generalizable to all cultural contexts.

In this chapter, we will first attempt to clarify terminology, then we will explore some of the issues and challenges faced by members of the LGBTQ community, including stigma and its pernicious role in the lives of LGBTQ individuals. We will examine queer theory and explore similarities and differences across sexual and gender identities. A closer look at the dynamics of "coming out" and of living as a transgendered person will be presented. In keeping with the structure of the other chapters, the narratives of Mateo and Andrea will be discussed at the end, capturing some of their struggles and experiences.

This chapter does not present original data; CQR methodology is not applied here. Of the 29 research participants we interviewed, eight self-identified as LGBTQ (four as gay, three as bisexual, and one as queer). None of the eight participants identified as lesbian or transgender. According to CQR guidelines proposed by Hill (2012), a minimum of nine to twelve participants is needed to proceed with an analysis, a criterion we did not meet.

▲ Clarification of Terms

It is important to highlight both the breadth and fluidity of sexual and gender identities. There are several nomenclatures and acronyms that are intended to inclusively represent the diverse and dynamic nature of sexual and gender identities. LGBTQ, for the purposes of this chapter, is a broad acronym that represents lesbian, gay, bisexual, trans/transgender, and queer-identified individuals. "Trans" is used as an umbrella term to capture the spectrum of gender-variant identities.

This section acknowledges the diversity, complexity, and evolution of this area of study. The terms are culturally informed, flexible, and subject to changes in meaning and construction over time. Before defining terms, we will examine the issues related to the distinctions between sexual identity and sexual orientation.

Definitions of sexual identity have evolved from emphasis on self-identification (with or without disclosure of a gay or lesbian label) to a multidimensional conceptualization that includes one's sexual attraction, sexual fantasies, and sexual activity, as well as one's emotional, romantic, and social preferences (Morgan, 2016).

Dillon and colleagues (2011) developed a model of sexual identity based on Marcia's more general model of identity development (discussed in Chapter 2). Characterized by flexibility and nonlinearity, the following five identity statuses were constructed: (a) *compulsory heterosexuality*, characterized by "heterosexual and heterosexism social assumptions," (b) *active exploration*, characterized by "purposeful exploration and evaluation of one's sexuality," (c) *diffusion*, characterized by "either a carefree or anxiety-provoking lack of personal or social commitments," (d) *deepening commitment*, characterized by "active exploration of personal and social identities," and (e) *synthesis*, in which "individual sexual identity, group membership identity, and attitudes toward dominant and marginalized sexual orientation groups merge into an overall sexual self-concept" (Morgan, 2016, pp. 264–265).

Savin-Williams (2011) emphasizes an interactive perspective, pointing out that while there are developmental similarities that all individuals share, each identity pathway is based on a unique combination of personal sexual orientation with numerous individual and group characteristics. Intersectional identities resulting from membership in multiple social groups such as race, gender, sexual identity, ethnicity, gender identity, age, and religion inform both one's identification experiences and one's resulting world views (Nadal, 2013).

Sexual orientation is no longer described using three categories of sexual orientation (heterosexual, bisexual, or gay/lesbian; Vrangalova & Savin-Williams, 2012). As noted above, updated definitions focus on multiple dimensions of sexual orientation, including sexual attraction, behavior, and fantasies; and emotional preference, social preference, self-identification, and lifestyle, consistent with, but not identical to, Kinsey and colleagues' (1948) seven-category sexual orientation continuum (which ranges from an exclusively heterosexual rating of 0 to an exclusively gay rating of 6; Morgan, 2016). Since Kinsey et al. made their contributions many decades ago, a temporal—past, present, and future—focus has been added, to allow for fluidity and shifts in orientation and identity that occur over time (Klein, Sepekoff, & Wolf, 1985, as cited in Morgan, 2016).

The terminology continues to evolve and refine. Explanations of relevant terminology are presented, intended to be inclusive. Though a bit of an oversimplification, the following statement may help clarify the range of possibilities and the terms used to denote them: "Sexual identity is who I go to bed *with*. Gender identity is who I go to bed *as*" (Kort, 2017).

- Gender—a social combination of identity, expression, and social elements related to masculinity and femininity. It includes gender identity (self-identification), gender expression (self-expression), social gender (social expectations), gender roles (socialized actions), and gender attribution (social perception). **https://lgbt. wisc.edu/documents/Trans_and_queer_glossary.pdf**
- Intersex—refers to a difference at birth between the sex chromosomes, the external genitalia, and/or the internal reproductive system that is not considered "standard" or normative for either the male or female sex. **https://lgbt.wisc.edu/ documents/Trans_and_queer_glossary.pdf**
- Asexual—(a) a sexual orientation whereby "a person does not experience sexual attraction or desire to partner for the purposes of sexual stimulation," (b) "a spectrum of sexual orientations where a person may be disinclined towards sexual behavior or sexual partnering." **https://lgbt.wisc.edu/documents/Trans_and_ queer_glossary.pdf**
- Pansexual—"A sexual orientation where a person desires sexual partners based on personalized attraction to specific physical traits, bodies, identities, and/or personality features, which may or may not be aligned to the gender and sex binary." **https://lgbt. wisc.edu/documents/Trans_and_queer_glossary.pdf**
- Bisexual—"A person emotionally, physically, and/or sexually attracted to males/men and females/women. This attraction does not have to be equally split between genders, and there may

be a preference for one gender over others." (That preference may shift over time.) **https://lgbt.wisc.edu/documents/Trans_and_ queer_glossary.pdf**

- Polyamory—refers to having romantic, emotional, and/ or sexual relationships with multiple partners and can include: open relationships, polyfidelity (having multiple romantic relationships with sexual contact restricted to those), and multiple primary/secondary relationships (a "secondary" relationship is distinguished from a "primary" relationship by having fewer expectations in terms of commitment, finances, emotional intimacy, and other factors). **https://lgbt.wisc.edu/ documents/Trans_and_queer_glossary.pdf**
- Gender queer—a person who identifies as neither male nor female; includes those individuals who consider themselves both genders, or neither. **https://lgbt.wisc.edu/documents/Trans_and_ queer_glossary.pdf**
- Gender fluid—gender identity is neither male nor female on a fixed basis. Person identifies as a male some days and female on other days, and some days as neither. **https://lgbt.wisc.edu/ documents/Trans_and_queer_glossary.pdf**
- Transgender—a person "whose behavior departs significantly from the norms of the gender suggested by his or her anatomy at birth" (Solomon, 2012, p. 599).
- Transsexual—a person who "has had surgery or hormones to align his or her body with a non-birth gender." (Solomon, 2012, p. 599)
- Transvestite—a person who "wears clothing usually reserved for the other gender" (Solomon, 2012, p. 599).

⚠ Stigma and Internalized Homophobia

LGBTQ-identified individuals experience both overt and covert stigma (Sue & Sue, 2015). For example, in 28 states it is legal to terminate an employee because the employer does not appreciate the gender of the person he or she is in love with (https://www.washingtonpost. com/news/parenting/wp/2017/03/29/homeless-rates-for-lgbt-teens-are-alarming-heres-how-parents-can-change-that/?utm_term=. cfedb7f0942d). The ongoing questioning, uncertainty, and confusion— on the part of both the self and others—can be emotionally exhausting and burdensome. Emotional vulnerability and mental health issues are likely sequelae, particularly when family support is lacking (Frost, Meyer, & Hammack, 2015). Increased levels of substance abuse, sexual risk, and suicidality have been reported among LGBTQ identified emerging adults (Meyer, Dietrich, & Schwartz, 2008, as cited in Sue & Sue, 2015). Even higher rates of suicide have been reported among Black and Latino/a LGBTQ identified youth.

Familial acceptance, on the other hand, helps fortify against depression, substance abuse, and suicidal ideation and behaviors (Ryan, Russell, Huebner, Diaz, & Sanchez, 2010). Although acceptance is associated with a range of salutary outcomes including positive self-esteem and health status, acceptance by family members is frequently in short supply, especially initially. Being misunderstood by one's social networks and/or rejected by family members can negatively affect romantic relationships, as manifested in increased conflict and decreased relational functioning and satisfaction (Frost et al., 2015).

In a qualitative study involving 99 gay and lesbian participants (mean age of 34.38, $SD=9.53$) in relationships that had endured on average 6.86 years ($SD=5.00$), one fourth of whom were married and most cohabitating, Frost (2011) asked the question, how does stigma and intimacy coexist and become integrated in relationships? Negative and positive strategies were identified by Frost et al., findings that were not dissimilar to earlier findings (e.g., Frost & Meyer 2009; Rostosky, Riggle, Gray, & Halton, 2007). Two of the four identified strategies were understood in positive ways: "positive stigma as a generative experience" and "stigma as an opportunity for (re)definition" (Frost, 2011, p. 7).

Based on the research findings of King (2001) and Pals (1999) (findings that are described in greater detail in Chapter 11), positive strategies emphasize opportunities for reframing experiences of stigma within the relationship (Frost, 2011). For example, the experience of lack of public recognition (e.g., being ignored as a family unit in a public setting) can lead to feelings of invisibility and accentuation of one's minority status (Frost, 2011). However, upon further discussion with one's partner, one can feel strengthened by the external stigma he/she is experiencing, an adaptive strategy associated with resilience. An adaptive strategy may also include seeking out safe spaces, communities, and rituals that serve to buffer the negative effects of stigma. Some participants also increased their feelings of empowerment and self-efficacy by seeking out opportunities to participate in politically oriented activities that addressed stigma and social justice issues.

Negative styles of adaptation were also identified. Individuals who felt burdened by stigma associated with their nonnormative identities were more likely to experience stress associated with their minority status. Conflict and dissatisfaction within the relationship were likely to be reported in these relationships (Frost, 2009, 2011, 2013). Frost (2011) also noted that "subtle aspects" of stigma could detract from the joy LBGTQ-identified individuals might experience during periods of accomplishment. Although stigma was not necessarily an ongoing drain on these relationships, it was likely to "contaminate" and detract from joyous experiences (p. 5).

Despite positive steps forward (as well as some backward steps on the political front), there remain questions and concerns as to whether discrimination against LGBTQ emerging adults is decreasing or is simply taking on less explicit tones, in the form of implicit prejudice and discriminatory practices—not unlike the way racism is often practiced in the United States today (Frost et al., 2015). Such less obtrusive acts may be just as pernicious as overt prejudice and perhaps even more disabling in that they are frequently internalized by the recipient and at times cannot be directly accessed and addressed. Internalized societal stigma is subtle and can increase stress levels and negatively impact relationship quality and satisfaction. Subtle stigma is also associated with "increased levels of conflict, loneliness, and sexual problems" (e.g., Frost & Meyer, 2009; Otis, Rostosky, Riggle & Hamrin, 2006; Todosijevic, Rothblum, & Solomon, 2005, as cited in Frost, 2011).

Microacts of aggression, a term originally developed to describe insulting and dismissing acts by non-Black Americans toward African Americans, is relevant to this discussion. These acts can be directed towards individuals who identify as LGBTQ in the forms of microassaults (e.g., "Have you ever had *real* sex?" or "I'm not homophobic, you are being too sensitive"), macroinsults (e.g., subtle glares of disgust or shock—sometimes unconscious or unintentional—when LGBTQ individuals show public displays of affection), and microinvalidations (e.g., nullifying feelings and experiences, as when a heterosexual says, "I'm not homophobic," after an LGBTQ person confronts them about a biased or hurtful statement; Kort, 2017).

In sum, stigma can be implicit and explicit and can result in pernicious effects among individuals in relationships that are nonheteronormative. LGBTQ-identified individuals frequently feel that their relationships are not accorded the same level of social support and recognition, nor the same political, moral, and legal standing as those of heterosexuals

(Herek, 2006, as cited in Frost, 2011). Because they are denied the same rights as heterosexual couples, same-sex couples are often relegated to second-class citizenship, which is likely to compromise their social and psychological well-being (Riggle, Rostosky, & Horne, 2010, as cited in Frost, 2011). To avoid dealing with stigma directly, many LGBTQ-identified emerging adults elect not to disclose their sexual identity and/orientation, a choice that is fraught with burden and stress (Meyer, 2003, as cited in Frost, 2011).

Much of the subtle stigma that LGBTQ emerging adults experience may be a result of heteronormative prejudice embedded in the language, literature, and assumptions of culture itself. Queer Theory seeks to address this.

▲ Queer Theory

Queer theory is an approach to literature and theory that attempts to "dethrone" heteronormative language as the standard. Queer theory enriches the emerging adulthood literature by bringing sexuality to the forefront; it affords us new ways to examine, critique, and discuss transitions to adulthood. According to Torkelson (2012), the study of sexual exploration during emerging adulthood has been diminished by heteronormative society, a society which passes judgment on certain ideas and practices, while privileging ideals such as opposite-gender relationships, traditional marriage, monogamy, and procreativity.

By challenging heterosexist assumptions, queer theory allows for the examination of relationships between sexuality and gender; it also offers greater opportunities for transgender studies. Torkelson argues that by challenging "normal" sexual identity during the period of emerging adulthood, a key cornerstone of queer theory, alternative models can emerge to highlight and inform societal expectations and norms. Queer theory attempts to elevate the importance of understanding sexuality for everyone who transitions to adulthood; researchers in turn can gain a better understanding of individuals whose paths to adulthoods might vary from normative models.

Queer theory acknowledges that the development of a sexual-minority identity varies from person to person. During emerging adulthood, the identities of queer-identified youth fluctuate significantly more than those of their heterosexual counterparts. Frequently, queer youth resist labeling or else construct identities that are distinctly different from current conceptualizations (Tolman & Diamond, 2001; Moore & Norris, 2005, as cited in Torkelson, 2012). Torkelson argues that queer theory offers an opportunity to increase our understanding as to how individuals experience the development of their sexual identities in relationship to their constructions of adulthood.

As Morgan (2012; 2016) points out, established milestones for the development of a sexual-minority identity include same-sex attraction, same-sex behavior, self-identification with a sexual-minority label, and disclosure to others. But some researchers, such as Torkelson (2012), argue that sexual identification may come before same-sex behavior, and Morgan emphasizes the diversity even within heterosexual sexual-identity development. Sexuality should perhaps be viewed on a continuum, a notion that is consistent with queer theory; as a result, many emerging adults might choose to reject traditional labels of sexuality and gender, highlighting instead the complexity, variability, and flexibility that is inherent to the experiences of many emerging adults of all sexual identities. For example, individuals, particularly women, are self-identifying as bisexual at increasing rates, a trend that may shift over time (Torkelson, 2012).

In sum, queer theory attempts to decenter the normative status of heterosexual traditions by directly articulating, rather than underplaying, the importance of sexuality for *all* individuals transitioning to adulthood. It also heightens our awareness of the circumstances nonheterosexuals and others with nonnormative sexual and gender identities face. It honors and addresses the complexity of sexuality both for researchers and for those who are coming of age.

▲ LGBTQ Relationships: Similarities and Differences

The universal uniting factor that all emerging adults share is the need to develop a sexual identity that fits. There has been interest in characterizing the sexual and romantic relationships of LGBTQ individuals, specifically in comparison to heteronormative individuals (Rith & Diamond, 2012). Overall, when group comparisons between sexual minority and heteronormative individuals are made, results reveal many similarities and some differences (e.g., Torkelson, 2012; Frost, 2015; Morgan, in press).

A majority of LGBTQ adolescents report that they have had sexual experiences in mixed-sex dating contexts, attributed most likely to mixed-sex attractions, interest in clarifying one's sexual identity, and/or need to cover up a sexual-minority identity (Morgan, 2017). With respect to number of same-sex relationships, LGBTQ adolescents and heterosexual adolescents have reported a comparable number of relationships (Morgan, in press).

Willoughby and James (2017) found little difference in the ways sexual-minority and heteronormative emerging adults speak about commitment, marital timing, and marital importance. Although there was a great deal of variation within each group, the sexual minority group, comprised of mostly men, "view[ed] the world similarly" (p. 168). Torkelson (2012) discusses the increasing practice of partnership by choice of LGBTQ individuals as opposed to legal partnership (i.e., marriage), with the intent of procreation.

Frost and Gola (2015) conducted a study that relied on multiple qualitative and quantitative measurements to assess the meaning of intimacy. Based on these markers, they found no differences between heterosexual and same-sex couples in the ways in which they live intimacy. The 150 individuals in the study who self-identified as LGBQ described the same relationship maintenance strategies, patterns of exclusivity, and factors leading to relationship breakups as heterosexuals. Similarly, Fagundes and Diamond (2013, as cited by Morgan, 2017) reported that heterosexual and same-sex couples reported the same likelihood of relationship violence and a similar association between sexual satisfaction and overall relationship quality (p. 4).

As discussed in the previous section on stigma, however, same-sex couples continue to experience a disproportional amount of social stigma, which seems to be based on assumptions of difference that are largely unfounded. What is common to the diverse experiences of same- sex couples is that their identity labels (LGBTQ) place them outside conventional norms and in turn they are vulnerable to shame, harassment, and lack of social support and public validation of their romantic relationships (Rith & Diamond, 2012). Differences between the two groups may be underreported given that comparative research has tended to rely on quantitative comparisons exclusively, a pattern that may not capture nuanced meanings of intimacy and other related constructs in these populations (e.g., commitment, sacrifice). In addition, the political and social contexts LGBTQ emerging adults are navigating must be considered when trying to make meaning of the reported results.

Differences between males and females have been reported in same-sex relationships. Adolescent girls, for example are more likely to report that their relationships emerged from their respective friendships and memberships in communities that are supportive of LGBTQ youth. Same-sex relationships between men are more likely to emerge from sexual encounters and tend to be characterized by less emotional attachment and intimacy between the partners and less social support than either same-sex relationships between two women or mixed-sex relationships (Morgan, 2016). In keeping with these results, same-sex adult males' relationships tend to be less sexually exclusive in comparison to same-sex female relationships; same-sex females' relationships tend to report higher levels of emotional connectedness, cohesion, and intimacy in comparison with male same-sex relationships (Rith & Diamond, 2012).

It is important to note that there is a need to move beyond the assessment of similarities and differences between LGBTQ and heteronormative emerging adults. Rather, specific sociocultural and interpersonal contexts of LGBTQ must be examined on their own merits (Umberson, Mieke, & Lodge, 2015). Understanding the interpersonal processes and mechanisms through which an individual's status as an LGBTQ-identified emerging adult affects the formation and development of intimate bonds is crucial (Rith & Diamond, 2012). Research efforts that explore intersectionalities between an individual's various group identities (e.g., cultural, ethnic, religious, socio-economic, etc.) and how they may inform sexual and gender identity are critically needed as well.

▲ Coming Out

Because of the stigmas and prejudices that exist on a widespread basis— and the risks attendant with these—coming out can be a stressful decision for LGBTQ-identified emerging adults who choose to take this step. The process of coming out—the open acknowledgement of one's sexual orientation—is not a one-time event, however; it is an ongoing process that must be addressed with each new context and relationship (e.g., change in job, change in social networks, the making of new work friends, etc.). LGBTQ-identified individuals are continually faced with choices about when and with whom to self-disclose (Sue & Sue, 2015;

Kort, 2017) With each new experience, feelings of vulnerability, shame, rejection, and stigmatization are likely to be aroused.

Black and Latino gay and lesbian youth are even more reluctant to come out, given their multiple minority-group memberships and the complexity and potential stigma associated with their multiplicity (Sue & Sue, 2015). Estrada, Rigali-Oiler, Arciniega, and Tracey (2011) reported that gay Mexican American males experience a greater degree of internalized homophobia, partially due, perhaps, to being members of a machismo-oriented culture (as cited in Sue & Sue, 2015). Religious affiliation also adds to the level of complexity and to the potential for rejection and/or stigmatization.

For transgender individuals, the coming out process unfolds over a longer period of time, and the process typically involves preparing their social networks and work colleagues for the physical changes that will be occurring (Budge, Tebbe, & Howard, 2010).

Coming out is a process that results in a series of complex cognitive, affective, and behavioral changes (Sue & Sue, 2015). In using the term "coming out," the implication is that one is in the process of learning to recognize and accept what one is; immutability is implied as the individual gears up for his or her "debut." This does not reflect the experience of many LGBTQ-identified youth; they come out at different times in their lives and, for many, the process is not always linear.

Although her theory has not been validated, Vivienne Cass's six-stage theory of gay and lesbian identity carries no connotation that such an identity is a fundamental way of being, determined prenatally or in early childhood (1979). She identifies the following stages: (a) identity confusion (Who am I?); (b) identity comparison (I am different); (c) identity tolerance (I am probably gay); (d) identity acceptance (I am gay); (e) identity pride (Gay is good, heterosexuals are bad); and (f) identity synthesis (My gayness is only one part of me).

It is important to note that with increasing social acceptance of sexual diversity, coming-out models and their applicability have been questioned, particularly given that these models do not address important intersectionalities such as race, ethnicity, nationality, religion, and socioeconomic class (Chun & Singh, 2010). However, given the fact that there are so few road signs to guide emerging adults and the clinicians who work with them, existing models may still be helpful, provided they are viewed in a way that acknowledges complexity and supports a nonessentialist orientation.

Overall, stage models of identity development have been criticized for being reductionistic and simplistic, as well as emphasizing linear growth. Increasingly, researchers are highlighting the fluidity of sexual orientation, the importance of contexts (e.g., prisons), and the need to view development as a nonlinear process. Furthermore, models that have been proposed have not acknowledged bisexual or transgender identity and have rarely addressed the significance of race, religious orientation, and ethnicity (DeBlaere, Brewster, Sarkees, & Moradi, 2010). Assumptions about coming out are based on predominantly White or White-identified lesbian, gay, bisexual, and trans individuals, with a paucity of discussion about cultural differences and how they affect the meaning, process, and role of coming out (e.g., the roles of individualism, independent identity, and separation from family of origin). In addition, it has been argued that the process of identity is inappropriately conflated with the group identification, and that it is necessary for LGBTQ-identified youth to engage with both individual and group identity processes, particularly given their past history of being an invisible minority group (Sue & Sue, 2015).

Given the complexity of sexual and gender identification, and given the pervasiveness and subtlety of social bias, it seems that no easy advice regarding coming out may be dispensed. Coming out is a continual and complicated process that is as individualized as the persons involved. Any attempt to offer support to an emerging adult engaged in this process must be informed by an acknowledgement of the intersectionalities of that individual, as well as by an understanding of the individual's unique psychology and web of social contexts. Certainly, more research needs to be done in this area to increase general sensitivity and understanding.

The same may be said for the topic of transgenderism, a topic rife with disagreement and misunderstanding.

▲ Transgender

Transsexualism is not a sexual mode or preference. It is not an act of sex at all. It is a passionate lifelong, ineradicable conviction, and no true transsexual has ever been disabused of it.
—Jan Morris, as cited in Solomon, 2012, p. 599

A male child who says, "I must be a girl because only girls want to do these things," is not showing evidence of transgender; he's showing evidence of sexism.
—Stephanie Brill, as cited in Solomon,
2012, p. 609

Transgender is an inclusive term that encompasses anyone whose behavior departs significantly from the norms of the gender suggested by his/her anatomy at birth. Gender dissonance, the experience of incongruity between who one *feels* one is and who one *is told* one is, can manifest itself in children as early as age 3, or even younger. Significantly, this experience of incongruence has been termed a disorder (gender identity disorder or GID) by clinicians, mental health professionals, and the medical community.

Although behavior that varies from gender norms is "tolerated" by society when children are very young, by age 7, children are pressured into expressing stereotypes consistent with their respective genders (Solomon, 2012). Pressure to be gender-conforming can burden and confuse a child; it can be emotionally and cognitively depleting, and emotional sequelae may follow (e.g., depression, anxiety, learning disabilities). Only one in four children given a GID diagnosis will show full cross-gender identification in adolescence, a statistic that highlights the instability, complexity, and fluidity of the behaviors and issues associated with gender dissonance (Solomon, 2012). Decisions related to raising children with GID diagnoses are immensely challenging.

Labels matter. As noted above, transsexual refers to a person who "has had surgery or hormones to align his or her body with a nonbirth gender," while transvestite refers to a person who "wears clothing usually reserved for the other gender" (Solomon, 2012, p. 599). Solomon (2012) asserts that the confusion in terminology between LGB and transgender is in part due to the fact that the tendency toward cross-gender expression and behavior is more prevalent amongst gay individuals than heterosexuals, which has turned transgenderism into a gay issue in many people's minds. One half of transwomen and a third of transmen are gay or bisexual.

The causes of gender dissonance are unknown. Although gender dissonance prevalence rates appear to be more common than in the past, that perception may be attributable to living in a globally interconnected world. Media celebrities such as Bruce Jenner/Caitlyn Jenner and Laverne Cox, the first openly transgendered actress to receive a

Primetime Emmy Award nomination, have certainly raised collective awareness related to transgender-related issues.

To review basic terminology, a transman is born a female and elects to become a man, whereas a transwoman is born a male and elects to become a female. It must be noted that these labels are considered demeaning by some, and therefore many prefer the terms "assigned male at birth" (AMAB) or "assigned female at birth" (AFAB) to describe one's birth status, and "affirmed female" or "affirmed male" to describe one's status after transition. Many individuals refer to the nontrans population as cisgender; the Latin prefix cis means "on the same side." Clinicians, mental health professionals, the medical establishment, and the general public alike need to be cognizant and sensitive of the meanings and political agendas associated with these terms.

Prevalence rates are difficult to determine due to the shame and secrecy associated with gender dissonance. It is estimated that 1 in 5 or 10 individuals who experience discomfort with their birth gender will pursue genital surgery and, as previously mentioned, one quarter of children who have received a psychiatric diagnosis of Gender Identity Disorder (GID) will show full cross-gender identification.

Transitioning refers to the process a trans person undergoes when changing their bodily appearance either to be more congruent with the gender sex they feel themselves to be and/or to be in harmony with their preferred gender expression (Kort, 2017). There are between 32,000 and 40,000 postoperative transwomen in the United States.

Natal females who transition can usually achieve a public perception of maleness once they develop facial and body hair and deepened voices. However, their sex organs are different from those of natal males; most cannot urinate while standing, and none can achieve a male orgasm. Natal males who become females often retain some male appearance because of their body size/shape and the thickness of their bones. Their postoperative genitalia, sexual response, and urination patterns, however, can be almost identical to genetic females. *Sex reassignment surgery* is a term used by some medical professionals to refer to a group of surgical options that alter a person's biological sex. (*Gender confirmation surgery* is considered by many to be a more affirming term.) In most cases, one or multiple surgeries are required to achieve legal recognition of gender variance. There are various medical options that can be considered, such as top surgery, bottom surgery, and hormonal medical therapy.

Some transgender individuals do not have surgery due to the financial costs. Top surgery ranges between $5,000 and $10,000, whereas bottom surgery ranges between $15,000 and $25,000. An increasing number of insurance companies have been covering gender-affirming surgeries. Sex changing interventions are considered "non-trivial." They involve both life-risks and risks to sexual sensation as well as a lifelong commitment to managing hormone replacement (Kort, 2017).

The following gender affirmative principles have been put forth to help guide both transgender individuals and the helping professionals who work with them. It is important to acknowledge that this area of inquiry is in transition and evolving. The principles include: (a) gender variation/diversity is normal, (b) gender can be fluid, and gender identity and expression can occur along a continuum, (c) dysphoria and co-occurring mental illness is largely the product of minority stress and lack of access to treatment, and (d) most of the symptoms regress when one validates and supports the principle of gender diversity and provides the individual access to medical treatment (Kort, 2017).

There has been increased emphasis on examining factors that facilitate the formation of positive LGBTQ identities among emerging adults. Resilient adaptations have been documented in the literature—although less so for transgender and queer individuals. Many LGBTQ-identified individuals can recognize and appreciate positive aspects of belonging to their respective communities and the accompanying social support that this belonging brings (Singh, Hays, & Watson, 2011), as well as the ability to create families of choice (Riggle et al., 2008, as cited in Sue & Sue, 2015). In addition, the opportunity to serve as positive role models and to demonstrate the sense of freedom that emanates from relinquishment of gender-specific roles has also been identified as a potential source of strength and resilience.

Some final words to consider before closing this topic:

> Masculinity and femininity are not locked in binary competition, but fused in collaboration. . . . I like to imagine a . . . future when gender-bending will not entail surgical procedures, hormone injections, and social disapprobation—a society in which everyone is able to choose his or own gender at any time. . . . If they wish to linger at the middle of a gender spectrum—physically psychologically or both—that too would be possible. (Solomon, 2012, pp .675–676)

On the other hand:

> Choice can be burdensome and exhausting and frightening,
> especially unaccustomed choice. . . . A piece of me thinks people
> are not good at choosing. . . . I likewise believe that choice is the
> only true luxury, that the striving inherent in decision-making
> gives decisions value.
>
> In America, choice is an aspirational currency and even
> knowing the weariness [and human biases] selection entails,
> I like to imagine a future in which we would be able to choose
> everything. I'd quite possibly choose what I have now—and
> would love it even more for having done so. (Solomon, 2012,
> pp. 675–676).

The following section takes the opportunity extract insights from our participants by taking a detailed look at two of our LGBTQ-identified participants, Mateo and Andrea.

▲ Mateo: Coming to America

Mateo is a 26-year-old gay male, born in Lima, Peru, raised in a middle-class "traditional" religious family, and living in the United States for the past 5 years. He identifies as a practicing Catholic and attends church approximately once a month. Mateo came to the United States. to further his education and to realize his hope of finding work in a management capacity in human services. He currently functions as an assistant manager in an organization related to human services, likes his job, and has received multiple promotions and raises along the way. Mateo self-identifies as gay and is currently in a relationship that he anticipates he will end, given his recent realization that his partner does not share his values and goals. He now believes their constructs of a romantic committed relationship are different, as are their levels of readiness to be in a committed relationship.

Mateo describes his ideal relationship as one in which each partner prioritizes the other and is willing to "make sacrifices" for the other and the relationship (sacrifice is a major theme for Mateo). The most important sacrifice a committed couple makes for each other is to give up their single lifestyle, according to Mateo. This includes avoidance of "risky" behaviors such as going to gay clubs; it also includes deleting online dating/app profiles and cutting off communication with gay friends who might serve as temptations, distractions, or hindrances to the relationship.

Mateo's construct of a committed relationship includes monogamy. Each member of the dyad is "a partner, a friend, someone you can trust, someone you can share time with." He is often disappointed by partners who are unwilling to be monogamous and change their "social and outgoing lifestyles." His most recent relationship will end because Mateo has just learned that his partner was lying to him and surreptitiously pursuing a lifestyle that was not in keeping with their mutually stated expectations and desires for the relationship.

> I thought we were really trying to have something formal and we
> talked about it, but that didn't happen. I found out he was still
> texting and meeting different people and having different dates
> and who knows what else. I feel very disappointed about it. He
> didn't want to commit to something serious.
> I felt that we both had something so I was very honest,
> I stopped seeing people. I felt emotionally satisfied with him.
> I liked him physically. I don't regret the experience . . . because
> I see it as an experience to learn. I see this a lot in the gay world.
> Because I am gay, I see a lot of promiscuity. . . . I see it as pleasing
> yourself.

Mateo initially viewed sex as an opportunity to create a connection with a potential partner. He now understands that for many gay men, it becomes "a little more physical and a little bit selfish, just to please yourself, so that's why you have random sex with somebody just because you feel horny."

Mateo describes a very difficult time when he made the decision to share his sexuality with his family at the age of 21. At the time, he was in a relationship with an older man, a relationship that lasted 3 years. In choosing to be in the relationship, he was forced to put his partner above his family and risk losing them—a sacrifice Mateo was willing to make.

> It was very new to my family and they were not comfortable with
> it. It was shocking for my family to know that I was gay. They
> relate gay with illnesses, people dressing as women, they always
> classify [it as] negative. . . . I had to teach them that a gay person

is not only illnesses, not only a person who wants to dress like a woman, not a person that wants to have sex with everybody.

In his early 20s, Mateo felt he had to show his family that being gay did not match their stereotypes (illness, promiscuity, cross-dressing) and described his attempts to reconcile as a type of "sacrifice," performed in order to maintain a positive relationship with his family. Mateo also expended much effort in trying to educate his parents about what being gay means to him. With time, family members embraced Mateo and his partner and viewed his partner as a member of the family.

Mateo describes the relationship with his partner as a happy one in which he felt content. His partner served as a mentor to Mateo and he was devastated when he learned that his partner was not being faithful to him. The experience left Mateo hurt and suspicious; he felt that he had to "shield himself" from similar experiences in the future.

Mateo's cumulative experiences with other gay men have left him less trusting and more cautious. He believes that for many gay men, it is all about "me, me, me" rather than "both, both, both." Mateo states, "It is hard for me to trust right now, I feel like everyone is the same, whatever."

Mateo currently views sacrifice as what he is willing to change about himself in order to be "good" with his partner. Mateo is hoping to have a secure, trusting relationship with someone who would give up a "promiscuous" lifestyle for him. They would refrain from "the dating/sex scene" and "hookup apps" in which "booty calls" are the norm. Although Mateo acknowledges the benefits of FWB and casual encounters, and enjoys such encounters, he frequently feels "empty" and "guilty" afterwards.

Mateo's ideal relationship is one in which a potential partner gives up the gay lifestyle for *him*, a stance that has left Mateo vulnerable to making errors in judgment. He does not seem to entertain the possibility that there is a potential partner out there who is also looking to have a lifestyle similar to the one he envisions for himself.

When Mateo is ready to commit to a relationship, he discontinues his "single" behaviors, and hopes his partner will do the same. Regarding commitment, Mateo states:

If you're really willing to put yourself in a relationship, to lose your single life, or stop doing whatever it is that you want to do . . . then [you] just have to compromise and tell the other person and share what you are going to do. It will be . . . like knowing if you're willing to have a serious relationship.

Mateo expects that in his 30s, his future job and his experiences with romantic relationships may well be different, but his values about relationships will remain constant. He "would love" to be married in his 30s, "building something together." He concludes: "Respect, sacrifices, honesty . . . all of those goals should be equally the same as my partner's. . . . You get married . . . when you really love the person a lot and you know that it is permanent, and that it is *the* person you want to have next to you."

Mateo espouses traditional ideas about romantic relationships and prioritizes monogamy, not unlike 50% of gay males in relationships in the United States (Kort, 2017). The notion that gay men will never find a monogamous gay partner may well be a heterosexist prejudice, as may be the belief that all relationships *should* be monogamous (Kort, 2017). Mateo has a clear construct of what he would like his relationship to be, but he is meeting roadblocks along the way. Has he internalized heterosexist prejudice? His identification as a practicing Roman Catholic man and a gay man may be an intersectionality that is contributing to ambivalence and internalized heterosexist prejudice. Mateo perceives that many gay men are looking for anonymous hookups and/or random sex, a source of frustration and vulnerability for him. Perhaps he will need to further explore how he reconciles and integrates his religious beliefs with his sexual identification as a gay male.

While there have been some progressive movements within the Catholic Church, the fact remains that same-sex behavior is still officially regarded as a violation of natural and divine law. For a person who takes both his religious identity and his sexual identity seriously, this discord cannot help but create intrapersonal conflict. In Mateo's native Peru, Catholicism is the official state religion, practiced by 85–90% of the population, and tends to be practiced somewhat conservatively. It is impossible to know to what degree Mateo has internalized his faith's proscriptions against gay lifestyle choices. Millions of others worldwide share his dilemma of trying to reconcile their religious faith with their identification as LBGTQ. Some are able to set the conflict aside, others are not. For those who are unable or unwilling to do so, "Experiencing a conflict between ethno-religious and gay identity can significantly impact health and well-being . . . [including] depressive moods, self-loathing, suicidal ideations, and feelings of social exclusion"

(Barton, 2010; Coyle & Rafalin, 2001; Schuck & Liddle, 2001, as cited in Pietkiewicz & Kołodziejczyk-Skrzypek, 2016, p. 1574).

Mateo is trying to become more intentional in his search for a partner. Having a thoughtful and committed relationship, one that incorporates monogamy, is a possibility for gay men (Duncan, Prestage, & Grierson, 2015); for Mateo, it likely will require a more targeted approach geared toward finding a like-minded partner, rather than trying to change partners to a perspective and lifestyle that they may not be ready or willing to assume. Mateo has become more judicious in his approach, and appears to be ready to make fewer premature assumptions about potential partners. He is now mindful about rushing into relationships, his previous style of entry. Given Mateo's multiple strengths, his clarity regarding the type of relationship he wants, and his ability to adapt—as evidenced by his history of thriving in a work arena and culture where he was initially a stranger in a strange land—it seems likely that he will eventually find what he is looking for.

The qualities Mateo seeks in a partner—a willingness to be monogamous, to give up a "promiscuous lifestyle," to make sacrifices, to be trustworthy, and to adopt shared goals—reflect the basic requirements of a committed relationship as stated by most of the 29 participants. Despite the many ways in which emerging adults seem starkly different from previous generations in their romantic lives, these basic requirements seem fundamentally unchanged from those of past centuries, and also seem unaffected by gender or sexual orientation.

▲ Andrea: Smelling Colors

Andrea is a 25-year-old bisexual woman—she says this is the first time she has identified herself this way out loud—who does not appreciate labels and views herself as romantically fluid. She is currently working as a child care provider in a job that provides her with a fair amount of work-related satisfaction. Her career aspiration is to become a chef. Andrea was raised in a working-class neighborhood in a religious Roman Catholic household with strong working-class values. She is proud of having worked hard in multiple industries since the age of 16; when younger she worked two jobs in addition to being a student. Unlike her parents, Andrea shares that religion does not play an important role in her current life. She is currently living with her family, with both parents and a younger brother.

Andrea has been in two long-term committed relationships, one with each gender. Interestingly, in her first relationship she described her male partner as a "dude" who enjoyed thrill-seeking, adventurous activities (he currently works as a helicopter pilot), and in her second relationship, she describes her partner, Patti, as a traditional female.

Andrea has been in short-term relationships since her relationship with Patti, and continues to experiment. She has been in both casual encounters and friends-with-benefits relationships. In sharing her narrative, she conveys frustration that people are "trying to be perfect" and as a result, there is lack of genuineness and authenticity. In turn, her experiences of the relationship become compromised. She states:

> Don't lie . . . just share things genuinely. You don't have to change who you are or the other person doesn't have to change who they are to be a 9.5 [on a scale of 1 to 10]. If it works, it works. No one is perfect. . . . You don't need to put on this persona.

Andrea feels strongly that it is important to be genuine, and that lying or hiding from yourself does not serve a relationship well. It ultimately leaves the two people with the task of "unraveling" the subterfuge and compromises their future together.

She refers to her first relationship of 2 years, which began when she was age 15, as one in which she "learned the most about everything. . . . I learned what love was, I learned what sex was. I learned what everything was with this person." She states that in the relationship she learned how to "smell colors"; she developed her inner capacity to see and understand in new ways.

> You are so blind to everything but as you get older you start valuing different things. I care about appearance, but that's not everything. It is so easy to be shallow when you're younger. . . . And not really understand the whole picture. It turns into a lifestyle, whoever you are with.

The relationship ended when Andrea's partner went to college. His mother, as Andrea relays, demanded that they break up, and he was a "typical dude" and consented to her wishes. "He listened to his mom, so it was like, okay, do I have a choice in this? He was kind of basically saying, 'My mom is breaking up with us.'"

When speaking of her ideal romantic relationship, Andrea shares that she has two ideals, one for a male partner and another for a female partner.

> I have two different ideals because it has to do with two different people. One would be a woman and the other would be with a man. . . . I don't know what they would look like, I guess.
>
> I would need to be into them physically and I would say the dude needs to be a little taller than me, and the female needs to be a little shorter than me. . . . And I would love to move to California and live by the ocean, and I would really want to be a chef so they would have to understand the food industry. [I would like to] have a family and just be happy, but not boring. It doesn't mean I have to be married. . . . I feel like marriage helps you, it is such a statement for society and your friends and your family and just people in general like your community. I don't need to be married for me.

That said, Andrea does have some clear ideas about what she wants in a wedding. If she did marry, she says, she would go to a justice of the peace, have a barbecue, and travel to Hawaii—she is quite clear about this.

In her second relationship, at age 19, Andrea describes that she knew she "liked girls." When she invited her partner over to visit with her at her house, her father forbade her partner "from ever coming here again. If you want to see her, you need to leave the house." Andrea states:

> So basically, he kicked me out in a way, without saying it. I was [in a frame of mind of "I love Patti"], and so I lived with her [for 6 or 7 months] and that was a huge thing for me, because I never lived outside of the house, and she was older, 7 years older than me.

Andrea moved in with Patti and essentially they "played house" together for 6 or 7 months. It took 5 months for them to get "everything together, getting stuff for the house, and after the house was 'together,' it felt like, 'Now what do we do?'" Andrea came to the realization that her relationship was an "infatuation." She was also deeply hurt when she discovered that her partner had deceived her and that in retrospect Patti was not an honest and forthright person within the relationship, a value that Andrea holds dear. Andrea made the difficult decision to return home to her family.

Andrea is currently struggling with how to be open with any type of relationship, including a romantic relationship, in part due to her experiences—in various contexts—with deception and lies. She says that romantic partners, in trying to present "perfection," often assume personas that are disingenuous.

> You need to let yourself be vulnerable, to make yourself open enough to let the other person in. [But] I feel like if you are super open, you are going to get super heartbroken in a relationship. If you take things fast [you will get hurt], and with women, you open up faster. So I am learning how to be less open. I need to stop listening to other people and having them put their two cents in about anyone that I like.
>
> I've grown some and I've learned some and I feel like my past relationships are like little pieces of me. We all take things from people. We all take something away from anyone in life, so I don't think I would ever regret anything, no.
>
> As you get older it is like, "This is who I am, take it or leave it." When [you were] younger, it is almost like you were naïve. You were this little girl, just a sweet little daisy or something, and then you are, oh look at all the daisies! And then you smell that color and go back, and then you know the daisies are not good colors, or [not] all of the daisies. Some of them are taller and some them are shorter, and you would go back and say, Oh these are not even daisies. These are just flowers. And then you appreciate flowers.

Andrea, it seems, is learning to see people for who they are and to appreciate what each "flower" has to offer her. A dominant theme with Andrea is the importance of being honest with others about who you are, and not trying to pretend to be a "daisy" when you are a different type of flower. She also recognizes the dangers of being *too* open and forthcoming, and seems to be trying to balance the two. Labels can be constricting to Andrea; for example, she is trying to experience the freedom of declaring her bisexuality without being bound by any preconceptions that the word might carry. She is optimistic that she will find satisfying partners in her life—she is, after all, making herself available.

While Mateo's and Andrea's narratives are distinctly different, they also share certain similarities. Both emerging adults are evolving in their points of view about their sexuality and what they are seeking from future partners. Both have been hurt by dishonesty in past relationships, by partners whose behavior contradicted what they stated they wanted in a relationship, and both seem to be in a place where they are reevaluating their own expectations for honesty in future relationships. Both came from homes that were fairly religious—both Roman Catholic—and both had to struggle with how to reconcile the teachings of the church with the choices they made. Mateo actively practices his religious faith, however, while Andrea doesn't. Both risked losing their families for their partners. Both also had a first major relationship with an older romantic partner who served as a mentor and taught them about love, sex, and disappointment, among other things.

Interestingly, neither Mateo nor Andrea described any particular struggles they had experienced in the world at large as a result of their LBGTQ-identified status. For both of them, it seemed their families were their greatest source of conflict and tension, though they seemed to have made peace with their parents after some initial turbulence. Both seem to be going through evaluative processes that share much in common with those of other emerging adults, regardless of sexual identification. They have accumulated some experiences with long-term intimate relationships and are using those experiences as roadmaps for what to seek and what to avoid in future relationships. Like most emerging adults, they are trying to decide to what degree their romantic futures will be colored by traditional expectations as opposed to new and self-written "rules."

▲ Summary and Conclusions

We continue to live in a heteronormative culture, though it is clear that today's emerging adults are much more receptive to sexual diversity than previous generations, with 79% of adults aged 18–29 now supporting same-sex marriage. Legal and social barriers persist, as do the pernicious consequences of stigma, both overt and subtle. Though more extreme forms of stigmatization are disappearing, the question remains whether they are simply being replaced by subtler and internalized forms of stigma, which can, in some ways, be even more pernicious.

Sexuality is a fluid phenomenon, with some individuals fitting neatly into heteronormative identities and others assuming nonnormative identities or choosing to remain flexible and open-ended about their gender and sexuality. LGBTQ-identification is not limited to one's sexuality or gender, nor to any specific behaviors or sexual acts. Rather, it is a complex and nuanced phenomenon that is colored not only by changing social norms and individual psychological factors but also by one's intersectionalities with various other identities, such as race, ethnicity, religion, and socioeconomic class.

With respect to LGBTQ-identified emerging adults, the ongoing questioning, uncertainty, and confusion—on the part of both the self and others—can influence well-being. Loneliness and feelings of isolation are common, particularly when family support is not forthcoming. Elevated levels of substance abuse, sexual risk, and suicidality have been reported among LGBTQ-identified emerging adults and even higher rates of suicide have been reported among Black and Latino LGBTQ-identified youth. Family support is particularly important at this juncture of development, and serves as an important buffer against stigmatization, both internal and external.

Many LGBTQ-identified emerging adults are seeking commitment, intimacy, love, and trust in romantic relationships, not unlike their heteronormative peers. As the two participants, Andrea and Mateo illustrate, LGBTQ-identified individuals may espouse traditional norms and seek to live traditional lifestyles that include monogamy and child(ren). Clearly, however, there are also differences in the ways that LGBTQ individuals experience and approach romance, as alluded to in the case of Mateo who feels frustrated by the lifestyles of many his LGBTQ emerging adult peers.

Given the complexity of both sexual and gender identity developmental processes and the forms and faces that stigmatization can assume, "coming out" is not a simple or easy process for LGBTQ emerging adults. Nor is it a "one-time" event. Rather, coming out is an ongoing process that must constantly be renegotiated with each new job, social relationship, and life situation. Transgender individuals have an especially challenging path to walk in this regard, as they must often prepare friends, family, and coworkers to accept overt changes, such as a newly identified gender, a new name, new ways of dressing/behaving, and/or physical/medical/surgical changes.

Society moves slowly in its acceptance and support of nonnormative behaviors and identities. Perhaps we can collectively learn a lesson from queer theory and from today's generation of emerging adults—that is, learn to view sexuality and gender in nonbinary terms. Rather than trying to fit individuals into pre-existing categories, perhaps we can entertain the fact that sexuality has been a fluid phenomenon across history and cultures, with some individuals fitting more neatly into heteronormative identities and others taking on nonnormative identities or choosing to remain flexible and open-ended about their gender and sexuality.

▲ References

Budge, S. L., Tebbe, E. N., & Howard, K. A. (2010). The work experiences of transgender individuals: Negotiating the transition and career decision-making processes. *Journal of Counseling Psychology, 57*(4), 377. doi:10.1037/a0020472

Chun, K. S., & Singh, A. A. (2010). The bisexual youth of color intersecting identities development model: A contextual approach to understanding multiple marginalization experiences. *Journal of Bisexuality, 10*(4), 429–451. doi:10.1080/15299716.2010.521059

DeBlaere, C., Brewster, M. E., Sarkees, A., & Moradi, B. (2010). Conducting research with LGB people of color: Methodological challenges and strategies. *The Counseling Psychologist, 38*(3), 331–362. doi:10.1177/0011000009335257

Diller, J. V. (2011). *Cultural diversity: A primer for the human service* (4th ed.). Belmont, CA: Brooks/Cole

Dillon, F. R., Worthington, R. L., & Moradi, B. (2011). Sexual identity as a universal process. In S. J. Schwartz, K. Luyckx, & V. L. Vignoles (Eds.), *Handbook of identity theory and research* (Vols. 1 and 2, pp. 649–670), New York, NY: Springer Press. doi:10.1007/978-1-4419-7988-9_27

Duncan, D., Prestage, G., & Grierson, J. (2015). Trust, commitment, love and sex: HIV, monogamy, and gay men. *Journal of Sex & Marital Therapy, 41*(4), 345–360. doi:10.1080/0092623X.2014.915902

Estrada, F., Rigali-Oiler, M., Arciniega, G. M., & Tracey, T. (2011). Machismo and Mexican American Men: An empirical understanding using a gay sample. *Journal of Counseling Psychology, 58*(3), 358–367. doi:10.1037/a0023122

Frost, D. M. (2011). Stigma and intimacy in same-sex relationships: A narrative approach. *Journal of Family Psychology, 25*(1), 1–10.

Frost, D. M. (2013). Stigma and intimacy in same-sex relationships: A narrative approach. *Qualitative Psychology, 1*(S), 49–61. doi:10.1037/2326-3598.1.S.49

Frost, D. M., & Meyer, I. H. (2009). Internalized homophobia and relationship quality among lesbians, gay men, and bisexuals. *Journal of Counseling Psychology, 56*(1), 97–109. doi:10.1037/a0012844

Frost, D. M., Meyer, I. H., & Hammack, P. L. (2015). Health and well-being in emerging adults' same-sex relationships: Critical questions and directions for research in developmental science. *Emerging Adulthood, 3*(1), 3–13. doi:10.1177/2167696814535915.

Fukuyama, M. A., & Ferguson, A. D. (2000). Lesbian, gay, and bisexual people of color: Understanding cultural complexity and managing multiple oppressions. In R. M. Perez, K. A. DeBord, & K. J. Bieschke (Eds.), *Handbook of counseling and psychotherapy with lesbian, gay, and bisexual clients* (pp. 81–105). Washington DC: American Psychological Association. doi:10.1037/10339-004

Hill, C. E. (Ed.). (2012). *Consensual qualitative research: A practical resource for investigating social science phenomenon.* Washington DC: American Psychological Association.

Kinsey, A. C., Pomeroy, W. B., & Martin, C. E. (1948). *Sexual behavior in the human male.* Philadelphia, PA: W. B. Saunders.

Kort, J. (2017, June). *LGBT and questioning clients: Clinical issues for the therapist, straight or gay.* Presentation at the Cape Cod Institute, Eastham, Massachusetts.

Morgan, E. M. (2012). Not always a straight path: College students' narratives of heterosexual identity development. *Sex Roles, 66*(1–2), 79–93. doi:10.1007/s11199-011-0068-4

Morgan, E. M. (2013). Contemporary issues in sexual orientation and identity development in emerging adulthood. *Emerging Adulthood, 1*(1), 52–66. doi:10.1177/2167696812469187

Morgan, E. M. (2016). Contemporary issues in sexual orientation and identity development in emerging adulthood. In J. J. Arnett (Ed.), *The Oxford handbook of emerging adulthood* (pp. 262–279). New York, NY: Oxford University Press.

Morgan, E. M. (in press). Same-sex relationships and LGBTQ. In *The Encyclopedia of Child and Adolescent Development.* New York, NY: Wiley.

Morgan, E. M., Steiner, M. G., & Thompson, E. M. (2010). Processes of sexual orientation questioning among heterosexual men. *Men and Masculinities, 12*(4), 425–443. doi:10.1177/1097184X08322630

Morgan, E. M., & Thompson, E. M. (2011). Processes of sexual orientation questioning among heterosexual women. *Journal of Sex Research, 48*(1), 16–28. doi:10.1080/00224490903370594

Nadal, K. L. (2013). *That's so gay! Microaggressions and the lesbian, gay, bisexual, and transgender community.* Washington, DC: American Psychological Association. doi:10.1037/14093-000

Pals, J. L. (1999). Identity consolidation in early adulthood: Relations with ego-resiliency, the context of marriage, and personality change. *Journal of Personality, 67*(2), 295–329.

Pew Research Center. (June 16, 2017). Same-sex marriage detailed tables, 2017. Retrieved from http://www.people-press.org/2017/06/26/same-sex-marriage-detailed-tables-2017/

Pietkiewicz, I. J., & Kołodziejczyk-Skrzypek, M. (2016). Living in sin? How gay Catholics manage their conflicting sexual and religious identities. *Archives of Sexual Behavior, 45*(6), 1573–1585. doi:10.1007/s10508-016-0752-0

Rith, K. A., & Diamond, L. M. (2012). Same-sex relationships. In M. Fine & F. Fincham (Eds.), *Family theories: A contextual approach* (pp. 125–148). New York, NY: Routledge.

Rostosky, S. S., Riggle, E. D., Gray, B. E., & Hatton, R. L. (2007). Minority stress experiences in committed same-sex couple relationships. *Professional Psychology: Research and Practice, 38*(4), 392.

Ryan, C., Russell, S. T., Huebner, D., Diaz, R., & Sanchez, J. (2010). Family acceptance in adolescence and the health of LGBT young adults. *Journal of Child and Adolescent Psychiatric Nursing, 23*(4), 205–213. doi:10.1111/j.1744-6171.2010.00246.x

Savin-Williams, R. C. (2011). *Identity development among sexual-minority youth.* In S. J. Schwartz, K. Luyckx, & V. L. Vignoles (Eds.), *Handbook of identity theory and research* (Vols. 1 and 2, pp. 671–689). New York, NY: Springer Science and Business Media. doi:10.1007/978-1-4419-7988-9_28

Singh, A., Hays, D. G., & Watson, L. B. (2011). Strength in the face of adversity: Resilience strategies of transgender individuals. *Journal of Counseling and Development, 20*(1), 20–27. doi:10.1002/j.1556-6678.2011.tb00057.x

Solomon, A. (2012). *Far from the tree: Parents, children and the search for identity.* New York, NY: Scribner/Simon & Schuster.

Sue, D. W., & Sue, D. (2015). *Counseling the culturally diverse: Theory and practice* (7th ed.). Hoboken, NJ: Wiley.

Torkelson, J. (2012). A queer vision of emerging adulthood: Seeing sexuality in the transition to adulthood. *Sexuality Research & Social Policy, 9*(2), 132–142. doi:10.1007/s13178-011-0078-6

Umberson, D., Mieke, B. T., & Lodge, A. C. (2015). Intimacy and emotion work in lesbian, gay, and heterosexual relationships. *Journal of Marriage and Family, 77*(2), 542–556. doi:10.1111/jomf.12178

Vrangalova, Z., & Savin-Williams, R. C. (2010). Correlates of same-sex sexuality in heterosexually identified young adults. *Journal of Sex Research, 47*(1), 92–102. doi:10.1080/00224490902954307

Vrangalova, Z., & Savin-Williams, R. C. (2012). Mostly heterosexual and mostly gay/lesbian: Evidence for new sexual orientation identities. *Archives of Sexual Behavior, 41*(1), 85–10.

Willoughby, B. J., & James, S. L. (2017). *Why emerging adults love marriage yet push it aside.* New York, NY: Oxford University Press.

10 ▲

For Better or . . . Not
Marriage and the Emerging Adult

A Toast to Justin and Kat

> *In marriage, two individuals commit to walking their unique paths,
> yet to somehow doing it together. Each partner invests in the other's
> efforts toward self-actualization, toward becoming the person they
> aim to be. The right partner makes you feel like the best version of
> yourself.*
>
> *The qualities that make Justin and Kat special individuals make them
> a special couple. Their independence pushes them to pursue their goals
> on separate paths. Their love for each other gives them a safe and joyful
> harbor to which to return, again and again.*
>
> *. . . A toast to the music of Justin and Kate's marriage: may any lapses
> in harmony be the seeds of new melodies yearning to be born.*
>
> Anonymous

The desire to marry is an enduring one for most emerging adults.
While the majority of emerging adults are not giving up on marriage,
they *are* delaying this profound and life-altering decision (Maatta &
Uusiautti, 2012). In the United States, 80% of emerging adults view
marriage in their life plan (Hymowitz, Carroll, Wilcox, & Kaye, 2013),
but 66% report that they do not feel ready to marry (Carroll et al.,
2009). For many less economically advantaged emerging adults,
marriage is no longer a goal they feel is within their reach (Cherlin,
2009, 2012).

As discussed in the introductory chapter, today's emerging adults
do not view marriage as a necessary precondition for adulthood. Carroll
et al. (2009) suggest that emerging adults view becoming an adult and
being ready for marriage as two distinct transitions; therefore, one cannot
generalize from one context to another. Emerging adults are increasingly considering alternatives to marriage (e.g., going solo; Willoughby

& Carroll, 2016; Willoughby & James, 2017), sometimes by choice, sometimes due to external constraints (e.g., poverty; Cherlin, 2012).

With marriage rates continuing to decline, especially among those emerging adults without college degrees and marketable job skills, a pattern of unstable cohabiting unions is emerging (Cherlin, 2009). Many of these unions involve childr(en) born outside of marriage. At the same time, marriages among those with college degrees appear to be more stable than in the recent past (Amato, personal communication, July 28, 2016). A split seems to be occurring: some emerging adults are embarking on a marital commitment path, a path associated with greater stability; other emerging adults, confronted with structural and internal challenges, are embarking on a path associated with greater instability and less predictability.

Gender and class differences persist: women continue to attach greater importance to being married as compared to men (Caroll et al., 2007; Marquardt, 2011), although more men (38%) than women (22%) state that it is easier to find happiness as a married person (Taylor, 2014).

The choice to marry during emerging adulthood is generally considered to be a net gain and is viewed as beneficial overall (Hymowitz et al., 2013). Gains in emotional, physical, and economic well-being are attributed to the emotional and fiscal support each member of the union can provide to the other. Closer analysis, however, reveals that these conclusions may not be sufficiently nuanced. Although factors such as improved quality of life, health, happiness, and lower levels of distress are typically associated with marital status, the connection is not clearcut. Recent studies reveal that *satisfaction with one's relationship status*, whether married or not, may be a better determinant of certain aspects of well-being (e.g., life satisfaction and distress) than marital status alone (Lehmann, Tuinman, Braeken, Vingerhoets, Sanderman, & Hagedoorn, 2015). Research questions need to be refined in future studies. Questions that are likely to be more revealing and clarifying include: "Which individuals are more satisfied with being single versus being in a relationship?" "Which aspects of being single or partnered make people more satisfied with their status?" and "How do transitions from one status to another affect status satisfaction" (Lehmann et al., 2015, p. 182).

Although the desire to marry is high among emerging adults in the United States, desire does not predict age of entry into marriage (on average 27 for women and 29 for men) (https://www.theatlantic.com/sexes/archive/2013/03/getting-married-later-is-great-for-college-educated-women/274040/). While over 70% of women desire marriage, only about 20% enter marriage within 4 years after initial assessment (Lichter, Batson, & Brown, 2004). The 29 participants interviewed in our study report that entry into marriage is informed by opportunity, external contingencies, and individual life circumstances (e.g., educational pursuits, financial constraints).

In this chapter, a brief history of marriage will be presented: how it has evolved and continues to evolve. We will also consider the future of marriage in relationship to emerging adulthood. Some of the theoretical paradigms undergirding marital relationships will be examined, and we will explore the meanings emerging adults attach to being married. Our 29 research participants will share their thoughts about their plans for marriage, and the results will be discussed within the framework of marital horizon theory and marital paradigm theory. Finally, we will consider issues such as marital competency, divergent paths, and alternatives to marriage.

▲ Marriage: A Brief Historical Perspective

In order to appreciate emerging adults' attitudes and beliefs about marriage, one must place them in a historical context. History informs emerging adults' beliefs, and those beliefs in turn influence relationship formation and related decisions and behaviors (e.g., educational pursuits, risk-taking; Willoughby, Olson, Carroll, Nelson, & Miller, 2012). Globally and historically, a wide diversity of marital norms and roles has evolved over the millennia, but here we examine three types of marriages, each designed for adaptation to specific environmental norms, roles, and contexts: institutional marriage, companionate marriage, and individualized marriage. Exploration of these three marriage types reveal gradual, incremental shifts over time toward decreasing social control over spouses, a trend that has been termed by Cherlin (2004) the "deinstitutionalization of marriage."

Institutional marriage is a structural arrangement that was designed to meet the basic survival needs of families and to uphold prevalent social structures. Prior to the Industrial Revolution, life in agrarian societies required family members to work together to provide for their basic needs (e.g., food, clothing, and housing; Amato, 2014). Roles were highly differentiated and prescribed, and spouses were selected for function more than affection. Women were expected to be self-sacrificing and to behave in a manner that focused on the maintenance and well-being of the family.

After the Industrial Revolution, individuals tended to migrate to cities for employment. At this time, *companionate marriages*—breadwinner-homemaker partnerships—became the norm. These marriages were less regulated by tradition. Spouses, to a greater extent, were tied to one another by affection, caring, and mutual dependence. Individuals within the marriage still adhered to strict gender norms, however, but the notion that marriage should be based on love between two partners was embraced, as were complementary roles and cooperative teamwork (Coontz, 2005, as cited in Amato, 2014).

In the 1960s and 70s, a period of economic growth and abundance, a third major shift in marital norms occurred. This change was characterized by an even sharper reduction in traditional, "tribal," familial, religious, and social influences (Amato, 2014, p. 42). Self-development and personal fulfillment became a new norm: marital partners were expected to meet each other's needs for growth and self-actualization. If either member of the couple failed to meet the other's psychological needs for self-growth, the marriage was considered a failure (Amato, 2014). Cherlin (2004) coined the term *individualized marriage* to describe these marital relationships. Many emerging adults today, particularly those who are well resourced, are still trying to work within the confines of this new paradigm (Amato, 2014).

▲ Prevailing Theories

In addition to historical models, theory can help ground us in our understanding of emerging adults and their beliefs and behaviors related to marriage in the 21st century. Two particular theories, *marital horizon* and *marital paradigm* theory, offer salient perspectives.

Marital horizon theory, which was discussed briefly in an earlier chapter, asserts that the nearer to marital readiness one perceives oneself to be, the more likely one will act in accordance with behaviors associated with marriage (Carroll, Willoughby, Badger, Nelson, McNamara, & Madsen, 2007). Three components determine one's marital horizon: (a) the importance of marriage to the individual (i.e., marital salience), (b) the desired timing of marriage within one's life course, and (c) the types of preparation the individual believes are needed before being ready to enter marriage (Carroll et al., 2009). Carroll and colleagues found that when comparing emerging adults with close marital horizons (mid-20s and later) to those with distant horizons (early 20s), the latter group was more likely to take part in permissive sexual activities, destructive drinking behavior, and drug use.

In addition to these considerations, marital readiness is influenced by a range of factors including family background, religious affiliation, and mutual love—which, for some emerging adults, includes finding an ideal partner, a "soulmate" (Hall, 2006)—and the pursuit of educational and career goals prior to marriage (ostensibly so that the couple will be better positioned for financial independence; Willoughby & Carroll, 2016). As will be discussed later in this chapter, the education and income levels of emerging adults inform the transition to marriage in important ways.

Although marital readiness is critical to understanding the decision to marry and is a significant predictor of later marital satisfaction (Waller & McLanahan, 2005, as cited in Willoughby & Carroll, 2016), little is understood about the criteria emerging adults use in making the *actual decision* to marry.

The *marital paradigm* theory, conceptualized by Willoughby and colleagues, expands on marital horizon theory and offers what the authors consider a more comprehensive paradigm. This theory posits that one's beliefs about *getting* married and *being* married, which are at least partially framed against the larger culture's paradigms, are what drives one's behaviors as related to marriage (Willoughby, Medaris, James, & Bartholomew, 2015).

When considering an individual's beliefs about *getting* marriage, three distinct and interconnected domains are proposed: marital timing, marital salience, and marital context. Marital timing refers to the anticipated timing of events such as the marriage proposal, the engagement, and the wedding itself, as well as the desirable length of time a courtship should last. Marital salience refers to the overall importance of marriage and getting married as compared to other life goals (e.g., education, career achievements, recreation), and marital context refers to the individual and relational circumstances within which one believes marriage should occur.

Three additional dimensions define ideas related to *being* married: marital processes, marital permanence, and marital centrality. Marital processes refer to expectations as to what will happen during the process of marriage, including beliefs about transition and adjustment, as well as how the partners will behave within the marriage (e.g., intimacy practices, sharing of housework, etc.). Marital permanence addresses the individual's beliefs about commitment and about the circumstances that might justify termination of the marriage. Finally, marriage centrality refers to the importance of marriage to the married individual and the significance of the role of the spouse in the married individual's life.

▲ Beliefs About Getting Married and Being Married

Marital beliefs are not static; they are susceptible to change over time. Emerging adults change their beliefs related to marriage salience, centrality, and context with some frequency. Willoughby et al. (2015) studied changes in marital beliefs over a 1-year period among 134 unmarried undergraduates attending a large Midwestern public university. Data was collected during four assessment periods, two relative to *getting* married (marital salience and timing), and two relative to *being* married (centrality and permanence). The authors reported significant changes in marital beliefs during this 1-year time period: emerging adults placed higher importance on marriage (marriage salience) and yet expected to place less importance on their marital role once they were married (marriage centrality), a finding that appears to be paradoxical. As the authors acknowledge, however, the apparent paradox may derive from a need to refine the measures used to assess marital salience and centrality. Further research is needed to determine how the marital beliefs of emerging adults affect the dynamics of their marriages and influence the amount of time, attention, and importance emerging adults devote to their marital roles as opposed to the other adult roles they assume.

Marital beliefs are linked to changes in emerging adult behaviors: binge drinking (beliefs related to marital salience), alcohol use (beliefs related to marital permanence), and pornography use (beliefs related to marital permanence; Willoughby et al, 2015). As noted previously, when emerging adults begin to anticipate entry into marriage, their compliance with adult social norms begins to increase; they engage in "anticipatory socialization"—that is, they are inclined to change their behaviors in accordance with the anticipated role they will assume (p. 227). It is important to note, however, that a significant minority of emerging adults do *not* shift their beliefs toward social compliance. For example, 25% of emerging adult participants specify that members do not believe that avoiding illegal drugs is necessary before being ready for marriage. Only about half of the participants endorsed the statement that avoiding drunk driving is a necessary prerequisite for marriage readiness; nearly half did not endorse the statement.

Willoughby et al. (2012) report other interesting findings about marital beliefs with respect to differences in beliefs between today's emerging adults and their parents' generation. Willoughby's research group studied 446 mothers, 360 fathers, and 536 nonbiologically related emerging adults, and reported surprising differences between the two generations in their views on marital salience and ideal marriage age. The *parents* reported a higher desired age for marriage—almost a year later than the ideal age reported by emerging adults—and also accorded lower importance to marriage as a life goal.

It may be that parents promote later entry into marriage, even if their own marriages were fulfilling, due to the belief that their children will be in be in a better position to sustain satisfying marriages if they prioritize education before entering marriage. Their assessment, on the other hand, may be based on concerns and fears related to the institution of marriage itself and the possibility of divorce in their children's future. Willoughby and James (2017) conclude that "collectively, parents and other family influences appear to be one of the key foundations on which emerging adults have built their internal conceptualizations of modern marriage" (p. 130).

Willoughby and colleagues (2012, 2015) have made meaningful inroads into understanding marital beliefs and how they may influence behaviors during emerging adulthood. Further replication and elaboration, however, is warranted. For example, the idiosyncratic characteristics of the 134 participants in the 2015 student study (e.g., 75% female, 64% Christian, 27% identifying either as atheist, agnostic, or no religious affiliation), raise concerns as to generalizability of the findings.

In the next section, our 29 emerging adults share their views and plans related to marriage. In general, they recognize that they are in a transitional period, one in which they are shifting from a primary identification with their families of origin to a recognition that they will soon be forming families of their own—a shift that will likely require both minor and major adjustments in their relationship alliances. In terms of marital horizons, they are nearly evenly split as to whether they have specific marital plans in mind or not.

▲ Participant Responses

Our 29 emerging adults spoke of their plans and expectations for marriage. They focused on whether or not marriage was on their horizon, and, if so, at what age. They also elaborated on the factors that informed their determinations. A single domain, *marriage, future plans*, emerged from the data. Perhaps the narrowness of the participants' responses was due to the specificity of the issue in question. None of the 29 participants were married at the time of the study, although marital status was not a consideration for participation in the study.

Marriage, Future Plans

All 29 emerging adults were asked to respond to two related questions: (a) "Do you have a life plan in terms of your romantic life?" and (b) "Do you expect to be married? If so, at what age?" Participants spoke of their hopes, expectations, and plans for their romantic lives. They discussed whether marriage was on their horizon and, if so, elaborated on the particulars. One category, *marital horizon*, was identified within the main domain.

Marital horizon

In expressing their ideas and dreams about their romantic lives, participants speculated as to how their romantic lives might unfold, specifically with respect to long-term committed relationships, marriage, and child(ren), yielding a *general* category. Many of the participants reported that with the passage of time and the influence of external and internal exigencies (e.g., current finances, career status, mental health status), they have re-evaluated and modified their original marital plans. Some, disinclined to make predictions about their futures, made the decision to have no plans at all, while others spoke of plans that called for a delay in their timeline for marriage. Their responses were organized into the following subcategories: (1) no marital plan, an undetermined horizon (2) a marital plan, a determined horizon.

No marital plan, an undetermined horizon. Fourteen of the 29 participants, approximately one half, spoke of having no set plan for marriage. They appeared to be open to a range of options (including alternatives to marriage), options that would afford them flexibility and the space to "flow." They did not have a predetermined marital finish line within their present field of vision.

In response to a variety of factors including long-term relationships that had ended, revised career considerations, and lack of financial resources and/or concerns about the debt that they had accrued, 6 of the 14 participants had shifted their marital horizons. Although most of this subgroup hoped to be married at some point in the future, uncertainty in their lives had caused them to move away from attachment to a concrete marital plan.

Angela (27) and Ellen (24) both re-evaluated their set marital plans after determining that greater flexibility was required in order to accommodate to new realities. Angela states:

> I guess this kind of goes with the theme of what I have been
> saying, that I thought that we would be definitely married or
> engaged at 27 or maybe 24, 25, especially because we have been
> together for so long. But now I think more practical. I understand
> that we have debt to pay off, that we should probably do
> [that] first.

Angela adds that, had she followed her initial plans, she would have been engaged 3 or 4 years ago. At an earlier age, she was more idealistic and less pragmatic in her thinking about the future, specifically with respect to marital horizons. Angela is appreciative of the fact that she can now assess her relationship using a more practical lens. She no longer has a set plan as to when she will get married; her priority is to have the couple's finances in order *before* entering a marital relationship with her long-term partner.

Ellen has shifted her perspective from a clear set of plans to a less sharply defined marital horizon. In viewing her previous romantic relationship against her current frame of mind, Ellen asserts that living in the present offers a more gratifying approach to being in a relationship.

> I have given up on that [a specific marital plan] because I realized
> that . . . there's the difference between me at 18 years old [*laughs*].
> [At that age] I was definitely really focused on the end goal . . .
> marriage, kids, family, all that stuff, you know. You know a, b, and
> c. [Now] I realize, like, it's more of a flow, and you just go with it,
> you know, don't try to plan things. . . . What I've learned is, don't
> try to plan your future with someone, because when you do, it

takes away from what's happening in the present, and that's so much more important than what's happening in the future.

In relationship to marital horizon, participants in this subcategory preferred having the emotional space to maneuver; heading toward a prescribed finish line with a specified time in mind was felt as too constraining and/or disappointing.

A marital plan, a determined horizon. Fifteen participants, also approximately half, spoke of having a marital plan that was generally associated with a specific chronological age. A few noted that while it was hard to know and plan for an exact date with respect to marriage, they nevertheless created timelines for themselves. Alana (21) states, "I think if I get married, probably it will be around 26. Or if I don't get married, then at some point I'll just give up at, like, 30, and if someone asks I'll say yes and just settle down." Tina (27) asserts, "I'd love to finish up this master's and get married in the next year, and, you know, maybe work and be married [for] a year or two, and then start having a family."

All 15 participants in this group identified either a specific age or narrow bandwidth of time with respect to marital horizon. While the women hoped to be married by or before age 30, the men envisioned being married in their early to mid-30s. Male participants did not express the same sense of time urgency as the women, who were more inclined to think about children and how children might be integrated into their marital plans. Greta (26) speaks to this issue. Concerned about the future and the possibility of feeling "rushed" into the decision to marry and have children, she states:

> I always thought that I would be married at 28, [and] I'd have kids at 30. I'm worried that I'm going to be rushed to steps that I thought I would have a lot of time to process through. . . . I feel like I'm going to meet someone when I'm 30 or older, if at all, and then I'm going to feel really rushed about my time frame in terms of having kids, and moving in with someone, and living with them, and being a married couple.
>
> I don't want to . . . meet someone at 34, get married at 35, have kids at 36. I don't know, that's not my plan. My plan is to meet someone by 30. . . . I don't like having that [time] crunch on me.

In order to determine whether age informed participants' marital horizons, the 29 participants were divided into two groups: the first consisted of participants ages 21–24, and the second of participants ages 25–29, yielding 16 and 13 participants, respectively, in the two groups. Differences between these two groups were observed with respect to marital horizons. Among the participants aged 21–24 years, six reported no specific marital plans for the future; among the participants 25–29 years of age, 10 reported no specific future marital plans. Among the younger group, 10 participants reported specific plans, and among the older group, three reported specific plans. A pattern emerges: in comparison to older emerging adults, younger emerging adults are more likely to endorse a specific marital plan, a finding that is consistent with the theoretical underpinnings informing marital horizon and marital paradigm theory.

▲ Analysis of Findings

Our 29 emerging adults expressed their marital goals for the future, goals that are likely to inform their future behaviors across a range of domains and activities (Carroll et al., 2007; Willoughby, Olson, Carroll, Nelson, & Miller, 2012). Results support the conceptual framework as articulated by Carroll et al. (2007) and expanded upon by Willoughby and colleagues (2015).

Beliefs about marriage with respect to timing, importance, and criteria for readiness color individuals' lives and life plans during their twenties (Willoughby & Carroll, 2016). "How emerging adults situate marriage into their long-term plans appears to shape the very nature, context and length of emerging adulthood itself" (p. 293). Research results suggest that younger emerging adults (21–24 years of age) are more likely to endorse predetermined marital horizons. As they get older, however, and their concerns and priorities shift, they reassess their initial hopes and plans. Participants evidenced a flexibility with respect to their marital horizons. Some had reached the age by which they anticipated being married and then revised their plans accordingly. While some readjusted those plans to target a later marital horizon, others concluded that they preferred to have no set plans, and to "live in the present."

As emerging adults navigate this transitional period of development, their beliefs about marriage can change as well. "If emerging adults vary in the way they think about marriage, they will likewise vary in the way such beliefs influence their intentions to engage in behavior and then, by extension, their actual daily behavior" (Willoughby & Carroll, 2016, p. 284). The conceptual models of marriage that emerging adults internalize may shift in response to new experiences and exposure to different worldviews. The implications of these modifications are not yet fully understood.

▲ Single or Partnered

Although the majority of emerging adults factor marriage prominently into their hopes, dreams, and plans, the choice to be single is on the rise; marriage is no longer universally desired and embraced (Lehmann et al, 2015). In the United States., individuals between the ages of 18 and 34 represent the fastest-growing group remaining single (US Census Bureau, 2006-2008, American Community Survey Three-Year Estimates, as cited in Klinenberg, 2012). Reasons cited for this increase in singlehood include: (a) the prizing of choice and the lessening of reliance on marriage as the only solution, (b) shifts in meaning and emphasis regarding the importance of independence and individuality, (c) increased opportunities for women in the workforce, and (d) a decrease in stigmatization associated with being single (Jamieson & Simpson, 2013). Poortman and Liefbroer (2010) suggest that the increase in the choice to remain single is due to the trend toward later marriages, either because a person ages past the ideal age of marriage, or because, after a stage of experimentation, relationships become less romanticized and less important as emerging adults find other ways to lead fulfilling lives.

The United States is not a world leader in terms of the prevalence of singlehood. In Sweden for example, 47% of all households consist of a single resident, in contrast to 28% in the United States. In Stockholm, Sweden's capital, 60% of the populace elects to live alone. Common to both countries is a history that values individualism and self-reliance (Klinenberg, 2012). In Sweden, however, the government has invested resources and energy in constructing affordable living arrangements that facilitate social interactions and address risks associated with loneliness (e.g., providing common spaces to congregate).

Many individuals who are living alone view their living spaces as sanctuaries from their stressful work lives (Klinenberg, 2012) and from the intensely networked, 24/7 lifestyle they feel pressured to participate in. These individuals are finding that living alone allows them both a welcome sense of solitude and the freedom to participate in social activities at a frequency and intensity level they desire. Rather than attenuating their connection to the world, they find that living alone actually affords them the space and time to reflect, to develop their ideas, and to forge *deeper* connections with people, organizations, and even themselves.

According to Klinenberg (2012), solo living arrangements have been helpful to individuals wishing to extricate themselves from problematic marriages and families of origin, while also giving them a safe and comfortable place from which to begin reintegrating into careers and romantic lives, on their own terms. Living alone is not the *only* route to discovering one's individual talents, drives, and desires, but an increasing number of people are discovering that solitude is more than just a way to restore energy and find sanctuary; it is also a way to discover new approaches for living and interacting with others.

▲ Diverging Pathways: The Intersection of Education and Class

For those emerging adults who do opt for the marriage path, marriage holds a different place in their trajectory than it held for previous generations. This view of marriage, research indicates, is not "working out" equally for all members of society.

Although most emerging adults are still electing to marry, closer analysis of marital patterns reveals that divergent pathways are emerging (Cherlin, 2014). These pathways are informed by socioeconomic status and education, with significant consequences. Many emerging adults, particularly those with limited economic resources, are finding that the risks of marriage outweigh the advantages. For example, while emerging adults increasingly believe that stable finances are paramount to a successful marriage, many emerging adult men are unable to secure stable, well-paid employment. Other perceived risks include the vulnerability of modern marriage due to high divorce rates, and the complications of bringing in children from other partnerships. Due to these and other risk factors, many low-income couples are choosing to cohabit instead.

Statistically, the average age of marriage and the rate of divorce have both increased, while the rate of remarriage has decreased (Farber & Miller-Cribbs, 2014). Massey and Shibuya (1995) report a link between male joblessness and lower rates of marriage (as cited in Joshi, Quane, & Cherlin, 2009). The rate of women having children outside of marriage has spiked significantly (Farber & Miller-Cribbs, 2014). Approximately one third of lower-income women over the age of 25 have had a child outside of marriage, while among higher-income women, the percentage has decreased to 5%. Approximately one half of unmarried mothers are cohabiting with the fathers of their children (Farber & Miller-Cribbs, 2014). These cohabitating relationships tend to be unstable and prone to ending in dissolution; only a third result in marriage within 5 years. Explanations for the increase in raising children outside of marriage are varied and include diminished stigmatization associated with cohabiting (Cherlin, Barnet, Burton, & Garrett-Peters, 2008).

For those emerging adults who do marry, rates of divorce are nearly twice as high for low-income emerging adults than their more affluent counterparts (Jackson, Trail, Kennedy, Williamson, Bradbury, & Karney, 2016), a finding attributed to both individual and structural barriers and stressors. While higher-income partners most often cite communication difficulties as the reason for their decision to divorce, low-income couples are more likely to cite stressors such as domestic violence, financial and employment difficulties, and/or criminal activity.

Education levels also heavily influence divorce rates. Within 5 years, 34% of women who marry without high school diplomas are divorced. For those who do have high school diplomas, 23% are divorced. And among women who have college degrees, 13% are divorced or separated 5 five years (Cherlin, 2009). Single parenting has doubled for women with low to moderate levels of education since 1965, whereas for well-educated women the statistics have changed minimally since 1965.

Amato (2014) astutely concludes that "we live in an era of clashing marriage cultures" (p. 43), and class is a key to understanding the polarization that has emerged. In sum, two very different pathways, informed by education levels and socioeconomic factors, are being charted. Cherlin (2009) notes that one pathway, more orderly and predictable, includes completing one's education, developing a career, marrying, and electing to have child(ren), in that sequence. The other pathway often includes a high school education that has not been completed, a series of unstable cohabitating relationships, and children before marriage (although marriage remains a goal), a pathway that increases the likelihood of becoming a single parent. The first pathway, on the other hand, allows for the completion of an advanced degree and the development of a career, factors that enable emerging adults to accumulate financial resources before raising children.

Most emerging adults hold marriage in high esteem. However, relationship turbulence and instability is greater when emerging adults are facing seemingly insurmountable structural obstacles. And according to Cherlin (2009), relationship turbulence and instability is greater in the U.S. than in any other nation.

▲ Marital "Success"

Passionate love gets us married, companionate love keeps us happily married.
—Lewandowski, Loving, Le, & Gleason,
2011, p. 38

Earlier we examined three types of historical marriage, with three different purposes and contexts: institutional marriage (sustenance and safety), companionate marriage (belonging and love), and individualized marriage (esteem and self-actualization). If emerging adults make the choice to marry, they can theoretically choose from amongst these three options, as well as from the various combinations and permutations these choices may inspire, as syntonic with their personal views and preferences. Statistics relative to the types of marriages emerging adults are entering have not been gathered to date. These would be difficult to capture: in all likelihood, most modern marriages are a mixture of the three options and shift over time. They are dependent on the needs of the married couple at a particular point in time, and are likely to shift as those needs change. For example, many couples may value individual pursuits and self-fulfillment. When child(ren) enter the unit, however, the partners may re-prioritize their needs, and marital dynamics may dictate a shift toward companionate marriage.

It must be pointed out, however, that the *dominant* "cultural model" of a successful marriage, as portrayed in media, literature, and entertainment, is one of an individualized marriage aimed at meeting high-level personal needs. Because of the influences of class described above, it tends to be those couples with higher income and educational levels who are more likely to be able to make such a model work. Even among that group, however, marital success is stumbling:

> Expectations about marriage have risen. . . . People now want marriage to satisfy their financial, emotional and spiritual needs. But while some people spend a lot of one-on-one time working on their marriage, and reap the benefits, most people spend less time, and things slowly decay. (Finkel, 2014, as cited in Brooks, 2016)

In short, while our demands and expectations for marriage are increasing, the investment of time and effort we are putting into our marriages is decreasing, hardly a formula for success. In depicting the polarization of marriage in current times, Finkel (2014) concludes that "the best marriages today are better than the best marriages of generations ago; however, the worst marriages are worse, and the average marriage is weaker than the average marriage of days of yore" (as cited in Brooks, 2016).

How does one measure marital "success"? The criteria by which some emerging adults measure successful marriages have changed and the requisite skills required to have a successful marriage have become increasingly complex. For example, in marriages that prioritize self-actualization, social support is an important consideration. Because support networks are diminishing (Putnam, 2000, 2015), emerging adults are increasingly reliant on their *partners* to fulfill all of their higher-order needs. And yet, as noted above, married partners are spending measurably less time together (Amato, Booth, Johnson, & Rogers, 2009, as cited in Finkel, Cheung, Emery, Carswell & Larson, 2015).

Building upon the tenets of Maslow's (1954, 1970) theory of human motivation, Finkel, Hui, Carswell, and Larson (2014) present a *suffocation model* that describes the fate of many modern, well-resourced marriages. Whereas in the past, the satisfying of lower-level needs (e.g., physiological, safety) was the focus and criterion for marital success, currently many emerging adults are seeking marriages that meet their highest needs for growth and self-actualization, and they are asking their partners to fulfill these needs (e.g., self-esteem, self-actualization).

Higher-order needs, such as understanding of the self and the other, require the substantial investment of time and psychological resources, both of which are in short supply in modern marriages. The authors conclude that most partners today are not investing the necessary time and psychological resources required for their relationships to thrive. Frustrations and tensions then build within the marriage. Using a suffocation metaphor, there is insufficient "oxygen" to allow the couple to survive and thrive.

Why are spouses spending less time, rather than more time, meeting these higher needs? A partial reason is the dearth of emotional resources available to each individual partner. Time constraints contribute to marriages that are beset by disappointment and limited by the emotional resources that each member can bring to the relationship (Amato, 2014). Finkel and his colleagues (2014, 2017) propose corrective solutions to this dilemma, including (a) revisiting the issues related to marital investment, and reallocating resources within the marriage; and (b) revising the couple's expectations, which may mean asking less of the marriage in terms of realizing the higher needs of the partners. Some of the partners' higher-level needs might be better met outside the marital relationship, using resources such as friends, support groups, and social/educational options.

▲ Marital Competence

What are the competencies needed to make a long–term marriage work? The skills that *get* you married are different from the skills and relationship qualities that *keep* you married (Lewandowski et al., 2011). Initially, romantic relationships may be fueled by passion and optimism. The two partners are likely to idealize one another—and marriage itself—to some extent. Over time, that idealization typically breaks down, and that is when the work of marriage begins. Some couples succeed at the long-term work and others do not. The range of competencies that leads to success is not particularly well understood.

Historically, the literature examining clinical interventions for couples in distress has proclaimed the importance of communication in marriage. In response, clinical intervention programs have been designed to address deficits in marital communication skills. However, such interventions have recently been called into question (Blanchard, Hawkins, Baldwin, & Fawcett, 2009). Communication-based models that stress the development of communication skills between partners— skills designed to help them correct non-adaptive communication styles—have not borne out their promise. A more nuanced and complex narrative emerges.

According to Carroll, Badger, and Yang (2006), the competencies that lead to good marital communication are multidimensional and are not strictly skill based. For example, negotiation skills do not work unless there is a firm basis of loving support and empathy between the partners. The reason communication breaks down in many marriages may not be from lack of skill, per se, but rather from an intrapersonal deficiency that is affecting the *motivation* of one or both partners to communicate effectively. In order to intervene effectively in such a scenario, the origin of the difficulties must be assessed and then addressed. Simply teaching generic communication skills is insufficient. One might wish to ask, for example, whether communication difficulties might be related to issues either or both partners may be experiencing with commitment and love.

Carroll et al. (2006) elaborate on this notion, pointing out that current models fail to account for factors such as "personal security and other-oriented virtues" that must be in place before a couple can effectively "negotiate." (p. 1029). In the absence of sustained commitment, empathy, and a sense of justice and fairness, skill-driven marital communications can become little more than business negotiations. There is increasing recognition in the clinical treatment literature that in order to help couples deepen their marital communication, there must be greater understanding of how individual and couple processes interface with one another, as well as an appreciation of the cultural contexts and developmental histories of both partners. Relational competence needs to be viewed as an "evolving capacity that begins early in life" and is rooted in the particulars of the partners' parents' marriages (Carroll et al., 2006, pp. 1028-1029). Structural impediments must also be considered.

▲ Michael and Angela

To conclude the chapter, we will shift from the theoretical to the specific: Michael and Angela, both participants in the study, who have been in a committed romantic partnership for 9 years. Their narratives touch on many of the issues we have discussed, such as the dynamics of marital horizons, the inherent challenges of the "capstone" model of marriage, and the career and financial difficulties many emerging adults are facing today. Both of these emerging adults, who were interviewed separately, describe the frustrations of being at a point in their lives where they feel ready to commit and are excited to move forward, preferably into marriage, but also feel stalled. A combination of individual, professional, and financial goals, as well as Michael's struggle to "get it together" career-wise, has left the couple frustrated. They habitually compare themselves to friends who seem able to move forward while they, Michael and Angela, remain stuck. Their ability to reflect pragmatically on the realities of their situation, while expressing the mutual love that keeps them together, encapsulates the complicated struggles many emerging adults face as they simultaneously embark on the paths of defining themselves, their values, their careers, and their commitment to a partner.

Michael and Angela, both 27 years old, have been in an exclusive relationship with each other since high school. Angela, the daughter of an Italian-American Catholic family, has successfully launched a career as an optometrist after completing her degree. Her parents, both of whom have associate degrees, allowed her to live away for college, but now prefer that she lives at home until she is married. Michael, a part-time bookkeeper on the cusp of completing his master's degree in accounting, is also from a Catholic family and lives at home with his parents. He is currently earning an annual salary in the low teens, and after a series of career changes, has accrued substantial student loan debt. Neither Michael nor Angela identifies as a practicing Catholic, but the decision to live "at home" appeases their parents and seems to make practical sense in terms of paying down Michael's loans and saving money to buy their own home.

Angela, whom Michael refers to as the "responsible one" in the relationship, sees herself as financially stable and enjoys her career. Although she would like to move out of her parents' home and/or travel, she is unsure about what next steps will look like for her. Initially she had a time frame in mind for getting engaged and buying a house, but now finds herself questioning the value of getting married at all—mostly because of the expense. As she watches her friends cohabitate, marry, and start families, she worries about being developmentally behind. She envisioned being married at age 26, with all the accoutrements of the American dream: an engagement ring, a house, and two children. Although Angela is sure of her long-term commitment to Michael, she has adjusted her marital horizons and is unsure of whether marriage makes sense at this point in her life.

Sometimes it is hard to watch people around you moving forward and moving out and get[ting] married . . . seeing people put things together more than us—that has been like a theme, you know, of difficulty with us, because, probably, I was waiting for him to figure out what he wanted to do. Part of it is, our relationship kind of changed so much that I do not even know what I want . . . if we will get married. I don't know that I want to move out with him, but I want us to be together and live together and be with him forever, but I do not really know exactly the terms of that.

In terms of their identity as a couple, Angela summarized, "We are not the same, but we are similar enough, like, we can get along and do things together, but support each other's weaknesses. We kind of round each other as a *we*." " Thinking about where their relationship stands, Angela shares, "When you talk to one of us, it is kind of like talking to both of us because I think, pretty much, we are on the same page."

Although optimistic and committed, both partners report dissatisfaction with their relationship overall, especially their sex life, due to the constraints of living at home and not being permitted privacy. They each report feeling "too old" to be "sneaking around," and are increasingly curious about what it might be like to have a "normal" routine of coming home to each other each night, rather than having to coordinate their after-work schedules. Michael shares his frustration on their relationship and on feeling "stuck":

I would say the first, you know, 3, 4, 5 years we were together, things were actually really perfect because we did not *expect* to be living away yet. We were both in college and you . . . are at that stage where it is okay [to] have to jump a few hoops. . . . I think we both thought, coming out of college, that we would get that ideal . . . that you [would] have a great-paying job and you can just leave the house. I would say right now it has changed, in that we are both living with the stress of the little things, you know . . . getting interrupted and feeling like we do not have a real space. . . . We were thinking . . . early on in our relationship [that] we were just happy to be together. . . . But now we are 27 going on 28 [and] the stresses . . . are very real and they suck. It is probably one thing that has put a strain on our relationship.

I mean, we love being together. I think we have figured that out, but we just feel like we have not started our future together and that is kind of frustrating because we are seeing some of our friends get married and get out and then we are sitting there wondering why we have not. . . . I think in my *mind* we are making the smart choice . . . but the emotional side is tough. . . . Even though our relationship has progressed to a point where we should be somewhere else, you know, we're stuck in like we are still 18. . . . I think that is the biggest stress for both of us, it certainly is for me.

While they are experiencing anxiety around their progress as a *we*, Angela and Michael both reflected on the importance of maintaining a sense of independence from each other. Angela cited the fact that they went to separate colleges, remarking that her education and career have been "the most influential things on our romantic life." She reflects that it was a "great thing" to not choose a college or graduate school based on the other's interests. Unlike Angela, Michael has struggled to find an academic/career track that feels like a good fit. His search for a career identity has put a strain on their relationship, but he is resolute on the importance of finding his own way, even if that means "disappointing" his partner:

You have to be willing to [disappoint your partner] just to make sure you are still your own person. . . . . You have to feel like you can be honest with that person and make your own decisions. . . . I think that a big thing you can come to realize is that there are going to be different points that you will get somebody upset, and it is going to be okay. You are going to survive. It is not that big of deal. It is more important, in the long run, to establish what you like and what you are into. . . . You certainly have to stand up for yourself and, you know, make sacrifices for yourself too.

The disparity in their career progress remains their most formidable obstacle. While Michael stands by his need to make independent choices, he seems to feel a sense of guilt or shame around not being able to contribute financially to a wedding and a house purchase. He is focused on a goal of being married and cohabiting by age 30, but feels he is currently "making up" for his inability to "get it together" earlier. Neither of Michael's parents went to college, and he believed that attending a prestigious university and pursuing certain academic tracks—which shifted from engineering to law to sociology, and ultimately to accounting—would land him in a lucrative career upon graduating. He talks about finally having a "solid job" squared away, now that he is completing graduate school, which helps him feel that he and Angela are finally on the "right track." With regret, he wishes he could tell his younger self to focus on the future, to learn to better navigate a "capitalistic society," and to consider the practical needs of a relationship sooner.

Angela acknowledges her disappointment in their current stagnation, but sees that placing blame will not help them move forward. She consoles herself by focusing on the future, and states that mutual emotional support is more important to a commitment than being financial equals. She does expect, however, that Michael will be able to support himself independently before the relationship can move forward:

> Luckily, I am making a lot of money [and] we both could probably
> be okay on that, but I need him to be able to at least support
> himself a little bit financially, because, you know, if anything
> ever happens between us, if anything happened to me. . . .
> I want to make sure that he would be okay, and also that we both
> contribute. I [think] he would have better self-worth too.

Michael and Angela find themselves tackling multiple issues emblematic of the complicated developmental stage of emerging adulthood. They are navigating the challenges of coming into their own as adults and professionals, while at the same time maintaining a committed relationship. They have had to adjust their marital horizons, and at this juncture neither Michael and Angela is sure that the pursuit of a legal document validating their commitment to each other makes sense. Still, Michael reflects, "Everything I do, you know, involves her. I think when you decide to be in a committed relationship you are talking about a future together." Angela concludes that the title and status of being married is not everything: "I do not feel like that title means much to me, because I know I want to be with him forever and really if we . . . are married or not, I do not think it will change how I feel."

Angela does however observe that people do not accord her the same level of respect as compared to her peers who are married, but have not had as long a relationship, and have not had to endure the frustrations of living in their parents' homes and all of the compromises and indignities that go along with that.

As individuals, Angela and Michael have grown, changed, and met milestones at different times and at different paces. While they are finally "on the same page" in terms of career and goals for the future, the path to this stage has been wrought with guilt and shame, resentment and frustration. At the same time, Michael and Angela are deeply committed to each other and see the value they bring to each other's lives via emotional support, friendship, and their vision of a future together.

Michael and Angela are a good illustration of some of the reasons today's emerging adults are marrying so late, as well as of some of the challenges inherent in making that decision. Though they have been committed to each other for 9 years, they are still working at putting all their "ducks in a row," in terms of finance and career, before they get married, a goal both of them state they enthusiastically desire. The "capstone" vision of marriage is clearly in evidence for them. Angela has completed her college and graduate work and is earning a living as an optometrist, a profession with a median income of over $100,000. Michael is finishing up grad school and has secured a "solid position," and yet they still don't feel ready to exchange vows—even though their present separate living conditions are causing them a great deal of stress and discomfort. One is tempted to ask, "What are they waiting for?" This raises several further questions that future research might address: What ideas about marriage may be affecting emerging adults' decision to wait? Are these ideas realistic? Do emerging adults idealize or romanticize marriage in any way, or perhaps the opposite? Is the tendency of emerging adults to treat marriage as a hard-to-reach capstone that can occur only when financial/career conditions are exactly right perhaps masking a reluctance to marry for other reasons? No doubt the answers are as complex as the questions.

▲ Summary and Conclusions

People want to be monogamous or promiscuous, they want kids or they don't want kids, they want this or they want that. For centuries, they had to hide those preferences and take everything as a package deal. Now you don't have to: It's literally pick and choose. Cut and paste the kind of life you want. Family life and love relationships are essentially becoming a build-your-own model.

—Stephanie Coontz, as cited by Finkel,
2017, p. 261

In summary, societal norms inform individuals' meanings associated with marriage. Norms are shifting and becoming more flexible as evidenced by the greater acceptance of alternatives to marriage, including casual sexual experiences, remaining single, cohabitation, and divorce (Hall, 2006). However, the vast majority of emerging adults still view marriage as a positive goal and figure it prominently into their life plans. Practical, vocational, educational, and financial considerations, however, along with emerging adults' view of marriage as a "capstone" rather than a "cornerstone" event, have had the effect of moving the age of marriage later for emerging adults. For many, as that marital horizon approaches and then slips into the rearview mirror, they are reassessing the desire to get married at all, and are choosing alternatives to marriage, such as singlehood and cohabitation.

The diversity of meanings attached to marriage not only influence marital behaviors, but also the likelihood of marital "success." Though emerging adults are "free" to choose from a variety of marital types, such as institutional, companionate, and individualized marriages, the overall cultural model has been shifting toward the latter. That is, couples tend to look to marriage to serve as a vehicle and a support system for finding meaning and personal growth. However, a number of factors are working against their success, such as income level, education level, increasing expectations and romanticization of marriage, and the shrinking of time and effort that married partners are actually investing in each other. As a result, while some marriages are stronger than ever, marriages, for others, have become weaker.

Our understanding of the competencies that lead to a good marriage are undergoing some revision. Whereas it was recently believed that communication is the cornerstone of a good marriage, and that communication can be improved by the teaching of skills, a more nuanced perspective is emerging, one that suggests that developmental, cultural, structural, and motivational factors must be taken into consideration.

The institution of marriage and how it is lived continues to evolve, creating both opportunities and challenges for emerging adults. Self-actualized marriages and diverging paths such as going solo serve as examples of the range of possibilities now available to emerging adults, and shed light on this evolving institution.

▲ References

Amato, P. R. (2014). Tradition, commitment, and individualism in American marriages. *Psychological Inquiry*, 25(1), 42–46. doi:10.1080/1047840X.2014.877812

Blanchard, V. L., Hawkins, A. J., Baldwin, S. A., & Fawcett, E. B. (2009). Investigating the effects of marriage and relationship education on couples' communication skills: A meta-analytic study. *Journal of Family Psychology*, 23(2), 203–214. doi:10.1037/a0015211

Brooks, D. (2016, February 23). Three views of marriage. *The New York Times*. Retrieved from https://www.nytimes.com/2016/02/23/opinion/three-views-of-marriage.html?mcubz=0

Carroll, J. S., Badger, S., Willoughby, B. J., Nelson, L. J., Madsen, S. D., & Barry, C. M. (2009). Ready or not? Criteria for marriage readiness among emerging adults. *Journal of Adolescent Research*, 24(3), 349–375.

Carroll, J. S., Badger, S., & Yang, C. (2006). The ability to negotiate or the ability to love? Evaluating the developmental domains of marital competence. *Journal of Family Issues*, 27(7), 1001–1032. doi:10.1177/0192513X06287248

Carroll, J. S., Willoughby, B., Badger, S., Nelson, L. J., Barry, C. M., & Madsen, S. D. (2007). So close, yet so far away: The impact of varying marital horizons on emerging adulthood. *Journal of Adolescent Research*, 22(3), 219–247. doi:10.1177/0743558407299697

Cherlin, A. J. (2004). The deinstitutionalization of American marriage. *Journal of Marriage and Family*, 66(4), 848–861. doi:10.1111/j.0022-2445.2004. 00058.x

Cherlin, A. (2009). *Marriage, divorce, remarriage*. Cambridge, MA. Harvard University Press.

Cherlin, A. J. (2012). Goode's world revolution and family patterns: A reconsideration at fifty years. *Population and Development Review*, 38(4), 577–607.

Cherlin, A. J. (2014). *Labor's love lost: The rise and fall of the working class family in America*. New York, NY: Russell Sage Foundation.

Cherlin, A., Cross-Barnet, C., Burton, L. M., & Garrett-Peters, R. (2008). Promises they can keep: Low-income women's attitudes toward motherhood, marriage, and divorce. *Journal of Marriage and Family*, 70(4), 919–933. doi:10.1111/j.1741-3737.2008. 00536.x

Farber, N., & Miller-Cribbs, J. E. (2014). 'First train out': Marriage and cohabitation in the context of poverty, deprivation, and trauma. *Journal of Human Behavior in the Social Environment*, 24(2), 188–207. doi:10.1080/10911359.2014.848693

Finkel, E. J. (2017). *The all-or-nothing marriage: How the best marriages work*. New York, NY: Penguin Random House.

Finkel, E. J., Cheung, E. O., Emery, L. F., Carswell, K. L., & Larson, G. M. (2015). The suffocation model: Why marriage in America is becoming an all-or-nothing institution. *Current Directions in Psychological Science*, 24(3), 238–244. doi:10.1177/0963721415569274

Finkel, E. J., Hui, C. M., Carswell, K. L., & Larson, G. M. (2014). The suffocation of marriage: Climbing Mount Maslow without enough oxygen. *Psychological Inquiry*, 25(1), 1–41.

Hall, S. S. (2006). Marital meaning: Exploring young adults' belief systems about marriage. *Journal of Family Issues*, 27(10), 1437–1458. doi:10.1177/0192513X06290036

Hymowitz, K. S., Carroll, J. S., Wilcox, W. B., & Kaye, K. (2013). *Knot yet: The benefits and costs of delayed marriage in America*. Charlottesville, VA: The National Marriage Project.

Jackson, G. L., Trail, T. E., Kennedy, D. P., Williamson, H. C., Bradbury, T. N., & Karney, B. R. (2016). The salience and severity of relationship problems among low-income couples. *Journal of Family Psychology*, 30(1), 2. doi:10.1111%2Fj.1741-3729.2009. 00581.x

Jamieson, L., & Simpson, R. (2013). *Living alone: Globailization, identity and belonging*. New York, NY: Palgrave Macmillan.

Joshi, P., Quane, J. M., & Cherlin, A. J. (2009). Contemporary work and family issues affecting marriage and cohabitation among low-income single mothers. *Family Relations*, 58(5), 647–661. doi:10.1111/j.1741-3729.2009. 00581.x

Klinenberg, E. (2012). *Going solo: The extraordinary rise and surprising appeal of living alone*. New York, NY: Penguin Books.

Lehmann, V., Tuinman, M. A., Braeken, J., Vingerhoets, A. M., Sanderman, R., & Hagedoorn, M. (2015). Satisfaction with relationship status: Development of a new scale and the role in predicting well-being. *Journal of Happiness Studies*, 16(1), 169–184. doi:10.1007/s10902-014-9503-x

Lewandowski, G. W., Jr., Loving, T. J., Le, B., & Gleason, M. (2011). *The science of relationships: Answers to your questions about dating, marriage, and family*. Dubuque, IA: Kendall Hunt.

Lichter, D. T., Batson, C. D., & Brown, J. B. (2004). Welfare reform and marriage promotion: The marital expectations and desires of single and cohabiting mothers. *Social Service Review*, 78(1), 2–25. doi:10.1086/380652

Määttä, K., & Uusiautti, S. (2012). Changing identities: Finnish divorcees' perceptions of a new marriage. *Journal of Divorce & Remarriage*, 53(7), 515–532. doi:10.1080/10502556.2012.682906

Marquardt, E. (2011). *One parent or five: A global look at today's new intentional families*. New York, NY: Institute for American Values.

Maslow, A. H. (1954). *Motivation and Personality*. New York, NY: Harper and Row Publishers.

Maslow, A. H. (1970). *Motivation and personality* (2nd ed.). New York, NY: Harper & Row.

Poortman, A., & Liefbroer, A. C. (2010). Singles' relational attitudes in a time of individualization. *Social Science Research*, 39(6), 938–949. doi:10.1016/j.ssresearch.2010.03.012

Putnam, R. D. (2000). *Bowling alone: The collapse and revival of American community*. New York, NY: Simon & Schuster.

Putnam, R. D. (2015). *Our kids in crisis*. New York, NY: Simon & Schuster.

Taylor, P. (2014). *The next Americal: Boomers, Millenials and the looming generational Showdown*. Washington DC: Pew Research Center.

Taylor, P., & the Pew Research Center. (2016). *The next America: Boomers, millennials, and the looming generational showdown*. New York, NY: Pew Research Center.

Willoughby, B. J., & Carroll, J. S. (2016). On the horizon: Marriage timing, beliefs, and consequences in emerging adulthood. In J. J. Arnett, (Ed.), *The Oxford handbook of emerging adulthood* (pp. 280–295). New York, NY: Oxford University Press.

Willoughby, B. J., & James, S. L. (2017). *The marriage paradox: Why emerging adults love marriage yet push it aside*. New York, NY: Oxford University Press.

Willoughby, B. J., Medaris, M., James, S., & Bartholomew, K. (2015). Changes in marital beliefs among emerging adults: Examining marital paradigms over time. *Emerging Adulthood, 3*(4), 219–228. doi:10.1177/2167696814563381

Willoughby, B. J., Olson, C. D., Carroll, J. S., Nelson, L. J., & Miller, R. B. (2012). Sooner or later? The marital horizons of parents and their emerging adult children. *Journal of Social and Personal Relationships, 29*(7), 967–981. doi:10.1177/0265407512443637

11 ▲
Divorce and Its Aftermath

You never know someone until you divorce them.
                    —Author unknown

The decision to marry is an identity investment with a range of possible meanings. (Magnusson, 1990, as cited in Pals, 1999). Many American men and women, as noted in the previous chapter, view marriage as representing a "capstone achievement" in life (Finkel, Hui, Carswell, & Larson, 2014, p. 13). Marriage is often used as a vehicle for attaining social prestige. The finding of love, as symbolized by marriage, is commonly seen as a route to self-fulfillment, personal growth, and/ or discovering one's life-meaning or purpose (Finkel et al., 2014, 2017; Mayseless & Keren, 2014).

In addition to the range of *meanings* that emerging adults attach to marriage, emerging adults also pursue a range of *pathways* to marital commitment. For some, the process can be linear and traditional, for others more investigational and/or spontaneous (Shulman & Connolly, 2013). In the context of a demanding, competitive sociopolitical climate, with the felt pressure to establish a career and lifestyle in a fluctuating global market, marriage may seem to some a stabilizing respite (Konstam, 2015), while for others it may be associated with dread or fear of failure. One's purpose for and pathway toward marriage undoubtedly inform one's decisions, thoughts, and emotions about divorce.

Divorce is very much on the radar screen of emerging adults as they contemplate marriage. While emerging adults are determined not to replicate the divorce rates of their parents' generation (Konstam, 2015), prevalence rates among emerging adults suggest that divorce continues to be a real and pressing issue for them (Schoen & Canudas-Romo, 2006). For men 15–24 years of age, the divorce rate is 3.8%, but for men 25–34 the rate increases to 23.7%. Similarly, for women 15–24 and 25–34 years of age the rate is 5.8% and 27.3% respectively (US Census Bureau, 2011).

These figures suggest that as the challenges of later emerging and young adulthood unfold, marriage continues to be difficult to sustain.

In this chapter, the impact of divorce on emerging and young adults—women in particular—will be discussed, including the influence of the divorce experience on individual development. Stigma will be defined and discussed in the context of divorce. Various potential outcomes of divorce will be explored. The narratives of nine women in their 20s and 30s will add dimension to the examination of the meaning and experience of divorce for today's emerging and young adults.

▲ Divorce and Emerging Adulthood

Dissolving a marital relationship can be daunting, particularly during a time in one's development already marked by instability, volatility, and uncertainty (Cherlin, Cross-Barnet, Burton, & Garrett-Peters, 2008; Konstam, Curran, & Karwin, 2015). While divorce may be a disruptive force associated with emotional turmoil and compromised well-being (Konstam, Karwin, Curran, Lyons, & Celen-Demirtas, 2016), it can also trigger positive shifts such as the enhancement of the self-concept (Schneller & Arditti, 2004), personal growth, accelerated identity development (Gardner & Oswald, 2006; Schneller & Arditti, 2004; Thomas & Ryan, 2008), and the discovery of new romantic love that is mutually fulfilling (Eldar-Avidan, Haj-Yahia, & Greenbaum, 2009; Maatta & Uustautti, 2012). In a longitudinal study, Gardner and Oswald (2006) determined that divorce can also improve psychological well-being for both men and women.

As discussed in Chapter 10, Finkel et al. (2014) argue that expectations of marriage have trended, in recent generations, toward a more individualistic model that emphasizes self-expression and self-development, particularly for those emerging adults who are well resourced. As individuals become better able to materially provide for themselves, they begin to ask more of their marriages, imposing additional stress on the union. In contrast to previous generations, when couples focused on basic needs such as safety and physiological resources, today's emerging adult couples increasingly focus on what Maslow (1970) classified as higher-level needs, such as esteem and self-actualization. Self-focused orientations (Mayesless & Keren, 2014), the quest for a meaningful life, and perfectionistic pursuits including the search for a perfect job and partner (Konstam, 2015), may leave emerging adults vulnerable to unrealistic expectations and accompanying frustrations. In addition, skills required to maintain a harmonious partnership may conflict with self-focused pursuits (Shulman & Connolly, 2013). Even as many of today's emerging adults have become more sophisticated in their quest for self-development and relational skills, their demands and expectations for marriage have risen as well.

Thriving in a marital relationship during emerging adulthood can be challenging, particularly in the current sociocultural environment. The stress of balancing a relationship with the demands of finding work and/or pursuing an education can affect the pace and quality of a marital relationship (Seiffge-Krenke & Luyckx, 2014). For those who marry at the younger end of the age spectrum, these challenges can be amplified. Amato and Previti (2003) note that "the negative consequences of marrying at an early age may be due to psychological immaturity, unstable employment, and a truncated spousal-search process" (p. 606).

Amato and Previti (2003) suggest that many emerging adults have an incomplete understanding of their partners prior to marriage, and learn "substantially more" after the wedding (p. 606). Once these couples begin living together as married partners, any of several common marital disruptions may arise. Amato (2010) identifies some of these as, "domestic violence, frequent conflict, infidelity . . . perceived relationship problems, a weak commitment, and low levels of love and trust" (Clements, Stanley, & Markman, 2004; DeMaris, 2000; Gottman & Levenson, 2000; Hall & Fincham, 2006; Kurdek, 2002; Lawrence & Bradbury, 2001; Orbuch et al., 2002; Previti & Amato, 2003, p. 652).

In the event that the partners ultimately decide on divorce, emerging adults need to come to terms with what it means to them when such an important relationship goes awry. Historically, individuals who divorce are vulnerable to deviance labeling (Yodanis, 2005). Particularly for women, fears of being negatively judged around their capacity to nurture their marital relationships leaves them feeling exposed (Gregson & Ceynar, 2009). Failure, shame, embarrassment, social devaluation, compromised self-esteem, and isolation (Gregson & Ceynar, 2009; Yodanis, 2005) are prevalent themes represented in the divorce literature.

▲ Divorce and Stigma

Stigma is a complex social construct that has been defined across a sweeping range of populations and contexts (Corrigan, 2004, 2005;

Frost, 2013; Goldberg & Smith, 2011; Sedlovskaya, Purdie-Vaughns, Eibach, LaFrance, Romero-Camyas, & Camp, 2013; Vogel, Bitman, Hammer, & Wade, 2013). Goffman (1963), for example, defines stigmatization as "the condition of being denied full social acceptance" (as cited in King, 2008, p. 58). According to Link and Phelan (2001), stigma includes "elements of labeling, stereotyping, separating, status loss, and discrimination [that] co-occur in a power situation" (p. 367), and can prevent individuals from fully functioning in society by limiting access to resources and support. Although stigma associated with divorce can be a major factor in identity development (Gerstel, 1987), there has been a paucity of research about the experience and outcomes of divorce and how these factors have shifted over the last twenty years.

Stigma may manifest as overt discrimination, or it may be internalized (Vogel et al., 2013). When cultural images associated with a group (such as divorced women) are tinged with negative stereotypes, prejudices, and discrimination, individuals tied to that group are likely to experience low self-esteem and poor self-efficacy (Corrigan & Kleinlein, 2005). Stigma needs to be considered not only in relation to how an individual is treated, but also in relation to how that individual *expects* to be received socially. Corrigan (2005) describes two distinct stigma experiences: public stigma and self-stigma. Public stigma consists of social constructs such as stereotypes, prejudice, and discrimination; it can be witnessed in the social discourse and behaviors of a group. Self-stigma, on the other hand, involves endorsing public stigma toward oneself. By internalizing stigma, the individual comes to believe that negative constructs about herself are true, and may then act in accordance with the prejudice (Corrigan & Kleinlein, 2005; Vogel et al., 2013). Internalized self-stigma may manifest in feelings of shame and limited integration with others (Kranke, Floersch, Kranke, & Munson, 2011, as cited in Vogel et al., 2013).

Public stigma and self-stigma are equally relevant in considering the impact of divorce on an individual's self-construct and ability to navigate in society. Goffman (1963) posited that "the divorced come to be seen and to see themselves as a less desired kind . . . reduced in our minds from a whole and usual person to a tainted, discounted one" (p. 3, as cited in Gerstel, 1987, p. 173). In an analysis based on interviews with 104 separated and divorced individuals diverse in socioeconomic status, education level, and employment status, Gerstel (1987) found support for Goffman's observation, and argues that although there has been a clear and significant decline in the disapproval of divorce, "informal relational sanctions" remain prevalent and common (p. 173). Typically, public stigma results in discrediting the divorced individual (Gerstel, 1987), while internalized self-stigma reduces the individual's sense of self-worth (Vogel et al., 2013). Stigma associated with divorce has been found to overshadow other defining features of an individual in a social context (Gerstel, 1987).

It must be noted, however, that many of these findings were made before most of today's emerging adults were born. More contemporary studies, such as a long-term study conducted by Thornton and Young-DeMarco (2001), reveal that there is greater acceptance of pre-marital cohabitation, childlessness, and divorce as valid options for American adults today.

Although divorce has become a more common, mainstream occurrence, it remains unclear whether stigmatization is still a relevant cultural phenomenon, and, if so, how such stigma presents itself today. It is also unclear whether and how divorce-related stigma impacts emerging adults who are building foundations that will inform future professional and personal choices. It is therefore important to ascertain whether today's emerging adults perceive themselves as vulnerable to stigma across multiple contexts, including work, family, "the dating scene," and social circles.

How do emerging adults integrate a powerful, often life-altering, experience such as divorce during a time of developmental instability and uncertainty? As in previous chapters, we will use qualitative data informed by CQR methodology (Hill et al., 2005) to probe more deeply into this subject matter. For this chapter, nine divorced women in the emerging and young-adult age range are interviewed, with these two research questions providing the structure:

1. What are the divorce-related experiences of emerging and young adult women, and how does the developmental period of emerging adulthood inform these experiences?
2. Does divorce-related stigma negatively impact the lives of emerging and young adult women, and, if so, how does it manifest in the lives of women who are in the throes of developing and consolidating an identity?

It is important to note that the research discussed in this chapter is based on interviews with women only. While emerging adult men also experience difficulty after divorce (Hetherington & Kelly, 2003), women—who are traditionally charged with maintaining and preserving intimate relationships—are more vulnerable to internalizing relationship outcomes (Hare-Mustin & Marecek, 1988; Josselson, 1996). Since it has been posited that women maintain their identity *by means of* their intimate relationships (Josselson, 1987; Jordan, 2010), their experiences of divorce can be expected to more clearly illustrate the depth of impact divorce has on personal and social development, especially at a time in life when identity has yet to fully take form.

In the next section, the thoughts and reflections of these nine emerging and young adult women will be summarized to illuminate their collective experience of divorce and its impact on their lives.

▲ Participant Responses

The following questions were posed to the nine participants: (a) What are the lived experiences of emerging and young adult women negotiating the process of divorce? and (b) Does divorce-related stigma negatively impact the lives of emerging and young adult women, and, if so, how does it manifest in the lives of women who are in the throes of developing and consolidating an identity? Two domains were generated: (a) *experiences of divorce: building foundations for self-development*, and (b) *divorce-related stigma*.

Experiences of Divorce: Building Foundations for Self-Development

All nine of the women interviewed described experiences that left them confronting feelings of failure and examining their past, present, and possible future. Jarring at times, their experiences ultimately led them to opportunities for introspection and examination of interpersonal relationships. Each woman reported having learning experiences that led to personal development and a richer understanding of herself, her choices, and the social sphere in which she navigates. Eight categories were identified with respect to this first domain: (a) unmoored, in transition, and seeking an anchor; (b) a convenient lens; (c) unrealized expectations: reality bites; (d) revisiting the self: a time for reflection and evaluation; (e) rebuilding, a process; (f) divorce, a defining passage; (g) putting the divorce in its place: stepping back, panning out; and (h) feelings of failure and embarrassment.

Unmoored, in transition, and seeking an anchor

Four of the nine women spoke of feeling unmoored and uncertain about the future prior to getting married. A *typical* category was created to capture their experiences. Women in this category described being unsure and unhappy in their single lives. They then sought control and/or stability—or gave in to pressure to solidify their relationships—via marriage. One of these women, Alicia, divorced at age 27, had been in an on-and-off, long-distance relationship with her ex-husband for nearly 10 years prior to getting married at age 23. She spoke of wanting to put down roots, but also of feeling fearful about being unable to find "that person" to start a family with: "If your goal is you want to have a family, you want to have a marriage, you want to have children, you want to build a life with somebody else, it's scary to think that maybe you won't have that in your 20s."

Nina, divorced at age 31, met her partner while studying abroad as an undergraduate. She described her courtship as romantic and swift. At the time, the relationship served as one of the few constants that had endured across her many life transitions, including graduation, relocation, and changes in employment, all of which came with no time for reflection:

> At one point rents were difficult and, you know, I think we just decided to move in together. So, it kind of snowballed at that point because then it was proposals and yeses and then there was a wedding and I showed up at it *(laughter)*.

Feeling "pressured" into marriage in order to clarify or stabilize their lives and relationships was another presenting issue in this category. Francine, a doctoral student from Europe who found herself without a place to live, sought refuge in what turned out to be a controlling marriage. Jennifer was pursuing an advanced degree at the time of her divorce at age 24, felt "talked into" marriage by her parents and her partner, with whom she had been in a relationship since high school. When her relationship seemed to stall, marriage seemed to be a way to move forward securely.

For these women, marriage seemed to offer a solution to some form of felt instability. Using marriage to solve a problem, however, did not have optimal results for them.

A convenient lens

Six of the nine women spoke of "knowing that there were unstated, problematic issues—red flags—in their relationships, but also of being unable to bring them into focus. Each of these women discussed the hopeful aspirations she had for her impending marriage based upon what she *chose to see* in her partner, while discarding inconvenient truths. These denied truths were reflected in how family and friends seemed to respond to the relationships, and were reinforced both personally and socially. A *typical* category, *a convenient lens*, was created to describe this experience.

Francine, divorced at age 30, acknowledged uncertainty about the relationship early in her relationship. She proclaimed, "I think I knew it was a car accident waiting to happen but I did it anyways." Despite suspecting she was in a "bad situation," Francine chose to move forward, and explained, "It was one of those things, those cliché things. I saw this side [of him] I wanted to see and thought [about] the . . . charming, nice side. And then once I was living with him . . . the other side came out."

Alicia (28), despite a rocky long-term relationship preceding her engagement, chose to see her marriage through a lens of hopefulness for change. Reflecting on her relationship, she stated, "You think that they're going to change, but people don't change."

Maureen, at age 29, a mother to a 2-year-old boy at the time of her divorce, spoke of her marriage relationship as a façade—the lens through which she presented herself to others. Although she realized early in the relationship that her fiancé was "psychologically and emotionally abusive," she stated, "He got along well with my family, and he got along well with my friends, and as far as outward appearances we were this really great happy couple."

The convenient lens through which these women were viewing their partner/relationship eventually became impossible to maintain.

Unrealized expectations: reality bites

Under this *typical* category, participants revealed how they found themselves in an unsatisfying situation, with defenses that were unsustainable. Seven participants suggested that their expectations, in some cases unrealistic, left them vulnerable to harsh realities. For these women, marriage was expected to have protective, transformative, and enduring qualities that were somehow inherent to the marital relationship and to the act of getting married.

Michelle, who divorced her partner at the age of 32 as part of the fallout of his drug addiction, talked about having a premarital checklist of qualities that she believed would position her for a successful marriage. Qualities she ascribed to her husband such as coming from a "good family," having an elite education and a respectable job, and appearing to be an "all-American" person, seemed to promise a failproof marriage. Similarly, Alicia expressed that her beliefs about marriage had a magical quality, resulting in disillusionment when she realized that all of her expectations around the "title of husband and wife [weren't] happening." She added:

> A lot of people, including myself, feel like going into a marriage is almost like a magic potion where this person that you know well enough and you are willing to spend your life with [is] all of a sudden going to do everything that you think they should be doing.

Fidelity proved to be an unsustainable expectation for three of the women. Amy, 27 at the time of her divorce, described herself as "blindsided" when she discovered "infidelity on his side" 2 weeks after moving ahead of her husband to a new city.

Four of the women described the emergence of distinct personal values that clashed with the direction of their marriages. They reported having false expectations that their partners and their marriages would keep pace with their own personal growth. For example, after her graduate school experience, Nina realized that her marriage had not grown and evolved in a way that was consistent with her own developing values. She explained that the married version of herself did not "gel" with the person she had grown into as a student, leaving her personal ambitions at odds with her marriage. Francine, a self-identified "free spirit," was wary of the conservative values revealed in her husband following marriage. She divorced her husband at age 30. With consternation, she noted, "He sort of saw the wedding ring as, 'Okay, now you're mine,' like I was property." Hope and expectations about marriage eventually came into conflict with reality for these participants.

Revisiting the self: a time for reflection and evaluation

On the path to divorce, five women spoke of *hiding behind* or losing themselves in their marriages, such that they eluded a critical period of self-reflection. A *typical* category was thus generated.

Both Maureen and Alicia spoke of hiding behind the identity of *a married woman*, and the status associated with the title. Describing her marriage as a "security blanket," Maureen talked about her habit of hiding behind a false front, presenting to others that her marriage was conflict-free while she struggled with doubts. Maureen reflected that she felt invested in taking care of her husband's emotional needs during the marriage, but that after her divorce her sense of self shifted:

> I live much more of my life. I'm not trying to put on a show anymore to everybody, so . . . I feel like more of a person and I feel like I've gone back to the person I was before I got into the relationship.

Alicia also felt as though she was "hidden away for a while." Like Maureen, she lost herself in her marriage, and in the process also lost contact with many of her supports. After a period of reflection and evaluation following her divorce, Alicia concluded that her "personality was weighed down" during her marriage. In the same vein, Nina reflected on her struggle to find herself after divorce:

> I was trying to dig into the well of reserves to remember the person I was, at least I thought I was. And in doing that, I gained a ton of strength . . . but I also definitely became a very different person on a number of levels.

For these women, pursuing a couple identity interfered with the development and maintenance of their individual identity.

Rebuilding, a process

Six of the women discussed the process of rebuilding a stronger, more defined, and more secure self in the wake of divorce, generating a *typical* category. Pursuing growth and self-actualization in their post-divorce period, these women endeavored to further their education, engage in therapy, support others, and rekindle relationships. Alicia stated that before moving forward, especially with romance, she needed to evaluate her own needs and behaviors: "I didn't want to run out and start dating. I wanted to look at the situation and see what I could have done differently—what I had done wrong, what I had done right." Francine also emphasized the importance of taking time off from dating to focus on rebuilding herself, stating, "I definitely was, like, *no dating* for a while. I mean I was exhausted . . . the last thing I wanted to do was try and date again."

Four of the women actively pursued support from friends, family, and fellow divorced individuals. Michelle recognized the value of rebuilding supportive friendships—especially with other women—that she had let slide during her marriage. She acknowledged, "Friendships are the most important thing to me now. They took a back seat when I was married and going through what I went through when I got divorced." Maureen renewed her connections with family and felt grateful for their support as she rebuilt her life as a single mother, noting, "[My divorce has] made me grateful for my parents, because . . . before you've been through something [like a divorce] you don't realize the lengths your family will go for you." Nina found that reconnecting with her mother was essential in writing the next chapter of her life, and shared how these conversations had helped her find closure and move on.

Francine discussed the importance of tuning out "external influences" while constructing a more distinct, self-committed identity in her post-divorce period. Therapy, friendship, and exploration of Buddhism helped Francine move forward with a new "meaning system." Jennifer reflected that therapy—both individual and couples counseling—allowed her to "compartmentalize" her divorce experience into "a very small part" of her newly constructed identity. This sentiment was echoed by Maureen, who identified therapy as a major source of support as she emerged from her marriage, and Nina, who found solace in bibliotherapy and feminist theory.

Divorce: a defining passage

Post-divorce, five of the women attempted to make meaning of their experiences and came to understand divorce as a defining passage, an opportunity to learn, evaluate, and engage in growth-related pursuits. Their accounts yielded a *typical* category and described a process by which the women emerged from feelings of failure and embarrassment into a more nuanced and balanced understanding of their experiences.

Francine and Alicia came to use a developmental framework to normalize and make meaning of their experiences, both their marriage and their divorces. Francine explained:

> It's like you were young and you made a stupid mistake . . .
> I think it was something that I knew I just had to be okay with . . .
> [but] I knew I had to do something drastically different so I didn't
> end up in that same situation again.

In going through her divorce alone, Amy, divorced at age 27, discovered her own resilience and capabilities, reflecting, "I guess going through this by myself made me realize that I am more capable of things than I thought I would be." Maureen felt that divorce created a version of herself she likes better, confidently stating, "I didn't fail, it was actually a success for me as a person, but it took therapy to help me see it that way." Similarly, Michelle saw important changes in herself, such as discovering and learning to live by her values. Feeling more "gracious" post-divorce, Michelle stated, "I have better perspective and have better relationships now, since I've been through this experience."

Putting the divorce in its place: stepping back, panning out

Seven women discussed how, over time, they continued the process of giving meaning to their divorce experiences. A *typical* category was thus generated to capture how using a wider lens empowered these women to appreciate the depth and scope of their experiences and/or to develop or refine perspectives on the self.

Two of the women, Nina, divorced at 31, and Carmela, divorced at age 29, independently described themselves as wearing "a badge of honor," attesting to their resilient capacity to find meaning. Nina added, "It's . . . sort of proof that you can pick yourself back up and you can find people to help support you." Carmela spoke of people being "honored" to know her, elaborating:

> Having gone through everything that I went through and still
> being able to . . . smile, and to have fun . . . And then they said,
> you went through it, and now you have three kids and you're
> going to school. . . . You did it. So, a lot of my friends . . . they feel
> honored actually.

Francine, divorced at age 30, contextualized her divorce alongside her many accomplishments:

> It's not like I'm, like, *oh I'm so proud I got married*, you know, I grew up so much. . . . I'm 34, three degrees, traveled around the world a few times. It's something that I did and it probably wasn't the wisest thing to do but it certainly could have been a lot worse. . . . It was a very big learning curve but by no means is it the biggest defining point of my life or anything. And sometimes I have to actually remind myself that I got married and divorced.

All seven women in this category group spoke of taking a longer view, and of coming to terms with their previous selves. Michelle, divorced at age 32, emphatically stated, "I don't regret it. And I definitely think it was something that I was supposed to go through so that I could grow as a person." Alicia, divorced at age 27, reflected, "The more time passes, the more positive things I am able to see from it." Jennifer, divorced at age 24, taking the long view, stated, "I would say that I think I learned a hell of a lot. . . . I think that it made me ultimately a better person." The positive aspects of divorce were clearly reflected in all of these participants' responses.

Failure, embarrassment, and being judged

Although the unraveling of each woman's marriage happened in a way that was specific to her circumstances and worldview, eight of the women encountered personal disappointments and self-doubt. A *general* category was generated to capture these experiences.

Four of the eight women questioned the origin of their embarrassment. Jennifer pointedly stated, "[My divorce] has been a source of embarrassment for me, and I'm not someone who is embarrassed by anything." In looking for answers, Carmela repeatedly asked herself, "What did I do wrong?" Maureen, divorced at age 29, indicated that her sense of failure was self-imposed. The expectations she had for herself were not met, which led to embarrassment: "I don't know if [my reactions are atypical] or if it's just something I put on myself. . . . I was embarrassed that my marriage failed."

Five of the women discussed concerns about being judged in their personal and professional lives. Jennifer and Michelle each described how their fear of being judged at work informed their decision to conceal their divorced status. Jennifer stated that discussing her divorce "would undermine me professionally in the eyes of those that I work with," while Michelle speculated, "They could look at me and go, wow, she made a bad decision and she obviously has a bad sense of judgment of people."

Nina, who took several years to recover from her divorce, commented on how she feared people would react when hearing of her plans to rebuild her life: "I was terrified to tell people . . . and I was always considering what people might think when I was thinking about putting back together my future." Carol, divorced at age 23, also explained that she avoided disclosing her divorce out of fear of "being judged" and "passed to the side." Alicia linked her feelings of failure and embarrassment to being young, rejecting advice, and overgeneralizing. She continued:

> [Marriage is] such a big commitment, and it's sort of one of the first big things that you're doing in your life, so if it doesn't work out you can almost overgeneralize and think that's going to be the way for everything else that you do.

These women feared that their "failure" at marriage could be seen as an evaluation on their overall competency, judgment, and decision making.

Divorce-Related Stigma

Within this domain, all nine participants spoke to the issue of stigma in ways that were idiosyncratic and specific to their personal experiences, yet common themes emerged. The analysis revealed five categories pertaining to this second domain: (a) self-stigma versus public stigma; (b) failure, embarrassment, and perception of blame; (c) religion and stigma; (d) non-disclosure and impression management; and (e) contextual considerations: "It would have been different if. . . ."

Self-stigma versus public stigma

All nine participants spoke of the contrast between self-stigma—stigma that is internalized and becomes a part of the individual's worldview—and public stigma, stigma that is ingrained in society's understanding of divorce (Corrigan, 2005) and experienced personally via social interactions. A *general* category was generated to capture all responses in which the participants mentioned fear related to stereotypes associated with divorce.

Seven women feared that they might be viewed as "crazy," "bitchy," "flakey," "irresponsible," "uncommitted," and/or "selfish" (among other labels), and that their divorce status might negatively impact their professional and personal lives, although they were unable to cite specific examples of experienced stigma. Only two of the seven women shared specific incidents of public stigma, and in these cases the women either neutralized or redirected the stigma. Nina and Michelle both experienced stigma in the form of insults and provocative questions while dating after divorce. According to Nina, "I was called bitter, angry, a bitch, a dyke. . . ." Michelle reported, "I've had guys say to me, 'Oh, you're divorced—even though it's been a while—so what are you, an angry woman now?'"

Internalized self-stigma proved to be a prevalent dynamic among the seven women who feared stigma. These women took specific precautions against discussing or revealing their divorced status, despite the fact that they had never reportedly observed or experienced the negative outcomes they anticipated. For example, although Francine initially claimed that she did not worry about feeling stigmatized for being divorced, she stated that she does not identify herself as divorced on dating sites. To this she added, "[S]o I guess I did think there was a stigma, since I didn't put it down. The whole point is to make yourself attractive, isn't it?"

Four of the women wondered whether they had invented the stigma they perceived, due to overthinking. As Maureen, divorced at age 29, describes it:

> I don't know if [my reactions are atypical] or if it's just something
> I put on myself. So it's hard for me to separate what people
> actually think from [how I interpret what they say]. . . . I told you
> that it was, like, hard for me to tell my friends; I think it's probably
> because I was embarrassed. Like, it's not something I got from
> other people, but, like, personally, I was embarrassed that my
> marriage failed.

While all nine women speculated as to what others might think or say about a young divorced woman, they were hard pressed to cite concrete examples from their lives. There was consensus among the women that the people with whom they chose to associate after their divorce would not treat a divorced woman according to their feared stereotypes. Carmela captured this perspective:

> A lot of people that I knew . . . they tell me that they would have never have thought I was divorced with three kids. I honestly . . . haven't had any comments or feelings, nothing of the kind, just because I'm divorced.

Perception of stigma and *fear* of stigma seemed to be stronger factors than actual stigma for these women, causing them to alter their behavior and their level of self-revelation.

Failure, embarrassment, and being judged

Eight of the nine women spoke of feeling as though they were failures, particularly at the time of their divorce. They discussed connections between perceptions of failure, feelings of embarrassment, and awareness of potential judgment. Hence, a *general* category was identified to reflect concerns related to failure. Nina, Maureen, and Carmela all described how their feelings of embarrassment were entangled with ideas of failure because they had witnessed successful marriages in their families. They wondered how others could make marriage work while they could not.

NINA: I think first the whole element of failure, there's just this air of, "I tried this endeavor, this big thing that a lot of people succeed at, or my family succeeds at . . . and otherwise I'm a very successful person. . . " I think, it's the element of failure that can be kind of embarrassing. But I also will say that I definitely wondered if people thought that maybe I wasn't a worthy partner because someone had left me. So that's embarrassing too. . . . That was definitely a big intersecting part of why [I felt] embarrassed . . . and [a] failure.

MAUREEN: It feels like you couldn't make it work [when] all these other people could make it work [and I considered myself a successful person in other areas]. . . . It wasn't something I felt from other people, it's just something I put on myself; it was embarrassing, you know, like, everyone else can make this work.

Carmela and Michelle discussed the intersection of blame and failure. Carmela stated, "I felt that [the marriage] was a failure because I felt that it was my fault that it didn't work out. . . . I kept asking, 'What did I do wrong?'" Michelle stated that she initially internalized the divorce as her fault, but, as with many of the other participants, she was able to shift her perspective over time:

I think maybe it's knowing more and realizing how I was lucky to get out of [the marriage] and where he is now. I know that it wasn't my fault, and I couldn't have stayed. There is much less sense of failure about it.

For most of these women, the sense of failure faded with time and reflection.

Religion and stigma

Six of the nine women spoke to the influence of religion and how it informed their experiences with divorce. A *typical* category thus emerged. Three of the participants discussed the impact of their connection to the Catholic Church. An additional three women spoke about religious values and how they can shape an individual's opinions of divorce. The frequency with which religion was discussed during the interviews was unexpected, considering that only one of our nine interviewees self-identified as actively religious.

Alicia, who was raised Catholic and continues to identify as practicing, shared, "It's hard because I am Catholic, so divorce is frowned upon, and . . . I can never get married in the Catholic Church again, so that's hard." When applying to a master's program at a Catholic college after her divorce, Nina explained her fears: "[Divorce] actually did affect my decisions because I thought I would be judged more harshly in the context of Catholicism than anything else." Carmela, also Catholic, was initially worried that her divorce would mean that she would not be allowed to attend church anymore. Though she feared being judged by her community, her priest was supportive:

I talked to my priest actually . . . and he said *you* should decide; you shouldn't not get a divorce just because you're Catholic. Nothing's going to stop you, we're not going to stop you from coming to church or anything like that.

Maureen, who does not identify as religious, suggested that religion still has a stigmatizing impact on the lives of divorced women. She suggested that strongly religious people are more likely to stigmatize individuals for being divorced:

> I kind of feel like there is a group of people that are not going to like divorce anyway, and you know, [these people have] more of a religious way of thinking. If someone is against you being divorced, you don't want to meet them anyway. Like, I'm not really into religious people.

Francine carries this argument one step further and explains that, whether one is religious or nonreligious, everyone is affected by societal values, which have been shaped by religion:

> Although I'm not religious at all and I don't believe in God, we live in a society where divorce is [regarded as bad]. . . . I sort of thought that, oh, whatever, I'm not religious, I'm not Christian, so why do I still subscribe to how society is heavily influenced by that? I think that [even] if you're not religious and you don't think you're influenced by it, [religious values are] the basis of our society and what it is organized around.

Nondisclosure and impression management

Six of the nine women spoke to the issue of nondisclosure and impression management in the wake of their divorce. Hence, a *typical* category was generated. Although the rationales provided for engaging in impression management were diverse, the anticipation of being judged negatively was a common reason. Each of these women actively concealed or controlled personal, divorce-related information in order to avoid the consequences of a stigmatized identity (Sedlovskaya et al., 2013). The choice to withhold information about their divorce experiences was also driven by the need for privacy.

Several of the women chose a nondisclosing stance in order to maintain an identity that they wished to convey to others. Fear of judgement informed their decisions, and some of the women expressed concern that self-disclosure would lead to pejorative stereotypes. For example, Carol, divorced at age 23, acknowledged that stereotypes exist for divorced women in general, and explained that she has heard people refer to divorced women as "flighty," "impulsive," "irresponsible," and "apathetic towards marriage." She defends her choice to not self-disclose:

I don't really disclose a lot of personal information very easily. I don't really tell anyone [about the divorce]. I usually avoid feeling that way, feeling like I'm being judged, feeling like I'm being sort of passed to the side.

Jennifer and Michelle spoke about the management of divorce-related information in their professional lives. Michelle stated that although "there's not a stigma around divorce anymore," she deliberately avoids sharing her divorced status with classmates and colleagues in order to mitigate potential judgment. Along these same lines, Jennifer stated:

I know statistically that half of people have gotten divorced, but I do think that there still is a big stigma around people who have, and I definitely think more so around young people, in the sense that you're brash and impulsive and things like that.

Themes of judging oneself and being judged by others in the wake of divorce were prevalent among all nine of the participants, suggesting that successful marriage still represents a significant social achievement for these emerging adults, even though its importance may be downplayed when they speak about it.

Contextual considerations: It would have been different if . . .

Each of the nine participants spoke to the importance of *context*, specifically how context can intensify or minimize feelings associated with stigma. A general category was created to reflect the participants' beliefs that their experiences with stigma *would have been different if* one or more features of their personal context had changed. For example, the participants consistently pointed to the importance of chronological age and how it influences the degree to which one is stigmatized. Participants hypothesized that older women (i.e., in their 50s or 60s), who have been married for a long time, are less vulnerable to stigma than younger women with children. Four of the nine women concluded that historical and developmental considerations can temper feelings associated with divorce-related stigma.

The identity of *mother* served as a common qualifier with respect to the experience of stigma. Three of the nine women speculated that they would have experienced an intensification of stigma had they been mothers. Maureen added credence to this belief, stating that the stigma she personally perceived and experienced was due to her being a young divorced mother: "I felt very much like, 'Oh my God. People are going to think I'm crazy because I'm going through a divorce with a 7-month-old. Like, I think it was very much my own stigma I put on it." Amy, divorced at age 27, found that her view of a "stereotypical" divorced woman applied only to women with children—whom she described as hierarchically "more divorced."

Environmental factors represented another perceived variable with respect to the experience of stigma surrounding divorce. Three of the nine women speculated that they would have experienced *more* stigma had they not lived in a major city. Two of the nine women asserted that living in American culture, as opposed to their more traditional cultures of origin, tempered their experience of stigma.

Certain attendant features of the participants' divorce experiences were regarded as more stigmatizing than the divorce itself. Michelle, for example, felt that her husband's narcotic addiction was more stigmatizing than her choice to get a divorce. Similarly, Amy indicated that explaining her ex-husband's infidelity triggered a greater experience of stigma and shame than admitting to being a divorced woman. Jennifer felt that her sense of stigma around divorce would not have been so notable if she were not getting remarried.

▲ Analysis of Findings

All of the nine women reported that prior to marriage they found themselves navigating an environmental context that mirrored their feelings of uncertainty and instability. Some of their narratives spoke to feeling pressured to be married, and then later becoming aware of problems in the marriage as their illusions about being married collapsed or as their marriages failed to keep up with their own personal growth. Divorce, though traumatic, was viewed as the key to unlocking a stronger sense of identity and competency. In the wake of divorce, several participants spoke of taking a long view and building foundations that supported their growth. Additionally, the women's experiences were peppered with a vague sense of having experienced stigma in their interactions with the public sphere, but also with a sense of self-stigmatization.

These results echo the assessment Gerstel (1987) offered more than two decades ago: "To argue that the divorced are no longer stigmatized is to misunderstand their experience" (p. 183). However, since the time Gerstel wrote her seminal article, subtle shifts have occurred in how divorce is lived and experienced, as evidenced by the narratives of the women in this study. In addressing the issue of stigma, a significant number of the participants denied its relevance; however, through their actions, self-perceptions, and experiences, stigma proved relevant. In other words, their behaviors and actions belied their cognitive assessments.

Prior to marriage, many of the women felt unmoored and sought solace and security in marital relationships; they expected that via marriage they would gain stability and a sense of permanence. Alicia's choice to marry, for example, appeared to be more influenced by anxiety about the future than by the actual status of her relationship. "I don't think we really knew what marriage would entail," she reflected, suggesting that the decision to marry may have been an attempt at finding an anchor. Marriage, for some, addressed the women's discomfort with the transience emblematic of emerging and young adulthood.

Although a preponderance of the women thought marriage would provide them a place of comfort, stability, status, and self-definition, they later realized that important developmental milestones had been deferred in the process. Their sense of self was not well developed prior to marriage. The partners did not view each other as a "distinct" and "connected" self (Pals, 1999, p. 301). In anticipation of gaining status and security, these women adopted unexamined ideas about marriage without envisioning how they or their partners might retain an *I* and *we* identity within the marital context. Using a "convenient lens," two thirds of the women entered marriage in the face of red flags, significant concerns that would need to be addressed (e.g., a very controlling partner, tumultuous long-term or long-distance relationships, unnoted substance abuse). Looking through a lens of convenience, and ignoring what they did not want to see, the participants forged forward.

Idealism and magical thinking—the idea that marriage would transform the partners or that an ideal partner might be found via a checklist of superficial attributes—represented some ways in which the women depersonalized the prospect of marriage while underestimating the role that shared values, goals, and interests play in producing salutary marital outcomes. They based their decisions to marry on what they might gain abstractly, without a realistic understanding of themselves, their partners, and/or their relationships. Thus, they were unprepared for the realities of marriage and found it difficult to relate to their partners in mutually satisfying ways.

Perhaps not surprisingly, a majority of the women did not rush to enter new romantic relationships after their divorces; rather, they took the time to reflect on who they were, and who they had become. Over half of the women described an evolution of their values through the divorce process, and spoke of discovering aspects of themselves that they had not considered, or had put on hold, before entering marriage. They revisited a process they had averted prior to their marriages, the development of a more differentiated *I*. In evaluating their relationships, their courtships, and their marriages, they reflected on how they themselves contributed to the decision to divorce, first asking, "What did I do wrong?" and later, "Who was I before and during this marriage?" Over time, the women gained important insights, clarified their evolving values, and enhanced their sense of self-determination. They became committed to learning to become a better *I*, and with that in mind pursued their own interests and goals.

Themes related to growth, capability, and renewed self-understanding were evident throughout the women's narratives about their divorce experiences. Emerging from a period of perceived failure, nearly all of the women came to see how the divorce process was actually a positive force in their lives. The meaning of divorce shifted from emphasis on feelings of failure and embarrassment to feelings of pride deriving from a sense of capability and growth. A majority of the women revealed that the divorce sparked a personal awakening, supporting findings reported in the literature (Gardner & Oswald, 2006; Hetherington & Kelly, 2003; Maatta & Uusiautti, 2012).

Once the women got past the initial crisis, they began to feel a sense of personal freedom. Without the previous perceived marital constraints, they discovered opportunities to "explore new challenges" (Thomas & Ryan, 2008, p. 211), including the continuation of their education, new jobs, and for some, new relationships. Although the women continued to face stigma-related adversity (Konstam et al., 2016), possibilities for personal growth became evident over time.

Regarding their experiences of stigma, the women *anticipated* being devalued and/or judged, as evidenced by their concealing and/

or failing to disclose their divorced status. Their responses are consistent with Corrigan's (2005) assertion that individuals belonging to a stigmatized group often attempt to avoid and/or minimize the effects of stigma by withholding information regarding their group membership. The participants seemed to become more aware of their stigmatization as they reflected back on their divorce experiences, though at the time of the actual concealment they may have acted without forethought. Given their initial denial that stigma against divorced women still exists today, their nondisclosing stance suggests a disconnect between their cognitive beliefs and their actions; the women internalized the stigma and were acting it out, perhaps semi-consciously.

Although a nondisclosing stance can serve a self-protective function, there is an emotional price associated with it (Link & Phelan, 2001; Scrambler, 1998, 2004). As proposed in the literature on stereotypes and prejudice (Bargh & Williams, 2006; Blair, 2002; Devine, 1989), this stance serves to keep feelings of failure, embarrassment, and shame in abeyance. However, its cost is that it perpetuates feelings of guilt, failure, and embarrassment and also deprives the individual of meaningful self-examination and social engagement. In the service of self-protection, non-disclosing women are engaging in a process that requires concealment of portions of their identities (Sedlovskaya et al., 2013).

The participants experienced dissonance between the expectations they had for their marriages and the personal failure they felt when confronted with reality. Many of the women in the study feared that their "failure" in marriage might predict future failures in both their personal and professional lives. A sense of shame, either overt or subtle, permeated several of the narratives.

Brown (2006) explains that shame often produces feelings of confusion, anger, fear, and self-judgment, as well as the need to hide the shame. Furthermore, she suggests that shame is frequently experienced as a complex of competing, conflicting expectations of the self, derived from rigid societal expectations—which, as our participants alluded to, are reinforced by societal structures (e.g., religious entities such as the Catholic Church). Thoits (1992) reports that both men and women (ages 18–55) tend to identify with, and take pride in, their marital status and to view themselves as responsible for their marriages and the quality of their intimate relationships. Thus, when the marriage fails, they presumably also feel responsible and suffer a concomitant loss of pride. The feelings of failure, shame, and embarrassment that pervade the narratives of the nine women confirm the underlying power of social expectations around the sanctity of marriage. Many of the participants, in the wake of divorce, felt compromised as women and questioned their capacity for intimacy. "Till death do us part," a cultural ideal, infiltrated their psyches and left them feeling inadequate when they failed to "go the distance."

Collectively, the women tended to contextualize their experiences of stigma related to divorce. This process of "qualifying" their experiences was self-protective, allowing them to de-intensify stigma-related feelings, such as embarrassment and fear of judgement. It allowed the women to make social comparisons and thereby gain perspective on their personal scenarios (Wills, 1981). Most of the participants felt their particular situation wasn't *as bad as it could be*. For two of the women, they ultimately assessed that their fears around being judged and criticized for their divorce were "ridiculous" or "silly," and they struggled to identify the source of their initial feelings of guilt and shame.

Organized religion was an unexpected focus in conversations around stigma. Specifically, for the two participants who identified as Catholic, the challenge of integrating the conflicting identities of "religious" and "divorced" was compounded by both self-stigma and public stigma. Stokes and Ellison (2010) point out that "American Catholics have lost much of their once distinctive conservatism toward family issues" (p. 1282), with more members selecting a personalized menu of values to adhere to in day-to-day life. However, despite this general shift toward a more accepting perspective, some of our interviewees still feared repercussions from the Catholic Church at the institutional level. Interestingly, other participants who did not identify as Catholic opined that "religious people" were more likely to harshly judge divorced women. This view could serve to help them diminish self-stigma by holding a particular group of people responsible for judging divorced women, rather than viewing divorce-related stigma as status quo.

Overall, themes of resilience and pride in overcoming obstacles prevailed, and while the women did feel vulnerable during the early stages of the divorce process, they were able to seek support and establish a stronger sense of self over the long term. As evidenced by the terms they used in describing their experience—"learning curve," "learning experience," "being young," "badge of honor"—the women acknowledged that their resilience was hard-earned, the result of engaging in the personal development work they had deferred during their marriages.

Each of the nine women engaged in a process of healing, which included revisiting their divorce experience and coming to see the role it played in their development as young adults. A majority of women in the study sought the help of either religious counsel, bibliotherapy, support groups, or a professional therapist. All of those women reflected on their therapeutic encounters with gratitude and attribute their increased self-esteem to these encounters. They described a process whereby they were able to work through feelings of failure, embarrassment, and shame, while redefining themselves and learning important life lessons along the way (Gregson & Ceynar, 2009; Josselson, 1996). Their self-definition no longer depended on their marital status, although for many, self-stigmatization and nondisclosure continued to reinforce the pernicious effects of stigma, denying the women a full opportunity for self-actualization.

Protective narratives play an important role in mitigating shame and vulnerability. It is important to understand that it was not following a traditional path that placed the women at risk (Pals, 1999), but rather their lack of self-assessment, development, and resources. A "convenient lens," such as ignoring red flags in the relationship or selectively focusing on a partner's positive qualities, may serve a protective purpose at the time of the marriage, but may result in feelings of guilt or blame when the marriage dissolves. In the aftermath of divorce, nondisclosure and concealment may protect against self-stigma and public stigma; the individual is walking a line between fear of exposure and defying culturally integrated stereotypes. Professionals working with emerging adults may have to straddle both dynamics while carefully identifying and teasing apart stigma-laced narratives.

Alicia, a participant in the divorce study, embodies a range of divorce-related experiences shared by other study participants and thus serves as a good illustrative case, the focus of the next section of this chapter. Six months after her divorce, Alicia reflected on the low self-esteem she experienced during her marriage and on the considerable personal and professional changes she and her spouse underwent. Initially thinking marriage would be a "magic potion" that would make her tumultuous relationship work, Alicia defensively ignored the warnings of others regarding red flags in her relationship. After years of emotional abuse and unaddressed affairs, Alicia finally reached a breaking point and pursued divorce. Feelings of embarrassment and failure, as well as a changing perspective on the Catholic Church, marked the challenges she faced along the way. Relying on a loyal group of supportive family and friends, as well as support from a women's group, Alicia was able to recover her sense of self and feel "stronger" than before. Her experience highlights the potential growth journey of the divorce experience.

▲ Alicia, an Illustrative Case

Alicia, a 28-year-old, white US Airforce veteran, was 14 when she started dating her ex-husband, also a serviceman. He was her first boyfriend, and the two dated on and off before becoming "serious" at approximately age 20. They married when Alicia was 23, the same year she completed boot camp. For the first 8 months of their marriage, they lived together in California, where Alicia was stationed, but when her husband found work in Boston, their relationship became long-distance for the next 3 years—including 2 separate years in which her husband was deployed in active combat. Two months after his return, the couple agreed to separate. A year later, they were divorced.

Reflecting back, Alicia was able to recognize symptoms of combat-related PTSD in her partner, including "classic signs" such as hypervigilance and social withdrawal, but it was other emergent qualities—his emotional distance and tendency to become "cold" and "almost egocentric"—that proved to be the most trying on their marriage. Alicia noted that he began "calling me names and acting like he hated me. It was just so sudden that I knew something big had changed." While in marriage counseling, Alicia discovered he had been having affairs with other women, which she remarked was "the last straw." Divorced for 6 months at the time of her interview, Alicia remarked, "I'm still finding stuff out randomly through the grapevine—that he was probably having affairs for years when I didn't even know."

Alicia, who identifies as a practicing Catholic, was married in the Church. Her divorce experience challenged her sense of connectedness to the organization, and while she feels disappointed that she cannot get married in the Church again, she remarks that an annulment is "just a piece of paper that gets sent to Rome." Ultimately, she believes that "nobody [in her Church community] looked at me like, 'Oh you can't get a divorce because you're Catholic,'" and that fear of reaction from her church community did not play a role in her decision to divorce.

Regarding stigma, Alicia feels that divorce has a "shock factor" for people her age. When she separated from her husband, she felt nervous about how she might be seen by people who didn't know her story, and by potential romantic partners. She shared, "I thought they would think something was wrong with me, that I wasn't marriage material or partner material."

While she feels that she was never judged for being divorced, and that divorce is not a shameful thing, Alicia did experience embarrassment due to being "so young" and disagreeing with friends and family who questioned whether her marriage was healthy. She reflects:

> I was just so resistant to seeing what everyone else saw. So
> I think . . . having to go back on that and admit that they were
> right and I was wrong and feeling like I failed my marriage at
> such a young age, that was the embarrassing part about it.

Like many of the young women in the study, her feelings of embarrassment were connected to a sense that she had failed. She worried that her failure in marriage might be perceived as a sign of her being a poor decision maker, or of being stubborn in failing to take the advice of others who "knew better."

Alicia sought support from multiple outlets during and after her divorce, including family, professional counseling, and a women's support group. In reconnecting with friends, Alicia observed, "It's almost like you were hidden away for a little while." The support group, in particular, had a normalizing effect on her experience of being a young divorced woman. Attending groups helped Alicia see where her story "fit" alongside the narratives of other women. It was Alicia's family, though, who were the first to observe a re-emergence of her personality—the "fun," "funny," and "outgoing" aspects of herself that seemed to be "weighted down" in marriage. Alicia reflected that when she was married she would become defensive if a family member noticed she wasn't "acting like herself," believing they didn't understand the complexities of her situation. Having gained some distance from the relationship, she now sees, "It's almost like in their eyes that I am recovering from a sort of sickness and getting better."

In the aftermath of divorce, Alicia sees herself not as "happier," but "stronger" and possessed of more insight into what she wants in a partner:

> I don't want to say happier that it happened, but it's made me a
> much stronger person, much more aware of myself and what I am
> capable of and the things that I want and I don't want. Looking

back and seeing the stuff that I settled with and accepted and allowed to go on are not things that I would ever do now. I have definitely taken a lot [of] personal insight on, "How could I let somebody treat me like that for so long?" There were a couple of years where he wasn't working, I was supporting him. . . . [In] my younger 20s, I didn't think I was good enough to not be treated that way. But I look now and I know my own value. And I started doing things for myself. . . . I have tried to look at [divorce] as positively as I can. The more time passes, the more positive things I am able to see from it.

Reflecting on her experience, Alicia's advice to other emerging and young adults who might be going through a divorce is practical. She challenges the magical, "convenient" thinking that she and others her age sometimes engage in when imagining marriage to be a transformative solution to a red-flag-laden relationship: "I think that's the biggest mistake that people make and that I made. Thinking that marriage is the solution to making things better."

Like many of the women in the study, her expectations of what marriage would be like for her and her partner were unclear and unrealistic. She was blindsided by his cheating and by her realization of the depth of emotional abuse she was experiencing, although friends and family seemed to be all too aware of the latter. Her marriage, which did not adequately address the needs of the two struggling people in it, was not enough to create an established life, a safe haven, or a strong sense of self.

At the time of the interview, Alicia disclosed that she is in a new romantic relationship with a partner who is also divorced and who also experienced being cheated on. She shared that while divorce is a turbulent experience, they both feel grateful for what they learned, especially about communication, the need for mutual support, and what it takes to make a relationship work.

In terms of my relationship with my boyfriend now . . . there is no dysfunction in the relationship. It is very communicative, it's very easy . . . we compromise, we don't disrespect each other, we don't yell. If we are in a disagreement, we talk it through, we don't scream and swear. It's different because we both know that those are things that lead to a divorce and lead to a marriage breaking apart.

Alicia now feels she is able to have both a romantic partner and a foundation to succeed in her personal goals and growth. She proclaimed:

> I have somebody now who encourages the things I want to do. . . .
> I'm not afraid to go after the things that I want to go after because
> I have somebody now who isn't putting me down constantly and
> saying I'll never make it.

▲ Summary and Conclusions

Divorce among emerging adults is a tumultuous process whose roots and causes are manifold. Sometimes divorce is the "inevitable" result of fundamental flaws in the relationship that were ignored or glossed when partners got married. Sometimes divorce flows from a failure of the partners to grow and evolve at the same rate and in the same direction once married. Many of our participants felt emotionally vulnerable; they entered their marriages without doing the necessary work of developing themselves, developing an *I* informed by individual interests and goals. Ultimately, though, despite the pain it typically involves, divorce can lead to personal growth and to numerous other positive outcomes once the crisis has been navigated.

The findings of the qualitative study reported in this chapter reveal that each of the nine emerging and young adult participants engaged in a rich process of personal growth and discovery through her experience of divorce. Their experiences, though nuanced and distinct, also spoke to the continued relevance of self-stigma and public stigma.

Navigating the stormy waters of emerging adulthood without an anchor, many of the women envisioned marriage as a safe harbor. However, their decision to marry—made at a time when their sense of self and their personal values had yet to be defined—also served to defer an important period of self-exploration and development. These young women shifted their focus instead to managing their relationships. Using a "convenient lens" and relying on magical thinking, they entered marriage without strong foundations that might have served both themselves and the marriage well.

Divorce brought with it a necessary period of working on the self, in which the study participants battled feelings of embarrassment and failure and then emerged more capable and self-aware. They eventually came to understand their marriage and divorce experiences in the context of a developmental framework, and now consider these painful experiences to be part of a "learning curve" toward self-understanding.

Although this chapter has focused on the lived experience of divorced emerging adult women, the choice to focus on women does not suggest that the process of divorce is less daunting for emerging adult men. Emerging adult men do mourn the dissolution of their marriage; they begin to mourn at a later point in time, and on average express their pain and grief indirectly rather than verbally, as compared to women (Doka & Martin, 2010). Whereas women tend to mourn the loss associated with divorce prior to physical separation or legal action, men tend to mourn the loss when physical separation has actually occurred.

In order to relieve the stress of divorce, emerging adult men are more likely to immerse themselves in work, and to engage in heavy drinking and pornography usage initially. Women, in contrast, are more likely to become depressed, emotionally and verbally expressive, and to seek professional help (Martin & Doka, 2000). Both emerging adult men and women do have the ability to learn and grow from their divorce-related experiences. Their processes toward growth are likely to differ (Steiner, Durand, Groves, & Rozell, 2015).

It is important to note that the results of our study do not indicate that divorce rates would be lower if women entered relationships better prepared, or having made more personal developmental progress. Each relationship is unique, and the success of a marriage is contingent on a range of factors inherent to both partners. These results do, however, suggest that women who enter marriage with a fuller and more textured understanding of themselves, their partners, and their relationship—including an awareness of their expectations—may be in a better place to make thoughtful, deliberate decisions prior to and during marriage. Attempting to establish one's own identity as one is simultaneously trying to build a committed partnership remains a challenge, regardless of one's level of insight, external supports, or dedication to one's marital partner.

The participants' reported experiences of marriage and divorce have significant clinical implications for those who wish to work with emerging and young adults. Deferred self-development and stigma-laced narratives, for example, may lead to negative outcomes unless supports are strengthened and individuals resume the pursuit of essential developmental milestones. In regard to stigma, the narratives of the nine women clarified that stigma remains relevant today and that it informed their experiences in complicated and, at times, contradictory ways.

The behavior of the participants often seemed inconsistent with their cognitive assessments of the role stigma played in their lives. At times they assessed that stigma has no place in a modern social construct, while at other times they anticipated harsh judgement from others. Some of the women struggled to identify actual examples of prejudice they had encountered, while at the same time taking steps to conceal their divorced status from others, especially in scenarios where others might be scrutinizing them, such as at work or on the dating scene. Tactics such as these suggest the continued existence of stigma— or at least the continued *fear* of stigma—while the inability to cite specific examples of stigma suggests perhaps that stigmatization may indeed be dissipating. Perhaps in bringing these women's stories to light, the narrative of divorce might become less "embarrassing" and might be seen more as a developmental journey with promising outcomes.

▲ Author's Note

The content of this chapter was published as Konstam, V., Curran, T., Karwin, S. (2015). Divorce and emerging adult and young women: Building foundations for self-development. *Journal of Divorce and Remarriage, 56*(4), 277–299 and Konstam, V., Karwin, S., Curran, T., Lyons, M., & Celen-Demirtas, S. (2016). Stigma and divorce: A relevant lens for emerging and young adult women? *Journal of Divorce and Remarriage, 57*(3), 173–194.

▲ References

Amato, P. R. (2010). Research on divorce: Continuing trends and new developments. *Journal of Marriage & Family, 72,* 650–666. doi:10.1111/j.1741-3737.2010.00723.x

Amato, P. R., & Previti, D. (2003). People's reasons for divorcing: Gender, social class, the life course, and adjustment. *Journal of Family Issues, 24*(5), 602–626. doi:10.1177/0192513X03254507

Bargh, J. A., & Williams, E. L. (2006). The automaticity of social life. *Current Directions in Psychological Science, 19,* 1–4. doi:10.1111/j.0963-7214.2006.00395.x

Blair, I. V. (2002). The malleability of automatic stereotypes and prejudice. *Personality and Social Psychology Review, 6,* 242–261. doi:10.1207/S15327957PSPR0603_8

Brown, B. (2006). Shame resilience theory: A grounded theory study on women and shame. *Families in Society: The Journal of Contemporary Social Services, 87*(1), 43–52.

Cherlin, A. J., Cross-Barnet, C., Burton, L., & Garrett-Peters, R. (2008). Promises they can keep: Low-income women's attitudes toward motherhood, marriage, and divorce. *Journal of Marriage & Family, 70*(4), 919–933. doi:10.1111/j.1741-3737.2008.00536.x

Corrigan, P. (2004). How stigma interferes with mental health care. *American Psychologist, 59,* 614–625. doi:10.1037/0003-066X.59.7.614.

Corrigan, P. W. (Ed.). (2005). *On the stigma of mental illness: Practical strategies for research and social change.* Washington, DC: American Psychological Association.

Corrigan, P. W., & Kleinlein, P. (2005). The impact of mental illness on stigma. In P. W. Corrigan (Ed.), *On the stigma of mental illness: Practical strategies for research and social change* (pp.11–44). Washington, DC: American Psychological Association.

Devine, A. G. (1989). Stereotypes and prejudice: Their automatic and controlled components. *Journal of Personality and Social Psychology, 56,* 5–18. doi:10.1037/0022-3514.56.1.5

Doka, K., & Martin, T. (2010). *Grieving beyond gender : Understanding the ways men and women mourn* (rev. ed.). London: Taylor and Francis.

Eldar-Avidan, D., Haj-Yahia, M. M., & Greenbaum, C. W. (2009). Divorce is a part of my life. . . . Resilience, survival, and vulnerability: Young adults' perception of the implications of parental divorce. *Journal of Marital and Family Therapy, 35*(1), 30–46. doi:10.1111/j.1752-0606.2008. 00094.x

Finkel, E. J. (2017). *The all-or-nothing marriage. How the best marriages work.* New York, NY: Penguin Random House.

Finkel, E. J., Hui, C. M., Carswell, K. L., & Larson, G. M. (2014). The suffocation of marriage: Climbing Mount Maslow without enough oxygen. *Psychological Inquiry, 25*(1), 1–41. doi:10.1080/1047840X.2014.863723

Frost, D. M. (2013). Stigma and intimacy in same-sex relationships: A narrative approach. *Qualitative Psychology, 1*(S), 49–61. doi:10.1037/2326-3598.1. S.49

Gardner, J., & Oswald, A. J. (2006). Do divorcing couples become happier by breaking up? *Journal of the Royal Statistical Society: Series A (Statistics in Society), 169*(2), 319–336. doi:10.1111/j.1467-985X.2006.00403.x

Gerstel, N. (1987). Divorce and stigma. *Social Problems, 34*(2), 172–186. doi:10.2307/800714

Goldberg, A. E., & Smith, J. Z. (2011). Stigma, social context, and mental health: Lesbian and gay couples across the transition to adoptive parenthood. *Journal of Counseling Psychology, 58*(1), 139–150. doi:10.1037/a0021684

Gregson, J., & Ceynar, M. L. (2009). Finding "me" again: Women's postdivorce identity shifts. *Journal of Divorce & Remarriage, 50*(8), 564–582. doi:10.1080/10502550902970546

Hare-Mustin, R. T., & Marecek, J. (1988). The meaning of difference: Gender theory, postmodernism, and psychology. *American Psychologist, 43*(6), 455–464. doi:10.1037/0003-066X.43.6.455

Hetherington, E. M., & Kelly, J. (2003). *For better or for worse: Divorce reconsidered.* New York, NY: Norton.

Hill, C. E., Knox, S., Thompson, B. J., Williams, E. N., Hess, S. A., & Ladany, N. (2005). Consensual qualitative research: An update. *Journal of Counseling Psychology, 52*(2), 196–205. doi:10.1037/0022-0167.52.2.196

Jordan, J. V. (2010) *Relational-cultural therapy.* Washington, DC: American Psychological Association Press.

Josselson, R. (1987). *Finding herself: Pathways to identity development in women.* San Francisco, CA: Jossey-Bass.

Josselson, R. (1996). *Revising herself: The story of women's identity from college to midlife.* New York, NY: Oxford University Press.

King, B. R. (2008). The influence of parental gender and custodial status on perceptual stigmatization: Are non-custodial mothers viewed more negatively than other parent types? *Journal of Divorce & Remarriage, 48*(3/4), 55–65. doi:10.1300/J087v48n03.04

Konstam, V. (2015). *Emerging and young adulthood: Multiple perspectives, diverse narratives* (2nd ed.). Cham, Switzerland: Springer International.

Konstam, V., Curran, T., & Karwin, S. (2015). Divorce and emerging adult and young women: Building foundations for self-development. *Journal of Divorce and Remarriage, 56*(4), 277–299. doi:10.1080/10502556.2015.1025897

Konstam, V., Karwin, S., Curran, T., Lyons, M., & Celen-Demirtas, S. (2016). Stigma and divorce: A relevant lens for emerging and young adult women? *Journal of Divorce and Remarriage, 57*(3), 173–194. doi:10.1080/10502556.2016.1150149

Link, B. G., & Phelan, J. C. (2001). Conceptualizing stigma. *Annual Review of Sociology,* 363–385. doi:10.1146/annurev.soc.27.1.363

Maatta, K., & Uusiautti, S. (2012). Changing identities: Finnish divorcees' perceptions of a new marriage. *Journal of Divorce & Remarriage, 53,* 515–532. doi:10.1080/10502556.2012.682906

Maslow, A. H. (1970). *Motivation and personality.* New York, NY: Harper & Row.

Mayseless, O., & Keren, E. (2014). Finding a meaningful life as a developmental task in emerging adulthood: The domains of love and work across cultures. *Emerging Adulthood, 2*(1), 63–73. doi:10.1177/2167696813515446

Pals, J. L. (1999). Identity consolidation in early adulthood: Relations with ego-resiliency, the context of marriage, and personality change. *Journal of Personality, 67*(2), 295–329.

Schneller, D. P., & Arditti, J. A. (2004). After the breakup: Interpreting divorce and rethinking intimacy. *Journal of Divorce & Remarriage 42*(1/2), 1–37. doi:10.1300/J087v42n01_01

Schoen, R., & Canudas-Romo, V. (2006). Timing effects on divorce: 20th century experience in the United States. *Journal of Marriage & Family, 68,* 749–758. doi:10.1111/j.1741-3737.2006.00287.x

Scrambler, G. (1998). Stigma and disease: Changing paradigms. *The Lancet, 352*(9133), 1054–1055. doi:10.1016/S0140-6736(98)08068-4

Scrambler, G. (2004). Re-framing stigma: Felt and enacted stigma and challenges to the sociology of chronic and disabling conditions. *Social Theory & Health*, 2(1), 29–46. doi:10.1057/palgrave.sth.8700012

Sedlovskaya, A., Purdie-Vaughns, V., Eibach, R. P., LaFrance, M., Romero-Canyas, R., & Camp, N. P. (2013). Internalizing the closet: Concealment heightens the cognitive distinction between public and private selves. *Journal of Personality and Social Psychology*, 104(4), 695–715. doi:10.1037/a0031179

Seiffge-Krenke, I., & Luyckx, K. (2014). Competent in work and love? Emerging adults' trajectories in dealing with work-partnership conflicts and links to health functioning. *Emerging Adulthood*, 2(1), 48–58. doi:10.1177/2167696813516090

Shulman, S., & Connolly, J. (2013). The challenge of romantic relationships in emerging adulthood: Reconceptualization of the field. *Emerging Adulthood*, 1(1), 27–39. doi:10.1177/2167696812467330050

Steiner, L. M., Durand, S., Groves, D., & Rozell, C. (2015). Effect of infidelity, initiator statue and spiritual well-being on men's divorce. *Journal of Divorce and Remarriage*, 56, 95–108. doi:10.1080/10502556.2014.996050

Stokes, C. E., & Ellison, C. G. (2010). Religion and attitudes toward divorce laws among U.S. adults. *Journal of Family Issues*, 31(10), 1279–1304. doi:10.1177/0192513x10363887

Thoits, P. A. (1992). Identity structures and psychological well-being: Gender and marital status comparisons. *Social Psychology Quarterly*, 55(3), 236–256. doi:10.2307/2786794

Thomas, C., & Ryan, M. (2008). Women's perception of the divorce experience: A qualitative study. *Journal of Divorce & Remarriage*, 49, 210–224. doi:10.1080/10502550802222394

Thornton, A., & Young-DeMarco, L. (2001). Four decades of trends in attitudes toward family issues in the United States: The 1960s through the 1990s. *Journal of Marriage and Family*, 63(4), 1009–1037. doi:10.1111/j.1741-3737.2001. 01009.x

United States Census Bureau. (2011). *Marital events of Americans: 2009*. Retrieved from: http://www.census.gov/prod/2011pubs/acs-13.pdf

Vogel, D. L., Bitman, R. L., Hammer, J. H., & Wade, N. G. (2013). Is stigma internalized? The longitudinal impact of public stigma on self-stigma. *Journal of Counseling Psychology*, 60(2), 311–316. doi:10.1037/a0031889

Wills, T. A. (1981). Downward comparison principles in social psychology. *Psychological Bulletin*, 90(2), 245. doi:10.1037/0033-2909.90.2.245

Yodanis, C. (2005). Divorce culture and marital gender equality: A cross-national study. *Gender & Society*, 19(5), 644–659. doi:10.1177/089124320527816

12 ▲
Summary and Syntheses

Rebecca Traister, author of *All the Single Ladies: Unmarried Women and the Rise of an Independent Nation* (2016), sums up her experiences in the process of becoming a "grown-up":

> By the time I walked down the aisle—or rather, into a judge's chambers—in 2010, at the age of 35, I had lived 14 independent early-adult years that my mother had spent married. I had made friends and fallen out with friends, had moved in and out of apartments, had been hired, fired, promoted, and quit. I had had roommates and I had lived on my own; I'd been on several forms of birth control and navigated a few serious medical questions. I'd paid my own bills and failed to pay my own bills; I'd fallen in love and fallen out of love and spent five consecutive years with nary a fling. I'd learned my way around new neighborhoods, felt scared and felt completely at home; I'd been heartbroken, afraid, jubilant and bored.
>
> I was a grown-up: a reasonably complicated person. I'd become that person not in the company of any one man, but alongside my friends, my family, my city, my work, and simply by myself.
>
> I was not alone.
>
> —Traister, 2016, *New York Magazine*

Traister's description of her emerging and young adulthood is a poignant illustration of the instability and complexity of romantic life that emerging adults are navigating today in their journeys toward adulthood. The path Traister embraced might appear to be nonlinear and characterized by haphazard choices. She has spent time alone and in relationship, "heartbroken, afraid, jubilant, and bored." There were many challenges along the way. But haphazard? Perhaps not. Traister has navigated her own unique path toward adulthood, quite different from the one her parents trod. A multiplicity of factors—historical, economic, sociocultural, and individual—have informed her journey and her identity as it continues to unfold.

Each generation, over the last century, has taken longer to assume the roles of adulthood than the previous one. Today's dearth of viable guidelines, in combination with a radically new set of social, economic, and cultural conditions, creates vast opportunities for experimentation, as exemplified in Traister's description of her journey toward adulthood. As previous chapters have emphasized, emerging adults are experimenting and innovating in their romantic lives. With no compass in hand, they are improvising. Their romantic lives do not follow clear linear pathways toward intimacy; rather, they tend to be circuitous, fluid, and flexible. Postponement of traditional markers such as long-term commitment and marriage can be seen as logical sequelae to this style of experimentation. Perhaps greater long-term fulfillment will be a sequel as well. It is too early to tell for whom and under what conditions greater fulfillment is likely to occur.

There is no one path toward an *I* or a *we* identity. We are in the midst of a technological shift that is changing the landscape of jobs, work environments and communities, and romantic relationships. Accommodations to such major changes are required. Shifting cultural, economic, and socioeconomic contexts have created the need for alternative solutions and ways of living. As Thomas Friedman (2016) pointed out, we are now in a race "with and against machines." New jobs will likely be in the STEM sector (science, technology, engineering, math) but will also require human empathy. Because no one can predict what the next big changes will be, the smartest posture may be to remain as open, nimble, and flexible as possible; to read the signs and be poised to adapt to the next new wave. But in so doing, one must realize that in this fast-changing world "small errors in navigation" can have a butterfly effect (Friedman, 2016, p. A25).

Emerging adults seem to intuitively understand this. They are taking an open and experimental stance in many areas of life, and yet they are also trying to be well prepared and trained, career-wise. Emerging adults, particularly those who are economically advantaged, are investing in careers that require education and training that extends into their 20s. Consequently, many are delaying romantic commitment and marriage. As we learned in Chapter 10, many parents of emerging adults approve of this approach, advocating for an even longer delay.

Recognizing that there is no uniform path to a happy and stable adulthood, this generation of emerging adults is more open to diverse choices than past generations have been, particularly in the romantic arena. They are more accepting of same-sex relationships, interracial relationships, and long-term singlehood. They are content to make their own choices, without feeling that their choices should dictate how others live.

Relational experiences such as "hooking up" and "friends with benefits" have appeared as common forms of romantic engagement among emerging adults (Claxton & van Dulmen, 2013). Cohabitation, which in the previous generation often led to long-term commitment, has become yet another transitory alternative for many emerging adults (Manning & Smock, 2005). Casual sexual and relationship encounters (CSREs) have not *taken the place* of committed relationships for emerging adults, but they are filling the vacuum created by the delay in commitment that many emerging adults are opting for (Armstrong, Hamilton, & England, 2010). Previous chapters have provided a context for understanding how these new "relationships" may or may not serve the needs of emerging adults during this transitional period of development.

As to when, how, and if emerging adults begin to move away from CSRE behaviors to more committed behavior, Carroll, Badger, and Yang (2006) suggest that there are two distinct periods: (a) becoming an adult and (b) readiness for a more committed long-term relationship. Regarding the latter, marital horizon theory as discussed in Chapter 10 can help inform our understanding of emerging adults and their CSRE-related behaviors. This theory posits that the readier for long-term commitment and marriage emerging adults perceive themselves to be, the likelier they are to engage in behaviors consistent with norms associated with such committed relationships (Carroll, Willoughby, Badger, Nelson, Barry & Madsen, 2007; Johnson, Anderson, & Stith, 2011). Emerging adults appreciate having choices; they also want to pursue authentic, purposeful, and meaningful lives. As their marital horizons draw closer, they tend to re-evaluate and shift their views and behaviors to align them more consistently with their goals and values. However, the mere fact that they are *approaching* their marital horizon does not necessarily mean they will *make the choice* to marry. Going solo is becoming an increasingly acceptable option for emerging and young adults (Hughes, 2014).

According to marital horizon theory, beliefs regarding the preparatory work needed to enter and maintain long-term relationships inform the behaviors of emerging adults. Hence, behaviors consistent with committed or marital relationships may be dormant for a period, only to be reawakened and refined at a time when emerging adults assess that they are ready to engage in such relationships (e.g., they have their vocational lives on track).

This final chapter will review and synthesize some of the major findings related to the romantic lives of emerging adults. What are some of the challenges they face in getting from *I* to *we*? In order to attempt to answer that question, several key concepts merit a second look: the shift from an individual identity to a couple identity, commitment, and sacrifice.

▲ Individual Identity

Establishing an enduring sense of self is a main developmental task of emerging adulthood. Emerging adults' diverse collections of past and current experiences, and the degree to which they have been integrated, strongly influence the identity construction process. And it *is* a process, not a one-time event. This process incorporates not only past experiences but the individual's dynamic responses to the constantly changing world around them (Chappell, Rhodes, Solomon, Tennant & Yates, 2003, as cited in Stokes & Wyn, 2007).

Complicating any understanding of identity is the fact that today's emerging adults exhibit multiple "selves" in a variety of contexts. Their "online" identity, for example, may be quite different from their work identity or their family identity. Each individual embodies many interwoven narratives, and, according to Josselson (1996), the growth of identity involves integrating these narratives as well as revising them to adapt to changing circumstances. It is not an easy task in a world where so many diverse models of identity are offered to emerging adults; where many ideologies, each with its own modes of dress, speech, and behavior, openly compete with one another; where the rules and conditions are constantly changing; and where so many options for expressing one's identity are available to emerging adults through computer-mediated communications (CMC) and other outlets.

▲ Couple Identity

While engaged in the difficult work of forging a personal identity, many emerging adults are also simultaneously learning to develop an identity as a member of a romantic couple. There is no single, defined path, nor is there a *preferred* path, toward a couple identity, should couplehood even be a goal. And many emerging adults in the United States are delaying, prolonging, or even abandoning exploration of a couple identity as they work toward solidifying a career identity or an educational identity. As with forming an individual identity, developing a romantic identity is rarely a linear process. As one explores and refines relationship skills, new options and possibilities that could not be seen before often emerge. Skills are reorganized and recombined, leading to more sophisticated relational abilities (Thelen & Smith, 1996).

The skills required to successfully sustain a romantic relationship take years to develop. This work often begins in earnest in adolescence, where individuals begin to experiment with the self in relationship. Through friendships and early romances, adolescents practice relational skills such as negotiating conflict, compromising, pursuing their own needs, respecting the needs of others, and negotiating tensions between the need for autonomy and the desire for connection (Connolly & McIsaac, 2009; Seiffge-Krenke & Shulman 2012, as cited in Shulman & Connolly, 2016). This work proceeds throughout the 20s, at least for those who have the "luxury" to engage in continued learning and romantic experimentation.

Many emerging adults feel that the transition from an individual identity to a couple identity should occur only when they have made sufficient progress in developing as an individual. Carroll, Badger, Willoughby, Nelson, Madsen, and Barry (2009), in a study of 788 college students from around the country, reported that emerging adults tend to believe they will be ready for long-term couplehood only after they have accomplished key tasks as a single person, including developing interpersonal competencies and becoming less self-interested. An additional level of complexity that must be considered is that the institution of marriage itself is "placed on too high a pedestal for some emerging adults to reach" and the list of requirements for a potential partner is ever expanding (Willoughby & James, 2017, p.107).

If this is the case, then perhaps the transition from an *I* to a *we* ought to occur sequentially for many emerging adults. After developing the self through exploration and discovery, one then becomes ready to authentically and volitionally shift to a couple orientation. There are competing points of view regarding this singular approach, however. For example, Tanner (2006) has pointed out that taking an extended time to experiment with romantic preferences and multiple partners may be correlated with later difficulties in compromising—a key to a successful long-term romantic relationship. Our nine divorced emerging adult women speak to the importance of self-development prior to marriage, although opportunities for clarity, growth, and redemption can occur after the experience of a divorce (Chapter 11).

A central tension in romantic relationships revolves around the desire for the partners to both seek connection and maintain autonomous selves, pursuits that may be at odds with each other (Baumeister & Leary, 1995). Baxter (1988) posits that a key task for partners in successful close relationships is to learn to negotiate tensions related to autonomy versus connection. As the partners try to develop a distinct *we*, they must also seek to preserve a distinct *I*.

In the initial stages of a relationship, each partner functions as an independent unit. As the relationship develops, the couple transitions to a state of *interdependence* whereby they come to rely on one another and work together to accomplish mutual goals. Concern shifts from self-interest to doing what is best for the other and for the relationship itself (Kelley & Thibault, 1978). Whitton, Stanley, and Markman (2002) suggest that partners can be considered a "couple" to the extent that they are willing to work together as a team. Our 29 participants, too, viewed *working as a team* as critical to the process of becoming a *we*.

Our participants also emphasized the need to preserve an individual identity when in a couple relationship. Maintaining one's own interests and goals and speaking up for one's own desires were two identified ways of maintaining and growing the *I* in the midst of a *we*.

Partners in romantic relationships strive for equilibrium (Kumashiro, Rusbult, & Finkel, 2008; Slotter, Duffy, & Gardner, 2014), in the process of trying to balance one's own needs, the needs of the partner, and the needs of the relationship itself, so that all three are met to the highest possible degree (Slotter, Duffy, & Gardner, 2014). Over time, though, the balance shifts for partners that are strongly identified as a couple. Losses and gains begin to be experienced differently; losses are no longer seen as subtractive to the self, and gains that benefit the partner more than the self are likely to be accepted and endorsed (Whitton, Stanley, & Markman, 2002).

According to Aron and Aron (1986, 1996), becoming part of a *we* can actually enhance the *I* in ways that solo living cannot do—for example, by introducing new resources, people, and opportunities. As the partners become closer, they begin to share their network of friends and interests, which, in turn, expands the sense of self for each. Partners also begin to integrate attributes of the other person into their own selves (Slotter & Gardner, 2009).

According to our research participants, external markers can be instrumental in helping partners discern when a transition to "couplehood" has occurred, and in cementing a joint identity. Outward signs such as publicizing a relationship on social media, sharing resources and living spaces, and including a partner in everyday narratives, particularly through the use of plural, first-person pronouns (we, our) were seen as telltale signs—for both the couple and the world at large—that a shift to a couple identity had occurred.

Irrespective of sexual orientation, most of our 29 emerging adults viewed their romantic relationships as central aspects of their identity. They also emphasized that the process of the becoming a *we* takes time and cannot be rushed. It involves the sharing of many types of experiences that slowly build a connection between the partners and help them find meaning and narrative in their joint existence.

To summarize: In a world where identity options abound and reliable guidance is notably absent, it is not surprising that emerging adults are taking longer than their parents did to solidify a sense of who they are as individuals. Many are still working this out even as they find themselves embroiled in intimate couple relationships. Forming a couple identity is *vastly* more challenging than it has been, given the lack of standard, uniform models and guidelines. Each couple feels, to some extent, the need to construct "couplehood" for itself—a demanding task.

The relationship itself can become the partners' greatest resource, however, for better or worse. If the relationship is a mutually supportive and growth-oriented one, each partner can learn to become a better *I* as the two partners are learning together to become a better *we*.

▲ Commitment

One of the key defining elements of a *we* perspective is commitment. Most emerging adults engage in several romantic relationships of varying degrees of commitment during this transitional period of development (Jamison & Proulx, 2013). Commitment is associated with many positive outcomes such as relationship satisfaction (Ruppel & Curran, 2012), improved functioning as a couple, and longer relationship duration (Corkery, Curran, & Parkman, 2011). Our 29 research participants identified commitment as a central element of any serious relationship.

Investment grows with commitment. The more committed emerging adults are to their partners, the likelier they are to invest in their relationships. When one invests in a relationship, one affirms the long-term viability and value of the relationship (Monk, Vennum, Ogolsky, & Fincham, 2014). Commitment to a romantic partnership fosters pro-relationship behavior, which, in turn, increases commitment. When commitment is high, the members of the couple are no longer "out for themselves," but rather are interdependent. They are less selfishly motivated and are more motivated to behave in ways that serve the other and the relationship. They are more likely to understand that cycles of "selfless" giving will yield mutual benefit over the long run, adding to the long-term stability of the relationship (Stanley, Rhoades, & Whitton, 2010).

Definitions of commitment vary from person to person and couple to couple. Our 29 research participants cited three defining qualities of a committed relationship: monogamy; working together as a team; and loyalty, trust, and respect. Although different aspects of commitment are emphasized by different individuals and couples, nearly all definitions of commitment include some understanding of putting one's own short-term needs aside for the long-term benefit of the relationship.

During emerging adulthood, romantic commitments tend to be marked by instability, confusion, and inner conflict, as the partners are learning what commitment means to them and also learning about their own ability and willingness to commit. Commitment is not an intellectual concept; it must be lived and learned through hard-won experience. It must be tested in the battleground of everyday romantic life.

As we learned in Chapters 3 and 4, two models have emerged as central to the literature on romantic commitment: interdependence theory (Thibaut & Kelley, 1959) and investment theory (Rusbult, 1983; Rusbult & Buunk, 1993). According to interdependence theory, commitment is influenced by a range of factors including the personality of each partner and the particular form of interdependence that develops between them (Thibaut & Kelley, 1959). Interdependence is at its highest when the individual has a strong desire to remain in the relationship, and when alternatives to the relationship are viewed as poor. The greater the interdependence, the greater the commitment to the relationship.

The investment model (Rusbult, 1983; Rusbult & Buunk, 1993) takes the position that commitment to a relationship is the product of increasing *investment* in the relationship. Through investment, resources (both emotional and physical) become tied to the relationship. The more invested the participants are in the relationship, the more motivated they are to preserve it.

In an attempt to improve upon the theoretical work of Rusbult, Johnson (1991) adds dimension to the concept of investment by proposing a three-part model that honors both the internal and external forces that act on a relationship. Emerging adults choose to stay in relationships because they *want to*, because they feel they *ought to*, or because they believe that they *have to*. Commitment remains the strongest predictor of persistence in romantic relationships (van Lange et al, 1997; Rusbult, Martz & Agnew, 1998).

▲ Sacrifice

Sacrifice is a concept closely tied to commitment. Relationally, sacrifice can be viewed as setting aside personal interests that conflict with the interests of the other person or the union. Willingness to sacrifice for the good of the relationship seems to be a relevant and significant measure with respect to commitment. Based on the response of the 29 research participants, emerging adults understand the importance of sacrifice in relationship and consider the learned ability to make adult sacrifices to be a marker of readiness for commitment.

Sacrifice increases investment in the relationship, which in turn contributes to greater commitment to the relationship (Monk et al., 2014). Greater commitment is associated with interdependence. As interdependence grows, the couple transitions from an *I* orientation to a *we* orientation. Thus, sacrifice becomes an important cog in the relationship.

Partners sacrifice out of a desire to continue the relationship. But more important than the act itself is the way the individual *interprets* sacrifice. Relationships tend to improve when the partners believe that sacrifice is an investment in the future of the relationship rather than a personal loss (Whitton et al., 2007). Conversely, when partners behave in a self-interested way, they exert less effort toward maintaining the relationship, which contributes to the decline of the relationship.

Sibley and colleagues (2015) suggest that, as with commitment, the process of romantic sacrifice is more experiential than conceptual. Our participants echoed this assertion. Through a lived accumulation of romantic experiences, they learned to negotiate their needs with their partners, as well as how to "perform" sacrifice. Most of them seemed to view sacrifice as an evolving process. Over time, they revised their understanding of sacrifice and were able to adjust their behaviors accordingly, though several of them noted that they had not yet been called upon to make a *large* sacrifice.

For most of our study group members, Kogan's concept of communal sacrifice was not yet applicable. An expectation of reciprocity was a feature of the way participants "performed" sacrifice. This is likely because they were still in a stage of self-focus and self-development, which, as Arnett (2000) points out, is characteristic of emerging adulthood. Some of the participants seemed to keep a running score as to who was giving more and who was giving less in their relationship. But as Kogan, Impett, Oveis, Hui, Goron, and Keltner (2010) point out, sacrifices made without expectation of direct reciprocation tend to be associated with higher levels of relationship satisfaction than those made on a quid pro quo basis. Monk et al. (2014) suggest the transformation to a communal attitude toward sacrifice is more likely to occur when there is a satisfaction with sacrifice and the presence of commitment.

Studies have linked sacrifice with several positive relationship outcomes, such as satisfaction and longevity, but, as pointed out earlier, the construct of sacrifice remains underexamined in the literature (Impett, Gable, & Peplau, 2005; Kogan et al., 2010; Stanley & Markman, 1992). Sacrifice is closely related to commitment; sacrifice leads to greater commitment, and commitment leads to a greater willingness to sacrifice. As partners adopt a stronger couple identity, they are increasingly likely to sacrifice for the benefit of the relationship.

Keeping contextual considerations in mind, most emerging adults would benefit from adopting an understanding of sacrifice that focuses on the gains to be had in the long run rather than on the personal loss one experiences when forgoing immediate gratification of one's needs. Contextual considerations *are* important, however. Emerging adults who have dealt with significant economic and familial hardships may lack either the skills or the desire to sacrifice for a romantic partner. They have not seen such sacrifices pay off within their realm of life experiences. For those who are struggling with substantial financial and emotional challenges, sacrificing for another person may seem too big a risk to take for the tenuous potential reward of forging a greater connection with a partner.

▲ Ambiguity and Risk

Risk is a fitting note on which to end the previous topic and transition to the present one, as risk is a theme that will carry through the remainder of the chapter. In the previous sections, we summarized some of the skills and dynamics that emerging adults must master in moving from an *I* orientation to a *we* orientation. What one is willing to *risk* in the service of a relationship is *particularly* relevant to 21st century emerging adults trying to establish and maintain romantic relationships. Risk is a crucial thread that is woven through all of the topics we have covered in this book.

Establishing and maintaining relationships has always carried elements of risk—risk of rejection, risk of choosing the wrong partner, and risk of loss—but today's emerging adults find themselves in a unique position when it comes to understanding and managing risk in relationships. The reason for that, to a large extent, is the absence of universally accepted romantic guidelines and models in today's society. Lack of guidelines leads to a profound state of ambiguity for emerging adults seeking long-term commitment.

Two partners entering a relationship today are likely to have substantially differing internalized ideas about commitment, sex, marriage, gender roles, and other important relationship elements. It would seem logical that a corresponding drive for clearer communication, aimed at resolving ambiguity, would have emerged among emerging adults. Clarification would seem to be a paramount consideration. But that does not appear to be the case. Rather, emerging adults seem to be leaning toward and favoring ambiguity. Perhaps that is because clarification entails risk. In the interest of avoiding risk, many emerging adults are allowing ambiguity to persist. In so doing, however, they may be incurring even greater risks in the future—risk of divorce, risk of bringing children into a dysfunctional marriage, and risk of long-term dissatisfaction. Many emerging adults may be engaged in trade-offs related to risk that they may not be aware of.

Scott Stanley (2016) frames the issue in a cogent way. He points out four factors that are combining in the early 21st century to create unstable relationships for emerging adults.

1. Stanley asserts that in recent years the rules for developing a romantic relationship are no longer well prescribed, culturally based, and marked by rituals and protocols. In the past, there were clear guidelines in place for meeting, dating, proposing, getting married, and being married—and for the behaviors that were appropriate at each stage of the relationship. The rituals helped ensure that each member of the couple knew where he or she "stood" with one another regarding the progress and status of the relationship. Today, the rituals have either disappeared or are being arbitrarily applied according to personal tastes. There is a far greater sense of relational ambiguity as a result.

2. Increasingly, emerging adults seem to *prefer* ambiguity because it helps them avoid two types of risk. The first is the short-term risk of rejection. Emerging adults worry that if they try to clarify and define the relationship, they may be rejected by the partner, who may have different ideas about the relationship. The second type of risk they seek to avoid through ambiguity is the risk of commitment itself, which they perceive as potentially dangerous.

3. As a result, during significant relationship transitions, emerging adults are more inclined to *slide* rather than *decide* (e.g., moving in together or having a child together). Instead of making conscious, well-discussed, and deliberative decisions, many emerging adults slide into romantic decisions in a nonintentional, ill-defined manner.

4. These nondeliberative decisions render it easier for emerging adults to get stuck in unstable, imbalanced, unsatisfying, and deeply flawed long-term relationships. Ambiguity can have a long-term cost.

Today's emerging adults do not know what it is like to grow up in an era of clearly prescribed romantic behaviors, and the burden falls on them to define their relationships for themselves every step of the way. This is a large responsibility at a time when they are also trying to define themselves as individuals and find their place in a volatile economy. Ambiguity is a more comfortable choice for many. And ambiguity may, in fact, be preferable in some situations. But, over time, ambiguity begins to carry more risks than explicitness.

▲ "The Commitment Talk" Revisited

This sometimes-mystifying tendency of emerging adults to choose ambiguity was evident in the way many of our research participants described "the commitment talk." Though most of our 29 emerging adults emphasized that they placed a high value on honesty, openness, and trust in a romantic relationship, the lack of explicit intentional behavior related to "the commitment talk" seemed to belie some of those stated values. Surprisingly, only about one third of the participants described their commitment talk as planned and intentional. Why is there a gap between behaviors and stated meanings and expectations of the participants?

Nelms, Knox, and Easterling (2012) suggest that avoidance of talk (and suppression of the corresponding feelings) functions to maintain the status quo. One possibility for the avoidance of a commitment talk among our participants is the fear that if feelings are openly discussed, the relationship might need to change or the behaviors of the partners might need to change. Another possibility, as mentioned previously, may be the fear of rejection or loss that can ensue when commitment levels are made explicit and the two partners need to contend with differences in levels of commitment. Once this disparity becomes explicit, there is an implied mandate to take appropriate action, which may entail a breakup if the disparity between the partners is unacceptable. As long as the talk is avoided, the status quo can be maintained.

In the absence of "the talk" or some other form of status-explicitness, however, the partners run the risk of finding themselves in an asymmetrically committed relationship (ACR).

▲ Asymmetrically Committed Relationships

An asymmetrically committed relationship (ACR) is one in which one of the partners is substantially more committed than the other. Though such relationships might be sustainable in the short term, there are long-term potential costs. Stanley and colleagues (2016) point out that when one partner is more invested than the other, exploitation and/or entrapment can occur, and there may be an unhealthy power differential. The partner with the lesser investment is able to disproportionately dictate the terms of the relationship.

According to Stanley et al., ACRs are more common now than at any time in the past 50 years, due, presumably, to the ambiguity inherent in many emerging adult romantic relationships. In a study of 315 unmarried, opposite-sex couples, Stanley and colleagues found that 35.2%, or 111 couples, to be in ACRs (in 72 of these, the male partner was less committed, in 39 the female partner was less committed). In these couples, a substantial difference (> 1 *SD*) was identified in the commitment levels of the partners as compared to couples who were more equally committed. Some notable findings emerged. For example, cohabiting couples and unmarried couples who had children together were more likely to be in ACRs comparatively. And both partners in the ACRs reported more conflict and aggression in their relationships, as well as lower relationship adjustment, than those who were not in ACRs.

In attempting to explain these unbalanced and unstable relationships, Stanley et al. suggest that in the absence of cultural scripts, customs, and rituals forcing commitment levels to be made explicit, many people are *sliding* into long-term unmarried relationships. These relationships often persist for years before one member of the couple is forced to admit, with pain and regret, that the other is "just not that into them."

The authors suggest that clarifying discussions can serve as an antidote to increasing risk within relationships. Such conversations obviously cannot happen too early in the relationship. On the other hand, as inertia starts to build for continuing a relationship, it becomes riskier to defer having a discussion about commitment levels. The avoidance of short-term risk begins to increase long-term risk. In the opinion of Stanley and colleagues, emerging adults today are erring on the side of waiting too long. And the longer they wait, the more reasons the weak-link partner has for avoiding "the talk."

▲ Cohabitation

As discussed in Chapter 3, cohabitation has become another example of relationship instability during emerging adulthood, particularly when failure to clarify commitment levels between the couple is at play (Manning & Smock, 2005). It has become de-linked from marriage. There is a wide range of reasons why emerging adults enter cohabiting relationships, including economic considerations and other convenience-related motives. Although emerging adults express the desire to form committed, trusting, authentic relationships that encourage growth for both partners, their desires are not always consistent with their behaviors. Stanley, Rhoades, and Whitton (2010) found that only a third of emerging and young adults came to cohabit via a pathway that was planned and intentional; the remaining two thirds of participants did so without deliberation and forethought—in other words, by sliding. The participants in the Stanley et al. study were inclined to enter cohabiting relationships via "inertia and "premature entanglement" (p. 252), a route that leaves them vulnerable to experience the relationship as constraining.

Stanley (2009, 2016) asserts that sliding into major milestones such as moving in together is not likely to be transformative to the relationship. He points out that the strongest commitments come about as the result of deliberate decisions that are made when both parties still have the freedom to choose, not when they find themselves constrained by their sliding behaviors. Focused and clear conversations foreclose alternative choices and increase the likelihood of "deciding" to enter a committed relationship, rather than "sliding into" one (Rhoades, Stanley, & Markman, 2009).

Having a clear conversation about commitment prior to cohabiting may more fully support the couple in navigating the difficult times that inevitably occur in any long-term relationship (Stanley & Rhoades, 2009; Stanley, Rhoades, & Markman, 2006). In the absence of such an explicit understanding of mutual commitment, however, the couple has no clear framework against which to view their difficulties, and dissolution of the relationship is a more likely outcome.

▲ Clarifying Conversations at Key Junctures

Honest and intentional communications at important relationship junctures (e.g., "the commitment talk," before moving in together, before having a child, etc.) can serve a protective function in keeping emerging adults aligned with their future aspirations and goals (Rhoades et al., 2009). Yet, as demonstrated by our participants, clarifying conversations are associated with potential risk for many emerging adults. Even when clarity in communication did occur for our 29 emerging adults, it frequently came from a tumultuous space within the relationship, and it did not always result in improved stability and satisfaction.

Given today's absence of clarifying rituals, emerging adults need new opportunities to become more self-aware and in sync with themselves and their partners. Toward that end, Fincham, Stanley, and Rhoades (2011) have developed a structured, prevention-oriented intervention, Project RELATE—designed specifically for college students to help them develop and sustain intimate relationships with romantic partners. The focus is on dynamic risk, as well as on protective factors that serve the development and maintenance of healthy romantic relationships (Fincham et al., 2011). The program emphasizes the value of making decisive choices, as opposed to sliding into romantic relationships. It is designed to help participants recognize the warning signs of "lapsing into unhealthy relationships" (p. 303), with the goal of helping them make intentional decisions *before* entering situations that create risk for them and limit future options (e.g., becoming pregnant, moving in with a partner, becoming economically codependent, etc.).

Clarifying conversations are not only relevant for long-term committed relationships. In friends-with-benefits relationships (FWBRs), for example, Knight (2014) observes that emerging adults are often unable to engage in clarifying conversations about relationship status and expectations, and thus "there is a mismatch between the expectations of openness and honesty in FWBRs and actual communication practice" (p. 271). Although honest and explicit relational talk may exceed the boundaries of FWBRs, Knight asserts that "the ability to engage in relational talk is important to the success of all relationships but may be especially salient in the management of FWBRs because of their ambiguous nature" and the complexity of feelings likely to be generated (Knight, 2014, p. 271). Emerging adults are negotiating a variety of ambiguous relationships; their ability to reflect and discuss these complex feelings seems to be lagging behind, with important repercussions.

▲ Marriage and Risk

In terms of ambiguity, marriage has one distinct advantage over cohabitating and other "sliding" relationships: it is an explicit, outward declaration of commitment. It entails planning, legal commitments, rituals, vows, and public acknowledgment. However, marriage is increasingly out of reach as an option for many emerging adults, particularly those with low-to-modest economic resources, and it seems to be a generally higher-risk endeavor than in the past. A combination of factors, as discussed in Chapter 10, has created a scenario whereby fewer emerging adults feel ready for marriage. At the same time, a two-tier structure seems to be emerging, in which only those of economic means feel able to choose marriage, while those without economic and educational means are tending to remain in higher-risk and less clearly defined romantic relationships.

Part of the reason for this is the redefinition of marriage that has been taking shape over the past several decades. Before the 1960s and 70s, most marriages were primarily functional in nature and tended to fit into the *institutional* or *companionate* molds. When *individualized* marriage became the new model, marriage was no longer just a social and economic institution, it was also viewed as a primary source of emotional fulfillment for the partners and a vehicle for personal growth. Willoughby and James (2017) suggest that the institution of marriage is perhaps now being "placed on too high a pedestal for some emerging adults to reach" (p. 107).

As expectations for marriage have continued to grow, marriage for many has shifted from being a *foundational* goal—one that can provide support for launching into careers, parenthood, and full adulthood—to being a *capstone* goal, one that is pursued only after all of one's other ducks are in a row. The popular cultural image of weddings has grown more elaborate and expensive, while jobs and careers are taking longer to solidify, creating a situation in which many emerging adults feel that a wedding is forever out of their financial reach. It is important to understand that these same emerging adults grew up at a time when divorce rates were increasing; many were raised in divorced households and want to avoid replicating divorce in their own lives. There appears to be a "perfect storm" of conditions that is making marriage less viable as a choice (even though most emerging adults still desire and envision marriage in their future): higher expectations for marriage, greater costs of getting married, and greater sensitivity to perceived risk of divorce than in the past. It is easy to see why many emerging adults are not willing or able to strike this risk/benefit option.

For those who *are* in a position to choose marriage, another set of risks inform their behaviors in relationships to risks associated with marriage. Many emerging adults view marriage as a vehicle for self-actualization; they seem to be asking more of their marriages, in terms of meeting their needs for growth and development. At the same time, they are relying less on other means of support, such as friends, extended family, and social institutions, placing them at risk (Finkel,

2017). They are, in effect, asking one person to meet all of their complex needs, and yet they seem to be putting less effort and energy, on average, into their marriages, due to shrinking time and psychological resources—a veritable formula for marital failure. As a result, Finkel (2014, 2017) concludes that the state of modern marriage is such that today's best marriages are better than the best marriages of the past; however, today's worst marriages are worse, and the average marriage of today is weaker than the average marriage in the past.

Clinical interventions designed to improve communication in distressed couples has not demonstrably led to lower divorce rates. A more important consideration in gauging the strength of a marriage may be the degree of investment, commitment, and sacrifice that each partner maintains toward the marriage. In addition, clarification related to the following questions may assist the couple in identifying areas of risk: What is each member of the couple expecting from the other? Are these expectations realistic? What supports can be put in place to help the couple meet its mutual expectations?

▲ Divorce and Risk

Avoiding the risk of divorce seems paramount in the minds of emerging adults as they consider marriage; this is evident from the literature and from our own research group. Fear of divorce seems to be one of the reasons emerging adults are more cautious about marriage than past generations were. The tradeoff here is worth examining. The desire to avoid dissolution of marriage is preventing many emerging adults from marrying, or else causing them to delay marriage until their life conditions are more stable. In the end, however, they may find themselves in the very situation they were trying to avoid: being romantically alone.

The responses of our nine divorced participants suggest the possibility that the negative cultural view of divorce might be contributing to the wish to avoid risk. Virtually all of the participants, after a period of grief and adjustment, came to view the process of divorce as a growth-oriented one. All of them felt they had become wiser, stronger, or more mature as a result of having gone through the process of divorce. Thus, the question is legitimately raised: Is it better to be married and divorced or to avoid the risk of divorce by avoiding marriage? While no one would suggest that divorce should be considered a welcome outcome of marriage, is the fear and avoidance of divorce warranted?

Negative perceptions of divorce can affect one's behavior not only in the premarital stage, but also in the postdivorce stage, in the form of stigma. Though most of our divorced participants reported that they no longer thought divorce carried substantial stigma, many of them continued to behave as if stigma were a significant factor in their lives. They seemed to attach risk to the idea of being honest about their divorce and thus were often reluctant to speak honestly about their divorced status to employers, new potential romantic partners, and others, for fear that they would be judged harshly. This raises a question: Is the cost of maintaining a nondisclosing stance commensurate with the perceived risk of revelation? These and other questions about divorce and risk avoidance would seem worthy subjects of future research.

▲ Conclusion

The focus throughout this text has been on the romantic lives of emerging adults. We have attempted to capture their values, attitudes, and behaviors, which, at times, seem baffling and contradictory. Why do they prize traditional marriage, for example, yet seem reluctant to embark on it? Why do they desire open, authentic honest relationships, yet seem to cling to ambiguity? Why do they value deeper qualities in potential partners, yet indulge in dating behaviors that emphasize the superficial? Our understanding is certainly incomplete.

Contradictions about romance abound during the emerging adulthood years. There is, at once, a valuing of long-term romance as well as a "decentering" of romantic relationships in the lives of emerging adults. In a 2014 study of single adults, aged 21–39, in Australia, Hughes concluded that although many of the emerging and young adults she interviewed were living alone, seemingly out of choice, they also viewed their singlehood as a preparatory stage for being in a committed relationship. The primary reason participants were living alone was understood to be failure to have found the "right" partner; in the meantime, they preferred living alone to living with family or friends. Living alone as a single person was viewed as a choice, but not an *ultimate* choice.

Based on her research and a review of the literature, Hughes (2014) argues that while emerging adults assign a high value to romantic relationships, they also tend to decenter these relationships. Because of an awareness that romantic relationships often do not last, emerging adults become reluctant to invest in them. Consequently, many tend to invest more in their own development and in non-romantic relationships, such as friendships. "Permanent" commitments such as marriage seem to be in conflict with the constant refining and redefining of the self that emerging adults feel called to engage in (p. 2). And yet they still desire these long-term committed relationships.

Single emerging adults with social capital, as we have discovered, are focused on their education/careers and establishing an autonomous identity, pursuits that are highly prized in modern individualistic societies such as the United States. In keeping with that goal, they are much more accepting of nontraditional relationships including nonmarital relationships, same-sex relationships, voluntary childlessness, and having children outside marriage than previous generations (Gubernskaya, 2010, as cited in Hughes, 2014). The reality, however, is that most emerging adults eventually do enter marital relationships. The search for a life-long partner tends to be an extended process for them, perhaps in part due to their idealization and romanticization of marriage. Whether or not they were currently in romantic relationships, the majority of participants in Hughes' study wanted a committed long-term relationship that would serve as an anchor in their lives. As we have observed with our 29 participants, traditional values related to monogamy, trust, and commitment persist in today's generation of emerging adults, as does the valuing of interdependence and growth within a relationship—and without.

Perhaps it is the tension between these opposing dynamics—the desire for a committed, growth-driven, trusting, long-term relationship and the need to protect oneself and continue to grow as an individual in the event that such a relationship never materializes—that best characterizes this generation of emerging adults and explains their sometimes contradictory-seeming behaviors and attitudes.

▲ References

Armstrong, E. A., Hamilton, L., & England, P. (2010). Is hooking up bad for young women? *Contexts, 9*(3), 22–27. doi:10.1525/ctx.2010.9.3.22

Arnett, J. J. (2000). Emerging adulthood: A theory of development from the late teens through the twenties. *American Psychologist, 55*, 469–480.

Aron, A., & Aron, E. N. (1986). *Love and the expansion of self: Understanding attraction and satisfaction.* New York, NY: Hemisphere Publishing Corp/Harper & Row Publishers.

Aron, A., & Aron, E. N. (1996). Self and self-expansion in relationships. In G. O. Fletcher & J. Fitness, (Eds.), *Knowledge structures in close relationships: A social psychological approach* (pp. 325–344). Hillsdale, NJ, US: Lawrence Erlbaum.

Baumeister, R. F., & Leary, M. R. (1995). The need to belong: Desire for interpersonal attachments as a fundamental human motivation. *Psychological Bulletin, 117*(3), 497. doi:10.1037/0033-2909.117.3.497

Baxter, L. A. (1988). Dyadic personal relationships: Measurement options. In C. H. Tardy (Ed.), *A handbook for the study of human communication: Methods and instruments for observing, measuring, and assessing communication processes* (pp. 193–228). Westport, CT: Ablex.

Carroll, J. S., Badger, S., Willoughby, B. J., Nelson, L. J., Madsen, S. D., & Barry, C. M. (2009). Ready or not? Criteria for marriage readiness among emerging adults. *Journal Of Adolescent Research, 24*(3), 349–375. doi:10.1177/0743558409334253

Carroll, J. S., Badger, S., & Yang, C. (2006). The ability to negotiate or the ability to love? Evaluating the developmental domains of marital competence. *Journal of Family Issues, 27*(7), 1001–1032. doi:10.1177/0192513X06287248

Carroll, J. S., Willoughby, B., Badger, S., Nelson, L. J., Barry, C. M., & Madsen, S. D. (2007). So close, yet so far away: The impact of varying marital horizons on emerging adulthood. *Journal of Adolescent Research, 22*(3), 219–247. doi:10.1177/0743558407299697

Claxton, S. E., & van Dulmen, M. H. M. (2013). Casual sexual relationships and experiences in emerging adulthood. *Emerging Adulthood, 1*(2), 138–150. doi:10.1177/2167696813487181

Corkery, S. A., Curran, M. A., & Parkman, A. (2011). Spirituality, sacrifice, and relationship quality for expectant cohabitors. *Marriage & Family Review, 47*(6), 345–362. doi:10.1080/01494929.2011.594213

Fincham F. D., Stanley S. M., & Rhoades G. (2011). Relationship education in emerging adulthood: Problems and prospects. In F. D Fincham & M. Cui (Eds.), *Romantic relationships in emerging adulthood* (pp. 293–316). New York, NY: Cambridge University Press.

Finkel, E. J. (2014, February 14). The all-or-nothing marriage. *The New York Times*, Retrieved from https://www.nytimes.com/2014/02/15/opinion/sunday/the-all-or-nothing-marriage.html?mcubz=0

Finkel, E. J. (2017). *The all-or-nothing marriage: How the best marriages work.* New York, NY: Penguin.

Friedman, T. L. (2016, November 2). Donald Trump voters, just hear me out. *The New York Times*. Retrieved from https://www.nytimes.com/2016/11/02/opinion/donald-trump-voters-just-hear-me-out.html?rref=collection%2Fcolumn%2Fthomas-l-friedman&action=click&contentCollection=opinion&region=stream&module=stream_unit&version=latest&contentPlacement=36&pgtype=collection

Hughes, J. (2014). The decentring of couple relationships? An examination of young adults living alone. *Journal of Sociology, 51*(3), 1–15. doi:10.1177/1440783314527656

Impett, E. A., Gable, S. L., & Peplau, L. A. (2005). Giving up and giving in: The costs and benefits of daily sacrifice in intimate relationships. *Journal of Personality and Social Psychology, 89*(3), 327–344. doi:10.1037/0022-3514.89.3.327

Jamison, T. B., & Proulx, C. M. (2013). Stayovers in emerging adulthood: Who stays over and why? *Personal Relationships, 20*(1), 155–169. doi:10.1111/j.1475-6811.2012. 01407.x

Johnson, M. P. (1991). Reply to Levinger and Rusbult. *Advances in Personal Relationships, 3,* 171–176.

Johnson, M. D., Anderson, J. R., & Stith, S. M. (2011). An application of marital horizon theory to dating violence perpetration. *Family Science Review, 16,* 13–26.

Josselson, R. (1996). *Revising herself: The story of women's identity from college to midlife.* New York, NY: Oxford University Press

Kelley, H. H., & Thibaut, J. W. (1978). *Interpersonal relations: A theory of interdependence.* New York, NY: Wiley & Sons.

Knight, K. (2014). Communicative dilemmas in emerging adults' friends with benefits relationships: Challenges to relational talk. *Emerging Adulthood, 2*(4), 270–279. doi:10.1177/2167696814549598

Kogan, A., Impett, E. A., Oveis, C., Hui, B., Gordon, A. M., & Keltner, D. (2010). When giving feels good: The intrinsic benefits of sacrifice in romantic relationships for the communally motivated. *Psychological Science, 21*(12), 1918–1924. doi:10.1177/0956797610388815

Kumashiro, M., Rusbult, C. E., & Finkel, E. J. (2008). Navigating personal and relational concerns: The quest for equilibrium. *Journal of Personality and Social Psychology, 95*(1), 94. doi:10.1037/0022-3514.95.1.94

Manning, W. D., & Smock, P. J. (2005). Measuring and modeling cohabitation: New perspectives from qualitative data. *Journal of Marriage and Family, 67*(4), 989–1002. doi:10.1111/j.1741-3737.2005. 00189.x

Monk, J. K., Vennum, A. V., Ogolsky, B. G., & Fincham, F. D. (2014). Commitment and sacrifice in emerging adult romantic relationships. *Marriage & Family Review, 50*(5), 416–434. doi:10.1080/01494929.2014.896304

Nelms, B. J., Knox, D., & Easterling, B. (2012). The relationship talk: Assessing partner commitment. *College Student Journal, 46*(1), 178–182.

Rhoades, G. K., Stanley, S. M., & Markman, H. J. (2009). Working with cohabitation in relationship education and therapy. *Journal of Couple & Relationship Therapy, 8*(2), 95–112. doi:10.1080/15332690902813794

Ruppel, E. K., & Curran, M. A. (2012). Relational sacrifices in romantic relationships: Satisfaction and the moderating role of attachment. *Journal of Social and Personal Relationships, 29*(4), 508–529. doi:10.1177/0265407511431190

Rusbult, C. E. (1983). A longitudinal test of the investment model: The development (and deterioration) of satisfaction and commitment in heterosexual involvements. *Journal of Personality and Social Psychology, 45*(1), 101–117. doi:10.1037/0022-3514.45.1.101

Rusbult, C. E. (1991). Commentary on Johnson's "Commitment to personal relationships": What's interesting, and what's new. *Advances in Personal Relationships, 3,* 151–169.

Rusbult, C. E., & Buunk, B. P. (1993). Commitment processes in close relationships: An interdependence analysis. *Journal of Social and Personal Relationships, 10*(2), 175–204. doi:10.1177/026540759301000202

Rusbult, C. E., Martz, J. M., & Agnew, C. R. (1998). The investment model scale: Measuring commitment level, satisfaction level, quality of alternatives, and investment size. *Personal relationships, 5*(4), 357–387. doi:10.1111/j.1475-6811. 1998.tb00177.x

Shulman, S., & Connolly, J. (2016). The challenge of romantic relationships in emerging adulthood. In J. J. Arnett (Ed.), *The Oxford handbook of emerging adulthood* (pp. 230–244). New York, NY: Oxford University Press.

Sibley, D. S., Springer, P. R., Vennum, A., & Hollist, C. S. (2015). An exploration of the construction of commitment leading to marriage. *Marriage & Family Review, 51*(2), 183–203. doi:10.1080/01494929.2015.1031424

Slotter, E. B., Duffy, C. W., & Gardner, W. L. (2014). Balancing the need to be "me" with the need to be "we": Applying Optimal Distinctiveness Theory to the understanding of multiple motives within romantic relationships. *Journal of Experimental Social Psychology, 52,* 71–81. doi:10.1016/j.jesp.2014.01.001

Slotter, E. B., & Gardner, W. L. (2009). Where do you end and I begin? Evidence for anticipatory, motivated self–other integration between relationship partners. *Journal of Personality and Social Psychology, 96*(6), 1137–1151. doi:10.1037/a0013882

Stanley, S. M. (2009, May 9). The DTR dance: Avoiding the talk [Blog post]. Retrieved from http://slidingvsdeciding.blogspot.com/2009/05/dtr-dance-avoiding-talk-i-wrote-in.html

Stanley, S. M. (2016, November 5). What happens when partners aren't equally committed. New study examines relationships where one is just not that into the other. *Psychology Today.* Retrieved from https://www.psychologytoday.com/blog/sliding-vs-deciding/201611/what-happens-when-partners-arent-equally-committed

Stanley, S. M., & Markman, H. J. (1992). Assessing commitment in personal relationships. *Journal of Marriage and the Family, 54*(3), 595–608. doi:10.2307/353245

Stanley, S., & Rhoades, G. (2009). Marriages at risk: Relationship formation and opportunities for relationship education. *What works in relationship education: Lessons from academics and service deliverers in the United States and Europe,* 21–44.

Stanley, S. M., Rhoades, G. K., & Markman, H. J. (2006). Sliding versus deciding: Inertia and the premarital cohabitation effect. *Family Relations, 55*(4), 499–509. doi:10.1111/j.1741-3729.2006.00418.x

Stanley, S. M., Rhoades, G. K., Scott, S. B., Kelmer, G., Markman, H. J., & Fincham, F. D. (2016). Asymmetrically committed relationships. *Journal of Social and Personal Relationships, 34*(8), 1–19. doi:10.1177/0265407516672013

Stanley, S. M., Rhoades, G. K., & Whitton, S. W. (2010). Commitment: Functions, formation, and the securing of romantic attachment. *Journal of Family Theory & Review, 2*(4), 243–257. doi:10.1111/j.1756-2589.2010. 00060.x

Stokes, H., & Wyn, J. (2007). Constructing identities and making careers: Young people's perspectives on work and learning. *International Journal of Lifelong Education, 26*(5), 495–511.

Tanner, J. L. (2006). Recentering During Emerging Adulthood: A Critical Turning Point in Life Span Human Development. In J. J. Arnett & J. L. Tanner (Eds.), *Emerging adults in America: Coming of age in the 21st century* (pp. 21–55). Washington, DC: American Psychological Association. doi:10.1037/11381-002

Thelen, E., & Smith, L. B. (1996). *A dynamic systems approach to the development of cognition and action.* Cambridge, MA: The MIT Press.

Thibaut, J. W., & Kelley, H. H. (1959). *The social psychology of groups.* New York, NY: John Wiley and Sons.

Traister, R. (2016). *All the single ladies: Unmarried women and the rise of an independent nation.* New York, NY: Simon and Shuster.

Van Lange, P. A., Rusbult, C. E., Drigotas, S. M., Arriaga, X. B., Witcher, B. S., & Cox, C. L. (1997). Willingness to sacrifice in close relationships. *Journal of Personality and Social Psychology, 72*(6), 1373. doi:10.1037/0022-3514.72.6.1373

Whitton, S., Stanley, S., & Markman, H. (2002). Sacrifice in romantic relationships: An exploration of relevant research and theory. In A. L. Vangelisti, H. T. Reis, & M. A. Fitzpatrick (Eds.), *Stability and change in relationships* (pp. 156–181). New York, NY: Cambridge University Press. doi:10.1017/CBO9780511499876.010

Whitton, S. W., Stanley, S. M., & Markman, H. J. (2007). If I help my partner, will it hurt me? Perceptions of sacrifice in romantic relationships. *Journal of Social and Clinical Psychology, 26*(1), 64–92. doi:10.1521/jscp.2007.26.1.64

Willoughby, B. J., & James, S. L. (2017). *The marriage paradox: Why emerging adults love marriage yet push it aside.* New York, NY: Oxford University Press.

APPENDIX A ▲

The material provided in this appendix describes the data sources used throughout the book. First, I describe the participants of the studies and then summarize the methodology used to gather and analyze the data. Appendix B, following Appendix A, provides demographic information about the 29 participants whose voices are heard throughout this text.

▲ Participants

In an attempt to expand the narrative about the romantic lives of emerging adults, 29 emerging adult research participants 21 to 29 years of age—diverse with respect to race, class, ethnicity, and sexual orientation—are represented throughout this text. These 29 participants comprised the "main" research group (a description of a second research group of nine divorced emerging adult women follows). At the time of the study, the participants were undergraduate or graduate students attending a large, public, urban, commuter university in the Northeast. The research participants differed somewhat from the middle-class undergraduate students attending private colleges that have typically been represented in the extant literature. This public institution serves a large number of minority students, first-generation college students, transfers, and immigrants—or children of immigrants—who speak languages other than English at home or with families. Students at this university are also diverse in terms of age and national origin. It is important to note that although many of the participants were dealing with challenging environmental circumstances, they persisted in their goal to complete their college or graduate degree, a characteristic that further distinguishes them as a group.

Of the 29 participants, 20 were women, eight were men, and one self-identified gender-queer person, ranging in age from 21 to 29 years ($M = 24.5$, $SD = 2.1$). Twenty identified as heterosexual, four as gay, one as lesbian, three as bisexual, and one as queer. All of the participants reported having been in romantic relationships that were at least 3 months in duration. At the time of the study, 15 participants were in committed relationships and 14 were single. Of those in a current committed romantic relationship, the average length of the relationship was 40.6 months, with a range from 7 to 108 months. Sixteen participants were working part-time while 10 were working full-time, and three were exclusively students. They represented a wide range of annual incomes from less than $10,000 to between $100,000 and $149,999.

With regard to socioeconomic status of family of origin, 15 participants identified as middle class, nine as working class, two as upper class, and three as poor. Twenty-two participants identified their national origin as the United States, while seven identified as non-US citizens. The sample was relatively diverse in race/ethnicity: 13 self-identified as non-Hispanic White, six as Asian, four as Hispanic/Latino, three as Black/African-American, two as multiracial/multiethnic, and one as Middle Eastern. (Refer to Table 1 for a detailed description of demographics of the participants.)

For Chapter 11, "Divorce and its Aftermath," a special group of research participants—specifically, divorced individuals—was required. The participants were nine emerging and young adult women ranging in age from 25 to 39 years ($M = 31.14$, $SD = 5.15$), all of whom were divorced between the ages of 23 and 32. The average period of time, postdivorce, was 4.38 years ($SD = 2.69$).

Seven of these women had earned a bachelor's degree or higher, with two pursuing doctoral-level degrees at the time of the study. Five participants were employed full-time, three were employed part-time, and one was temporarily unemployed. None of the women were remarried; one was cohabitating and planning to marry within the year. While seven of the participants had no children, two did have children (one and three respectively). With respect to income distribution, five women reported incomes between $20,000 and $49,000, two reported incomes between $80,000 and $100,000, one (cohabitating) reported a joined income of $149,000, and one preferred not to disclose her income. Three of the participants were minorities, two Latina and one Asian; the remaining six were Caucasian.

▲ Methodology

Both of the studies received approval from the Institutional Review Board. An email was sent to the university community describing the studies and the criteria for entry. Also, flyers inviting participants were hung in strategic sites across the campus (e.g., gyms, coffee shops). The technique of chain-referral sampling was utilized to maximize the sample's representation of the population (Penrod, Preston, Cain, & Starks, 2003). If a potential participant was interested, he or she contacted the researcher by email or phone. Further information regarding the study was then provided, along with an opportunity to ask questions. If the student continued to express interest in participating, a consent form was sent and, upon receipt of the signed form, a phone interview was scheduled. For both the 29 emerging adult participants and the nine divorced participants, a semi-structured, open-ended interview was conducted by phone; interviews lasted approximately 60–90 minutes.

Consensual qualitative research methodology (CQR; Hill, Thompson, & Williams, 1997) was employed to capture the range of narratives related to the romantic relationships of emerging adults and to explore how these narratives unfold and change during the emerging adulthood years. CQR, which is grounded in constructivist and postpositivist epistemologies, was the driving methodology used in analyzing all of the interviews with both groups: first, the methodology used with the 29 participants is described, followed by a description of the methodology used with the nine divorced research participants.

CQR is classified as qualitative research because it relies on open-ended interview questions and small group samples, and it proceeds inductively (Hill, 2012). CQR incorporates multiple viewpoints and stresses the importance of context. It allows for the examination of subjective attitudes, experiences, values, and beliefs, while also providing the objective rigor of the consensus of a research team. Lastly, CQR is an accessible rigorous methodological approach, that is easily applied and replicated, and allows for the integration of other qualitative methods (Hill, Knox, Thompson, Williams, Hess & Ladany, 2005).

The specific steps of CQR are as follows: A research team is chosen, an interview protocol is developed and pilot-tested, criteria for selecting participants are developed, participants are recruited, interviews are conducted, and transcriptions are completed. The researchers then engage in a process of "within-case" analysis, which is followed by cross-analysis by the research team. Within-case analysis include: developing domains or identifiable topic areas, identifying core ideas for each participant, verifying domains and core ideas for each participant by auditor(s), and revising those domains and core ideas based on feedback received. Cross-analysis includes, after reaching consensus, developing categories within domains across all participants, checking the cross-analysis by auditors, and making revisions based on feedback received. With CQR, the researchers are asked to specify whether categories are *general* (apply to all, or all but one, of the participants), *typical* (apply to at least half of the participants), or *variant* (apply to at least two or three of the participants, depending on the initial size of the participants). With respect to the original data that is analyzed and discussed throughout this text, categories are identified as either *general*, *typical*, or *variant* (Hill, 2012).

Not unlike the methodology used for the 29 emerging adult participants, researchers solicited participants via an email sent to the student body of the urban public university described above. Participants were then selected from among the email respondents based on qualifications such as age range (21–39) and divorce status. Seven women met the study criteria. In order to reach the recommended sample size of nine to 15 participants (Hill et al., 2005), two additional women were selected, using convenience sampling, to make a final total of nine women.

The nine participants were given a semi-structured, open-ended interview by phone; interviews lasted approximately 60 minutes. Interviews were initially conducted in rotating pairs with the author and her team, and then completed individually. As in the case of the 29 participants, members of the research team recorded, and later transcribed, the responses for coding and analysis. The questions were aimed at uncovering information about demographics, experiences of divorce, thoughts/feelings related to divorce, "real" and "imagined" reactions from others, and anticipated reactions from people they meet anew regarding their divorce.

▲ Team Members

The team members for both groups were comprised of master's level students in Mental Health Counseling, doctoral level students in Counseling Psychology, and the author. Consistent with CQR methodology, each of the teams had an assigned auditor. Team members were trained in CQR theory and methodology by the author. All researchers coded the first interview transcript independently. For the purpose of reducing bias, the remaining transcripts were coded by two or three members of the team. All of the team members met to discuss domains and compare core ideas to ensure the efficacy of the process. After reaching consensus, the teams identified categories that best represented the core ideas across the participants. The teams then met collectively, and in focused discussions further refined the categories until consensus was reached. For both studies, an auditor was selected to assist the team to reach consensus concerning the analysis of the data.

▲ References

Hill, C. E., Thompson, B. J., & Williams, E. N. (1997). A guide to conducting consensual qualitative research. *The Counseling Psychologist, 25*(4), 517–572. doi:10.1177/0011000097254001

Hill, C. E., Knox, S., Thompson, B. J., Williams, E. N., Hess, S. A., & Ladany, N. (2005). Consensual qualitative research: An update. *Journal of Counseling Psychology, 52*(2), 196–205. doi:10.1037/0022-0167.52.2.196

Hill, C. E. (Ed.). (2012). *Consensual qualitative research: A practical resource for investigating social science phenomena.* Washington, DC: American Psychological Association.

Penrod, J., Preston, D. B., Cain, R. E., & Starks, M. T. (2003). A discussion of chain referral as a method of sampling hard-to-reach populations. *Journal of Transcultural Nursing, 14*(2), 100–107. doi: 10.1177/1043659602250614

Appendix B ▲

Table 1 Demographics

Age	Relationship Status	National Origin	Primary Work Status	Income	Race/Ethnicity	Gender	Sexual Orientation
22	Relationship > 1 year	US	Student	≤ $20,000	White	F	Bisexual
21	Single	Non-US	Full-time	≤ $20,000	Asian	M	Heterosexual
24	Single	US	Part-time	≤ $20,000	Hispanic/Latino	F	Bisexual
26	Relationship ≤ 1 year	US	Part-time	≤ $30,000	White	F	Heterosexual
24	Single	US	Part-time	≤ $20,000	White	F	Heterosexual
23	Relationship ≥ 1 year	US	Part-time	≤ $20,000	Black	F	Heterosexual
25	Relationship ≤ 1 year	US	Full-time	≤ $20,000	Multiracial	Queer	Queer
24	Single	US	Part-time	≤ $40,000	White	F	Heterosexual
24	Single	US	Part-time	≤ $10,000	White	M	Gay
23	Relationship ≥ 3 years	US	Full-time	≤ $40,000	White	M	Gay
22	Relationship ≥ 3 years	US	Part-time	≤ $10,000	White	F	Heterosexual
23	Single	US	Student	≤ $10,000	Asian (Indian)	M	Heterosexual
24	Single	US	Student	≤ $10,000	Hispanic/Latino	F	Gay
24	Single	US	Full-time	≤ $50,000	White	F	Heterosexual

22	Relationship ≥ 1 year	US	Part-time	≤ $10,000	White	F	Heterosexual
26	Single	US	Full-time	≤ $70,000	Hispanic/Latino	F	Heterosexual
22	Relationship ≥ 3 years	Non-US	Part-time	≤ $20,000	Black	F	Heterosexual
22	Single	Non-US	Part-time	≤ $10,000	Multiracial	F	Heterosexual
28	Single	US	Full-time	≤ $30,000	Hispanic/Latino	F	Heterosexual
25	Single	Non-US	Part-time	≤ $30,000	Asian (Indian)	M	Gay
28	Relationship ≥ 5 years	US	Full-time	≤ $30,000	White	F	Heterosexual
27	Relationship ≥ 9 years	US	Full-time	≥ $100,000	White	F	Bisexual
26	Single	Non-US	Part-time	≤ $30,000	Hispanic/Latino	M	Gay
27	Relationship ≥ 9 years	US	Part-time	≤ $20,000	White	M	Heterosexual
27	Single	US	Full-time	≤ $30,000	Multiracial	F	Heterosexual
21	Relationship ≥ 4 years	Non-US	Part-time	≤ $10,000	Multiracial	F	Heterosexual
26	Single	Non-US	Part-time	≤ $20,000	White	F	Heterosexual
25	Relationship ≤ 1 year	US	Full-time	≤ $20,000	White	F	Heterosexual
27	Relationship ≥ 1 year	US	Part-time	≤ $10,000	White	F	Heterosexual

INDEX ▲